Black Interdictions

Black Interdictions

Haitian Refugees and Antiblack Racism on the High Seas

Philip Kretsedemas

LEXINGTON BOOKS
Lanham • Boulder • New York • London

Published by Lexington Books
An imprint of The Rowman & Littlefield Publishing Group, Inc.
4501 Forbes Boulevard, Suite 200, Lanham, Maryland 20706
www.rowman.com

86-90 Paul Street, London EC2A 4NE, United Kingdom

British Library Cataloguing in Publication Information Available

Library of Congress Cataloging-in-Publication Data

Names: Kretsedemas, Philip, 1967- author.
Title: Black interdictions : Haitian refugees and antiblack racism on the high seas / Philip Kretsedemas.
Description: Lanham, Maryland : Lexington Books, [2022] | Includes bibliographical references and index. | Summary: "Black Interdictions exposes the antiblack racism that was latent in the US government's Haitian refugee policies of the 1980s and the 1990s, setting the tone for the criminalization of migrants and refugees in the new millennium"—Provided by publisher.
Identifiers: LCCN 2021056689 (print) | LCCN 2021056690 (ebook) | ISBN 9781793630728 (Cloth) | ISBN 9781793630742 (paperback) | ISBN 9781793630735 (ePub)
Subjects: LCSH: United States—Emigration and immigration—Government policy—History. | Refugees—Government policy—United States. | United States—Emigration and immigration—Political aspects. | Racism against Blacks—United States. | Immigration enforcement—United States. | Return migration—Haiti. | Haitians—Civil rights—United States.
Classification: LCC JV6483 .K7397 2022 (print) | LCC JV6483 (ebook) | DDC 325.73—dc23/eng/20220118
LC record available at https://lccn.loc.gov/2021056689
LC ebook record available at https://lccn.loc.gov/2021056690

For Analise and Isabelle

Contents

List of Tables

Preface

The contents of this book are, sadly, just as relevant at the time of this writing as they would have been forty years ago. In 1981, the US government launched its first operation to interdict Haitian refugees on the high seas and in 2021 it is continuing to do so. Policies designed to safeguard public health, in light of the COVID-19 pandemic, are being implemented in a way that targets Haitian asylum seekers, similar to the HIV travel ban that was introduced in the early 1980s.

The transition from the Trump to the Biden administration held out some hope for a kinder and more generous immigration policy, and these hopes have been borne out in some ways. But this book also shows that US immigration and refugee policy is riven with stubborn continuities that are epitomized by the treatment of Haitian asylum seekers. From the beginnings of the Haitian refugee crisis in the 1970s, the US government has held to a policy of discouraging and deterring Haitian asylum seekers and it has been prepared to use unprecedented measures to meet this goal. In my attempt to explain these policies, and the legal arguments used to justify them, I have had to juggle two very different sensibilities—producing an analysis that is attuned to the timeliness of these policies but which also directs attention to histories of exclusion that are easily obscured if you limit your focus to the present moment.

There is a tension running between these two aspects of my analysis that resonates throughout the book, and which is reflected in the way I got involved in this research in the first place. In the late 1990s, I became involved in a number of research and community outreach projects that were focused on documenting the impact of the 1996 welfare and immigration laws for Haitian immigrants in the South Florida area. I was working, at the time, for a nonprofit in Miami-Dade County that advocated for the rights of welfare recipients. This work was funded by grants from big, established foundations and enmeshed in networks that included government policy-makers, social service professionals, and academicians. I first learned about the challenges facing Haitian migrants and refugees through the lens of the policy questions and grant research objectives, as they had been defined by these networks.

The explanatory framework I use in this book comes from a different place. It is something that I first encountered as frustration or a critical sensibility that was hovering on the margins of academic theory and the policy world. It is a knowledge borne of suffering that doesn't make much sense until you attune yourself to that suffering. In the course of writing this book, I have undergone a number of life transitions that have opened me up, even more, to this way of seeing.

Many people have attuned me to this critical sensibility; some have pointed me in the direction of specific books and theorists, or have raised arguments that connect the dots between race, refugees, and immigration in ways that I never thought about before. But there are also people that have sensitized me through their patience with my limitations and by the way they model their openness to critical knowledges that hale from unconventional sources. One of these mentors is longtime community activist Mike Chaney, who is one of the originators of the Twin Cities Juneteenth celebration. Mike befriended me as a graduate student at the University of Minnesota and gave me a very practical introduction to black community organizing, by living and working alongside other people who were rehabilitating abandoned houses in neighborhoods that were neglected and overpoliced. There is much more I could write about this time in my life, but it will suffice to say that it gave me the experience-based knowledge which made it possible for me to connect with the critical sensibility that I encountered, many years later, in the writing of Afropessimist scholars. The mentorship I received from Mike Chaney was carried on by Arthur Paris, who collaborated with me for many years in the production of the newsletter for the Association of Black Sociologists, as well as Ronald Walters who oversaw some of my early research on welfare reform and Haitian immigrant communities. I am also very grateful to Mark Dow who introduced me to the world of critical immigration enforcement studies and for underscoring the centrality of the Haitian experience, as well as David Brotherton (who has collaborated with me on two coedited projects) who has always been very persistent about nudging me in the direction of a more critical analysis.

I am especially grateful to Tamara Nopper and Rahsaan Mahadeo for their patience and collegiality over the years, taking the time to introduce me to important readings and perspectives in Black Studies. Khalil Saucier and Tryon Woods have played an invaluable role in helping me to connect theories of antiblackness to an analysis of refugee interdictions. Tryon, in particular, was instrumental in directing me toward readings that added much more depth to my treatment of black mobilities. I am grateful to Eve Zasoba for keeping me up to date with the latest happenings in Biden-era policy on Haitian refugees and supplementing these policy updates with an uncompromising critique of US foreign policy. I also want to thank Payal Banerjee, Sofya Aptekar, and Lisa Park for their openness to including some of the arguments I advance in this book in a mini-conference on the theme of "Critical Migration Studies" that was held as part of the proceedings of the Eastern Sociology Society's annual conference in 2020. Finally, I want to thank Becca Beurer, the acquisitions editor at Lexington Press and Carter Moran, acquisitions assistant, for their patience and confidence in this project, as well as the advice of the anonymous peer reviewers who offered their advice at various stages in the writing of the manuscript. But I want to emphasize that I take responsibility for the contents of this book. Writing is both a collective and solitary process. I would not have written this book were it not for the encouragement of others, but the words I have written are, ultimately, my own and any errors and aporias that the reader may come across, in the pages ahead, should be attributed solely to me.

Introduction

Black Interdictions

JAN TING: I think the Haitians are being treated differently . . . because the Bush administration has intelligence which suggests that there is a potential for a mass migration because of . . . conditions in Haiti and it's not in the best interest of the individuals that they make this hundreds of mile journey in these leaky boats. It's not in the interest of the United States to have these hundreds or thousand[s] of individuals land on our shores. . . . And one thing that we can do besides interdiction on the high seas is to make it more difficult for those who do arrive in the United States; and one thing that can be done is to deny parole for these individuals so that the word goes out there is not a possibility of parole. . . . And it's hoped that this will have a deterrent effect and encourage people not to get into these small boats and risk their lives on this journey to the United States.

GWEN IFILL: When you say that the U.S. government has credible intelligence that there are conditions in Haiti that would lead to a mass exodus, what kind of conditions? Are we talking about political conditions, economic conditions?

JAN TING: Well, all of the above. It almost doesn't matter. I mean the reality is conditions in Haiti potentially will drive significant numbers of individuals out into the high seas looking for a way to get to the United States.

—Handling Haitian Refugees, PBS NewsHour[1]

The interview excerpt that I have used to introduce this book is taken from a PBS NewsHour episode that aired in the fall of 2002. Jan Ting was offering commentary on the George W. Bush administration's deterrence agenda, which was informed by his experience serving in the Immigration and Naturalization Service (INS) under the prior Bush administration about a decade earlier.[2] Ting's commentary is derivative, in some ways, of the

1

security conscious climate of the post 9/11 era, but he also provides a succinct description of the US government's Haitian refugee policy from the
late 1970s to the present day. He makes no bones about the fact that the US
government was treating Haitians differently than any other asylum seeker
group. He asserts that the possibility of a Haitian mass migration is sufficient
to justify the government's position on deterring Haitian asylum seekers.
Most significant, he describes a strategy for deterring these unwanted migration flows which operate under the presumption that all of the fleeing Haitians
really are "migrants" and not refugees, and with no consideration for whether
these deterrence strategies violate international refugee law.

This policy agenda has, arguably, been inflected the partisan-ideological
leanings of different administrations. For example, the interdiction strategies of the Clinton administration were informed by a greater concern for
the humanitarian treatment of Haitian refugees than those of the Reagan
era, which were mainly framed as strategies to curb "illegal immigration."[3]
There are also some noteworthy differences in the refugee policies adopted
by the Trump and Biden administration—one of the main ones being the
Biden administration's decision to renew Temporary Protected Status (TPS)
for Haitians, and for many other displaced populations, that had been slated
for termination by the Trump White House.[4] Even so, the Biden administration, and the Obama administration before it, has held to the same deterrence
agenda for Haitian refugees that the US government began implementing in
the late Carter era.[5] One of the main goals of this book is to render these continuities more transparent for the reader. I also want to emphasize, from the
outset, that antiblackness is going to figure prominently in my explanation of
the US government's Haitian refugee policies.

I am using the term "antiblackness" and not, simply, "racism" because I
want to pay attention to an imaginary, sentiments, and relations of power that
are singular to the exclusion and control of bodies that have been racialized
as black. Instead of showing how all nonwhite groups are mutually alienated
from whiteness, I am going to call attention to a kind of exclusion that sets the
black condition apart from all other nonwhite populations. I realize this argument may strike some readers as unnecessarily trenchant. It runs against the
grain of how critical scholars, especially in the fields of migration and refugee
studies, have theorized race. It also creates complications for a politics that
emphasizes the common interest that vulnerable, racialized populations have
for a more equitable social existence. My contention, however, is that it is
not possible to work together for equity and justice if we are not prepared to
grapple with the divisive history of the black/nonblack binary. We should
also be mindful of how the instinct to avoid dealing with the singularity of
the black experience participates in the orders of knowledge and power that
have been fostered by antiblack racism.

Later in this chapter, and in the chapters that lie ahead, I am going to provide a theoretical framework that adds more depth to these propositions. Before I get into these arguments I want to provide more context for the Haitian crisis and the exceptionally exclusionary policies that the US government has used to control the movements of Haitian refugees.

Jan Ting's justification for these policies revolves around concerns about an unsolicited, mass migration from a nearby Caribbean nation. These are legitimate concerns. Given Haiti's history of economic and political instability, it is not difficult to see why tens of thousands of Haitians would be motivated to flee to the United States or any nearby nation in search of a better life. But it also bears noting that the US government—which includes its ties to international development agencies, multinational corporations, and its investments in global security—has played a role in perpetuating the desperate conditions that Haitians are trying to escape.

It is well known that Haiti is the first, and only, modern nation-state to be created as the result of a successful slave revolution. As a condition for being recognized by the international community, the Haitian state was forced to pay exorbitant sums of money to Western nations—mainly France—in compensation for losses due to the emancipation of the enslaved peoples that had been transformed into citizen-subjects of the new Haitian state.[6] Consequently, the Haitian state began its life on the verge of bankruptcy. Haitian aspirations for self-government have been consistently thwarted by the despotic forms of government that have adapted to this situation of resource scarcity, as well as the neocolonial interventions of the United States, which has sent troops to occupy Haiti several times throughout the course of the twentieth century.[7] So it is important to keep in mind that the US government's refugee policies are just one feature of a multilayered problem.

First, there is the unwillingness of the United States, and many other nations, to extend the same kind of welcome to Haitians that has been afforded to other displaced people. Second, there is an unwillingness to grapple with the root causes of this displacement, and to come terms with the complicity, of the United States and other Western nations, in undermining Haitian economic development and aspirations for self-government. As a result, many Haitians find themselves in a devastating catch-22, being unable to survive in an economy that, for decades, has been ranked as the poorest in the Western hemisphere, as well as having to contend with a chronically unstable and authoritarian state system that many Haitian expatriates have described as neofascist,[8] and also having to contend with border enforcement strategies that frustrate their ability to find a better way of life elsewhere. The desperateness of this situation is comparable to that of many other displaced populations. But for Haitians, these problems are exacerbated by the unprecedented measures that the US government has taken to prevent them from pursuing their asylum claims, chief among them being the practice of interdicting Haitian refugees on the high seas.

AN UNPRECEDENTED EXPERIENCE

Ronald Reagan's decision to have the Coast Guard intercept Haitian refugees on the high seas was a watershed moment in the history of US immigration and refugee policy. Reagan administration officials were aware that there was no precedent for these operations in the history of US immigration policy. But as Kristina Shull has explained, Reagan's advisers ended up using the legal ambiguity of the interdictions to their advantage.[9] Although the government had never treated a refugee population this way before, there was nothing in US Constitutional law that expressly prohibited it from doing so.

The executive order for *The Interdiction of Illegal Aliens* that President Reagan issued on September 29, 1981,[10] inaugurated the US government's first immigration control initiative that operated outside of its geopolitical borders. The strategy behind the interdictions was controversial but proved effective. If the government apprehended refugees outside of its territorial jurisdiction it could free itself of obligations to constitutional and international law that might limit its ability to control their movements.

Many national origin groups have been apprehended under the US government's interdiction operations, but Haitians have been its primary focus. In its first year of operation, the Reagan-era interdictions exclusively targeted Haitians.[11] In the years that followed, the Coast Guard began to apprehend refugees from Cuba, the Dominican Republic, and China among other groups. Publicly available data on these interdiction statistics have reported conflicting estimates, but they all show that Haitians were interdicted in larger numbers than any other national origin group.[12] According to a US Department Homeland Security report, Haitians composed 77 percent of all the "illegal aliens" that were apprehended by the interdiction operations that were authorized by Reagan's executive order (1982–1991).[13] According to this same report, Haitians were the single largest national origin group that were apprehended by all of the US government's interdiction operations that were carried out between 1982 and 2009, exceeding over 116,000 people.[14] The next most frequently targeted group were Cuban refugees, but their numbers for this same period time were less than two-thirds the size of the Haitian interdicted population, at 67,466.[15] These disparities, in the way that Haitians were targeted by the government's interdiction practices, are also reflected in the federal policy response to Haitian and Cuban refugees.

When they first began to arrive on the shores of South Florida in the 1980s, Cuban-Mariel refugees were compared, unfavorably, to the white, upper class and politically conservative refugees who fled the Castro regime in the early 1960s.[16] Al Pacino's portrayal of Tony Montana in the 1983 film *Scarface* also helped to establish the stereotype of Cuban-Mariel refugees as desperate, criminals with ties to the international drug trade.[17] These associations between Cuban refugees and crime set the stage for a hostile context of reception. But throughout the 1980s and into the early 1990s, the Marielitos still benefited from an open arms asylum policy that had been created to facilitate the incorporation of earlier cohorts of Cuban refugees.[18]

In contrast, the US response to the Haitian refugee crisis is better described as a closed door policy that went to unprecedented lengths to stop Haitian boats from entering US waters, which used more stringent criteria for assessing Haitian asylum claims than used for other national origin groups and which was determined to repatriate as many Haitian refugees as possible, even after they touched ground in the United States.[19] The wet foot/dry foot policy, which was devised by the Clinton administration in 1994,[20] provides a good example of these double standards in the US government's treatment of Haitian refugees. Under this policy, Cuban refugees were allowed to apply for asylum if they reached the shores of South Florida, while Haitians were denied this right if they did the same.

These disparities also surface in policies that were, by and large, beneficial for Haitian refugees. The Mariel boat lift that was carried out by the Carter administration, for example, was, arguably, the most genuinely humanitarian response of the US government to the Caribbean refugee crisis. In stark contrast to the Haitian interdictions, the boatlift operation rescued both Cuban and Haitian refugees at sea, brought them to the US mainland, streamlined their access to asylum, and assisted with their integration into Floridian society. But there were also some noteworthy differences in the integration process for both groups of refugees. Cuban-Mariel refugees who were rescued by the boatlift were immediately eligible for legal permanent residence due to the provisions of the 1966 *Cuban Adjustment Act*.[21] Haitians who were rescued by the boatlift, on the other hand, had to wait until the enactment of the 1986 *Immigration Reform and Control Act* (IRCA) before they were able to access the same pathways to legal status.[22] This disparate treatment is also reflected in the US government's schizophrenic policy on Haitians at the time of the boatlift.

During the same time that President Carter authorized the boatlift, Haitian nonprofits in the Miami area were raising a legal challenge to another Carter-era program—infamously dubbed the "Haitian program"—which was used by the INS to streamline the removal of thousands of Haitian refugees who were "clogging up" the immigration courts.[23] And just one year later, the Reagan administration began its interdiction operations which were designed to undermine Haitian asylum claims by ensuring that Haitian refugees never touched ground in the United States to begin with.

WHY ANTIBLACKNESS MATTERS

So what does antiblackness have to do with the disparities that I have just described? Haitians may have been singled out for exclusion by the US government, but every single black refugee who has plead for asylum to the United States has not been subjected to this treatment. It could be argued that the Haitian predicament is not really about blackness but about a combination of factors that is singular to the Haitian experience, which sets them apart from other Afro-Caribbean, Afro-Latinx, and African groups. On this point, I think it is worth noting that I have experience working on projects that have surfaced problems that are specific to Haitian immigrants and refugees.

The early years of my sociology career were focused on documenting the problems that US law and policy was creating for the Haitian community in South Florida.[24] Many of the Haitians that I interviewed, in the course of my research and community outreach work, believed that they were victims of a kind of ostracism that was specific to Haitians. Even if they were being marginalized for their blackness, it was because of the uniquely Haitian dimensions of this blackness, which led them to be associated with an alien culture and with problems (disease and disorder) that set them apart from a multicultural US citizenry.[25]

This tendency to focus on Haitian-ness rather than blackness is understandable if you focus on the way that borderlines of race, class, nationality, and culture are experienced in the daily lives of many Haitian migrants and refugees. But if you situate Haitian otherness historically, it is difficult to separate this experience of otherness from the qualities that have defined the black predicament in the modern world.

The treatment of the Haitian state by the world's powers over the past 300 years has to be viewed in light of the role that the Haitian revolution played in disrupting the transatlantic slave trade. The unprecedented response of the US government to Haitian refugees also has to be viewed in light of the unprecedented nature of the crisis itself. The US government has devised policies for incorporating many other kinds of racialized foreigners. For example, the Reagan administration legalized almost 3 million undocumented Mexican migrants during the same time that it was carrying out its interdiction operations for Haitian migrants, and in the Carter era, the US government adopted laws and policies that assisted with the integration of thousands of Indo-Chinese refugees.[26] The Haitian refugee crisis, on the other hand, marks the first time in US history in which the government had to contend with an unsolicited, mass scale flow of black bodies from another nation.

Antiblack animus can be factored into the government's Haitian refugee polices as a sensibility that was triggered by the population scale of the crisis. In other words, antiblackness became more salient once the government was forced to contend with tens of thousands of black bodies rather than the demands of smaller clusters of petitioners or with a more "controllable crisis" that occurred at a greater distance from the geopolitical borders of the United States. This population scale is relevant to the way that Afropessimist scholars have explained the problem of (anti)blackness. Rather than describing blackness as a subjective experience, it is treated as a condition that is radically alienated from the very idea of subjectivity.[27] All forms of personhood and individuation—the rights-bearing subject, the private individual and consumer—are premised on the exclusion of blackness. Hence, blackness takes the form of a fungible detritus which exists to enhance the life ambitions of properly human subjects.[28] I will elaborate on this theoretical perspective in the pages that lie ahead, but the important point for now is that this understanding of blackness maps very well onto the notion of a problem that is conceptualized on a population scale—a depersonalized mass that threatens the happiness of individual subjects.

To shed a little more light on this way of framing the problem, let me return to the exchange between Jan Ting and Gwen Ifill from PBS NewsHour that I used to introduce this chapter. In that exchange, Ifill, a storied journalist and PBS anchorperson, asks Ting whether the government intelligence about the likelihood of Haitian mass exodus was based on unstable political or economic conditions. Ifill was undoubtedly aware that the US government's interdiction policy for Haitians was premised on the idea that Haitian boat people were economic migrants and not "true" refugees who were fleeing political persecution. Jeffrey Kahn reads deeper into this policy rationale when he writes that, "the narration of Haitian suffering as purely economic became part of the justification for enormous state investments in new forms of migrant policing."[29] Kahn explains how the "economic problems" that were used to explain the Haitian exodus were conceptualized and integrated within explanatory models that championed the free market forces that were propelled by the interest-seeking pursuits of private individuals.[30] This way of conceptualizing the economic roots of the Haitian crisis imposed a sharp distinction between the economic pursuits and interests of private individuals, and the problem of political persecution, which targeted people for their publicly held beliefs and their participation in the civic life of a nation. The preference for an economic explanation also made it possible for government officials to put the Haitian crisis at a great distance from questions of rights—especially the rights accorded to refugees under international law.

But this is another of the many reasons why Ting's commentary on the government's Haitian refugee policy is so striking. In his response to Ifill's question, Ting insists that it does not matter whether Haitians are fleeing for economic or political reasons—either way the possibility of a mass scale exodus of Haitian refugees poses a problem to US security that requires a deterrent policy response.

Although Ting appears to be contradicting the government's policy discourse on economic migrants versus political refugees, he also provides a very frank description of the concerns underlying this discourse. If you read government policy in light of Ting's commentary, it stands to reason that federal policy-makers were using the "economic migrant" rationale as a way to avoid their obligations to international refugee law so that they could, more effectively, justify their Haitian deterrence strategy. INS officers (and the Department of Homeland Security officials that would take over from them[31]) were committed to treating the Haitian exodus as a population management problem regardless of whether Haitians were fleeing for political and economic reasons, and this "problem" was premised on the assumption that Haitian refugees were "undesirables" who were uniquely unsuited for integration into US society. Although Ting does not make any allusions to the undesirability of Haitians, these sentiments are more explicit in the internal memos of Carter-era INS officials and Reagan-era officials (including President Reagan himself) who laid the foundations for the governments' Haitian refugee policies.[32]

The concern that Ting evinces for the safety of Haitian refugees also plays into a depoliticized narrative about the causes of their displacement. What concerned the INS the most is the way that refugees were endangering their lives by taking to the high seas, but not the reasons why they would risk their lives in the first place. Court documents and news journalism stories are replete with examples of these desperate conditions, which are just as bad today as they were forty years ago.

For example, there is the story of a man who is identified only as "Yves."[33] Yves was harassed by the police and Haitian citizens affiliated with the Tonton Macoutes—a paramilitary force that reported directly to President Duvalier—because he was a known Aristide supporter and had followed the orders of a priest affiliated with the National Front for Change and Democracy. Yves was targeted for harassment throughout the 1980s. In February 1991 the breaking point came. He was injured trying to protect the priest from an assault involving over twenty armed civilians. After that incident, Yves began to receive a series of death threats that he took very seriously. In the spring of 1992, he fled Haiti in the middle of a night, bribing his way on board a boat headed for the United States with five bowls of pasta. He was one of the lucky ones. After being detained at the US naval base in Guantanamo for over two months, he was released to the US mainland, and began a new life in the greater Los Angeles area.

There is the story of woman who goes by the alias "Rosaline" who fled Haiti in 2016. Roseline was beaten and raped by a group because of her known political affiliations.[34] When it became apparent to Roseline that the police would do nothing to help her, she decided to flee the country with her husband. Instead of taking the nearby, heavily policed, waterways to South Florida, Roseline and her husband took a much longer and more arduous trek to the US border through Central America and Mexico. She gave birth along the way and ended up becoming one of the many asylum-seeking families with children that were turned away by the Trump administration. Her story, unfortunately, is more typical of the Haitian refugee experience. Trump administration officials used an unprecedented interpretation of public health policy to deny entry to migrants out of concern that they could be carriers of COVID-19. Similar to the ban on entry for HIV-infected migrants, this policy was used, almost exclusively, to bar the entry of Haitian migrants and asylum seekers. Rosaline was returned to Haiti where she continues to live in fear of retaliation from her persecutors and is making plans to, hopefully, one day re-enter the United States.

There is also the story of Sergeant Bienvenue Theodore which appears in one of the supporting documents that is cited in a precedent setting federal court decision from 1980.[35] Bienvenue fled Haiti because he feared retaliation from the government because he reprimanded a soldier under his command about firing on striking workers. This soldier thought the workers deserved to be fired on. Bienvenue did not overtly take the side of the workers, but observed that labor disputes were not a military matter. The soldier that Bienvenue reprimanded decided that Bienvenue should be punished for harboring treasonable sentiments against the Duvalier regime. This solider denounced Bienvenue to the government and shortly thereafter, Bienvenue was forbidden to speak before the officers that were under his command. After Bienvenue saw how his superiors were prepared to undermine his authority for the sake of politics, he became increasingly fearful for his future and safety in Haiti and ended up joining the ranks of the "boat people" who were fleeing to the United States.

Each of these stories illustrates how the tendrils of authoritarian power can pervade any facet of social life in Haiti. If you view these incidents from the perspective of the 1951 Refugee Convention, it may seem easy enough to say that all of these people are being persecuted for their political beliefs. But these beliefs do not have to take the form of public speech. They can be beliefs that a person is reputed to have, based on information gathered through informal gossip networks, or in the case of Sergeant Bienvenue, you can be targeted due to the connotations of an informal exchange that was not necessarily intended as a statement of political position. Bienvenue, like many other Haitian refugees, was not formally charged with sedition or some other "political crime."[36] He was punished for not conforming, in a convincing enough manner, to the informal organization of authoritarian power that has been established, over many decades by the Tonton Macoutes.

The power of the Macoutes is absolute because it mirrors the absolutism of the Duvalier regime. Francois Duvalier was famous for making statements in which he identified his personage with the spirit of the Haitian nation.[37] Similar to a feudal-era monarch, Duvalier described his body as a symbolic expression of the body of the nation and his will as the will of the nation. It follows that you could not be a true Haitian if you were not loyal to Duvalier. The Macoutes, in turn, were understood by Duvalier to be an extension of himself, which meant that any Haitian who refused the commands of a Macoute was defying Duvalier. This authoritarian organization of power also has to be viewed in light of the fact that the Macoutes were an unpaid paramilitary force. Instead of issuing the Macoutes a salary, the regime granted this paramilitary force license to raise their own revenue through extortion of the general population as well as access to resources channeled through the state by foreign entities.[38] This is one reason why the authority of the Macoutes blurred the lines between political control and economic exploitation.

Any Haitian could be targeted for contradicting the opinion of a Macoute or of someone affiliated with the Macoutes. Or they could be targeted because they refused a Macoute, or someone affiliated with the Macoutes, access to something they wanted, whether this was financial resources, property, or their own labor.[39] Moreover, as Kahn has pointed out, when the Duvalier regime retaliated against people, it targeted entire neighborhoods and family networks.[40]

This organization of power requires an analysis of political economy rather than one that treats political persecution and economic deprivation as separate and distinct problems. Economic privilege is organized through social and political networks, and the same goes for economic exploitation. The ability to access resources and exploit others is largely determined by your location in an informal organization of power that emanates from the ruling regime and is also conditioned by a political culture fostered by many decades of authoritarian government. This informal organization of power makes certain people vulnerable both to extreme immiseration and persecution. Kahn makes a comparable argument in his analysis of the economic discourse that has been used to explain the root causes of the Haitian refugee crisis.[41] Theories of antiblackness take this analysis a step further, to focus attention on the social ontology that undergirds these political-economic relations.

Moon-Kie Jung, for example, makes a compelling contrast between the nineteenth-century class struggle that pitted white workers and bosses against each other versus the dilemma of the black slave.[42] Whereas the class struggle could be described as a conflict between people of unequal standing over the means of production, the slave was treated *as* a means of production—a nonperson that had no claim on the interests at stake in this political struggle.

Afropessimist theory makes a similar point, which is that the predicament of the black slave cannot be adequately explained by theories of economic exploitation that take the white working class as their starting point.[43] The black slave could be used to generate profit, satisfy private desires, to bolster the status or political influence of their owner, or any combination thereof. The foundation for this predicament is a social ontology that understands blackness as the antithesis of Being. Blackness lies outside of history, reason, agency, and civilized culture—it is everything that the modern subject is not. But for this same reason, blackness pervades modern life, as a radically depersonalized substratum of flesh and energies that can be molded to suit the interests of nonblack/human subjects.

All of these arguments draw attention to the order of rank between human and subhuman types that undergirds the modern economy, and which defines the threshold between rights-bearing persons who use and consume commodities, and nonpersons who have been converted into commodities. The relationships between these persons and nonpersons describe an economic order, with antiblackness serving as the cosmological imaginary that has been used to rationalize this order. Antiblackness is not simply a justification for the unequal distribution of resources, though it plays a role in perpetuating these inequities. More important, it defines the borderline between order and chaos and produces the meta-narratives that are used to conceptualize this borderline.

The organization of power under the Duvalier regime provides a unique insight into how the legacies of antiblackness have played out in more recent history. The Duvalier regime was invested in its own brand of black nationalism that was culturally conservative, virulently anti-communist, and was also constructed in opposition to the liberal, cosmopolitan culture of lighter-skinned Haitian elites. Like many other postcolonial Afro-Caribbean nations (as well as the post-civil rights culture of the United States) the Haitian state was invested in the project of creating black citizen-subjects. From an Afropessimist perspective, this would be a contradiction in terms—in which blackness is integrated into modern subjectivity instead of defining its outer limits. As some Black Studies scholars have pointed out, this contradictory situation is a pervasive feature of contemporary black politics, marking a divide between black subjects who have a privileged relationship to the state, and a larger population that suffers the brunt of institutionalized racism.[44] This is one reason why blackness can be understood as a prism of visibility (created by antiblack racism) for making distinctions between persons and nonpersons that can even cut through populations that are nominally categorized as "black." The functionaries of the Haitian state, for example, can control the public discourse on black identity, while being structurally protected from violence, deprivations, and stigma that are routinely suffered by the Haitian masses, which revolve around the specter of blackness.

The legacies of antiblackness that I examine in this book are not as complex as the ones I have just described. I will be examining court decisions and policies devised by networks of elites—who are predominantly white, male and upper class—that have been used to control the flow of Haitian refugees into the United States. The legacies of antiblackness that inform these decisions are more directly connected to concerns about protecting a mostly white citizen population from an unwanted flow of black noncitizen bodies.

It is also important to keep in mind that my research is focused on policies that have been crafted by the executive branch of the US government. So my analysis of antiblackness is going to be focused on decisions and rationalizations that usher from centers of political authority. My analysis is also focused on the law. To be more specific it is focused on the jurisprudence of the federal courts and a discretionary authority to shape policy that is not strictly regulated by the law. Questions of border control and refugee rights are the practical focus of most of these policy decisions and legal deliberations. But I also want to show how these decisions and deliberations are informed by the social ontology that I described earlier. Whispering through the formalities of the law there are decisions being made about the kinds of people who deserve to be protected by the law.

Economic considerations enter into these decisions, for example, as it concerns the distinctions the courts have made about "economic migrants versus refugees" and concerns about the fiscal burden of refugee populations. But these decisions also draw attention to the ways that political authority (and legal and policy decisions as an arm of this authority) is used to conceptualize the economy and to define its scope and limits. This process has more to do with the way that economy is ordered and imagined, rather than with the influence of economic factors on government policy.

Many researchers, for example, have shown how migrant "illegality" is shaped by economic incentives and informal recruitment processes that have become an institutionalized feature of local labor markets across the United States.[45] But interdiction operations are a very different creature. Interdiction strategies make sure that displaced people never even get the opportunity to become undocumented migrant workers. The economic value of these operations for the government has more to do with "keeping the wrong people out" than with maximizing their utility as exploitable and disposable workers. It is also important to underline that the US government has been willing to spend hundreds of millions of dollars over the past several decades to fund these operations.[46]

I have made a point of emphasizing how the driving concerns for these operations transcend economic considerations, but these concerns also provide an insight into the cultural underpinnings of the modern economy. Over the last few decades, many researchers and theorists have argued that more attention needs to be paid to the sociocultural contexts for economic transactions.[47] There are some connecting threads between these insights, and the arguments advanced by feminist scholars about the need to critically examine abstract, universalist discourse (which includes economic formulae) from the vantage point of socially grounded positionalities.[48] Feminist economists, in particular, have pointed out that the modern economy is reliant on a discourse and accumulation strategies that are ruthlessly indifferent to the natural environment and the lived, socioeconomic experience of the majority of the world's inhabitants.[49] Viewed in this light, "economic growth" can be described as a process which has created unprecedented concentrations of wealth and decision-making authority, which has been aided by meta-narratives that obfuscate and rationalize the material damages that have been wrought in the name of this "growth." In the case of refugee policy, these meta-narratives have been used to make distinctions between populations that deserve a place—as social beings, political subjects, and economic actors—in the modern world, and others that can be treated like useless detritus. The law, which is the focus of my analysis, is one of the many institutions that play a role in circulating these meta-narratives. In the next section, I explain how I am going to go about surfacing these meta-narratives in legal texts, by re-contextualizing their contents and calling attention to their conspicuous silences.

LEGAL STORYTELLING AND BLACK INTERDICTIONS

The way I approach the study of the law has been informed by critical theories and methodologies that have been used to examine many kinds of marginalities. One of the starting points for this approach is the Critical Legal Studies movement, which crystallized in the late 1970s and helped to lay the theoretical and epistemological foundations for Critical Race Theory and intersectionality theory, which also originated from the work of legal scholars.[50] Michelle Crenshaw, for example, who is widely regarded as one of the founders of intersectionality theory, focused much of her early research on antidiscrimination court cases that ignored the unique positionality of black women. Critical Race Theory, which overlaps in many ways with intersectionality theory, has been used to produce revisionist histories of the way the law has been used to construct race and perpetuate the marginality of Asian, black, Latinx, and indigenous populations. Feminist legal studies is another important intervention that was influenced, in part by the Critical Legal Studies movement and is a recognized influence on Critical Race Theory, but it was also influenced by currents of feminist theory from outside the field of legal studies—similar to the role that black feminist thought played for intersectionality studies.

One connecting thread for all of these critical perspectives is their concern for exposing the historical contingency of the law. The law's proclivity for a universalist language—which addresses an abstract rights-bearing subject—is situated historically and in light of actually existing inequalities that can operate along lines of race, class, gender, and sexuality, along with other axes of social difference. As a result, the law is located within a cluster of interests, sentiments, and cultural narratives, and it is read in light of these contexts, which are usually "redacted" from the language of the law. One of the goals of this analysis is to show how the law is used to construct arguments that nullify the experience of marginalized people and to expose the disjuncture between the language of the law and the practical application of the law, as it is experienced by these people.

I also want to emphasize that, although the study of the law and federal policy is a running theme of most of my research, that I am sociologist by training and my areas of expertise, which include race studies and migration and refugee studies, appeal to a broad, interdisciplinary audience. This is why my approach to the critical study of the law is going to be supplemented by sociological theories of race and migration, Black Studies approaches to the study of race and insights from an interdisciplinary body of scholarship that has been used to theorize migrant and refugee mobilities and border control. I also want to foreground Critical Race Theory as an important influence on my approach to the study of the law, and especially the work of Derrick Bell, who had an important influence on the field of Black Studies.

Derrick Bell belonged to the cadre of lawyers who led the fight against Jim Crow segregation in the state and local courts.[51] Bell believed that narratives about the inevitable demise of racism, that were widely shared by his colleagues and allies, were doing more harm than good. He introduced the permanence of racism thesis as an alternative to the brand of racial justice advocacy that was being encouraged by most liberals and by the more institutionalized segments of the civil rights movement.[52]

Bell's permanence of racism thesis appears to be constructed on top of a paradox. It insists that racism is permanent, but this advice is intended to provide a new and more realistic set of strategic goals for racial justice activism—on the premise that is possible to challenge the very same racism that, he insists, is "permanent." Bell used this thesis to say "no" to triumphalist liberal narratives about the end of racism that held sway in his time. But this "no" also became a starting point for new interventions that are guided by a belief in the emancipatory potential of collective action.

Bell used many analytic and narrative techniques to communicate his arguments, which can be summed up by the practice of legal storytelling,[53] including socio-legal commentary on the issues of the day, the use of hypothetical scenarios to point out the limitations of the political status quo, and the use of fictional characters and science fiction allegories to present an alternative reading of historical events and present-day problems. Bell's arguments were often informed by a close reading of empirical nuances and macro-contextual factors that were ignored by other scholars, as evidenced by his analysis of the geopolitical and ideological interests that led US elites to converge in their support for the desegregation agenda that was launched by *Brown v. Board of Education* decision.[54]

The goal of legal storytelling, as Bell explains it, is not simply to call attention to overlooked empirical details. The ultimate goal is to present a new meta-conceptual framework for interpreting these empirics. This is what Bell was doing by insisting that the permanence of racism is a more instructive premise for racial justice activism than the prevailing premise about the inevitable demise of racism. Bell's thesis on the permanence of racism should not be read as a predictive statement; it introduces something on the order of a Kuhnian paradigm shift into the analysis of race and racism—a new premise from which to generate theory, to interpret empirical data, and to devise legal strategy.

The meta-conceptual aims of legal storytelling are also informed by lived experience. The overarching goal of the meta-conceptual reframing is to produce a narrative that is better aligned with this experience, and the positionality that informs it. Bell's insistence on the permanence of racism, for example, was informed by his frustrations about the inability of civil rights litigation to alter deeply engrained patterns of race and class inequality. As Michelle Alexander has explained, Jim Crow segregation was never really dismantled, but reinvented in the form of mass incarceration, and Jim Crow itself was just one of the many manifestations of the afterlife of slavery that permeate the US social structure.[55] Viewed in this light, the aim of legal storytelling is to provide a meta-conceptual framework that can shine a light on an experience of oppression which has been excised from official accounts of the historical record.

The analysis that I provide in this book is inspired by the examples of legal storytelling that can be found in the work of Bell and many other critical race scholars. My use of this method, however, is not nearly as adventurous as Bell's. I am not going to rely on hypothetical scenarios or narrative techniques from the world of fiction writing. My analysis will be confined to the content of legal and policy documents, and supplemented by secondary research, government statistics, and archival data. But the way I am going to analyze and interpret these documents is consistent with the goals of legal storytelling. I will be reading them against the grain, through juxtapositions with legal documents and histories of lawmaking which call attention to patterns of argumentation that would not be as easy to see if you confined your analysis to bodies of jurisprudence that are specific to immigration or refugee law.

As I noted earlier, my approach to the law is also informed by sociological theories of race, Black Studies scholarship, and theories that have been used to explain the control of migrant and refugee mobility. Out of this diverse pool of theories, Afropessimist theory—which comes out of Black Studies— warrants additional commentary, since it poses some important challenges to contemporary treatments of race. Critical Race Studies, feminist legal theory, and intersectionality studies all, to varying degrees, emphasize the importance of examining the law from the vantage point of a marginalized standpoint. As I noted above, this sensibility also informs Derrick Bell's contributions to Critical Race Theory.

Afropessimism, on the other hand, denies the possibility of constructing or affirming something like a black standpoint or subjectivity.[56] As I explained previously, Afropessimism treats blackness as the nether-zone of modernity—the absence against which the active presence of the modern subject is foregrounded. The puzzle that is put forward by Afropessimism is not very different from the one introduced by Gayatri Spivak in her well-known essay, "Can the Subaltern Speak?"[57] The Afropessimist answer to this question would be a decisive "no." Blackness is treated as the depersonalized substratum of existence that is always being canceled out by discourses that appear to speak on behalf of the universal, and even, in some cases, on behalf of blackness itself.

Although Derrick Bell had more appreciation for a black standpoint than Afropessimist theory, the Afropessimist analysis shares something in common with Bell's permanence of racism thesis. It is concerned with defining the terms of a problem. Viewed from an Afropessimist perspective, the aim of legal storytelling is not to affirm a black standpoint that has been marginalized by the law and which should be recognized by the law. Instead, the aim is to describe the defining feature of a predicament, created by antiblack racism, that leaves people thoroughly abandoned by the law—as nonpersons who are denied a subjective experience that could be recognized by the law. This problem requires a more thoroughgoing solution than "integration" or "reform" of the law. It requires a rethinking of the meta-narratives that inform the scope and limits of the law, as well as the very purpose of the law.

I am also going to show how this predicament is perpetuated by the silences of the law: the things left unsaid and questions left unaddressed that allow the movements of black bodies to be controlled by policies and practices that are not held accountable to the law. You cannot plumb the depths of these silences if you attend only to the empirical details about the black experience that they have been used to suppress. It is also necessary to challenge the meta-narratives, about race and the law that have normalized these silences, and tell a new kind of story that renders them problematic.

This way of thinking about the relationship of blackness to the law is reflected in the cover art for the book; abstract columns of white text, excerpted from federal court cases, set against a gray background that is as dreary, perhaps, as the dimensionless horizon of the Atlantic Ocean if you have been sailing on it for far too many days. Some of the text comes from court cases that are central to the legal struggle over the government's Haitian interdiction policies. Other parts of the cover art text come from cases that were used to justify Jim Crow segregation and the rightlessness of black slaves. The point of situating all of these excerpts adjacently, using blurred italicized type that makes them barely distinguishable from one another, is to emphasize a continuity. I am also using the cover art to illustrate the dominion of the law, by calling attention to the texts that constitute the corpus of the law—the expression of its immanent form.

The entire book revolves around the analysis of these texts. I want to explain how these legal texts defined the problem of racial discrimination, refugee rights, and the government's concerns about border security, in a way that systematically erased the problem of antiblackness and its relevance for the government's unprecedented policies for Haitian refugees. This is why it is important to emphasize the dominance of the official discourse, because I am concerned with rendering, as clearly as possible, the terms of a problem which has been perpetuated by this discourse.

My treatment of this problem also helps to explain the way I use Haitian refugee stories, and black American narratives about racial oppression throughout the book. I use these stories to introduce many of the chapters, and to provide more context on the problems that I examine in the body of each chapter. But I want to emphasize that I am not trying to provide a representative account of the way that Haitian refugees experienced the interdictions or describe the composite features of a black refugee subjectivity that could be generalized from this experience. I also do not want to produce a romanticized narrative of black resistance that understates the durability and pervasiveness of antiblack racism. When I use examples from Haitian refugee stories and other Black narratives, I am concerned only with exposing the distance and disjuncture between these narratives and the official discourse of the law that has silenced them.

The silencing of Black narratives provides a clue about the double meaning of this book's title, *Black Interdictions*. In the most practical sense of the term, "interdiction" refers to exterritorial border enforcement practices that are typically carried out on the high seas.[58] Any noncitizen, regardless of race or nationality, could, potentially, become a target of these interdiction practices. I devote several chapters to tracing the history of these interdiction practices, but they are not the primary focus of the book.

I am more concerned with examining another kind of interdiction that is intimately related to the theorization of (anti)blackness. This second kind of interdiction calls attention to an antiblack animus, and a tactic for controlling black mobility, that can be traced to the inception of the US republic. These interdictions are not the exclusive preserve of the Coast Guard or the US Presidential office; they can be effected by all of the institutions and circuitries of power that constitute modern society, which includes the law, educational institutions, health, and social service delivery systems, and the techniques that are used to regulate labor markets, among many other examples.

The otherness evoked by this second kind of interdiction is connected to the distinction between "fully human" and "less than human" types that was formalized by the scientific racism of the eighteenth and nineteenth centuries.[59] This kind of interdiction refers to a way of ordering the social world that is predicated on the elimination of blackness, but which also requires blackness as a way of marking the limit point of the human—and it is not specific to an immigration control strategy. It describes all of the ways, practical and symbolic, in which modern institutions have relied on blackness to define that which lies beyond the bounds of the tolerable, and must be kept there.

Blackness, in this view, is not just the other of the citizen. Blackness is the radically depersonalized backdrop for both the citizen and the immigrant (the latter being admitted as a potential candidate for citizenship). This second kind of interdiction illustrates how the meaning of oppression changes significantly when it is viewed through the lens of the black condition, rather than being viewed through the lens of immigrant and refugee rights. I aim to show that there is something singular about the predicament of blackness, about its standing before the law, and its relationship to the state and very idea of political agency, which is different than the predicament of the immigrant. But on the other hand, I also want to show how the predicament of blackness has laid the groundwork for exclusions and marginalities that have been imposed on a larger population of racialized noncitizens.

For example, the US government's policies for Haitian refugees became a testing ground for detention practices, discourses on criminality, and restrictions on noncitizen rights that set the stage for the present-day deportation regime.[60] European governments have also looked to the Haitian interdictions as a model for how to manage their own "refugee problem," setting the stage for exterritorial enforcement operations that are currently being used to intercept refugees on the Mediterranean Sea, and with a special concern for controlling the movements of black/African peoples.[61]

When I examine the proliferation of these policies, my goal is not to show that we are in an era in which there is no longer any practical difference in the hardships experienced by black and nonblack migrants and refugees. Instead, I am going to emphasize the chronological sequencing of this process. Policies and practices of unprecedented severity are imposed on blacks *first*. I am also going to show that the black/nonblack binary remains intact, even when these policies and practices are extended to nonblacks. Instead of relativizing the black/nonblack distinction, this approach underscores the explanatory value of blackness, which is an argument I develop in more detail throughout the book.

Organization of the Book

In chapter 1, I provide a more thorough discussion of the theoretical framework that informs my treatment of blackness, mobilities, and the law. I use this discussion to rethink the way that migration and refugee scholars have tried to explain the problem of migrant mobility, statelessness, and the "otherness" of immigrants and refugees. In this discussion, I use several examples from antebellum law to describe the pained and complex relationship between blackness and the law, which provides the foundations for the analysis I pursue in the rest of the book.

In chapters 2–6, I provide a critical re-telling of the US government's Haitian refugee policies—and the legal challenges to these policies—which proceeds in a rough chronological order. Chapters 2 and 3 examine several of the earliest legal challenges to the US government's Haitian refugee policy. Both chapters are focused on the "Haitian program" that was created by the INS in the late 1970s. In chapter 2, I situate the courtroom battles over the Haitian program in light of a legal history that dates to the early 1800s. In this review, I show that many of the progressive legal precedents that were brought to the defense of Haitian refugees hail from a jurisprudence on immigrant rights that systemically excluded blacks. I use the de facto, nonblack framework for this jurisprudence to shed some new light on how the legal challenges to the Haitian program were adjudicated and why they all failed.

Chapter 3 situates these same legal challenges in light of jurisprudence on alien excludability that originates in the late 1800s and matures in the early twentieth century. The main argument I make in this chapter is that excludability provides an important starting point for theorizing the relationship between (anti)blackness and the marginality of migrants and refugees, and I introduce the concept of radical exclusion as a way of explaining this relationship. In contrast, critical migration scholars have placed much more emphasis on the problem of deportability, and they have not come to terms with the histories of antiblack racism that explain why the vast majority of deportable subjects fall on the "nonblack side" of the black/nonblack binary. I develop this argument further, in the body of the chapter, with a re-telling of US jurisprudence that traces points of intersection—and divergence—between the precedents established by the Chinese exclusion laws, and the discourse on excludability that was used to justify the mass removal of Haitian refugees under the US government's "Haitian program."

In chapter 4, I examine a series of federal court cases that challenged the interdiction operations of the Reagan-Bush administrations. This chapter covers the peak period of the Haitian interdictions (early 1980s through early 1990s). My analysis focuses on the (ex)territorial arguments that were used to justify the interdictions. I show how questions about the territorial jurisdiction of US law indirectly referenced—and obscured—an antiblack subtext which recalls the racist discourse on the "jurisdictional limits" of the court authority that was introduced by the 1857 *Dred Scott v. Sandford* decision.[62]

Chapter 5 continues with the history of the Haitian interdictions, in the late 1990s, focusing on the federal court decisions for *Cuban American Bar Association (CABA) v. Christopher*[63] which concluded in 1995. The CABA decision was initiated by the complaints of Cuban refugees who had been interdicted and were being detained at the US military base in Guantanamo Bay Cuba, and their lawsuit was joined by legal advocates representing Haitian refugees who were also being detained at Guantanamo.

Comparisons between the government's treatment of Cuban and Haitian refugees are a central theme of this chapter. Although Cubans have, historically, benefited from a more lenient asylum policy than Haitians, the CABA decision was a watershed moment in which Haitian refugee policy was used as a precedent for the treatment of Cubans and, by extension, all other refugee populations. I use my re-telling of this case history to highlight the explanatory value of blackness. I show how policies shaped by a history of (anti) blackness can proliferate to the nonblack side of the black/nonblack binary but without eroding the categorical distinction between black and nonblack. I also expand on this argument to explain how the US government's interdiction operations established precedents that became a routinized feature of the entire immigration system—resulting in what is often described today as "crimmigration."[64] Building on the arguments advanced in all the prior chapters, I explain that the criminalization of immigration can be connected to enforcement practices and a racialized understanding of crime that has historically been used to control black mobility.

In chapter 6, I provide a more contemporary example of how the US government's Haitian refugee policies have established precedents for the treatment of black and nonblack migrants and refugees. My analysis in this chapter is focused on two Trump-era policies and the legal challenges that were levied against them. One of these policies is the Migrant Protection Protocols (more popularly known as the remain-in-Mexico policy) which was directly influenced by Reagan-era Haitian interdiction operations and has been used to control the mobility of Central American refugees. The second policy issue concerns the Trump administration's efforts to cancel the TPS of Haitian, Sudanese, Nicaraguan, and El Salvadoran nationals.

I use the legal struggle over both of these policies to add more depth to arguments that were made in the prior chapters. I show, for example, that the refugees and migrants who were targeted by both of these policy decisions have been maneuvered into a kind of marginality that is qualitatively different than that of the deportable migrant. They are not being incorporated into the United States under a condition of legal precarity. Instead, they are either being prevented from entering the United States (making it impossible for them to become deportable subjects) or they are being ejected on the premise that they had never been officially admitted to the United States (a criterion that alienates them from the rights that are afforded to deportable subjects). The main goal of this analysis is to show how policies and practices that were first applied to black refugees have been expanded to a larger and more diverse migrant and refugee population.

Chapter 7 provides a closing discussion that reflects on the legacies of the Haitian interdictions for immigration and refugee law in the post-Trump era. In this discussion I emphasize that the most important thing that my analysis has to offer these policy debates is a new meta-theoretical and ethical framework. Because antiblackness is a constitutive feature of the modern episteme, it cannot be reduced to a particular "side" in these debates. This is why, throughout the book, I make a point of showing how antiblack sensibilities were justified, normalized, or erased by arguments used to defend immigrants, and even in some cases, by arguments used to defend Haitian refugees. This is one reason why the challenge of making antiblackness salient—for legal strategy or as a framework for rethinking migrant and refugee rights—requires something on the order of a paradigm shift. The challenge is not simply how to make the law more inclusive or force policy-makers to own up to their bias, but to interrogate the social ontologies that have defined the practical scope and limits of the law, which would also require us to confront questions like: "Who is the law truly intended for?"

In order to generate a meaningful answer to these sorts of questions it is necessary to critically reflect on some of the foundational premises of democratic government, modern progress, and the very idea of what it means to be human. Chapter 7 explores these questions to reflect on the limits of the possible as it's been defined by immigration and refugee policies of the present day.

The price paid for entertaining policy solutions that operate within the sphere of the possible is that one has to accept the limits of society, culture, and politics, as defined by an established constellation of powers. As a result, one is never in a position to challenge, or adequately explain, operations like the Haitian interdictions which do not play by the rules of the possible. In order to properly frame the ethical, policy, and political questions raised by the interdictions, it is necessary to think beyond the limits of the possible—as well as questioning how these limits were constituted in the first place. The analysis of antiblackness is an indispensable part of this process. When used to its best effect, this analysis pulls back the curtain on breathless narratives about the problems of the day, to show us that the present moment is just the fragment of a larger process that has been unfolding for several centuries. If we are truly committed to stopping these destructive processes from repeating we must first be prepared to see them in their fullness, which is the chief aim of this book—to bring the defining features of a problem more clearly into view.

NOTES

1. PBS NewsHour, "Handling Haitian Refugees," October 30, 2002, accessed September 29, 2021, https://www.pbs.org/newshour/show/handling-haitian -refugees.

2. Ting was appointed to the position of assistant commissioner of the INS by the George H. W. Bush administration in 1990 and served until 1993. After serving, he returned to his faculty of law position at Temple University and became a more active figure in Republican politics in the new millennium. Temple University Directory, "Jan Ting: Professor Emeritus," accessed September 29, 2021, https://law.temple.edu /contact/jan-ting/.

3. Exemplified by the humanitarian discourse that was used to frame the objectives of Operation Sea Signal and the Supreme Court's rebuttal of refugee complaints about Sea Signal and the camps at the US Naval Base in Guantanamo Bay Cuba. See chapter 5 for a more detailed discussion. The "illegal immigration" discourse that was used to frame Reagan-era interdiction strategies is discussed later in this chapter as well as in chapters 3 and 6.

4. See discussion in chapter 6.

5. Each of the book's chapters builds on this argument, which is summarized in chapter 7. Chapter 6 provides a more detailed look at continuities spanning Obama-, Trump-, and Biden-era policies, including the Obama-era precursors for the Trump-era remain-in-Mexico policy and also how Trump-era exclusions that targeted Haitian asylum seekers were intensified under the Biden administration.

6. Patrisse Cullors, "Abolition and Reparations: Histories of Resistance, Transformative Justice, and Accountability," *Harvard Law Review* 132 (2018): 1684.

7. Brenda Gayle Plummer, *Haiti and the Great Powers, 1902–1915* (Baton Rouge: Louisiana State University Press, 1988).

8. Jeffrey Kahn, *Islands of Sovereignty: Haitian Migration and the Borders of Empire* (University of Chicago Press, 2019), 36–38.

9. Kristina Shull, "Nobody Wants These People: Reagan's Immigration Crisis and America's First Private Prisons," PhD diss, University of California-Irvine, 2014, 49–54.

10. Executive Order No. 12324, 3 C.F.R. 46 FR 48109 (1981), Comp., p. 180.

11. One hundred and seventy-one Haitian refugees were interdicted within the first year of the operation. These numbers escalated to the tens of thousands by early the 1990s. US Department of Homeland Security, USCG Migrant Interdiction Statistics, "Table 534. Coast Guard Migrant Interdictions by Nationality of Alien," Originally accessed May 2011: http://www.uscg.mil/hq/cg5/cg531/AMIO/FlowStats/currentstats.asp/ Reposted at this link and accessed November 21, 2020. https://view.officeapps.live.com/op/view .aspx?src=http%3A%2F%2Fwww2.census.gov%2Flibrary%2Fpublications%2F2011 %2Fcompendia%2Fstatab%2F131ed%2Ftables%2F12s0534.xls.

12. Between 1982 and 2011 the Coast Guard interdicted just under 6,000 Chinese, 36,000 Dominican, and approximately 11,000 Mexican and Central American and just over 67,000 Cuban migrants and refugees, compared to over 116,000 Haitians. US DHS. *USGC Migrant Interdiction Statistics*. Interdiction statistics reported by the Bureau of Transportation recorded a smaller number of Haitians interdicted in the peak years of 1991–1994, and these statistics also cover a different time span (1991–2001). But they still show that Haitians were the single largest interdicted population during this time frame (exceeding 78,000 people, with the next largest interdicted population being Cuban refugees at just under 51,000 people). Bureau of Transportation Statistics. "Table 5.1 U.S. Coast Guard Migrant Interdictions at Sea, Calendar Years 1991–2001."

13. Ibid.

14. Ibid.

15. Ibid.

16. Portes, Alejandro, and Alex Stepick, *City on the Edge: The Transformation of Miami* (Berkeley: University of California Press, 1993), 18–37, 89–122.

17. Damarys Ocaña, "An Unfortunate Icon," *The Guardian*, December 10, 2008, https://www.theguardian.com/commentisfree/cifamerica/2008/dec/10/scarface-al -pacino-anniversary-latinos. It also bears noting that 1983's *Scarface* was a remake of 1940s Al Capone gangster film of the same name and the parallels it made between the Italian mafia and Cuban organized crime implicitly situated in Montana on the "nonblack" side of a black/nonblack binary. The following source uses its critical race analysis to make a different argument but it also documents the parallels I have just described. Roberto Dainotto, *The Mafia: A Cultural History* (London: Reaktion Books, Limited, 2015), 181–183, 192–197.

18. The open arms policy was established by the 1966 Cuban Adjustment Act Public. L. No. 89-732, 80 Stat. 1161 For a discussion, see Alberto Perez, "Note and Comment: Wet Foot, Dry Foot: The Recurring Controversy," *Nova Law Review* 28 (2004): 442–444.

19. All of these conditions are discussed in more detail in chapters 2-4 of this book, but also see: Carl Lindskoog, *Detain and Punish: Haitian Refugees and the Rise of the World's Largest Immigration Detention System* (Gainesville: University Press of Florida, 2018); Shull, "Nobody Wants These People," 41–80.

20. Perez, "Note and Comment: Wet Foot, Dry Foot: The Recurring Controversy."

21. *Cuban Adjustment Act*, Pub.L. 89–732, 80 Stat. 1161 (1966).

22. *Immigration Reform and Control Act*, Pub.L 99–603, 100 Stat. 3359 (1986). Shull, "Nobody Wants These People," 47, citing Gilburt Loescher and John Scanlan, "Human Rights, U.S. Foreign Policy, and Haitian Refugees," *Journal of Interamerican Studies and World Affairs* 26, no. 3 (1984): 313–356 at 344.

23. This program is discussed in chapters 2 and 3. See also the overview provided by *Haitian Refugee Ctr. v. Civiletti*, 503 F. Supp. 442 (S.D. Fla. 1980).

24. During 1998–1999 I served as policy and communications director for the Human Services Coalition of Dade County and, among other things, became involved in community-based research, public education, and advocacy projects addressing the needs of African American, Latinx, and Haitian welfare recipients. As an outgrowth of this work, I became lead researcher for a project that documented the impact of the 1996 welfare and immigration reform laws on the South Florida Haitian immigrant population, funded by the Scholar-Practitioner Project of the W.K. Kellogg Foundation. I continued this research through 2002, after taking up a faculty position at Florida Memorial College, which is South Florida's only historically black college or university. For a summary report, see Philip Kretsedemas, "Haitian immigrants and welfare services in Miami-Dade county," W.K. Kellogg Foundation website, July 2001, accessed September 29, 2021, file:///C:/Users/pkret/Downloads/1623706%20(3).PDF.

25. Philip Kretsedemas, "Language Barriers and Perceptions of Bias: Ethnic Differences in Immigrant Encounters with Welfare System," *Journal of Sociology & Social Welfare* 32 (2005): 109–123; "Avoiding the State: Haitian Immigrants and Welfare Services in Miami-Dade County," in *Immigrants, Welfare Reform, and the Poverty of Policy*, eds. Philip Kretsedemas and Ana Aparicio (Westport, CT & London: Greenwood-Praeger, 2004), 107–136.

26. For one account, see Pia Orrenius and Madeline Zavodny, "Do Amnesty Programs Reduce Undocumented Immigration? Evidence from IRCA," *Demography* 40, no. 3 (2003): 437–450; *HRC v. Civiletti*, 503 F. Supp. 442 (S.D. Fla. 1980), 516–517.

27. Jared Sexton, "Unbearable Blackness," *Cultural Critique* 90, no. 90 (2015): 159–178; Calvin Warren, *Ontological Terror: Blackness, Nihilism and Emancipation* (Durham, NC: Duke University Press, 2018); Frank Wilderson, *Afropessimism* (New York: Liveright Publishing/W.W. Norton, 2020), 191–210.

28. Building on the work of Saidiya Hartman which I treat in more detail in chapter 1. For an introduction to the concept of black fungibility, see Sarah Jane Cervenak

and J. Kameron Carter, "Untitled and Outdoors: Thinking with Saidiya Hartman," *Women & Performance: A Journal of Feminist Theory* 27, no. 1 (2017): 45–55.

29. Kahn, *Islands of Sovereignty*, 47.

30. Kahn, *Islands of Sovereignty*, 27–54.

31. The Department of Homeland Security, which incorporated the INS bureaucracy as part of a broader security mandate, was in the process of being formed during the time of Ting's October 2002, PBS NewsHour commentary. The proposal to form the DHS was issued in June 2002 and the DHS began operations in March 2003. Charles Perrow, "Disaster after 9/11 The Department of Homeland Security and the Intelligence Reorganization," *Homeland Security Affairs* 2, no. 1 (2006): 1–29.

32. *Civiletti*, 503 F. Supp. 442, 510–516; Shull, "Nobody Wants These People," 41–80.

33. Lucille Renwick, "Haiti Memories: Searching for a New Life, Hundreds of Refugees Have Arrived in L.A. With Their Stories of Despair and Brutal Treatment Back Home," *LA Times*, August 21, 1994, accessed September 24, 2021, https://www .latimes.com/archives/la-xpm-1994-08-21-ci-29766-story.html.

34. Nicole Phillips and Tom Ricker, *The Invisible Wall: Title 42 and Its Impact on Haitian Migrants* (San Diego, CA: Haitian Bridge Alliance, Quixote Center and UndocuBlack Network, 2021). Accessed September 19, 2021, file:///C:/Users/pkret/ OneDrive/Documents/Writing%20&%20Research/Black%20Interdictions/Chapter% 20Drafts/Completed%20Drafts/The-Invisible-Wall.pdf, 38–40.

35. Michael Posner, *Violations of Human Rights in Haiti*, A Report of the Lawyers Committee for International Human Rights to the Organization of American States. November 1980, accessed September 25, 2021, https://ufdc.ufl.edu/AA00001006 /00001/2j, 16–17. This report was cited several times in one of the first federal court decisions to challenge the US government's Haitian refugee policies. *Civiletti*, 503 F. Supp. 442 at 481, 483 and 523.

36. Posner, *Violations of Human Rights in Haiti*, 6 and 12–14.

37. Ibid., 7–8.

38. Kahn, *Islands of Sovereignty*, 34–40; Nicolas Rossier, "Conversation Part 2: Jean-Bertrand Aristide on Haiti in the Earthquake's Aftermath," *The Nation/Grit TV*. November 22, 2010. Accessed September 19, 2021, https://www.youtube.com/watch ?v=1EP_hrhRgg0.

39. Posner, *Violations of Human Rights in Haiti*, 12–15.

40. Kahn, *Islands of Sovereignty*, 39.

41. Kahn, *Islands of Sovereignty*, 27–54.

42. Moon-Kie Jung, "The Enslaved, the Worker and Du Bois's Black Reconstruction: Toward an Underdiscipline of Antisociology," *Sociology of Race and Ethnicity* 5, no. 2 (2019): 157–168.

43. See n28 and 29 and also, Saidiya Hartman, *Scenes of Subjection: Terror, Slavery, and Self-Making in Nineteenth-Century America* (New York: Oxford University Press, 2007); P. Khalil Saucier and Tryon Woods. eds., *Conceptual Aphasia in Black* (Lanham, MD: Lexington, 2016).

44. Roy Bryce-Laporte, "Black Immigrants: The Experience of Invisibility and Inequality," *Journal of Black Studies* 3, no. 1 (1972): 29–56; Julian Go, ed.,

Rethinking Obama (Bingley, UK: Emerald Group Publishing, 2011); Jared Sexton, "Proprieties of Coalition: Blacks, Asians, and the Politics of Policing," *Critical Sociology* 36, no. 1 (2010): 87–108.

45. Sébastien Chauvin and Blanca Garcés-Mascareñas, "Beyond Informal Citizenship: The New Moral Economy of Migrant Illegality," *International Political Sociology* 6, no. 3 (2012): 241–259; Nicholas De Genova, "Migrant 'Illegality' and Deportability in Everyday Life," *Annual Review of Anthropology* 31, no. 1 (2002): 419–447.; Douglas Massey, Jorge Durand and Karen Pren, "Explaining Undocumented Migration to the US," *International Migration Review* 48, no. 4 (2014): 1028–1061.

46. In the Clinton era the US government spent half a billion dollars to construct living quarters on the Naval Base at Guantanamo Bay to house tens of thousands of Haitian and Cuban refugees, not counting the funding it provided for other refugee holding facilities in Central America and the funds it provided to Caribbean and Latin American governments to assist with the diversion of these refugee flows. Christina Frohock, "'Brisas del Mar': Judicial and Political Outcomes of the Cuban Rafter Crisis in Guantánamo," *Harvard Latino Law Review* 15, no. 39 (2012): 39–83 at 50. More recently the US government has spent tens of millions of dollars to create living facilities on the Mexican side of the US-Mexico border to house migrants and refugees who are being diverted from entry into the United States via the Migrant Protection Protocols (aka the remain-in-Mexico program) which does not include funding provided to international humanitarian organizations and the Mexican government to assist with services intended to facilitate the return of these migrants to their home nations or funding provided to other governments to assist with "third country" diversion strategies for refugees. Department of Homeland Security, "Assessment of the Migrant Protection Protocols (MPP)," *Publications Library*, October 28, 2019, accessed January 1, 2021, https://www.dhs.gov/publication/assessment-migrant-protection-protocols-mpp; Claire Felter and Amelia Cheatham, "Can 'Safe Third Country' Agreements Resolve the Asylum Crisis?" *Council on Foreign Relations*, August 29, 2019, accessed January 4, 2021, https://www.cfr.org/in-brief/can-safe-third-country-agreements-resolve-asylum-crisis#:~:text=Asylum%20seekers%20are%20required%20to,them%20back%20to%20that%20country. For a more comprehensive treatment of these diversion strategies, which account for policy and spending of other Western industrialized nations, see Thomas Gammeltoft-Hansen and Nikolas Tan, "The End of the Deterrence Paradigm - Future Directions for Global Refugee Policy," *Journal on Migration and Human Security* 5, no. 1 (2017): 28–56.

47. For one account of this paradigm shift, see Viviana Zelizer, "How I Became a Relational Economic Sociologist and What Does That Mean?" *Politics & Society* 40, no. 2 (2012): 145–174.

48. Dorothy Smith, *Writing the Social: Critique, Theory, and Investigations* (Toronto: University of Toronto Press, 2000), 45–69.

49. Marilyn Waring, *If Women Counted: A New Feminist Economics* (San Francisco: Harper & Row, 1988).

50. Mark Tushnet, "Critical Legal Studies: A Political History," *Yale Law Journal* 100 (1990): 1515; Stefancic and Delgado Richard Delgado and Jean Stefancic,

Critical Race Theory an Introduction, 3rd ed. (New York: New York University Press, 2017), 4–6.

51. Derrick Bell, "*Brown v. Board of Education* and the Interest Convergence Dilemma," in *The Derrick Bell Reader*, eds. Richard Delgado and Jean Stefancic (New York: NYU Press, 2005), 30–39.

52. Derrick Bell, *Faces at the Bottom of the Well: The Permanence of Racism* (New York: Basic Books, 1992).

53. Legal storytelling is a term coined by Delgado and Stefancic, based on their interpretation of Bell's writing, which Bell subsequently embraced as an epistemology that informs his work. Richard Delgado and Jean Stefancic, "Derrick Bell's Chronicle of the Space Traders: Would the US Sacrifice People of Color if the Price Was Right?" *Univ of Colorado Law Review* 62 (1991): 321; Derrick Bell, "Chronicle of the Space Traders" in *The Derrick Bell Reader*, eds. Richard Delgado and Jean Stefancic, (New York: NYU Press, 2005), 57–72.

54. Bell, "*Brown v. Board of Education* and the Interest Convergence Dilemma."

55. Michelle Alexander, *The New Jim Crow: Mass Incarceration in the Age of Colorblindness* (New York: The New Press, 2012) 1–19.

56. Wilderson (elaborating on insights from Saidiya Hartman) has insisted that blackness is constituted as an object in relation to subjects; it cannot have a subjectivity of its own. Frank Wilderson, *Afropessimism* (New York: Liveright Publishing/W.W. Norton, 2020), 191–210. Although this is a valuable insight, I also think it is important to emphasize that this subject/object distinction is constructed through language and power rather than being an inherent property of the black body—which leads to the understanding that people who are embodied as black can have subjective orientations, so long as these subjectivities do not affirm their experience of (anti) blackness. This insight is consistent with the Fanonian metaphor of the white mask covering the black face. Black bodies access social space through nonblack personas, but the same institutional processes that enable these nonblack personas militate against the formation of subjectivities that are informed by a singularly black experience of embodiment. I make this same point in chapter 1 using the contrast between refugees that happen to be black and the black people who happen to be refugees.

57. Gayatri Chakravorty Spivak, "Can the Subaltern Speak?" *Die Philosophin* 14, no. 27 (2003): 42–58.

58. As I explain in chapter 6, there are also exterritorial border control practices that take place inside the sovereign territory of other nations. The US government's efforts to contain flows of Central American refugees within Mexico are one example of these "interdiction-on-land" strategies, which have a history that is almost as old as its "interdiction-at-sea" operations. See Joseph Nevins, *Operation Gatekeeper and Beyond: The War On "Illegals" and the Remaking of the U.S. – Mexico Boundary*, (Routledge, NY: 2001).

59. Ronald Judy, *(Dis)Forming the American Canon: African-Arabic Slave Narratives and the Vernacular* (Minneapolis, MN: University of Minnesota Press, 1993), 1; Warren, *Ontological Terror*, 76–87.

60. Lindskoog, *Detain and Punish*; Jenna Lloyd and Alison Mount, "The Caribbean Roots of U.S. Migration Policy," *NACLA Report on the Americas* 51,

no. 1 (2019): 78–84, https://www.tandfonline.com/doi/abs/10.1080/10714839.2019
.1593695?journalCode=rnac20.

61. Jeffrey Kahn, "The Caribbean Roots of European Maritime Interdiction,"
Society for Cultural Anthropology: Refugees and the Crisis of Europe, June 28,
2016, https://culanth.org/fieldsights/the-caribbean-roots-of-european-maritime-inter-
diction. African refugees are not the only national origin groups targeted by these
interdictions, but similar to the Haitian case, they are the predominant target of these
operations. Africans are also heavily overrepresented in the statistics of refugees who
have died trying to cross the Mediterranean. International Migration Organization
(IOM), Missing Migrants: Tracking Deaths Along Migratory Routes, https://miss-
ingmigrants.iom.int/; EUNAVFOR MED—Operation SOPHIA Six Monthly Report:
June 22 to December 31, 2015 at 23, https://migrantsatsea.org/tag/maritime-interdic-
tion/; UNITED network, Fatal Policies of Fortress Europe, http://unitedagainstrefuge
edeaths.eu/.

62. *Dred Scott v. Sandford*, 60 U.S. 393 (1857).

63. *Cuban American Bar Association v. Christopher*, 43 F.3d 1412 (11th Cir.
1995).

64. Juliet Stumpf, "The Crimmigration Crisis: Immigrants, Crime and Sovereign
Power," *American University Law Review* 56, no. 2 (2006): 367–419.

Chapter 1

Navigating the Chasm

Antiblackness, Mobilities, and the Law

Capt. J. B. Brunt, who resided near my master, had a slave named John. He was his body servant, carriage driver, &c. On one occasion, while driving his master through the city,—the streets being very muddy, and the horses going at a rapid rate,—some mud spattered upon a gentleman by the name of Robert More. More was determined to be revenged. Some three or four months after this occurrence, he purchased John, for the express purpose, as he said, "to tame the d--d nigger." After the purchase, he took him to a blacksmith's shop, and had a ball and chain fastened to his leg, and then put him to driving a yoke of oxen, and kept him at hard labor, until the iron around his leg was so worn into the flesh, that it was thought mortification would ensue. In addition to this, John told me that his master whipped him regularly three times a week for the first two months—and all this to "tame him." A more noble looking man than he, was not to be found in all St. Louis, before he fell into the hands of More; and a more degraded and spirit-crushed looking being was never seen on a southern plantation, after he had been subjected to this "taming" process for three months. The last time that I saw him, he had nearly lost the entire use of his limbs.—*Narrative of William W. Brown, a Fugitive Slave. Written by Himself*[1]

JOHN'S STORY

I have begun this chapter with one of the many horrifying stories that are recounted in the fugitive slave narrative that has been attributed to William Brown.[2] The story of John the carriage driver depicts the experience of black people who have been much less fortunate than the Brown. Without Brown's

narrative these stories would very likely have been swallowed up by the sanc-
timonious justifications of the slave trade that were being circulated by the
slave owning classes.

For this book, Brown's narrative is important because it calls attention
to the intimate relationship between the extreme violence of slavery and an
experience of controlled mobility. Brown's narrative is in many respects a
travel log, which shows how the movements of enslaved people were dic-
tated by their masters and also how slavery was defined by a series of violent
transits, beginning with the forced migration of Africans to the "new world."
Brown gives many accounts of how he was taken by his masters on cross-
country treks to perform various duties, how other blacks were purchased as
slaves along the way or discarded at the convenience of the master, and how
slaves were punished because they did not conform, precisely, to the demands
placed on their mobility.

This oppressive experience of mobility is a defining feature of John's story.
John begins his role in this story as a function of his master's mobility—a
carriage driver. But he commits an error in the transport of his master that
offends another white male of some wealth and social standing. This "gentleman," Robert Moore, decides to purchase John from his current master for the
sole purpose of punishing him, and the punishment that John receives is so
brutal that he is rendered immobile, losing the ability to use his arms and legs.

John's new master clearly took personal offense at having mud splashed on
him. The punishment he meted out to John was also, clearly, in excess—by
any "humane" and reasonable measure—of the gravity of John's error which,
if we are to believe Brown's narrative, was not intentional (and the punishment was grotesquely excessive even if John's actions were intentional).
The punishment meted out to John also had nothing to do with an interest in
exploiting his labor. From a strictly utilitarian perspective, it makes no sense
for a white man of means to invest his money in a new "property" (the body
of a black man), for the purpose of rendering this property incapable of laboring. But this is exactly what John's new master did.

Robert Moore's personhood had been offended by the actions of John, who
he regarded as a nonperson. Moore could not respond to this situation in a
more reasonable way without according some dignity to John, and in order to
do this he would have to confront the antiblack sentiments that had made it so
easy for him to see John as a subhuman commodity that existed to serve the
wishes of fully human subjects. John's status, as the property of another, was
grounded in a sensibility that cannot be explained by a pragmatic economic
reasoning. There is, first of all, a racist order of rank—or what many Black
Studies scholars have called, an antiblack, social ontology[3]—that determines
who will be a commodity and who will be the owners and consumers of these
subhuman commodities. If this order of rank is violated, the entire chain

of economic transactions on which it relies is threatened. Mobility is the medium through which this barbaric melodrama plays itself out.

In the context of this story, white privilege manifests itself in an expectation of dignified and unimpeded movement, and in the ability to control the movements of the nonpersons who are charged with facilitating these movements. To be black, on the other hand, is to be caught in a predicament—which is supported by institutionalized networks of power and a deeply engrained cultural sensibility—in which your mobility is controlled by people who relate to you from the other side of an unbridgeable, social divide.

The narrator of John's tale eventually finds his way to freedom. William Brown escapes to Canada and his story, which is eventually contracted to a Boston publisher, becomes an important document for the abolitionist movement.[4] In addition to being a trenchant denunciation of chattel slavery, Brown's narrative presents the reader with an archetype of black liberation as self-willed mobility. It resonates with the pattern of movement that Ralph Ellison has used to describe the collective consciousness of the black American experience.[5] According to Ellison, this pattern of movement is not a cultural tradition or an identity.[6] It just reflects the way that black people tend to respond to the challenges they collectively face, using similar tactics that are animated by a yearning for freedom.

It is not difficult to see the connections between this black American pattern of movement and the Haitian refugee experience. Like William Brown's narrative, these refugee stories have been narrated as a struggle for a freer way of living that is made possible by daring acts of mobility. One example is the story of Natalie and Gregory Beaubrun that has been documented by the Guantanamo Public Memory project.[7] Natalie and Gregory, who are brother and sister, fled Haiti with their parents in the wake of the instability and persecution that intensified after the first military coup that was led against President Aristide in 1991. They recall their family fleeing after police raided the village where they were living in Haiti. Natalie was so young at the time that she has very few detailed memories, but she recalls seeing police brutalize her mother. Gregory, who was a few years older, remembered a bit more. He did not recall his parents telling him they were leaving. He explains:

> All I really remember is we packed our stuff, and then we were on the boat. And I remember the boat journey was a long scary journey, in the middle of the night. Rain storms . . . Ship rocking. At one point the ship . . . was about to tilt over. Water just hit us from one side . . . and everyone running to the other side grabbing buckets, throwing water off the boat. It was a pretty dramatic scene.[8]

Natalie and Gregory's boat was intercepted by the US Coast Guard the next day. The boat was sunk and everyone on board was taken to a navy ship and transported to the US military camp at Guantanamo Bay, Cuba. After a period of detention that may have lasted weeks or months, Natalie and Gregory's family was released to the United States. They were probably among the first several thousand Haitians whose asylum cases were processed normally in the weeks immediately following the coup—before the issuance of the Kennebunkport Executive Order that allowed the Coast Guard to repatriate all Haitians intercepted at sea without screening their asylum claims.[9] As is the case with many refugee stories that end reasonably well, this policy context fades into the background of Natalie and Gregory's story. What they remember is the experience of flight, the hardships, and the small acts of heroism that made it possible for them to have a new life in the United States.

Collette Brutus's voyage across the Caribbean Sea was just as harrowing.[10] She was fifteen years old at the time, a few years older than Gregory. But unlike Gregory she fled to the United States unaccompanied by either of her parents, though her father had encouraged her to leave. She remembers the name of the boat, *C'est La'vie*, which reflects the sense of humor and stoicism of the Haitian people, and of her traveling companions in particular. After the boat disembarked from the dock, Collette saw one of her friends running toward it, hoping to board. Collette dove in the water, swam to her friend, and swam back with her to the boat. Collette's friend was extremely grateful for being "saved" in this way, but they both knew there was no guarantee that they would survive the trip. It so happens that Collette's story ended well (since she lived to tell her tale) but three months after Collette and her friend landed in the United States, thirty-three Haitians who attempted the same journey drowned at sea.[11] Like Natalie and Gregory's boat, the *C'est La'vie* was rocked by tumultuous storms. Collette recalls seeing waves as big as buildings. There was a Catholic and a Voodoo priest on board the ship. They each offered their own brand of spiritual protection from the storm and spent much of the journey arguing about theology.

Collette was a month at sea. Her boat landed on the South Florida shores sometime in August 1981. She recalls being met by US immigration officers who she thought were very friendly; they took everyone to the detention center at Krome. What Collette did not know, at the time, is that most other refugees were paroled into the United States, which meant that they could live freely with family, friends, or sponsoring organizations while their cases were being processed. At the time, the policy of detaining asylum seekers was directed exclusively at Haitians.[12] Nevertheless, Collette's attitude toward the entire venture was one of gratitude and she had a reason to feel lucky. A few weeks later, the Reagan administration issued the executive order that inaugurated the Haitian Migrant Interdiction Operation (HMIO). If the *C'est La'vie* had begun its journey at that time, it would not have been allowed into US waters.

CONTROLLED MOBILITY

For Collette, sea travel presented an opportunity for freedom, which is not very different from the fugitive lines of flight made possible by the underground railroad. Her journey across the Caribbean Sea can be located within a long tradition of unruly Diasporic movements that has been described by Paul Gilroy and Julius Scott.[13] Both of these scholars have shown how sea travel and the communication networks of port-side communities allowed black people to think and act outside of the strictures of colonial society. Scott, in particular, has shown how these relationships between sea travel and the black freedom struggle played out in the era of the Haitian revolution.

The interdiction operations that were inaugurated by the Reagan administration changed this relationship in some very significant ways. The extra-territorial space of the high seas was leveraged in favor of national governments, as a space in which refugees could be subjected to enforcement practices that did not have to abide by national or international law. Instead of holding out the promise of liberatory movement, the seas were converted into carceral laboratories.

Fugitive slaves like William Brown faced a similar dilemma. The freedom that many ex-slaves hoped to find in free states—or in Canada—was bittersweet. Even when a black slave was manumitted, and could procure legal documents to show that their freedom had been authorized by the law, they were still haunted by the alienating stigma of blackness. The free black populations of the antebellum era suffered racist violence, chronic unemployment or precarious employment, and were barred from many aspects of public life.[14] For many whites, the very idea of a free black was an anomaly that had no place in US society, which is why many of the laws enacted to control black movement in the antebellum era were focused on free blacks.[15] Under slavery, blacks were subject to controls that coercively integrated them, as a servile caste, into white social and economic life. The controls imposed on free blacks, on the other hand, were used to keep them at a distance from whites. Like the black refugee, free blacks were an unwanted population, and the tactics used to control both populations gravitated in the same direction—deterrence, detainment, and expulsion.

The predicament I have just described offers more insight into the plasticity of controlled mobility. In some instances, controlled mobility arrests movement and in other cases, it is used to govern a very fluid kind of movement. So it stands to reason that the most important feature of controlled mobility is not how far and wide a body is allowed to move. What matters most are the conditions under which the body is able to move. The object of controlled mobility can be highly mobile, so long as this mobility is not self-directed.

The transatlantic slave trade, for example, radically accelerated the inter-continental mobility of African people. Because of the slave trade, millions of African people were forcibly imported into the Americas. Beginning in the late eighteenth century, the US government tried to stop some of these prac-tices. The Coast Guard's first interdiction operations, which began in 1794, were focused on intercepting ships that were transporting African slaves into the United States.[16] It is not difficult to see how these interdiction operations could be justified by a humanitarian interest in preventing the exploitation of enslaved black people. But it is important to consider how this solution to the problem of black slavery was informed by the same unilateral prerogatives as that of the slave traffickers.

Most nineteenth-century US elites who thought slave trafficking should be criminalized also believed that black people were uniquely unfit candidates for migration to the United States, whether forced or free.[17] The same human-itarian impulses that led many of these elites to oppose slavery also led them to endorse plans for the mass deportation of the US-born black population and other policy priorities that minimized the black presence within the flow of free migrant labor to the United States. The end result is that controlled mobility pervaded all aspects of the struggle over slavery—in the way that enslaved blacks were imported into the United States and how they were deployed by their masters, as well as in the interdictions used to prevent their importation to the United States and in the programs that were used to deport free and enslaved blacks to Africa. Parallels can be drawn to the treatment of refugees in the present day.

The interdicted refugee can be held indefinitely in detention centers that fall outside of the legal jurisdiction of the nation-state, which was the fate of Haitian refugees held at the US military base in Guantanamo Bay, Cuba.[18] These detainees can also be transferred from one facility to another, as deemed necessary by the US government, or they can be deported "home" or to a third nation if US officials are able to make a repatriation or resettle-ment agreement with another national government. On rare occasions, the interdicted refugee can be admitted to the United States. Some of these refu-gees are paroled into the United States so that they can pursue their asylum claim before the immigration courts or to receive medical treatment. Harold Koh provides a poignant example with his story of Silieses Success, who was held in a camp for HIV-infected Haitians at Guantanamo Bay and was relocated back and forth between Guantanamo and hospitals on the US main-land. According to the official transcript, these relocations were coordinated for the sake of tending to her medical condition, but they were carried out in complete disregard for her mental or physical health and with no concern about the death of her infant, which was caused by the treatment she received at Guantanamo.[19] This tragic story shows that maritime interdictions do not completely arrest the movement of the refugee. After they are intercepted by the Coast Guard, the refugee just transitions from one type of mobility to another: their self-directed movement is supplanted by an externally directed movement, which is entirely controlled by the state.

SITUATING CONTROLLED MOBILITY WITHIN MIGRATION AND CRITICAL RACE STUDIES

Broadly defined, there is nothing about controlled mobility that runs against the grain of established theories of migrant mobility. The sticking point arises with the proposition that antiblackness is a paradigmatic feature of this kind of mobility. In other words, controlled mobility is not just a predicament that disproportionately effects black populations; it is a mobility regime that is inextricably intertwined with the history of antiblack racism. This means that the black body has to be understood as the prototypical object of administration for the exercise of power that produces controlled mobility.

The migration studies literature, on the other hand, tends to theorize mobilities in light of factors that operate at a higher level of abstraction than racial-ethnic categories (as well as, for that matter, gender, class, and sexuality). For example, there may be a history of seasonal migration that is specific to Mexican farm workers, but the concept of seasonal migration is not treated as if it is a unique product of the migratory dynamics of Mexican farmworkers, and the way that these migrations have been regulated by the state.[20] A similar observation can be made about most research on unauthorized migration, or migration propelled by the dynamics of family reunification or the migration of visa holders who have been categorized, by policy makers, as "high skilled workers."[21] This is a habit of thought that pervades the field of migration studies: that migrant mobilities have a (social) life unto themselves that can be conceptually distinguished from the populations that are doing the migrating. This premise has been artfully used by many theorists and researchers to conceptualize and document new patterns of global migration. I am not arguing that the findings generated by this scholarship are theoretically invalid. I am trying to make a more nuanced point: the way this scholarship conceptualizes mobility does not provide an adequate starting point for the problems I am grappling within this book.

The refugee studies literature is, arguably, more attuned to group-specific patterns of movement because people often flee in groups, and their displacement has usually been shaped by a particular history of group relations. Research on statelessness, for example, can be used to diagnose a condition that is endemic to an entire sociocultural population, as evidenced by the case of the Kurds and the Rohingya.[22] Even so, most of the research on these populations is not informed by a theory of racism and racial stratification, and especially not one that operates on a world-historical scale.

When the refugee studies literature engages the problem of racism it is usually contained within an analysis of contexts-of-reception and obstacles to integration.[23] Even when the refugee studies literature takes race seriously, it conceptualizes racism as a problem that is experienced the same basic way by all racialized populations, or in some cases, as a problem that is inherent to the refugee category itself. As a result, it becomes possible to write about the racialization of refugees, and to analogize the predicament of one refugee population to another, without having to reflect on differences in the ways bodies can be racialized—apart from the question of their refugee status.[24] Not surprisingly, these kinds of analyses have little or nothing to say about antiblack racism. Meanwhile, explanations of refugee displacement tend to follow the same pattern as the migration studies literature.

International law treats the refugee as a displaced person who happens to be black, female, Nigerian, a single mother, Muslim, and so on. Displacement is not understood to be a chronic feature of an entire population's experience that follows from the way they have been categorized. Instead, displacement is usually depicted as a tragic turn of events that effects a subcategory of people in these populations. So, we have a problem of displaced Iraqis or displaced Somalians, but not displacement as a constitutive feature of the Iraqi or Somalian experience. The state bureaucracy also requires the particulars of the refugee's experience to be converted into a narrative that comports with national and international refugee law. Researchers have documented the stress and confusion this process causes for asylum seekers who are often forced to reinvent their life stories, to make them legible for the asylum bureaucracy.[25]

These dilemmas are symptomatic of an epistemological commonsense that cuts across the migration and refugee studies literature. There is a relationship between this commonsense and another phenomenon which has been described as methodological nationalism.[26] The connecting thread has to do with the political-administrative prerogatives of the nation-state and the way these prerogatives come to define scholarly objects of study. The flow of migrants and refugees is a special concern for the state administration, because these movements raise thorny questions about legal status and political membership that carry implications for immigration and refugee law, border security, citizenship law, and so on. As a result, migrant and refugee mobilities are conceptualized from the vantage point of the nation-state. Consequently the very idea of mobility becomes associated with movement across international borderlines, involving populations that are defined by the legal statuses assigned to them by the state (seasonal workers, work visa holders, unauthorized migrants, noncitizens who adjust through family reunification, etc.).

Within the critical literature on globalization, migration, and displacement, there is a more pronounced emphasis on how patterns of spatial mobility are shaped by the organization of the global economy and how they correlate with other patterns of stratification that operate along lines of race, class, and gender. For example, Zygmunt Bauman and Mark Duffield have explained how globalization has accelerated the mobility of investment capital and amplified the exit power of multinational corporations, while also creating new forms of centralization and spaces of confinement.[27] Duffield, in particular, has explained why this global system should be understood as a racist stratagem that is geared toward confining populations in racially circumscribed territorial zones.[28] Ronen Shamir, who advances a comparable line of argument, has produced one of the most detailed conceptualizations of the global stratification of mobility.[29] Shamir explains how access to mobility has become a new axis for the organization of inequality on a global scale. Following this premise, Shamir is able to map the continuities between restrictions on the mobility of black, native-born populations (via mass incarceration, the politics of urban development, and welfare reform) and restrictions on the mobility of migrants and refugees.

These theories make a break with the methodological nationalism that has hampered many conceptions of mobility. But they continue to replicate an epistemological commonsense in which theories of mobility—even if they are being used to critique the practices of state and corporate actors—are conceptualized on a more abstract scale than the populations that are doing the moving (or whose ambitions of free movement are being frustrated by the state). For example, the phenomenon of restricted mobility, as theorized by Shamir, describes a technique of control that is not specific to black populations, Latinx migrants, or Arab-Muslim refugees. These populations may be subjected to restrictions on their mobility which vary by degree of intensity, but the factors that explain this condition of restricted mobility are essentially the same for all of these groups.

This may seem to be a fine point, but it carries important implications for the analysis I am pursuing in this book. The key distinction is whether you understand the mobility regime as a thing that is imposed on an already-racialized population, or whether you understand race as an axis of difference that is being constantly generated and reshaped by these mobility regimes. If you take the former route, it is not possible to produce a race analysis (i.e., an analysis that explains race). Instead, you are using your analysis of mobility to describe disparities that vary by race. On the other hand, if you take the latter route, you are using the mobility regime to explain race which, among other things, means coming to terms with the reflexive and generative relationship between the mobility regime and the racist imaginary that informs it. Viewed in this light, controlled mobility is not a regimen of power imposed on populations that are already categorized as black. Instead, controlled mobility is a regimen of power that actively constitutes blackness as a condition of unfreedom—reinforcing a chain of associations between blackness, rightlessness, and externally directed movement.

This proposition is my attempt at restating one of the core arguments advanced by Afropessimist theory, which is that slavery makes blackness.[30] One point that follows from this proposition is that racial categories are constantly being made and reshaped by machineries of power and domination. This argument is similar, in some ways, to Michael Omi and Howard Winant's explanation of the reflexive interplay of structural and cultural forces that drive the process of racial formation.[31] One important difference, however, is that the Afropessimist argument about slavery is not describing a history of power that can be abstracted from blackness. Omi and Winant, in contrast, theorize race in the same way that many migration scholars theorize mobility. They have produced a theory that can explain the meaning of race in virtually every spatio-temporal context, because the theorization operates at a higher level of abstraction than all of the racial categories that are subsumed under their theory.[32]

In contrast, the argument that "slavery makes blackness" is attuned to factors that are immanent to antiblack racism. The transatlantic slave trade is not used to illustrate a set of factors that are more abstract than the slave trade itself. Instead, (anti)blackness is understood to be a unique product of the tear in the fabric of meaning that was produced by the transatlantic slave trade and the orders of modern knowledge that coalesced in tandem with it. This early modern period could be described as the sociocultural equivalent of the big bang—a singular event that produces a new world of meaning which recodes all that came before rather than being determined by it. The structural organization of the modern racial order has to be traced to this period, which established the paradigm within which it operates.

Another important implication of this argument is that (anti)blackness is baked into the structural and cultural foundations of this order from the very beginning, defining the constitutive exterior of the modern Human. Blackness is associated with all of the regressive and stultifying things had to be cleared out of the way so that the Human could make its entrance on the scene of history. In this regard, blackness does not describe another kind of peoples, but a host of illegible qualities that rule out the very possibility of peoplehood, civilizational advancement, political agency, and so on.[33] But this banishment of blackness from the realm of the Human is accompanied by another process whereby blackness is reincorporated as a radically depersonalized strata of commodified bodies that are used to make the very same world they are excluded from. Jared Sexton sums up this predicament in the following way:

> Blackness indicates: existence without standing in the modern world system. To be black is to exist in exchange without being a party to exchange. Being black means belonging to a state that is organized in part by its ignorance of your perspective. . . . Reduced to what would seem its essential trait, blackness is a kind of invisibility. Taken seriously, these facts about blackness are enough to make problems for anyone who wants to talk about blackness as founding a tradition. *Conceptualized not as a shared culture but as the condition of statelessness,* blackness would seem to deny the perspective that is necessary to communicate a tradition.[34] (Emphasis added)

Sexton is describing a radically alienated condition that reverberates through all of the institutions and knowledge systems of the modern world. He describes this predicament as a kind of statelessness, but it is clearly not the same kind of statelessness that is described by reports issued by the United Nations High Commission on Refugees (UNHCR).[35] For the UNHCR, and international law more generally, statelessness is a tragic situation that a person can fall-in and fall-out of. The same is true for the forced displacement of the refugee.[36] One becomes a refugee due to exceptional circumstances that uproot a person from their normal habitat, and one ceases to be a refugee once you are able to resume your life in that habitat or if you are able to resettle elsewhere. Within this universe of meaning, black refugees are refugees, first and foremost. Put another way, they are understood to be refugees who happen to be black. Their predicament can be remedied by the assignment of legal status that rescues them from their rightless existence, and this is because the problems they are suffering have more to do with their status as refugees than as black people.

Sexton, on the other hand, is describing a predicament that follows the black refugee even if they are granted asylum. The unarmed, black US citizen or legal permanent resident who is killed by the police, because they appear to be a dangerous criminal, is just as good an example of the problem of black statelessness as the Haitian refugee who is interdicted on the Caribbean Sea. The connecting thread between these two situations is not defined by a political, legal, or socioeconomic status which could define their place inside a social order. The connecting thread is that both people have been relegated to a zone that defines the outer limits of this social order—a zone in which the formal and informal rules that govern interactions between the fully incorporated members of this order do not apply.

Of course, not all black people are exposed to the hazards of black statelessness in the same way, and the vast majority do not experience the extremes that I've used to illustrate the condition. There are also many black people who are buffered from the worst hazards of this condition by the other privileged statuses they happen to occupy. But the problem of blackness, as theorized by Sexton and other scholars, is a condition that exceeds and overflows all of these protections.[37] It is a condition that leads all of the people, who are caught up in it, to gravitate ineluctably toward statelessness, barring the presence of countervailing forces. Once you cross the threshold at which a body cannot be recognized as anything else but black, the hazards of statelessness reach their zenith. So if you are trying to understand the Haitian interdictions through the lens of Sexton's analysis it is important to attend, first of all, to the blackness of the black refugee. Instead of trying to understand the displacement of refugees who happen to be black, we must attend to the predicament of black people who happen to be refugees.

This is another way of saying that antiblackness is a durable substratum of the modern world that has produced a social reality unto itself. It is the cipher that explains the social order from which it is excluded, and which can be used to decode the structures that always appear to transcend it. This is why the blackness of the black refugee has to be factored into the explanation of their predicament, even though the salience of their blackness is always being obfuscated by the discourses that produce the "black refugee" as an object of knowledge. It also follows that there is a kind of mobility that is part and parcel of this antiblack social reality. Controlled mobility is my attempt to describe the defining features of this condition.

Controlled mobility is my starting point, but it recedes into the background of my analysis for the rest of the book, and this is mainly because it is not a legal construct. It is a regimen of power that can be traced to a largely unregulated sphere of socioeconomic relations that is subject to the desires and dictates of private persons, and to the public officials who are vested with the sovereign authority to act on behalf of these individuals. Instead of being created by the law, controlled mobility is a mode of power that is shielded from public scrutiny by the law. This is why the relationship between antiblackness and the law is plagued by silences, which I am going to discuss in the next section.

SILENCES AND OCCLUSIONS: THE APORIAS OF THE SLAVE AND THE LAW

In the introduction, I explained why the kind of legal storytelling I am going to pursue in this book is geared toward exposing the silences of the law. These problematic silences are also referenced by the title of this chapter—the chasm. The chasm is, above all, a chasm of misunderstanding that has led the Western intellectual canon to systematically ignore the problem of antiblackness.

Patricia Tuitt provides an insight into this problem when she calls attention to the role that the legal complaints of enslaved people have played in shaping the modern system of law.[38] The slave is categorically excluded from the pantheon of rights-bearing persons who are the intended subjects of the law. Even so, Tuitt contends that the modern system of law revolves around the figure of the slave. She argues, using the slave as her primary case in point, that the historical development of the law has been driven by the "reluctant labor of repressed, subjugated individuals . . . who would conventionally be perceived as subjects on which the law merely acts."[39]

Tuitt's observation makes for a fitting comparison with the legal history of the Haitian interdictions, which was driven by the complaints of refugees whose mere right to file suit was seriously questioned by the US government. Barring a few exceptions, the Herculean efforts of Haitian refugees to challenge the US government's policies failed.[40] So from one perspective, it could be argued that the US government was effective in undermining the legal personhood of the refugees. But these legal challenges also forced the government and the federal courts to generate new interpretations of established jurisprudence that became a part of constitutional law, which included precedents that clarified the rights of excludable aliens.[41] None of this would have happened were it not for the agency of Haitian refugees.

It is also significant that Tuitt sees the plight of the modern day refugee as comparable to that of the antebellum- and feudal-era slave.[42] For Tuitt, the refugee and the slave (as well as the illegalized migrant) are all examples of social types that have been "constituted in law only in terms of their exclusion."[43] She goes on to explain that the reluctant labor of these legal quasi-persons has been systematically excluded from most accounts of the history of modern law. In accordance with many critical race scholars, she observes that when it comes to "the sale and barter of human slaves and the oppression and domination of other excluded groups" there has been an "almost total erasure of that legacy from the institutional memory of the law."[44]

Khalil Saucier and Tryon Woods provide another account of this erasure which is more specific to the black condition. They have likened this problem to a conceptual aphasia that permeates the institutional and intellectual culture of the modern world.[45] Aphasia, conventionally defined, is a loss of ability to understand or communicate, which is usually the result of physical trauma. Building on this metaphor, it can be argued that the transatlantic slave trade and the histories of antiblack violence that outlived chattel slavery are the sociocultural equivalent of a blow to the head which has traumatized every facet of modern society.

This problem comes to a much finer point than the one described by Tuitt. The excluded subjects described by Tuitt include slaves but are not limited to slaves. Her account of the slave and law is also not specific to the trans-atlantic trade of African slaves. Like the migrant and refugee scholarship I discussed earlier, Tuitt produces a theory of slavery that is abstracted from the problematic relationship between blackness and the modern order of things.[46] The black slave is included, as a subcategory of the larger class of subjugated peoples that are described by her theory, but the blackness of the slave adds nothing of great significance to Tuitt's theory. This tendency in Tuitt's writing does not take away from the important contributions she has made to the study of race and the law. Even so, it is important to note that the conceptual aphasia discussed by Saucier and Woods can operate even within scholarly writing that appears to be addressing issues of direct relevant to the black condition. Tuitt's writing is one such example; another even more prominent example is the writing of Hannah Arendt.

Hannah Arendt is one of the few scholars of her stature, and of her era, who drew attention to the silence on the transatlantic slave trade that is endemic to the Western canon of social and political theory.[47] In her historiography of modern totalitarianism, Arendt traces the connection between the racism of European colonial administrations in Africa, and the anti-Semitic ideologies and governing strategies of German far right nationalists, which reached their fruition in the Third Reich.[48] Arendt's writing has proved useful for scholars who have been looking for a way to bring the history of European racism into the study of human rights and the present-day politics of refugee law and policy.[49]

Even so, Arendt's historiography of the European colonization of Africa is marked by some troubling silences. She begins her telling of this history in the late nineteenth century, to describe the competition between European nations for territory in Africa.[50] This starting point allows her to criticize the imperial ambitions of an already established community of nation-states. But she does not extend her critical eye to the early phase of European exploration and colonization, which dates to the sixteenth century. As a result, she remains silent on the founding acts of violence that prepared the way for the modern nation-state. Furthermore, when Arendt does, occasionally, reference this history of violence, it is relativized in a way that minimizes the culpability of European colonizers. She notes, for example, that European genocides of African tribes were no more extreme than the acts of mass violence that these tribes regularly visited on each other.[51]

Similar kinds of silences show up in Giorgio Agamben's scholarship on sovereignty and bare life. Agamben describes the dilemmas of people who have been abandoned by the law, and exposed to the unmitigated power of the social order from which they are excluded.[52] As Frank Wilderson has pointed out, Agamben's theory marks yet another incident in which scholarship that seems especially relevant to the black condition ends up navigating around the problem of antiblack racism.[53] In a nutshell, Wilderson puzzles at how Agamben can produce a history of sovereign power and bare life that skips over the transatlantic slave trade.[54]

Many scholars have made connections between the genocidal violence of European colonization and the ideologies and political process that prepare the way for the Third Reich and the Jewish Holocaust. Arendt's race analysis may have its pitfalls but, as I've just noted, she makes these connections in her analysis of modern totalitarianism.[55] Similar connections have been made by scholars who have studied the history of scientific racism and right-wing nationalism.[56] Agamben, on the other hand, traces a genealogy of power and absolute domination that begins in ancient Rome and ends in the Nazi concentration camp, but which has nothing to say about the violence that produces the black body as the Other of the modern Human.[57] This tendency also surfaces in Agamben's writing on states of exception. In this work, he touches on the US history of black slavery, but only to make a point about the admiration of Nazi intellectuals for the consolidation of power under the executive office by the Lincoln administration in its campaign to end the Civil War.[58] Although Agamben's observations on this matter are well sub-stantiated, it is curious, nonetheless, that he problematizes the machinations of power that were used to dismantle chattel slavery in the United States, but does not critically examine the machinery of racial domination that was intrinsic to the institution of slavery.

These silences in Agamben's writing invite comparisons with the conceptual aphasia that surrounds the Haitian interdictions. As Kristina Shull has pointed out, some of the most influential critical treatises on the history of US migration policy and the rise of the contemporary deportation regime have little, if anything, to say about the Haitian refugee crisis.[59] These studies give the impression that the Haitian refugee crisis is just so much empirical garnish that adds nothing of substance to the argument they are making. This is the same impression that is given off by Agamben's aphasia concerning the violence that produced the black nonperson.

In Agamben's defense, it could be argued that he is being held to a comple-tist standard that is impossible to achieve. No scholar can incorporate every conceivable, relevant empirical detail into their theory of a given social phenomena. But again, the point that Wilderson makes is that the details that Agamben repeatedly steers around are not incidental to his theory at all: they are the shock waves emanating from an epochal transformation in the organization of the world system and its orders of knowledge and power which *should* be a matter of concern for any theory of sovereignty and bare life. Ironically, but also quite appropriately, these silences prove Wilderson's point. They can be read as the lingering effects of the metaphysical holocaust that has, for many centuries, defined the scope and limits of the modern intellectual project—and which contemporary scholarship has only begun to interrogate.

The problem surfaced by Wilderson underscores the pervasive under-theorization of the black condition. The problem is not simply that the law has erased the agency of subjugated people from its institutional memory, as Tuitt contends. The problem is that even when theorists like Agamben call attention to the predicament of people who have been abandoned by the law, these interventions ignore the black condition (and it bears noting that Tuitt's proposition about people who are "constituted in law only in terms of their exclusion" is directly informed by Agamben's scholarship[60]). So when all is said and done blackness is excluded by the law, and it is also excluded by the critical scholarship that has attempted to shine a light on all of the quasi-persons who have been excluded by the law.

ANTIBLACKNESS AND THE LAW

Calvin Warren's writing on antiblackness and the law provides an important intervention on the problem I have just described.[61] One of Warren's core theses concerns the distinction between the being of the law and the Law of Being. The being of the law describes what we usually take as the actually existing components of the law: its articles of constitution, amendments, jurisprudence, legislative acts, and all of the quasi-legal documents (institutional policies, memos, executive orders, etc.) that are not strictly regulated by the law but which can become objects for legal deliberation. These legal documents are addressed to an abstract, rights-bearing subject and they are governed by a self-referential body of norms and precedents that are generated by the law, as described by Niklas Luhmann's systems theory.[62]

The Law of Being, on the other hand, is not something that issues from the autopoiesis of the law. It is rooted in a metaphysics that precedes and exceeds the law. The Law of Being locates the Law (and the modern order, more broadly) within an evolutionary or cosmological teleology that delineates its higher purpose and indicates who it is truly intended for. As Warren has explained, the Law of Being pronounces an existential judgment on blackness which has the effect of an interdiction.[63] Blackness is denied any standing before the law, and this condition of abject rightlessness opens the door for the regimen of power that produces controlled mobility.

Immanuel Kant's writing on race and progress provides a good illustration of this metaphysical imaginary that informs this interdiction on blackness. Insofar as the Law is intended to facilitate the progress of Humankind toward the universal ideal, it is intended "for all." But according to the scientific racism of the eighteenth and nineteenth centuries, the universal was embodied by Humans whose ideal qualities were modeled after a white, European civilizational norm.[64] Within Kant's evolutionary treatises, blackness (or "Negroid" traits) are an index of those inferior qualities that will inevitably pass away as Humankind realizes its full potential.

As Ladelle McWhorter has explained, Kant's racist sensibilities are indicative of a sea change in the understanding of race that occurred in the mid-to-late eighteenth century and which also had a pronounced influence on many US elites.[65] Rather than being viewed as the property of a people who shared a similar history and culture (similar to Johann Herder's theory of nationality)[66] race was increasingly defined in morphological terms and guided by advances in natural philosophy, taxonomy, and the biological sciences. It's also important to keep in mind that this new way of understanding race crystallized during the same time that European intellectuals were coming to terms with the "civilizational" differences of non-European peoples that had been encountered through Europe's many colonial exploits. These encounters gave rise to a racialized, topographical imaginary that made it possible to plot the geographical scope of European civilization.[67] Another outcome, which is more relevant to Warren's theory, is the production of evolutionary taxonomies that divided the human species into morphological types, and ranked them according to their capacity for civilization.[68]

These taxonomies provide a stark illustration of the Law of Being, which the being of the law is bound to respect. According to these racist treatises, black or "Negroid" morphology was a sign of inferior traits that could not be modified by sociocultural context. Put more simply, the law of the state must cede to the natural laws of evolution and biology. Similar to Agamben's theory of homer sacer, the black biological other is completely abandoned by the law. To use Warren's terminology, the black other is excluded by the Law of Being, which is rooted in an evolutionary teleology that had the imprimatur of scientific objectivity and plain "good sense."

To illustrate, Warren discusses the Supreme Court's opinion in the *Dred Scott v. Sanford* decision, which upheld the legality of fugitive slave laws.[69] Dred Scott, an enslaved black man, sued for his freedom on the basis that his owner had taken him to a state that did not recognize the legality of slavery. Justice Taney, who issued the majority opinion, in this case, argued that the reasons why Scott could not claim the same rights of a "free white man" was not simply a matter of law. He explained that belief in the inherent inferiority of blacks was so widely held among the US white population that it did not require legal codification.[70] He also issued this telling statement:

[The Constitution] cannot introduce any person, or description of persons, who were not intended to be embraced in this new political family, which the Constitution brought into existence, but were intended to be excluded from it.[71]

Taney calls attention to a contradiction between the letter and the spirit of the law. Warren explains that this contradiction is epitomized by the dilemma of the antebellum era "free black" who was manumitted by the slave master but was not regarded as a citizen of the same standing as the free white male.[72] Taney addresses this same dilemma when he speculates on the prospect of Dred Scott "being freed" by the laws of non-slave holding states. For Taney, the fact that the law creates circumstances whereby some blacks can gain freedom runs counter to their true purpose.[73] Hence, legal codifications have to be interpreted in light of the sovereign intentions under which they were first crafted.

The sovereign authority that I have just referenced is a central feature of Agamben's theory. For Agamben, the primacy of the sovereign over the law produces the wretched situation of complete abandonment by the law.[74] One of Agamben's chief accomplishments is writing a theory of sovereignty back into a theory of the law, and in a way that illustrates its relevance for the modern era (rather than being treated as a regressive throwback to the feudal or ancient world). Warren, on the other hand, explains that a critical theory of sovereign power is not sufficient in of itself to explain black rightlessness. One must also account for the antiblack social ontology (the Law of Being) that informs the desires and anxieties that operate through sovereign power.

The antiblack Law of Being is rarely discussed by the law. The law proceeds as if it is addressing an abstract, universal rights-bearing subject, but it produces practical results that agree with an antiblack animus. So at one and the same time, the Law of Being is kept at arm's length from the official record of the law and is also allowed to speak through it. Warren has described these tendencies as a distortion that is foundational to the law.[75] For a point of illustration, he returns to Justice Taney's opinion in the Dred Scott decision.

Taney's decision on Dred Scott overruled the decision of a lower court that had decided in Scott's favor.[76] He argued that the lower court was in error because the matter lay beyond the court's jurisdiction.[77] Dred Scott's complaint was based on an argument about territorial jurisdiction; that he should be granted freedom because he had been transported from a "slave" to a "free" state.[78] Taney, on the other hand, brought up the matter of jurisdictional authority to make a point about the kinds of people who could legitimately bring complaints before the federal courts. He insisted that the federal courts only had the authority to hear the complaints of US citizens and, of course, Scott was not a citizen.

Taney's interpretation of jurisdictional authority does not hold up under inspection—at least, that is, if one takes his argument at face value. Throughout the nineteenth century, the federal courts routinely heard complaints that had been filed by noncitizens, and the Supreme Court issued a number of decisions that favored alien petitioners.[79] But it is also important to note that all of the noncitizens in that era who received favorable decisions were white or nonblack aliens who had migrated freely to the United States. Taney's argument about jurisdictional authority was not addressed to these kinds of noncitizens.

Although Taney used the citizen/noncitizen distinction to couch his argument, his practical point of reference was the free/slave distinction. On one hand, this may appear to be an error in Taney's reasoning, in which he mistakenly conflates different kinds of legal statuses. But earlier in this same decision, Taney argued that blacks were racially unfit for citizenship and that, even if the law allowed for the possibility of "black citizenship," the mere existence of this kind of legal subject ran counter to the spirit of the law. As a result, Taney's reflections on "jurisdictional authority" became a vehicle for an existential judgment. It was Scott's questionable status as a human being and not his legal status that was the fundamental issue at stake for Taney. Viewed in this light, the citizen/noncitizen and free/slave distinctions are not just two different pairs of legal statuses. The citizen/noncitizen is a construct of the law. But in Taney's opinion, the slave is disqualified from citizenship on the grounds of innate, racial characteristics that the law is powerless to modify.

Taney's statements about black inferiority could be interpreted as inflammatory dicta. It also bears emphasizing that he describes antiblack sentiments as an informal body of opinion that are capable of exerting their influence without having to rely on the force of law. Even so, Taney resorts to the jurisprudence on jurisdictional authority to provide legal justification for his final decision. The practical result of this decision, which forces Scott to live the rest of his life as a slave, is consistent with Taney's virulent antiblack sentiments. But this racist commonsense is communicated by a jurisprudence that could, hypothetically, be used to disqualify the petitions of any noncitizen—regardless of race or free/slave status.

This is an important example of how the letter of the law can be used to both enable and obfuscate antiblack animus. Taney's jurisdictional argument returns Scott to the absolute authority of his master—making it clear that the mere act of traveling to a "free state" does not change Scott's status as a slave. But even though Taney opines about black inferiority, he does not explicitly justify the nullification of Scott's freedom of movement on the grounds of his blackness. He ventriloquizes his antiblack sentiments through his argument about jurisdiction and Scott's status as a noncitizen.

In the generations that have passed since the Dred Scott decision, the relationship between controlled mobility and the law has become more complicated to trace. Court decisions that subjected Haitian refugees to the dictates of controlled mobility have been justified by a language that is not just race-neutral but which also, at times, seems to go out of its way to affirm the antidiscriminatory norms of the post-civil rights era, or which justifies interdictions as being in the best interest of refugees, or which insists that Haitian refugees are having their asylum claims processed in accordance with international law, even though the government has no obligation to honor these rights.[80] Consequently, the extreme measures that have been used to void the rights and control the movements of Haitian refugees are normalized and made to seem comparable with the treatment of other migrant and refugee populations who have not actually been subjected to these same policies and practices. This is one reason why controlled mobility can be understood as a repressed subtext of the law.

Throughout the book, I use a number of bridging arguments to bring this repressed subtext into view. In chapter 2, I discuss a body of elite opinion which I refer to as "the prohibition on black migration," to illustrate how the imperatives of controlled mobility formed the backdrop for the rise of a de facto nonblack migration regime in the nineteenth century. In chapter 3, I use the concept of radical exclusion to explain how controlled mobility operates through the jurisprudence on excludability, which coalesced in the late nineteenth and early twentieth centuries (and set the stage for the treatment of Haitian refugees in the years prior to the Reagan-era interdiction program). In chapter 4, I explain how controlled mobility was enabled by (ex)territorial legal arguments that were used to justify the government's interdiction operations. And in chapters 5 and 6, I use controlled mobility as a framework for examining forms of migrant criminality and border enforcement practice that can be traced to the legacy of the Haitian interdictions. These are all concrete examples of what I aim to accomplish with my approach to legal storytelling. In the process, I also want to call the reader's attention to a chasm that runs through the legal personage of the racialized alien.

The refugee who happens to be black is rendered legible in the eyes of the law through a discourse that takes the nonblack subject as the norm. So it is not just that black refugees receive worse treatment than nonblack refugees. The bigger problem is that the black refugee is subjected to antiblack animus while being inserted in subjectivities that deny the existence of this animus. They must endure arguments that use nonracial euphemisms to pronounce judgments on their blackness or they become the subject of arguments that try to help them by cloaking them in the mantle of nonblack deservingness.

This problem is another one of the animating concerns of my approach to legal storytelling. I want to show how the law routinely eviscerates a black perspective on the problem of rightlessness. The point of doing this, however, is not to argue for the impossibility of black agency; I want to do the opposite. Instead of providing the reader with an escapist image of black agency—that is capable of magically overcoming all of the problems I examine in this book—I want to affirm the explanatory value of blackness. What I mean, more precisely, is that you cannot counter the ontological degradation of blackness by denying this denigration, which is a denial in which dominant institutions also want to participate. You have to use the fact of this denigration as the starting point for a way of making knowledge that affirms the explanatory value of the black condition. So instead of allowing the denigration of blackness to serve as the silent, constitutive exterior of the law—which, as Fred Moten has explained, relegates blackness to the status of a perpetually "unasked question"[81]—you engage in critical interventions that convert this silence into a source of questions.

There is a paradoxical quality to this process which is similar to what Derrick Bell was doing with his permanence of racism thesis.[82] As I explained in the introduction, Bell was not trying to dissuade black people from struggling against racism; he wanted to provide a better meta-narrative about the problem of racism that could lay the groundwork for a more mature and effective kind of antiracist activism. This same sensibility is reflected in this excerpt from the closing pages of *Black Skin, White Masks* in which Fanon writes:

Man is a *yes*, I will never stop reiterating that. *Yes* to life. *Yes* to love. *Yes* to generosity. But man is also a *no. No* to scorn of man. *No* to degradation of man. *No* to exploitation of man. *No* to the butchery of what is most human in man: freedom. Man's behavior is not only *reactional*. And there is always resentment in reaction. Nietzsche had already pointed that out in *Will to Power*. To educate man to be *actional*, preserving in all his relations his respect for the basic values that constitute a human world, is the prime task of him, whom having taken thought, prepares to act. (Original emphasis)[83]

Some Afropessimist scholars might take issue with the optimistic overtones of this passage, especially given Fanon's appeal to a "human world" as an aspirational framework for the black freedom struggle. I will also leave aside, for the purpose of this discussion, the gendered standpoint of Fanon's mode of address, which he never interrogates.[84]

I want to call attention to the curiously affirmative nature of Fanon's pessimism. He makes it very clear that the willingness to say "yes" is predicated on the strength to say "no." The strength to say "no," which is directed at things that cannot be tolerated and that must be changed, is another one of the defining features of my approach to legal storytelling. Nietzsche's idea of a "pessimism of strength" provides an important insight into this way of seeing.[85] Like Fanon, Nietzsche describes a pessimism that is geared toward transformation, not resignation. It allows for the possibility that the emancipatory potential of the Human could be salvaged from the wreckage of history, and that even if this is not possible, then the Human will have to be replaced by something better. But one thing that this ethos of transformation does not tolerate is optimism that refuses to allow its ideals to be interrogated in light of the actually existing reality that they have helped to create. This means that Fanon's appeal to Humanity will have to face up to its complicity in creating an antiblack reality if it has any role to play in the process of black liberation. This is the same challenge that I am going to pose to the US legal system with my analysis of the government's Haitian refugee policies.

NOTES

1. William Wells Brown, *Narrative of William W. Brown, a Fugitive Slave. Written by Himself* (Boston: The Anti-Slavery Office, 1847), 28–29.

2. Historians and literary scholars have raised questions about the authenticity of these narratives, many of which were heavily edited for a white, reading public by white liberal intellectuals with a specific ideological agenda. For one account of how scholars have struggled with these issues, see Lawrence Aje, "Fugitive Slave Narratives and the (Re) presentation of the Self? The Cases of Frederick Douglass and William Brown," *L'Ordinaire Des Amériques* 215 (2013): 1–45. Having acknowledged these problems, it is still possible to use these stories as a window into the brutalities of the slave trade. Saidiya Hartman's reflections on how to contextualize these narratives in tandem with other texts are very instructive and similar to the approach I take in this book. See Saidiya Hartman, *Scenes of Subjection* (Oxford: Oxford University Press, 1997), 10–13.

3. P. Khalil Saucier and Tryon Woods, "Introduction: Racial Optimism and the Drag of Thymotics," in *Conceptual Aphasia in Black*, eds. P. Khalil Saucier and Tryon Woods (Lanham, MD: Lexington Press, 2016), 1–34; Jared Sexton, "The Social Life of Social Death: On Afro-Pessimism and Black Optimism," *In/Tensions Journal* 5 (2011): 1–47.

4. See the account of the public uses of William Brown's narrative in Aje, "Fugitive Slave Narratives and the (Re) presentation of the Self?," 35–44.

5. Ronald Judy, *(Dis)forming the American Canon: African-Arabic Slave Narratives and the Vernacular* (Minneapolis: University of Minnesota Press, 1993), 50–53.

6. Ibid.

7. Guantanamo Public Memory Project, "Natalie and Gregory Beau Brun: At Guantanamo, 1992," New York: Columbia University's Institute for the Study of Human Rights, accessed September 24, 2021, https://gitmomemory.org/stories/natalie-and-gregory-beaubrun/.

8. Ibid.

9. Harold Koh and Michael Wishnie, "The Story of Sale v. Haitian Centers Council: Guantanamo and Refoulement," in *Human Rights Advocacy Stories*, eds. Margaret Satterthwaite and Deena Hurwitz (Eagan, MN: Westlaw and Foundations Press, 2008), 385–432 at 394–395.

10. Wilkine Brutus, *A Boat Voyage: A Haitian Refugee Story*, "Episode 1 - Child of the Sea: Haiti to Cuba," May 3, 2018, accessed September 26, 2021, https://www.himalaya.com/album/a-boat-a-voyage-a-haitian-refugee-story-1760211.

11. Gregory Jaymes, "Thirty-three Haitians Drown as Boat Capsizes Off Florida," *New York Times*, October 7, 1981, accessed September 26, 2021, https://www.nytimes.com/1981/10/27/us/33-haitians-drown-as-boat-capsizes-off-florida.html.

12. This policy history is discussed in chapters 2 and 3, focusing on the mandatory detention practices that were introduced by the late Carter-era "Haitian program."

13. Paul Gilroy, *The Black Atlantic: Modernity and Double Consciousness* (Cambridge, MA: Harvard University Press, 1993); Julius Scott, *The Common Wind: Afro-American currents in the age of the Haitian Revolution* (New York: Verso, 2018).

14. Calvin Warren, *Ontological Terror: Blackness, Nihilism and Emancipation* (Durham, NC: Duke University Press, 2018), 78–83, 131–142.

15. Daniel Kanstroom, *Deportation Nation* (Cambridge, MA: Harvard University Press, 2009), 76; Scott, *The Common Wind*, 190–192.

16. Joanne Van Selm, Betsy Cooper and Kathleen Newman, *The New "Boat People": Ensuring Safety and Determining Status* (Washington, DC: Migration Policy Institute, 2006) at 71.

17. See Fred Kaplan, *Lincoln and the Abolitionists* (New York: HarperCollins, 2017). The history of this body of opinion is discussed in more detail in chapter 2.

18. Mark Dow, *American Gulag: Inside US Immigration Prisons* (Berkeley, CA: University of California Press, 2005); Naomi Paik, "Carceral Quarantine at Guantanamo Legacies of US Imprisonment of Haitian Refugees, 1991–1994," *Radical History Review* 115 (2013): 142–168.

19. Harold Koh, "The Human Face of the Haitian Interdiction Program," *Virginia Journal of International Law* 33 (1993): 483–490 at 488–489. Naomi Paik has provided more context on this callous treatment, which shows that US policy and administrative opinion toward the detainees was premised on the assumption that they were fated to "die soon," regardless of how well they were cared for. Paik. "Carceral Quarantine at Guantanamo."

20. For one of the few macro-historical, cross-national accounts of the history of seasonal and circular migrations, see Saskia Sassen, *Guests and Aliens* (New York: New Press, 1999).

21. For some examples, see Ajaya Sahoo, Dave Sangha, and Melissa Kelly, "From 'Temporary Migrants' to 'Permanent Residents': Indian H-1B Visa Holders in the United States," *Asian Ethnicity* 11, no. 3 (2010): 293–309; Nina Glick Schiller, Linda Basch, and Cristina Szanton Blanc, "From Immigrant to Transmigrant: Theorizing Transnational Migration," *Anthropological Quarterly* 68, no. 1 (1995): 48–63; Robert Smith, *Mexican New York* (Berkeley: University of California Press, 2006);

Leah Vosko, Valerie Preston, and Robert Latham, eds. *Liberating Temporariness?: Migration, Work, and Citizenship in an Age of Insecurity* (Montreal: McGill-Queen's Press, 2014).

22. Barzoo Eliassi, "Statelessness in a World of Nation-States: the Cases of Kurdish Diasporas in Sweden and the UK," *Journal of Ethnic and Migration Studies* 42, no. 9 (2016): 1403–1419; Abul Hasnat Milton et al., "Trapped in Statelessness: Rohingya refugees in Bangladesh," *International Journal of Environmental Research and Public Health* 14, no. 8 (2017): 942.

23. Justine Dandy and Rogelia Pe-Pua, "The Refugee Experience of Social Cohesion in Australia," *Journal of Immigrant & Refugee Studies* 13, no. 4 (2015): 339–357; Ransford Danso, "From 'There' to 'Here': An Investigation of the Initial Settlement Experiences of Ethiopian and Somali Refugees in Toronto," *GeoJournal* 56, no. 1 (2002): 3–14; Linh Nghe, James Mahalik, and Susana Lowe, "Influences on Vietnamese Men: Examining Traditional Gender Roles, the Refugee Experience, Acculturation, and Racism in the United States," *Journal of Multicultural Counseling and Development* 31, no. 4 (2003): 245–261.

24. Reza Barmaki, "Criminals/Refugees in the Age of Welfareless States: Zygmunt Bauman on Ethnicity, Asylum and the New 'Criminal,'" *International Journal of Criminology and Sociology Theory* 2, no. 1 (2009): 251–226; Mark Duffield, "Racism, Migration and Development: The Foundations of Planetary Order," *Progress in Development Studies* 6, no. 1 (2006): 68–79; Liz Fekete, "The Emergence of Xeno-Racism," *Race & Class* 43, no. 2 (2001): 23–40; Nikos Papastergiadis, "The Invasion Complex: The Abject Other and Spaces of Violence," *Geografiska Annaler. Series B, Human Geography* 88, no. 4 (2006): 429–442.

25. Deirdre Conlon, "Becoming Legible and 'Legitimized': Subjectivity and Governmentality Among Asylum Seekers in Ireland," in *Migrant Marginality: a Transnational Perspective*, eds. P. Kretsedemas, J. Capetillo and G. Jacobs (New York: Routledge, 2013), 186–204.

26. Andreas Wimmer and Nina Glick Schiller, "Methodological Nationalism and Beyond: Nation–State Building, Migration and the Social Sciences," *Global Networks* 2, no. 4 (2002): 301–334.

27. Zygmunt Bauman, *Liquid Modernity* (New York: Polity, 2000); Duffield, "Racism, Migration and Development: The Foundations of Planetary Order"; Saskia Sassen, *Globalization and Its Discontents* (New York: New Press, 1999).

28. Duffield, "Racism, Migration and Development."

29. Ronen Shamir, "Without Borders? Notes on Globalization as a Mobility Regime," *Sociological Theory* 23, no. 2 (2005): 197–217.

30. Saucier and Woods, "Ex Aqua"; Jared Sexton, "People of Color Blindness: Notes on the Afterlife of Slavery," *Social Text* 103, no. 28:2 (2010): 31–53.

31. Michael Omi and Howard Winant, *Racial Formation in the United States*, 3rd ed. (New York: Routledge, 2014).

32. This argument presents a different way of getting at a comparable point made by other scholars, who have raised concerns about the way racial formation theory emphasizes the fluidity of race and understates the durability of whiteness and anti-blackness. See Joe Feagin and Sean Elias, "Rethinking Racial Formation Theory: A

Systemic Racism Critique," *Ethnic and Racial Studies* 36, no. 6 (2013): 931–960; Saucier and Woods, "Introduction: Racial Optimism and the Drag of Thymotics."

33. In the early colonial period, "race" was understood to be a civilizational quality specific to Europeans that was absent among indigenous African peoples. Black Africans were not viewed as an "alien race" but as "nonpeoples" who were incapable of producing a "racial identity." See Mahmood Mamdani, *When Victims Become Killers: Colonialism, Nativism, and the Genocide in Rwanda* (Princeton: Princeton University Press, 2001), 3–20. This argument is broadly consistent with the Afropessimist thesis on the deontological status of blackness in relation to white European culture. See Sexton, "The Social Life of Social Death"; Sebastian Weier, "Consider Afro-Pessimism," *Amerikastudien/American Studies* 59, no. 3 (2014): 419–433; Wilderson, "The Prison Slave as Hegemony's (Silent) Scandal."

34. Sexton, "The Social Life of Social Death," n1 at 37.

35. A good example being the UNHCR's annual report on global displacement. See UNHCR, "Global Trends in Forced Displacement, 2019," accessed November 29, 2020. https://www.unhcr.org/globaltrends2019/.

36. Stateless and displacement are sometimes referenced interchangeably but, under international law, they describe categorically different situations and are enumerated separately in the statistics gathered by the UNHCR ("Global Trends in Forced Displacement 2019"). The stateless person is not recognized as a citizen by any nation but is not necessarily displaced. Displaced people, on the other hand, enter into a de facto condition of statelessness when they are forced to flee their home nation (or even if they become internally displaced), but it is presumed that they will be able to reclaim their status, as citizens of their home nation.

37. See Hartman, *Scenes of Subjection*; Saucier and Woods "Ex Aqua"; Sexton, "The Social Life of Social Death"; Weier, "Consider Afro-Pessimism"; Wilderson, "The Prison Slave, Hegemony's (Silent) Scandal."

38. Patricia Tuitt, *Race, Law, Resistance* (New York: Taylor & Francis Group, 2004), 1–20.

39. Ibid., 2.

40. Most of the decisions that were sympathetic to Haitian refugees were issued by District Courts, which include cases like *Haitian Refugee Ctr. v. Civiletti*, 503 F. Supp. 442 (S.D. Fla. 1980) and *Louis v. Nelson*, 544 F. Supp. 973 (S.D. Fla. 1982) which contested policies implemented prior to the Reagan-era interdictions, and decisions issued in the interdiction era itself, such as *Haitian Centers Council, Inc. v. McNary*, 807 F. Supp. 928 (E.D.N.Y. 1992). The Second Circuit Court's decision on *Haitian Centers Council, Inc. v. Mc Nary* (969 F.2d 1350 [1992]) is the only occasion at which an appellate level court issued a decision that is strongly sympathetic toward the cause of the refugees and bolstered the sympathetic arguments of a lower court decision. All other circuit court decisions erred in favor of the government's justification for the interdictions, with the Supreme Court being the most consistently supportive of the government's position. See chapters 4 and 5 for a discussion of this legal history.

41. Examples include the acknowledgment by the Eleventh Circuit Court appeals that excludable aliens had a First Amendment right to legal counsel (*Jean v. Nelson*

727 F.2d 957 [11th Cir. 1984]) and arguments on behalf of the Fifth Amendment, due process rights of interdicted refugees that were issued in *Haitian Centers Council, Inc. v. McNary*, 807 F. Supp. 928 (E.D.N.Y. 1992); *Haitian Centers Council, Inc. v. Mc Nary* (969 F.2d 1350 [2nd Cir. 1992]).

42. Tuitt, *Race, Law, Resistance*, 4, 20. 55–70.

43. Ibid., 3.

44. Ibid., 3–4. Also see Michelle Alexander, *The New Jim Crow: Mass Incarceration in the Age of Colorblindness* (New York: The New Press, 2010); Derrick Bell, *Faces at the Bottom of the Well* (New York: Basic Books, 1992); Dorothy Roberts, *Killing the Black Body: Race, Reproduction, and the Meaning of Liberty* (New York: Vintage, 1998). This argument is also a running theme of the Afropessimist scholarship that I cite in this chapter.

45. Saucier and Woods, "Introduction: Racial Optimism and the Drag of Thymotics."

46. My treatment of Tuitt's theory is also informed by Calvin Warren's reading of her work. Warren, *Ontological Terror*, 71–73.

47. Hartman, for example, credits Arendt for drawing attention to the "social question" of American racism, and its roots in the transatlantic slave trade—though she also goes on to critique the limitations of Arendt's analysis of the social and its relationship to the political sphere. Hartman, *Scenes of Subjection*, 169 and 242. The analysis of the European colonization and its consequences for the political dilemmas of the present day is also the running theme of Arendt's work, which continues to inform contemporary scholarship on race and nation. Hannah Arendt, *Crises of the Republic* (New York: Harcourt & Brace, 1969), 58–62; *The Origins of Totalitarianism* (New York: Harcourt Inc.: 1966), 123–304; Richard King and Dan Stone eds., *Hannah Arendt and the Uses of History: Imperialism, Nation, Race, and Genocide* (New York: Berghahn Books, 2007).

48. Arendt, *Origins of Totalitarianism*, 123–304.

49. For an example, see Ida Danewid, "White Innocence in the Black Mediterranean: Hospitality and the Erasure of History," *Third World Quarterly* 38, no. 7 (2017): 1674–1689.

50. Arendt, *Origins of Totalitarianism*, 185–221. Arendt's discussion of "race-thinking before racism" (which precedes this historiography and delves into a history of "racialist" national ideologies in Europe that is divorced from an analysis of whiteness or blackness; *Origins*, 158–184) also inverts a persistent theme of Afropessimist theory, which is that racism makes race. See Barnor Hesse, "Preface: Counter-Racial Formation Theory," in *Conceptual Aphasia in Black: Displacing Racial Formation*, eds. P. Khalil Saucier and Tryon Woods (Lanham, MD: Lexington Press, 2016), vii–xi.

51. Arendt, *Origins of Totalitarianism*, 191–207.

52. Giorgio Agamben, *Homo Sacer: Sovereign Power and Bare Life* (Stanford, CA: Stanford University Press, 1998).

53. Frank Wilderson, *Red, White, and Black: Cinema and the Structure of US Antagonisms* (Durham, NC: Duke University Press, 2010), 38–49.

54. Ibid., 39–40.

55. Arendt, *Origins of Totalitarianism*, 158–266.

56. Richard Hofstadter, *Social Darwinism in American Thought* (Boston: Beacon Press, [1944] 1992); John Jackson, Nadine Weidman, *Race, Racism and Science: Social Impact and Interaction* (Camden, NJ: Rutgers University Press, 2005).

57. Agamben, *Homo Sacer*.

58. Giorgio Agamben, *State of Exception* (Chicago: University of Chicago Press, 2005), 20–21.

59. Kristina Shull, "Nobody Wants These People: Reagan's Immigration Crisis and America's First Private Prisons" (PhD Diss., University of California-Irvine, 2014), 51n31. Shull makes note of this silence in Aristide Zolberg's *A Nation by Design* (Cambridge, MA: Harvard University Press, 2009) and Daniel Kanstroom's *Deportation Nation* (Cambridge, MA: Harvard University Press, 2009); though her observation could be applied to many other accounts of the rise of the post-Cold War deportation regime, including Nicholas De Genova and Nathalie Peutz eds., *The Deportation Regime* (Durham, NC: Duke University Press, 2010) which is framed by an extensive discussion of Agamben's theory of sovereign power and bare life.

60. Tuitt, *Race, Law, and Resistance*, 3.

61. Warren, *Ontological Terror*, 62–109.

62. Niklas Luhmann, *Law as a Social System* (Oxford: Oxford University Press, 2004).

63. Warren, *Ontological Terror*, 76–87.

64. For a discussion, see Ladelle McWhorter, *Racism and Sexual Oppression in Anglo-America: A Genealogy* (Bloomington, IN: Indiana University Press, 2009), 82–86. For more context on the scientific racism of this era, which has influenced by the treatises of natural philosophers like Blumenbach, Buffon, and Linneaus, see Jackson and Weidman, *Race, Racism and Science*, 8–23.

65. McWhorter, *Racism and Sexual Oppression in Anglo-America*, 75–90.

66. Johann Herder, *JG Herder on Social and Political Culture* (Cambridge: Cambridge University Press, 1969). Charles Taylor has, arguably, played the most decisive role in bringing Herder's theory back into the contemporary conversation around culture and political community. See Isaiah Berlin, *Philosophy in an Age of Pluralism: The Philosophy of Charles Taylor in Question* (Cambridge: Cambridge University Press, 1994), 1–3.

67. Jackson and Weidman, *Race, Racism and Science*, 4–23.

68. Ibid., 7–12, 35–60.

69. *Dred Scott v. Sandford* 60 U.S. 393 (1856) as discussed by Warren, *Ontological Terror*, 76–87.

70. *Dred Scott*, 60 U.S. 393 at 407–408 as quoted by Warren, *Ontological Terror*, 82.

71. *Dred Scott*, 406 as quoted by Warren, *Ontological Terror*, 84.

72. Warren, *Ontological Terror*, 27–28, 65.

73. *Dred Scott*, 60 U.S. 393 at 406–408.

74. Agamben, *Homer Sacer*. It also bears noting that this predicament of being abandoned by the law is very different than the injunction to abandon oneself to the law, which as Warren explains (by way of the legal theory of Jean Luc Nancy) is an

essential obligation of the citizen-subject. Abandoning oneself to the law is, effectively, the willingness to be wholly subjected to the sovereign desire that animates the law. Through this act of abandonment, the citizen-subject affirms their place in the social body in whose name the law is authorized to rule. Warren argues that the nothingness of blackness before the law makes such an act of abandonment impossible. Put another way, black people cannot abandon themselves *to* the law because they have, already in advance, been abandoned *by* the law—being illegible as a subjects of the law. Warren, *Ontological Terror*, 63–71.

75. Warren, *Ontological Terror*, 77–79.

76. This being the Circuit Court of the District of Maryland; *Dred Scott*, 60 U.S. 393 at 423.

77. This argument is encapsulated by *Dred Scott*, 480–485, but it bears noting the jurisdictional argument is a running theme of the entire decision. Also see Warren, *Ontological Terror*, 80–82.

78. *Dred Scott*, 397–399.

79. I discuss this case history in more detail in chapter 2, focusing on cases in which the Supreme Court evoked the federal supremacy clause to overrule local laws restricting the right of noncitizens. Some noteworthy examples of these nineteenth-century decisions which favored both white and Chinese noncitizen plaintiffs include *Martin v. Hunter's Lessee* 14 U.S. 304 (1816); *Chy Lung v. Freeman* 92 U.S. 275 (1875); and *Yick Wo v. Hopkins* 118 U.S. 356 (1886).

80. This is a summary of patterns in federal court opinion that are examined in more detail in chapters 2–6 and are of special relevance to the following cases: *Jean v. Nelson*, 472 U.S. 846 (1985); *McNary v. Haitian Refugee Ctr., Inc.*, 498 U.S. 479 (1991); *Cuban American Bar Association v. Christopher*, 43 F.3d 1412, 1419 (11th Cir.).

81. Fred Moten, "Blackness and Nothingness," *The South Atlantic Quarterly* 112, no. 4 (2013): 737–780.

82. Bell, *Faces at the Bottom of the Well*.

83. Fanon, *Black Skin, White Masks*, 222.

84. Madhu Dubey, "The 'True Lie' of the Nation: Fanon and Feminism," *Differences* 10, no. 2 (1998): 1–12.

85. For a discussion, see Joshua Dienstag, "Nietzsche's Dionysian Pessimism," *American Political Science Review* 95, no. 4 (2001): 923–937. This proposition also has to be read in light of Nietzsche's theory of health, which does not reduce to a conventional physiological or psychological diagnosis. Deleuze is a guide here; see Gilles Deleuze, *Pure Immanence: Essays on a Life* (New York: Zone Books, 2005), 53–102.

Chapter 2

Sovereign Bodies and the Law

A Prehistory of the Antiblack Racism Underlying the US Government's Haitian Refugee Policies

The Haitians allege that the actions of the INS constitute impermissible discrimination on the basis of national origin. They have proven their claim. This court cannot close its eyes, however, to a possible underlying reason why these plaintiffs have been subjected to intentional "national origin" discrimination. The plaintiffs are part of the first substantial flight of black refugees from a repressive regime to this country. All of the plaintiffs are black. . . . None of the over 4,000 Haitians processed during the INS "program" at issue in this lawsuit were granted asylum. No greater disparity can be imagined.—*Judge James King, Haitian Refugee Center v. Civiletti*[1]

JUDGE KING'S COMPLAINT

In the judicial opinion on the US government's Haitian refugee policies, there are occasional moments of candor about the problem of racism. The passage from the 1980 District Court decision on *Haitian Refugee Center v. Civiletti* that I used to introduce this chapter is a rare case in point. In his opening statement, Judge King contends that the federal government viewed Haitians differently than all other refugee populations and singled them out for exclusion because they were black.

Judge King's statement also highlights a tension that runs through the history of the US government's Haitian refugee policies. On one hand, there is the testimony of Haitian asylum seekers—that was cited in great detail by Judge King—which provides compelling evidence of political persecution. And on the other hand, there is a pattern of decisions made by US policy-makers which is remarkably indifferent to these claims, which is one reason why Judge King was so frustrated.

One of the reports that King cites in his famous decision recounts the story of a Haitian professor of history who was ruthlessly interrogated by members of the Haitian president's privately organized paramilitary outfit, the Tonton Macoutes. The professor explains how he was ushered into a room that was occupied by someone in an army uniform and two other people in "civilian clothes."[2] The man in the uniform repeatedly accused the professor of being a communist and demanded "a list of names." The professor tried to explain that "no such people existed" because he was not a communist and did not have any connections to communist operatives, but this admission did not persuade his captors. He was beaten by the men in civilian clothes every time he was unable to answer their questions and, according to the professor's account, he was subjected to this treatment for a period of over two weeks before he was finally released.

A Haitian legal expert who was interviewed for the same report summed up the situation neatly enough, observing that "a communist is anyone who is deemed not to sufficiently support the Duvaliers."[3] Not surprisingly, this legal expert, who was living in exile at the time, wanted their name kept out of the report. It also bears noting that, for much of its existence, the Duvalier regime governed under a state of emergency, and one of the security measures it enacted—"the Loi Anti-Communiste"—stipulated that any persons found guilty of uttering statements publicly or privately in support of anything that could be construed as communism or anarchism would be charged with crimes against the state and face possible execution. In the late 1970s, many Haitians were accused of having communist sympathies by anonymous sources that were not required to provide any evidence of the facticity of their claims. The history professor is one of the many victims of these surveillance practices.

The professor, whose story I just told, was fortunate enough to have his case heard by Canadian authorities. The outcome of his case is not documented in the report but we know that, at the very least, he was granted an asylum hearing in which he was allowed to present evidence of persecution that was carefully considered by an immigration judge. During this same period of time, the INS was implementing a policy—informally dubbed the "Haitian program"—that was geared toward streamlining the removal of as many Haitian refugees from the United States as possible. This was the program that Judge King was charged with evaluating.

King's decision is distinguished by its frank commentary on the racist bias motivating the government's Haitian refugee policies. Although King does not use the term "antiblack racism," he insists the blackness of the Haitian refugees has to be factored into the reasons why the government was willing to go to such extraordinary lengths to reject their asylum claims. Throughout his decision, King also makes a point of favorably contrasting the way that nonblack migrants and refugees have been treated by the US government in comparison to Haitians.[4]

HRC v. Civiletti was decided in 1980. Several years later, language from this decision was still being featured prominently in the framing strategies of social movement groups that were contesting the US government's Haitian refugee policies. Bayard Rustin, writing on behalf of the A. Philip Randolph Institute, borrowed from King's analysis of government racism in a statement given to the Congressional Subcommittee on Immigration, Refugees and International Law in 1984.[5] In this statement he referred to *HRC v. Civiletti* as a "celebrated decision" that had won the respect of civil rights and labor rights activists across the United States.[6] Leaders from the International Ladies Garment Union, the AFL-CIO, the NAACP, the National Council of La Raza, the American Jewish Committee, the Catholic Bishop's Committee on Migration, and the newly formed Haitian Refugees Coalition also spoke at this hearing, which was being used to discuss the merits of a house bill, H.R. 4853, that would grant permanent residence to Cuban and Haitian refugees and migrants who had been living in the United States, in legal limbo, for many years.[7] These other speakers did not feature Judge King's decision as prominently as Bayard Rustin, but they all delivered the same message, which is that Haitians were legitimate refugees, that they had been treated unfairly by the US government, and that racism was one of the underlying motives for this unfair treatment.

Jerome Audige, executive director of the New Jersey Haitian American Cultural Association, made a uniquely important contribution to the public hearing. He began by identifying himself as a "political refugee from the Republic of Haiti."[8] Although this may have been a basic statement of fact, it underscored the point that political persecution was a very real problem in Haiti, pushing against the narrative that most Haitian asylum seekers were economic migrants.

Audige went on to describe the double bind that many Haitian refugees were experiencing in the United States. They had been forced out of Haiti by government persecution and had not been granted asylum by the US government. Audige explained that many of these Haitians had become part of the US undocumented population. He emphasized that these people were being treated like nonpersons ("nonpersons" is the only word that was underlined in his testimony) and that they were being forced to work for less than minimum wage, "under 18th century conditions, because they are taken advantage of by greedy charlatans."[9]

The term "Afropessimism" would not be coined for another twenty-five years or more,[10] but the precursors for an Afropessimist analysis are present in Audige's statement. One clue is Audige's emphasis on the nonpersonhood of Haitian refugees, which resonates with Afropessimist arguments about the social ontology that associates blackness with the subhuman. Another important clue is Audige's assertion that undocumented Haitians are laboring under "eighteenth-century conditions," which is an allusion to slavery. By referencing the eighteenth century in particular (because Audige could have just as easily referenced the nineteenth) he invites his audience to make a connection between the plight of Haitians today, and the oppressive conditions that their ancestors suffered prior to the Haitian revolution.

Audige is locating the Haitian refugee experience within a history of antiblack oppression that predates the phenomenon of the undocumented migrant. Once you start framing things this way you have to contend with the problems of black people who happen to be refugees and not the problem of refugees who happen to be black. Bayard Rustin points toward a similar analysis when he emphasizes the connections between the racism suffered by Haitian refugees and the African American population. Viewed in this light, it is more important to understand the defining features of a problem shared by black people who could be immigrants or native born—and who experience a statelessness that is not strictly defined by a citizen/noncitizen status.

In this chapter, I am going to describe a legal, policy, and political-cultural context that is attuned to the problem of black rightlessness, which overflows the distinction between slave and free, and between citizen and noncitizen. This goal is communicated by the chapter's subtitle, "A Prehistory of the Antiblack Racism Underlying the US Government's Haitian Refugee Policies." It is admittedly a rather long and awkwardly worded subtitle, but its awkwardness is symptomatic of the problem I am trying to describe. In order to surface the antiblack context for Haitian refugee policies, it is necessary to look beyond the confines of immigration and refugee law—and this is because legal precedents that have been used as a starting point for defending migrants and refugees are focused on the situation of nonblack migrants.

There is nothing in the letter of the law that prevents these "nonblack" legal precedents to be applied to black refugees, but as I show later in this chapter and in the chapters that follow, these precedents were of no help whatsoever for the majority of Haitian refugees who tried to contest their expulsion and exclusion. Building on my discussion of antiblackness and the law, from chapter 1, I argue that there is a black/nonblack binary that operates through the law that is enabled by the prerogatives of sovereign power. This relationship between sovereign power, antiblack sentiment, and the law has produced a pattern of decisions that normalize black rightlessness, that have become a part of the corpus of the law, as well as spaces of radical exclusion that are shielded from the oversight of the law. I am going to situate the Haitian refugee policies of the 1980s—that Judge King was deliberating on—in light of this history of antiblack, sovereign prerogatives which can be traced to the inception of the US republic—and which also has a special relationship to the events of the Haitian revolution.

The kind of legal storytelling I am doing in this chapter is concerned with tracing relationships between bodies of law that are not usually located within the same history. I think this project can be described as the narration of a "prehistory" for at least two reasons. First, it is concerned with Haitian refugee policies (e.g., "the Haitian program") that predate the interdiction operations that were inaugurated by the Reagan administration in 1981. Second, it situates these policies in a history of the law, antiblackness, and sovereign power that predates most treatments of anti-immigrant racism in the United States. I also want to emphasize that the story I am going to tell is defined by its continuities. Although the "Haitian program" was implemented on the US mainland, its objectives and the arguments used to rationalize it were not much different from the maritime interdiction operations that were implemented just a few years later. The sentiments underlying the Haitian program can be connected, in turn, to a history of prohibitive attitudes toward black migration that date to the earliest period of the US republic. In the next section, I explain how I am going to reframe US immigration law, in order to make room for this analysis.

PHANTOM NORMS AND ANTIBLACK RACISM: REFRAMING THE PLENARY POWER DOCTRINE

Hiroshi Motomura's discussion of the government's Haitian refugee policies provides an apt starting point for my analysis, and this is because of its insights as well as its aporias.[11] Motomura contends that judges who challenged the government's Haitian refugee policies relied on an established, but questionable tradition of introducing phantom norms into their interpretations of US immigration law. The practical utility of these phantom norms is that they allow judges to navigate around the government's authority to exclude migrants and refugees, but without having to directly confront the constitutionality of these exclusionary decisions.

The government's constitutionally protected right to discriminate on noncitizen admissions can be traced to the Plenary Power doctrine, which was articulated by the Supreme Court in an 1889 decision defending the exclusions that had been introduced by the *Chinese Exclusion Act*.[12] The Plenary Power doctrine gave the government a legal loophole that was defended by constitutional law, but which allowed the government to make decisions about immigrant admissions that were not strictly accountable to constitutional law.

Motomura explains how judges have used phantom norms to limit the sovereign authority that has been authorized by the Plenary Power doctrine. When judges attempt to strengthen the rights of people who are being denied entry to the United States, they often make arguments that borrow from constitutional law but are not squarely framed as constitutional arguments. Instead, legal norms that are indirectly informed by constitutional rights are used to guide the interpretation of statutory law.[13] Later in this chapter, I will explain how these legal tactics were used to protect Haitian refugees. But in the process, I am also going to show that these tactics were unable to dismantle the government's policies and only, at best, delayed the removal of the Haitians they were used to defend.

The ineffectiveness of phantom norms, in the Haitian case, is one reason why Motomura insists that arguments for immigrant and refugee rights have to become more bold about confronting the Plenary Power doctrine. This approach can be divided into two steps. First, it is necessary to acknowledge that the Plenary Power doctrine has given the government the authority to use race, among other criteria, as grounds of refusing admission to the United States. Second, this acknowledgment must be accompanied by a more clearly defined jurisprudence that limits the scope of this authority by accounting for other constitutional norms that could apply to migrant and refugee populations.[14] On this point, Motomura's argument resonates with an observation raised by Giorgio Agamben. Unlike many other Western nations, US law has left the sovereign powers of the federal government (and the executive office in particular) almost completely unregulated.[15] Agamben and Motomura agree that constitutional law should be used to better regulate these powers rather than creating loopholes that give them free reign over the law.

Motomura applies his phantom norms argument to many of the same cases that I discuss in this and the next chapter, and I find that his argument is amply corroborated by a close reading of these cases. My analysis, however, draws attention to an antiblack subtext that is relevant to Motomura's argument but which he never directly addresses.

Motomura situates the predicament of the Haitian refugee within a legal history that begins with the Chinese exclusion laws of the late nineteenth century.[16] Viewed in this light, the government's Haitian refugee policies can be explained as the re-emergence of an exclusionary treatment that is specific to the history of the Plenary Power doctrine. I argue, on the other hand, that the government's treatment of Haitian refugees has to be situated within a history of controlled mobility that dates to the earliest period of the US republic. The overarching point that I want to make with this argument is *not* that the Plenary Power doctrine and the racist exclusion of Chinese and other Asian immigrants are of no relevance for the US government's treatment of

Haitians. Throughout the book (this chapter included), I use the history of the Chinese exclusions to contextualize my explanation of black rightlessness.

Nevertheless, Motomura's insightful argument is hampered by an oversight that pervades the scholarship on immigration law, as well as the fields of migration and refugee studies. He produces an analysis that takes the legal predicament of the nonblack person as its starting point, and he assimilates the predicament of the Haitian refugee into this framework. As a consequence, he does not consider that the relationship of black people to the law is qualitatively different from that of the nonblack migrant. So he ends up producing an analysis that treats migrant rightlessness (and Haitian refugee rightlessness as a subcategory of migrant rightlessness) as a problem that is defined by contradictions that are internal to the law. I aim to show, on the other hand, that black rightlessness has to be situated in light of a practice of power and a racist imaginary that operates outside and on the margins of the law. The analysis that I provide in the rest of the chapter attempts to bring this context more clearly into view.

The bulk of the chapter is devoted to a review of progressive Supreme Court decisions on immigrant rights that date to the early nineteenth century. I am going to show that all of these decisions were addressed to populations that were located on the nonblack side of a black/nonblack binary. I am also going to explain why the US government's response to Haitian refugee flows in the late twentieth century can be located within a history of controls on black mobility that were propelled by ideologies of black inferiority and also by fears of slave revolts that were closely related to the events of the Haitian revolution.

Before I delve into this history, I am going to provide a brief summary of two of the earliest challenges to the US government's Haitian refugee policies. The goal of this review is to introduce the arguments and legal precedents that I am going to re-contextualize in the rest of the chapter. The first set of cases that I am going to discuss begins with the Southern District Court of Florida's 1980 decision in *Haitian Refugee Center v. Civiletti*[17] that was famously issued by Judge King, and which concludes with a decision by the Fifth Circuit Court of Appeals.[18] The second set of cases concerns policies that were being put to similar ends by the Reagan administration in the first few months of its first term. This case history also begins with a decision by the Southern District Court of Florida, in *Louis v. Nelson*—issued by Judge Eugene Spellman—and concludes with a decision by the US Supreme Court.[19]

THE HAITIAN PROGRAM AND
THE "HAITIAN PROBLEM"

The issues at stake in *Haitian Refugee Center v. Civiletti* revolve around the INS's "Haitian program" that began in the late Carter era, during the same period of time as the Mariel boatlift.[20] The Civiletti decision dates the origins of the program to the spring and summer of 1978, explaining that it was established "for the purpose of disposing of a backlog of asylum claims filed by Haitian immigrants."[21] INS officials testified that this backlog had developed in a climate of regulatory uncertainty, concerning new guidelines for processing asylum claims for "excludable aliens" that had not yet been issued.[22] INS officials routinely referred to this situation as the "Haitian problem" and used the terms "Haitian program" and "Haitian problem" interchangeably.[23]

The INS diagnosis of the "Haitian problem" helps to clarify the goals of the Haitian program. The statement of findings presented in the Civiletti case indicates that the program was not just designed to clear a backlog of asylum cases but to accelerate the removal of Haitians from the United States.[24] Consider the following summary, as described by Judge King:

> Among the records kept were the documents introduced as Defendants' Exhibit 79. On a single sheet, a person in the Travel Control section kept track of the Form I-589 Asylum Applications processed that day. The controlling presumptions of the Haitian Program are evident from these forms. *On the bottom of each sheet there are spaces for entering the day's total. But those spaces only provide for recording the total denials; no attempt was made to record granted applications.* Moreover, there is a section of the form for recording disposition of those asylum applications which had been completed with a statement before a hearing officer. Two possible classifications are provided for: doubtful and denied. There was no place to record cases which were granted. But then there was no need to record that which would never occur under the Haitian Program. (Emphasis added)[25]

In the same way that plea-bargaining expedites criminal adjudications by increasing the number of guilty pleas,[26] the "speed up" in the processing of Haitian asylum cases increased the number of Haitian refugees who were slated for removal from the United States.

Judge King argued that the Haitian program contradicted the spirit of international refugee law, which starts from the premise that displaced people have suffered some extreme form of hardship which could qualify as persecution under international law, and that these candidates for asylum are deserving, at the very least, of having their claims heard.[27] The Haitian program, in contrast, operated on the presumption that Haitians were not legitimate refugees. In fact, the policy of categorizing Haitians as economic migrants rather than refugees was invented by the architects of the Haitian program.[28]

The economic migrant label is characteristic of the cool, bureaucratic language that was used to facilitate the "speed up." But the Haitian program's overarching goal was informed by a more alarmist set of concerns.

Communications between INS officials indicated that Haitian refugees, in their eyes, posed an imminent threat to the security of the United States. In his recommendations for prosecuting the smugglers of Haitian refugees, INS Deputy Director Mario Noto urged federal attorneys to seriously consider

> THE DIMENSIONS OF THE HAITIAN THREAT. [Trial attorneys] should give the U.S. attorneys more data and background as to the importance of Haitian cases.—Volatile—show that these are unusual cases dealing with individuals that are threatening the community's well-being-socially & economically. (Original emphasis)[29]

This understanding of the uniquely "volatile" nature of the "Haitian threat" is a recurrent theme in the opinion of the INS officers and other federal officials. It surfaces in the statement of evidence provided in *HRC v. Civiletti*.[30] Examples of this threat discourse also surface in Kristina Shull's analysis of the Reagan-era interdiction program (including excerpts from President Reagan's diaries and the memoirs of attorney generals who served under Reagan).[31] Mark Dow notes that, during this same period of time, the federal government often assigned military personnel to sit in the audience of court cases involving its Haitian policies, to impress upon the presiding judge the sensitive nature of the security concerns that were at stake in these cases.[32]

Judge King expressed frustration at the lack of substantiating evidence for these alarmist concerns, describing them as "nothing short of fantastic," and went on to argue that they were steeped in racial prejudice.[33] But this is also the point at which the limitations of King's race analysis become more apparent. His discussion of racial prejudice leads him in the direction of bias theory, which treats racism as an irrational belief system held by a deviant minority of individuals.[34] As a consequence, King did not consider how the racist sentiments he was criticizing could be engrained within the law itself. He also fell into the trap described by Motomura.

On one hand, Judge King paid deference to the constitutionality of the Plenary Power doctrine, which allowed the government to use race as a basis for refusing admittance to the United States.[35] And on the other hand, he argued that the government was engaging in blatant acts of racial discrimination that violated the constitutional rights of immigrants and refugees.[36]

To support this argument, King cited a history of legal precedents which is traceable to the Supreme Court's 1886 decision on *Yick Wo v. Hopkins*.[37] Motomura traces the phantom norm problem to this same genealogy of decisions.[38] King argued that these legal precedents operated in the same spirit as a more recent history of progressive court decisions—dating from *Brown v. Board of Education* onward[39]—which dismantled racial restrictions in many areas of US law including migration quotas, citizenship, voting rights, and access to public space. Framed in this way, the blackness of Haitian refugees becomes legible as a protected category which should grant them access to the same constitutional rights as black citizens and other racial minorities who are residing in the United States. But the government did not consider Haitian refugees to be US residents. According to its argument, non-residents were not entitled to the constitutional considerations cited by King.[40]

One way to sum up this difference of opinion is that King wanted to treat Haitian refugees like a protected resident-minority group whereas the government wanted to treat them as aliens who had not been admitted to the United States. The odd thing about this argument, at least on its face, is that it is not about the racial minority status of Haitians, it is about their residence. But the race question (and more to the point, the question of antiblack racism) echoed through these questions of residence. The question of whether an asylum seeker had "entered" the United States or not was uniquely important for Haitians because Haitians were much more likely, than other refugee groups, to be subject to mandatory detention. Translated racially, it would appear that the question of entry was decided in a much stingier and more restrictive way for black bodies. Although Judge King took issue with the blatant racial disparities produced by this policy, his bias-oriented race analysis did not give him the best perspective to diagnose this problem—which had more to do with an institutionally engrained relationship between sovereign and legal authority rather than with the unreasonable attitudes of a few "maverick" decision makers.

The higher courts, on the other hand, were not even comfortable broaching the question of racism. This tendency comes across clearly enough in the Fifth Circuit Court case (*Haitian Refugee Center v. Smith*[41]) that heard the government's appeal of King's original decision. It bears noting, however, that the reason why the Fifth Circuit avoided the question of racism was different than that of the government. The government wanted to avoid the subject of racial discrimination so that it could continue its plans for the mass-scale removal of Haitian refugees from the US mainland. The Fifth Circuit Court, on the other hand, wanted to eliminate the question of racial discrimination, as a precondition for allowing the Haitian plaintiffs to pursue their claims against the government.

The Fifth Circuit agreed with Judge King that the INS Haitian program had treated Haitian asylum seekers unfairly. But it also dismissed King's commentary on racial prejudice as being irrelevant to the fundamental issues at stake in the case. The court reasoned that the most appropriate constitutional consideration at play was not the equal protection clause of the Fourteenth Amendment, but due process, which was more salient to the protections of the Fifth Amendment.[42] The court also argued that due process was a weaker standard than that of equal protection. Due process could not guarantee that Haitian asylum seekers receive a comparable outcome to that of other national origin groups,[43] but it did require the government to adhere to its own, advertised standards for processing asylum claims. This decision agreed with King's charge that the government had failed to consider Haitian asylum claims on their individual merits. Nevertheless, the judges of the Fifth Circuit refused to consider whether racism had anything to do with this treatment. The court's attitude toward Judge King's decision is summed up in its closing statement, which describes King's commentary about the callousness of the government's policy as "harmful dictum."[44]

These maneuvers provide a good illustration of how the problem of black rightlessness was routinely excised from courtroom deliberations over the government's policies. Judge King put the problem of racism at the forefront of his decision, but without questioning the institutionalized nature of this racism or its ontological foundations. As a result, antiblackness was reduced to a matter of individual bias that could vary from one decision-maker to another. The Fifth Circuit Court took things a step further. It narrowed down the constitutional rights that were available to Haitian refugees and eliminated race as a basis for making any complaint against the government's policies. The legal avenues for the refugees' complaints about government racism were narrowed down even further by the next series of cases I am going to discuss.

CHALLENGING THE DETENTION OF HAITIAN ASYLUM SEEKERS

The issues raised by *HRC v. Civiletti* resurfaced in the deliberations of *Louis v. Nelson*, which was decided by the Southern District Court of Florida in 1982.[45] The plaintiffs in this case were contesting policies that were implemented after the discontinuation of the Carter-era Haitian program. The question of residence, which lingered in the background of the Civiletti decision, jumped into the foreground of *Louis v. Nelson*. The main issue of contention was the policy of holding Haitian asylum seekers in detention centers instead of allowing them to be released on parole into the South Florida community while they were waiting for their cases to be decided.

Between May and July 1981, the INS introduced a new policy of detaining all refugees who, in its opinion, did not have a clearly compelling case for asylum.[46] Although this policy was applied to all refugee populations, the vast majority of the refugees detained were Haitian. Judge Spellman, who presided over the District Court case, cited evidence submitted by the plaintiffs which demonstrated that there was a strong statistical correlation between Haitian ancestry and the likelihood of being detained.[47]

Spellman found that Haitians had been treated unfairly by the new detention policy of the INS. But he also found that the statistical disparity in the
way the detention policy was applied was not sufficient evidence of there
being a racist intent to discriminate.[48] Spellman went on to explain that the
plaintiffs' complaint was better supported by a due process argument rather
than an equal protection argument. This argument echoed the reasoning of the
Fifth Circuit Court in *HRC v. Smith*, which substituted the question of racial
discrimination (appealing to the Fourteenth Amendment) with a less racially
charged complaint about due process (that appealed to the Fifth Amendment).

Unlike King, Judge Spellman did not try to depict the Haitian asylum
seekers as rights-bearing US residents. Instead, he accepted the government's
premise that these were people who had not been formally admitted to the
United States. But he went to craft an argument that held the government
accountable for making major changes to its detention and parole policy
that did not abide by the stipulations of the Administrative Procedures Act
(APA).[49] This argument could be described as a ghostly parallel of a due
process argument that did not require a rights-bearing subject. The "process"
that had been violated did not concern a plaintiffs individual right to a fair
and transparent hearing; it had more to do with the government's obligation
to be consistent in its administrative practice and to make a good faith effort
to clearly communicate policy changes in a timely manner.

This was a very different argument than the one advanced by King, but
when viewed in light of Motomura's analysis, it was just another version of
a phantom norm. Spellman's APA argument was the closest thing to a Fifth
Amendment due process argument that he was able to introduce to the case,
given his concession to the excludability of the Haitian plaintiffs. The practical result was that Spellman was able to check the sovereign authority that
the federal government wielded over immigration law, but without having to
get into a thorny debate over the constitutionality of this authority. As a result
of this decision, all of the Haitian refugees who were part of the class action
suit were released on parole, and the INS was granted a thirty-day period to
develop and advertise a new policy that was in compliance with the procedures of the APA.[50]

The INS promptly complied with Judge Spellman's order to comply with
the APA and rolled out a reframed version of its detention policy before the
end of the thirty-day moratorium.[51] The INS also appealed Spellman's decision to the Eleventh Circuit Court of Appeals, and the case was subsequently
heard by the Supreme Court. Both courts defended the INS' detention policy
for Haitian refugees.

In *Jean v. Nelson* the Eleventh Circuit Court of Appeals offered its critical evaluation of Judge Spellman's ruling. The court began its opinion by
noting that the only remaining issue of concern in the case was whether the

government had violated a Fifth Amendment guarantee to equal protection and due process.[52] Although Judge Spellman had determined that these Fifth Amendment protections did not apply to the case at hand, he had argued that they could potentially apply to any case involving excludable aliens.[53] The Eleventh Circuit, in contrast, evoked the Plenary Power doctrine and argued that excludable aliens do not have Fifth Amendment rights and that the statutory authority granted to the attorney general allows them to exclude on the basis of race or national origin if they so choose.[54]

When the Supreme Court heard the appeal of *Jean v. Nelson*, it took issue with the way that the Eleventh Circuit Court had pitched its argument. This criticism was of no practical relevance for the Haitian plaintiffs. The unanimity of the higher courts about the legality of the detention policy was so resolute that they ended up getting into a debate about which court had produced the best defense of the policy. Despite agreeing with Eleventh Circuit's position, the Supreme Court found that the judges of the Eleventh Circuit could have reached the same decision without relying so heavily on constitutional law.[55] The issue that seemed to have struck a raw nerve for the Supreme Court was the Eleventh Circuit's argument about the government's constitutionally protected right to exclude immigrants because of their race. In its opinion, the Supreme Court made a very different point. Instead of insisting on the government's right-to-be-racist, it emphasized that the INS' new detention policy had been implemented in a race-neutral manner.[56]

On its face, this appears to be a very strange argument. On one hand, the Supreme Court wanted to avoid the appearance that the government's policies were being guided by racist motives. In this regard, it seemed to be paying deference to the same antidiscriminatory norms that Judge King had incorporated into his impassioned critique of the government's policies. But according to the Supreme Court's own argument, Haitian refugees had no legal standing to raise complaints about racial discrimination, because they were not US residents. So, the court appeared to be going out of its way to insist that the government was abiding by a set of race-neutral norms that had no legal foundation, at least, not when it came to excludable refugees. This argument bounced back and forth between a series of seemingly contrary propositions. Haitian refugees had no grounds to complain about racial discrimination. But it so happens that the government's policies were not discriminatory anyway. But the antidiscriminatory norms that the government was abiding by were also not legally binding and could not serve as the basis for a complaint against the government. But these were all moot considerations because the government's policies were not racist to begin with, and so on.

Basically, the Supreme Court wanted to craft an argument that produced the same effect as the Eleventh Circuit's prior decision, while avoiding the bald-faced argument about race and the government's sovereign powers that the Eleventh Circuit used to ground this argument. This could also be described as a phantom norm argument in reverse, in which the Supreme Court sought to defend the government's sovereign authority over immigration law, but without having to get into a prickly argument about the constitutionality of this authority. The reason why the majority of Supreme Court justices wanted to avoid this issue became more apparent when considering the dissenting opinion that was issued by Thurgood Marshall.

Justice Marshall began his opinion by agreeing with the Eleventh Circuit. He observed that the Plenary Power granted to the government on matters of immigration clearly *does* allow for discrimination on the basis of race, national origin, or any other social characteristic of concern for the deciding officials.[57] But having made discrimination an explicit subject of deliberation, Marshall argued that this right-to-be-racist has to be reconciled to other features of constitutional law that forbid racial discrimination.[58] This argument hinges on the understanding—which was even acknowledged by the Eleventh Circuit[59]—that excludable aliens have some standing, no matter how precarious, before the law. Justice Marshall's argument allowed for the possibility that some acts of discrimination against foreign nationals would be constitutionally protected by the Plenary Power doctrine, but not all. By insisting that Plenary Power must be reconciled to the antidiscrimination stipulations of constitutional law, he was advancing an argument that would further extend the powers of judicial review over the immigration decisions of the executive office which would probably, over the long term, strengthen constitutional protections for excludable aliens.

Marshall's dissent in *Jean v. Nelson* is an important precursor for the argument that Motomura advances with his critique of phantom norms. The gist of the argument is that the government's right-to-be-racist must be recognized and made an explicit focus of legal deliberation, so that it can be regulated. The Supreme Court majority in *Jean v. Nelson* probably wanted to avoid this possibility, which explains why it took issue with the way the Eleventh Circuit Court had framed its argument. The Supreme Court majority realized that by making the Plenary Power doctrine so transparently central to its argument, the Eleventh Circuit had created an opening for it to be challenged and reigned-in.

FEDERAL SUPREMACY AND NONCITIZEN RIGHTS

The Supreme Court's decision on *Jean v. Nelson* concludes the first part of my "prehistory." Jean is the last major decision that deals with Haitian refugee policies that were implemented before the maritime interdictions that were inaugurated in September 1981. This early series of cases is important because it introduces issues and arguments that resurface in the challenges that were levied against the interdiction policies of the 1980s and 1990s. But these early struggles over the government's Haitian refugee policies can also be understood as the repetition of a much older assemblage of power practices, sovereign desires, and patterns of argumentation. The rest of the chapter is devoted to this other "prehistory," which predates and overflows the history of the Plenary Power doctrine. In my re-telling of this prehistory, I am going to situate the government's Haitian refugee policies within a historical context that can account for the black rightlessness of the Jim Crow and antebellum eras.

A good starting example is the maneuver that the Supreme Court used in *Jean v. Nelson* to avoid dealing with the "race question." This maneuver is not unique to immigration law. It is characteristic of decisions that have undermined the rights of black slaves and free blacks. The 1896 *Plessy v. Ferguson*[60] decision, which I discuss later in this chapter, used a similar tactic by interpreting egalitarian legal principles in a way that justified Jim Crow segregation.

The dicta concerning race in Plessy avoided the transparent antiblack racism of the 1857 *Dred Scott v. Sandford* decision.[61] Even so, the end result in both cases is that black plaintiffs were abandoned by the law. The Supreme Court's *Jean v. Nelson* decision produced a similar effect when it defended the government's decision to define the legal meaning of excludability in a way that categorically applied to Haitian refugees, to roll out an entirely new policy of mandatory detention that was also categorically applied to Haitians, to insist that these policies were in keeping with the antidiscriminatory norms of the post-civil rights era, and also that Haitian refugees had no right to question any of this because of the way the government had defined their excludability.

All of these decisions—Dred Scott, Plessy, and Jean—are different versions of an interdiction that runs to the heart of the problematic relationship between blackness and modernity. These interdictions impose controls on the movements of black bodies, and in the process, they relegate blackness to the margins of the law and the public, political sphere. This predicament complicates the legal strategy advocated by Thurgood Marshall and Hiroshi Motomura, because black migrants and refugees are not only vulnerable to exclusions that have been justified by the Plenary Power doctrine. Black people are also peripheral to much of the case law that is intended to *protect* immigrants, refugees, and other noncitizens. In order to explain why black people have been peripheral to this latter, more progressive, body of law, it is necessary to surface a racist subtext and a history of power that have been largely ignored by legal scholars. This problematic relationship between blackness and the progressive currents of immigration law helps to explain why the phantom norms that had been used, with varying degrees of efficacy, to protect nonblack migrants, failed when it came to the predicament of Haitian refugees.

In order to properly frame this problem I am going to tell a different story about the relationship between race, the law, and sovereign power that decenters the Plenary Power doctrine. I am going to argue that US immigration law has been shaped by two distinct varieties of sovereign power. One of these forms of sovereign power is reflected in the Plenary Power doctrine. This is the kind of sovereignty that Justice Marshall and Motomura (and Agamben among many other progressive scholars and jurists) have found so problematic. But there is another history of sovereign power, that is laced through the history of US immigration law, which has been put to very different ends than the Plenary Power doctrine. You have to understand the interplay between both of these forms of sovereign power to understand the problem of black rightlessness and the de facto, black/nonblack binary that pervades the US migration regime.

To begin this story, I am going to return to Justice Marshall's dissent in the Supreme Court decision on *Louis v. Nelson*. Marshall focused on the tension between the constitutionality of the Plenary Power doctrine and the constitutional guarantee of equal protection under the law.[62] Although this equal protection argument can be traced to the Fourteenth Amendment, the most relevant starting point for US immigration law is the Supreme Court's 1886 decision in *Yick Wo v. Hopkins*.[63]

The main issue of contention in the Yick Wo decision was a local ordinance that regulated the licensing of laundry services. According to the plaintiffs, the ordinance was being implemented in a way that exclusively targeted Chinese laundry business owners.[64] The Yick Wo Supreme Court found this correlation between race and the revocation of laundry licenses to be sufficient evidence of an intent to discriminate that violated the equal protection clause. Consequently, the Yick Wo decision established the argument that all persons residing under the territorial jurisdiction of the US government were entitled to the protections of the Constitution.[65]

The Yick Wo decision was approvingly cited by Justice King[66] and also by Judge Marshall in his dissent,[67] and it figures prominently in legal scholarship that has criticized the government's policy on Haitian refugees.[68] In all of these opinions and decisions, Yick Wo has been evoked as a bulwark against the government's Plenary Power over immigration law. But this desire to align Yick Wo with a constitutional rights argument that is opposed to the sovereign power of the US government masks are more complex story—because the Yick Wo decision was also supported by an argument that affirmed these sovereign powers.

Although the Plenary Power doctrine predates the Yick Wo decision, the sovereign powers that were endorsed by Yick Wo predate the Plenary Power doctrine. These powers were favorably discussed by Supreme Court decisions that are traceable to the early nineteenth century and are connected to legal disputes that began in the 1790s. Instead of focusing on the federal government's right to exclude noncitizens, these sovereign powers affirmed the primacy of federal over local law and are connected to the Supremacy Clause described by Article IV of the US Constitution.[69]

The Supremacy Clause, and the principle of federal preemption that derives from it, is concerned with ensuring that local laws operate within the framework of constitutional law. As it is typically interpreted, this means that local laws should not conflict with legislation that has already been enacted by the federal government.[70] It so happens that the federal government did not occupy the field of immigration lawmaking until 1875.[71] Even so, the Supreme Court had begun issuing arguments concerning the federal government's special prerogatives to decide on matters concerning noncitizen property rights and international commerce (which involved international migration flows) as early as 1816.[72] Furthermore, in the Yick Wo decision, this argument about "federal supremacy" was not made through reference to an actually existing, federal law but to a treaty agreement between the Office of the President and the Emperor of China, concerning the recruitment and treatment of Chinese migrant laborers.[73] Hence, the sovereign authority affirmed by Yick Wo was not the lawmaking powers of the legislature, but the decisions of the executive branch which are exercised within the scope of its discretionary authority.

This relationship between the Supremacy Clause and the discretionary powers of the executive branch is similar to the arrangement described by the Plenary Power doctrine. These powers are acknowledged by the Constitution, and they have been authorized by constitutional law. But the Supreme Court has also argued that these powers are an inherent property of the government, rather than an authority bestowed on the government by the Constitution. This is precisely the argument that the Eleventh Circuit made in *Jean v. Nelson* when it insisted that Haitian refugees have no right to due process or equal protection. Consider the following excerpt:

> For centuries, it has been an accepted maxim of international law that the power to control the admission of foreigners is an *inherent attribute* of national sovereignty. . . . We therefore see no reason for concluding that the traditional conceptions of national sovereignty relied on by the Supreme Court in its early decisions in this area have been significantly eroded. . . . Because *this "undefined and undefinable" sovereign power does not depend on any constitutional grant of authority*, there are apparently no limitations on the power of the

federal government to determine what classes of aliens will be permitted to enter the United States or what procedures will be used to determine their admissibility. (Emphasis added)[74]

In making its case, the Eleventh Circuit drew on a number of precedent decisions that affirm a sovereign authority over immigration that can be traced to the Plenary Power doctrine.[75] But it is significant that this passage begins by insisting on a sovereign right which has existed *for centuries*. By pitching its argument this way, the Eleventh Circuit was insisting that constitutional law was beholden to a principle of sovereign authority that predates the US republic. The court underscored this point when it insisted that this sovereign power "does not depend on any constitutional grant of authority." It also bears noting that one of the precedent decisions it cited, *Knauft v. Shaughnessy*,[76] argued that sovereign power over immigration was a property, specifically, of the executive branch of government (rather than a power conferred on the President's Office by the Congress). This understanding of sovereignty is also a feature of the federal supremacy argument, and it helps to explain why the Supreme Court had cultivated a sophisticated jurisprudence about the government's sovereign power on matters concerning noncitizen rights decades before the Plenary Power doctrine.

This jurisprudence on federal supremacy provides a new perspective from which to engage Motomura's argument about phantom norms. The phantom norm is, by definition, a construct of questionable legal standing. It is modeled after constitutional law but it is inserted into field of lawmaking (e.g., immigration law) in which there are few established legal precedents to support it. The federal supremacy argument is similar to the phantom norm in that it has a loose relationship to constitutional law. But it would be inaccurate to describe it as a questionable legal construct and it does not attempt to legitimate itself by imitating the rights discourse of constitutional law. Instead, the federal supremacy argument relies on a long-established jurisprudence concerning the government's sovereign authority over the law.

Whereas the phantom norm describes a problem within the law, the federal supremacy argument directs our attention to forces and sociopolitical considerations that impinge on the law from a larger social reality, which are mediated via the government's sovereign authority. The federal supremacy argument has also played a role in most of the progressive Supreme Court decisions on immigrant rights that Motomura attributes to the work of phantom norms. So, although I do not discount the phantom norm argument, I argue that the federal supremacy argument adds an important dimension to this jurisprudence on immigrant rights, which is not explained by the phantom norm argument—and which carries special relevance for an explanation of the antiblack subtext of US immigration law.

Plenary Power has been used to restrict migration flows and noncitizen rights. In contrast, the federal supremacy argument has been used to check the authority of state and local governments in favor of noncitizens.[77] Plenary Power is usually evoked in the name of the citizenry, whereas federal supremacy has been used, on balance, to defend the immigrant. But there is one important connecting thread that runs between these citizen and noncitizen beneficiaries of the government's sovereign powers, which is that black people have been excluded, historically, from both of these populations. Black people begin their history in the US republic as a population that is deemed to be uniquely undesirable, as citizens or immigrants. One consequence of this predicament is that legal arguments that have been used, historically, to protect immigrant and refugee rights have not done a good job of addressing the problem of black rightlessness. It is not possible to explain the US government's Haitian refugee policies without bringing this history more clearly into view. In the rest of the chapter, I am going to expand on this argument in two ways: by paying special attention to the way that blacks have been excluded from the US migration flow and by showing how US immigration law has revolved around the problems faced by non-black migrants.

My review is going to focus on Supreme Court decisions that have used the federal supremacy argument to protect immigrants from restrictive, local laws.[78] I have divided this time line into four periods, which begin in the late eighteenth century and end in the late twentieth century, around the same period of time that the Civiletti and Nelson cases were being adjudicated.

WHITE PROPERTY RIGHTS AND THE PROHIBITION ON BLACK MIGRATION

The application of the federal supremacy argument to the question of immigrant rights begins in the early 1800s. All of the cases in this era involved disputes over the right of foreign nationals to sell, transfer, or will their US property holdings to persons of their choosing. In all of these cases, the Supreme Court issued decisions in favor of the noncitizen property holder (see table 2.1).

These cases were usually propelled by disputes between the US and for-eign-born family members over the legitimacy of a property transaction that had been initiated by one of the foreign-born members. All of the noncitizens involved in these property disputes were white people of British or European nationality. During this same period of time, most black people living in the United States were the property of white land owners. The free black population of this era was also targeted by local laws that imposed restrictions on

Table 2.1 Decisions Concerning Local Laws Governing Noncitizen Property Rights

		Nationality of Noncitizen Property Owner or Claimant	*Local Law Restricted Noncitizen Rights*	*Outcome Favored Noncitizen Property Owner or Claimant*
Year	Case			
1813	*Fairfax's Devisee v. Hunter's Lessee*	British (UK)	No	Yes
1816	*Martin v. Hunter's Lessee*	British (UK)	No	Yes
1817	*Chirac v. Chirac*	French	No	Yes
1826	*Governeur's Heirs v. Robertson*	British (UK)	No	Yes
1830	*Spratt v. Spratt*	British (UK) and Irish	No	Yes
1879	*Hauenstein v. Lynham*	Swiss	No	Yes
1890	*Geofroy v. Riggs*	French	No	Yes
1901	*Blythe v. Hinckley*	British (UK)	No	Yes

Source: Table generated by author. Data or cases from Federal Register and justia.com.

the political and legal rights, including property rights.[79] The policing of the white/black color line, via the One Drop rule, is an apt case in point.

The One Drop rule revolved around the idea of "blood fraction," which was a proportional estimate of the quantity of "black blood" in a person's ancestral lineage.[80] It began to cohere as a legal institution in the early 1800s,[81] around the same time that the Supreme Court was issuing its decisions for most of the cases described in table 2.1. The jurisprudence on the One Drop rule eventually settled on a nationally accepted standard of "no more than a one sixteenth fraction" of black ancestry to qualify as a white person, but blood fraction criteria were established by the local courts and varied considerably from state to state in the early 1800s.[82]

In this same era, state and local governments were the driving force behind immigration law, and these lawmaking powers were informed by ideas about the inherent sovereignty of state and local governments.[83] So the same local authorities that were determining the standards for "white personhood" were also devising laws and policies concerning the recruitment and regulation of immigration flows. These two terrains of lawmaking shed more light on the antiblack context for the Supreme Court's earliest rulings on noncitizen property rights. The local culture of lawmaking on race and legal personhood ensured that only foreign-born persons who were demonstrably white would be in any position to make claims about their property rights, and this is not just because most blacks were barred from owning property. Blacks were also excluded from the flow of foreign-born persons into the United States.

This latter factor, the exclusion of blacks from the migration flow, did not rely entirely on the law to produce its effects. It relied on a discretionary authority that was guided by a well-established body of opinion on black inferiority. Although this body of opinion does not surface in the legal deliberations over alien property rights, it was an important feature of the sociopolitical context for these decisions. To explain further, I will take a closer look at one of these cases.

The first cases concerning alien property rights heard by the Supreme Court were *Fairfax's Devisee v. Hunter's Lessee* and *Martin v. Hunter's Lessee*. Both cases revolved around the same dispute, concerning the legal ownership of a tract of land in Virginia that had been purchased by the family and associates of a British citizen.[84]

Of the two cases, the Martin decision is the most significant because, in it, the Supreme Court established the primacy of Supreme Court jurisprudence over that of state and local courts. This argument was grounded in the court's interpretation of Article III of the Constitution, which addresses the need for a supreme, federal court.[85] Ironically, this argument which is so important for the genealogy of the Supreme Court jurisprudence on federal supremacy does not actually cite the Supremacy Clause of Article IV. The substance of the case is also not directly relevant to the issue of federal preemption, because there was no conflict between federal and local law. The Supreme Court found that Virginia State law agreed with its position, that foreign nationals had the right to purchase, sell, and will property to other parties.[86]

The court was primarily concerned with describing the structure of government that was intended by the Constitution. It noted, for example, that "the Constitution was not . . . carved out of existing State sovereignties, nor a surrender of powers already existing in State institutions."[87] Instead, the court observed that the Constitution established a new "general government" invested with "paramount and supreme authority" relative to state governments.[88] It also observed that two of the key areas in which the authority of this government clearly superseded the sovereign powers of the states were on matters of constitutional law and treaties between the US and foreign governments.[89] The latter concern is most relevant to the Martin decision.

The opening statement of the Martin decision refers to peace treaties signed by the US government.[90] The court went on to argue that treaties must be authorized by a supreme government and that interpretations of Virginia law that restricted the property rights of foreign nationals conflicted with the agreements that the US executive office had made with the British government. The end result was an argument that affirmed the sovereign authority of the federal government over local lawmakers and which protected the interests of foreign-born property holders. This argument established a template that was used by a series of Supreme Court decisions that span the nineteenth century, ending with *Blythe v. Hinckley* in 1901[91] (see table 2.1). In this same era, US elites were using their sovereign authority, in a very different way, to control black mobility. Thomas Jefferson's political career and views on race provide a good entry point into this other social reality.

At the time that the Supreme Court was fashioning the federal supremacy argument, Jefferson was an influential figure among US elites. He served as governor of Virginia, though he did not hold office when the Fairfax and Martin cases were making their way through the Virginia courts.[92] Jefferson's Presidential term ended shortly before the Supreme Court decided *Martin v. Hunter's Lessee*, but his Democratic-Republican Party occupied the Presidential office during the same period of time that the Supreme Court decided Hunter and several other immigrant property right cases.[93]

Jefferson was also a staunch supporter of immigrant rights. He was one of the most prominent critics of the 1798 *Alien and Seditions Acts*, and he appealed to the public outrage over the acts in his 1800 Presidential campaign.[94] It bears noting that the acts were unpopular due to restrictions on civil liberties they imposed on the entire citizen population, and not just for their restrictions on noncitizen rights. The scope of these restrictions calls attention to the continuum of legal personhood in which the citizen and the immigrant were both situated. Hence, restrictions on citizen and immigrant rights could be interpreted as attacks on the same kind of rights-bearing subject, and it is important to keep in mind that the prototypical rights-bearing subject of US law, in that era, was white, propertied and male.[95] There was also an antiblack subtext running through this principled defense of immigrant rights.

Jefferson, and many of the other elites who opposed the Aliens and Seditions Acts, were slave holders who were staunchly opposed to any movement to improve the legal standing of the black population.[96] Many of these elites enlisted black slaves in their campaign to defeat the Federalists, who had enacted the Aliens and Seditions Acts, by adding the "votes" of these slaves to their own. Fred Kaplan has explained that these "slave votes" (each counting as three-fifths of a free person's vote) helped secure Jefferson's narrow victory in his 1800 Presidential campaign.[97]

The Haitian revolution was also an important part of the backdrop for the Aliens and Seditions Acts. One of the concerns that led the Federalists to draft the acts had to do with a group of ships containing several hundred blacks from the French colony of Saint Domingue that had anchored near the US mainland.[98] A few years earlier, state lawmakers enacted a series of laws that were stoked by similar concerns about the migration of "French Blacks" who were associated with insurrectionist stirrings in the slave populations of Saint Domingue (i.e., revolutionary-era Haiti).[99]

Although anxieties about these "French blacks" set the stage for the Aliens and Seditions Acts, the contingent of Southern slave holders who opposed these acts made a sharp distinction between the cause of the French masses and that of black emancipation. Jefferson and his allies supported the French revolution. But they opposed the Haitian revolution and forged alliances with slaveholding elites that had fled Saint Domingue for the US and French-controlled territories of North America.[100] This sharply polarized view of the French and Haitian revolutions provides a good illustration of the black/white binary that defined the US political culture of the post-revolutionary era, which would mutate into a black/nonblack binary in the decades to come.

Jefferson's attitudes toward the Haitian revolution also should be situated in light of his views on race, which were widely shared by other elites of his day. Ladelle McWhorter has shown that Jefferson's views on black otherness were informed by biological and morphological theories of racial inequality that had been popularized by Linnaeus, Blumenbach, and Kant.[101] McWhorter has also shown that his views on race were informed by British and French ideas about race struggle which predate European scientific racism and which were rooted in a sociopolitical understanding of race.[102] According to Jefferson, blacks would always be a dangerous, unassimilable race because of the bitter resentments created by the transatlantic slave trade, but this political analysis only reinforced his understanding of the "black" and "white" races as radically different, biological and morphological types.

These views on race carried important consequences for Jefferson's views on black migration. Jefferson believed there was no conceivable future in which whites and blacks could freely coexist, that was unclouded by the threat of civil disorder, and his conviction on this matter was underscored by his belief in black otherness as a pre-social, biological property. Jefferson was also an anti-slavery moralist: a body of opinion that was widely held by white elites of his day. Anti-slavery moralists were critical of slavery in principle but did not support an abolitionist agenda.[103] Instead of emancipation followed by the granting of citizen rights to blacks, most anti-slavery moralists favored a gradual process of manumission combined with the repatriation of freed blacks to Africa or the Caribbean. These repatriation projects were often described as "mass deportations" or "voluntary deportations." The American Colonization Society (ACS) was the main political vehicle for these projects in the nineteenth century.

The ACS was founded in the early 1800s, as a private society, and was sustained by membership fees.[104] The ACS, with funding and logistical assistance of the US government, carried out a series of African colonization projects throughout the 1800s: one of its main accomplishments being the founding of the nation-state of Liberia in 1822.[105] The organization was supported by a string of antebellum-era US presidents, starting with

Jefferson, followed by James Monroe and James Madison, who became president of the ACS in 1830, after stepping down from his Presidential post.[106] The ACS was also endorsed by a politically diverse group of elites, like Lincoln and Whig party leader Henry Clay who were genuinely committed to limiting the spread of slavery in the United States.[107] But the ACS drew criticism from abolitionists for advancing the interests of the slave-holding classes.[108] As Kaplan notes, "[m]embership in the society didn't alone reveal whether someone was pro or anti-slavery. The glue that bound members together was their commitment to white supremacy and a black-free America."[109]

The ACS program of voluntary deportations can also be read in light of the political culture of the US slaveholding classes, which favored a weak central government. This political philosophy helps to explain why Jefferson could fiercely criticize the expansion of the government's deportation powers over aliens, vis-à-vis the Alien and Seditions Acts, and also support ACS' proposals for the mass deportation of blacks.[110] Under the ACS, black deportations would be coordinated by a civil society organization that was rooted in the networks of private citizens and that, presumably, would not contribute to the centralization of the federal government. It also bears emphasizing that the Haitian revolution, and its aftermath, was an important part of the backdrop for the ACS' program of black, mass deportations.

The Haitian revolution, which was well underway during Jefferson's first term as president, played a key role in shaping white elite opinion about the political necessity of imposing controls on black migration.[111] Jefferson and other US elites were also, undoubtedly, aware that many black people in the Southern states had fled across the Caribbean Sea to fight in the Haitian revolution and that the Haitian revolutionaries welcomed and encouraged these solidarities.[112] The leadership of the post-revolutionary Haitian state also paid close attention to the state of "race relations" in the United States and found common cause with the insurrectionist stirrings of the black US population.[113]

This combustible situation helps to explain the contradictory positions that were adopted by many white elites on the subject of race and slavery in the early nineteenth century. Slavery was widely believed to be a dangerous and unsustainable institution, but the United States remained committed to a slaving economy nonetheless. And these contradictions continued into the postbellum era. Blacks could, on one hand, be treated as a population that was entitled to citizenship, while also being viewed as a population that was inherently unfit for citizenship. These ambivalent and contradictory opinions about blacks and citizenship set the stage for the next phase of the history of the jurisprudence on federal supremacy, when its arguments—which had first been used to protect the rights of white aliens—were extended to nonblack minorities.

CONSTITUTIONAL RIGHTS AND THE
NONBLACK NONCITIZEN

In the late nineteenth century, the jurisprudence on federal supremacy was joined by a new argument, which drew on the equal protection clause of the Fourteenth Amendment. The Fourteenth Amendment was adopted after the Civil War to facilitate the incorporation of black, former slaves, which is why its language of "equal protection" was widely understood as a prohibition on racial discrimination.[114]

In the late nineteenth century, the Supreme Court began to extend the equal protection clause to noncitizens. These decisions invited comparisons between the noncitizen and the black other for whom the Fourteenth Amendment had been originally designed, and these comparisons carried two implications. The first implication is that the noncitizens who were deserved the protections of the Fourteenth Amendment were racial minorities themselves and potential victims of white racism. The second implication was that noncitizens were "like" racial minorities, simply because they were noncitizens, and could face discrimination due to their noncitizen status, regardless of their race. Both of these tendencies played out from the 1880s onward as the equal protection argument was used to protect the rights of Chinese and white, European immigrants.

The 1886 *Yick Wo v. Hopkins*[115] decision played a crucially important role in shaping this body of legal opinion. Yick Wo is significant because it is the first Supreme Court decision to extend the protections of the Fourteenth Amendment to noncitizens, which is why it is not surprising to see it enlisted in arguments that criticize the government's treatment of Haitian refugees. But if one takes a closer look at the reasoning behind Yick Wo and situates it in the context of its times, it becomes more apparent that Yick Wo was protecting the rights of people who belonged to the nonblack side of a black/nonblack binary.

This may seem like a strange proposition if you focus on the way that Yick Wo leveraged the Fourteenth Amendment. As I have already noted, this maneuver invites comparisons between black people and racialized immigrants, and Haitians clearly fall into both categories. But the Yick Wo constitutional rights argument was also joined by a federal supremacy argument that had been consistently used throughout the early nineteenth century to protect the property rights of white immigrants.

The role played by the supremacy argument does not completely void the progressive significance of Yick Wo, but it makes for a more complicated story. Viewed in this light, Yick Wo is not just a story about how the Constitution was brought to the defense of vulnerable noncitizens. It is also a story about how the sovereign powers of the US government that had been used to protect the rights of white immigrants, and were still being used in the time of Yick Wo to perpetuate black rightlessness and to keep blacks out of the US migration flow, were cautiously expanded to protect the rights of *some* nonblack immigrants. To explain further, it will be necessary to take a closer look at the contents of Yick Wo.

The Yick Wo decision struck down a local ordinance regulating laundry businesses that discriminated against Chinese migrants. But this decision was not the first instance in which the Supreme Court had taken an interest in the treatment of immigrants who were also nonblack racial minorities. The federal supremacy argument had been put to these purposes several decades prior to Yick Wo in a series of cases revolving around port-of-call fees that local governments were imposing on steamship passengers (see table 2.2). The fees were intended to discourage the migration of indigent persons who were associated with crime and sickness, as well as persons of questionable morality. Some of the case summaries for these decisions made explicit reference to "social problems" associated with Chinese migrants.[116]

This series of cases begins with an 1837 decision, *New York v Miln.*[117] This case is distinguished for being the only decision issued by the Supreme Court in the 19th century which sided with local governments over the federal government on a question that concerned noncitizen rights. The Court ruled that port-of-call fees fell within the city's sovereign authority to ensure the security and public health of its residents. This authority was supported by an argument about the "police powers" of local government.[118]

The discourse on police power and that of federal supremacy stem from the same genealogy of state power.[119] Within the context of US law, however, the police powers argument is limited by the territorial jurisdiction of local government. The federal supremacy argument, in contrast, is more wide-ranging and is, by definition, a "supreme authority" to which local governments must pay deference.

In *New York v. Miln* the Supreme Court paid tribute to the supremacy of federal over local sovereignty but did not find that municipal port-of-call fees infringed on this order of authority.[120] The Court reached a very different decision, however, for the four subsequent cases it heard on this subject between 1849 and 1883 (see Table 2.2). In these decisions the Supreme Court struck down port-of-call fees because they interfered with the federa governments interest in regulating international commerce (with steamship passengers being treated as units of commerce).[121] This argument was comparable to the "treaty powers" argument that was raised in the immigrant property rights decisions of the early 19th centiry (see Table 2.1), and it was sometimes combined with the references to the U.S. government's diplomatic relations with foreign governments.[122]

Most of these port-of-call cases were filed on behalf of a multi-national group of passengers[123], but one of them, *Chy Lung v. Freeman*[124] was filed by a group of plaintiffs composed entirely of Chinese immigrants. This 1876 decision is important because it is the first instance in which the Supreme

Table 2.2 Antebellum and Jim Crow-Era Decisions That Ruled against Local Laws Restricting Noncitizen Rights

Constitutional Rights and Federal Supremacy Argument

Year	Case	Nationality of Noncitizen Plaintiffs	Local Law
1886	Yick Wo v. Hopkins	Chinese	Business licensing
1915	Truax v. Raich	Austrian	Employment Quota
1941	Hines v. Davidowitz	Italian and unspecified European nationality	Alien registration
1941	Oyama v. California	Japanese	Land law
1948	Takahashi v. Fish & Game Comm'n	Japanese	Gaming licensing

Federal Supremacy Argument Only

Year	Case	Nationality of Noncitizen Plaintiffs	Local Law
1849	Passenger Cases	British	Port-of-call fees
1876	Henderson v. Mayor of New York	Scottish/British and Misc. Unspecified	Port-of-call fees
1876	Chy Lung v. Freeman	Chinese	Port-of-call fees
1883	People of NY v. Compagnie Generale Transatlantique	French and Misc. Unspecified	Port-of-call fees
1924	Asakura v. Seattle	Japanese	Business licensing

Source: Table generated by author. Data or cases from Federal Register and justia.com.

Court evokes the supremacy of the federal government in a way that specifically protects a nonblack, noncitizen group.

The next decision in this case history that focuses on nonblack, noncitizens is *Yick Wo v. Hopkins.* As I explained previously, Yick Wo is famous for bringing the equal protection clause to the defense of noncitizens. The decision begins by stating:

> The guarantees of protection contained in the Fourteenth Amendment to the Constitution extend to all persons within the territorial jurisdiction of the United States, without regard to differences of race, of color, or of nationality. Those subjects of the Emperor of China who have the right to temporarily or permanently reside within the United States are entitled to enjoy the protection guaranteed by the Constitution and afforded by the laws.[125]

But as I have already noted, Yick Wo did not rely exclusively on a constitutional rights argument. It combined this rights argument with a federal supremacy argument that had been consistently used by the Supreme Court for over seventy years (at the time of the Yick Wo decision). If you situate Yick Wo within the history of decisions that preceded it (see tables 2.1 and 2.2) it becomes more apparent that the constitutional rights argument was supplementing a supremacy argument that the Supreme Court had been using to protect immigrant rights since the early 1800s. This is why it is not surprising the Yick Wo court cited the Supreme Court's prior decisions in the port-of-call series of cases (and especially Chy Lung) to substantiate its argument.[126] These influences also show up in the discussion of the US government's treaty with the Emperor of China.

> By the third article of the treaty between this Government and that of China, concluded November 17, 1880, 22 Stat. 827, it is stipulated: "If Chinese laborers, or Chinese of any other class, now either permanently or temporarily residing in the territory of the United States, meet with ill treatment at the hands of any other persons, the Government of the United States will exert all its powers to devise measures for their protection, and to secure to them the *same rights, privileges, immunities and exemptions as may be enjoyed by the citizens or subjects of the most favored nation,* and to which they are entitled by treaty." (Emphasis added)[127]

Similar to the World War II-era Bracero program and the North American Free Trade Agreement, the treaty described in Yick Wo is a product of decisions made by the executive branch of the US government which does not require ratification by the Congress. This treaty also contained a guarantee of equal treatment that resonates with the language of the Fourteenth Amendment (see italicized excerpt above) but which is specific to the treaty itself. As a consequence, the US government was not committed to honor these rights any longer than it deemed necessary. It so happens that the US government decided to terminate this treaty just a few years after the Supreme Court ruled on Yick Wo.[128]

The government was also under no obligation to extend the rights, guaranteed by the treaty, to any other noncitizen population or national origin group. As it concerns black migrants, however, the main problem was not that they were denied rights extended to Chinese immigrants, but that the US government had no interest in recruiting them in the first place. So rather than restricting black immigrant rights or restricting black migration (which presumes that there was a flow to restrict), it would be more accurate to say that US policy-makers used their discretionary authority to convert the possibility of black migration into a non-event.

Labor historians have explained how the US government turned to Chinese labor and other racialized populations to substitute for the slave labor that had been eliminated by the Emancipation Proclamation.[129] But it would be misleading to describe these strategies, simply, as practical attempts to make up for a shortfall in the labor supply. There were black worker populations in the Caribbean that the US government could have drawn on to fill its growing need for low wage labor in the postbellum era, but it did not avail itself of these opportunities.[130]

Gerald Horne has shown that there was a body of elite opinion, in the late 1860s that found black labor to be "inappropriate" for the postbellum era, noting that "the Negro had fulfilled his destiny in building the productive forces on the mainland and could now be ushered off stage as bonded labor from China would proceed to hold sway."[131] These sentiments help to explain why blacks were largely excluded from the migrant flows of the late nineteenth century, despite the fact that no law had been enacted to prohibit black migration. The idea that blacks should be "ushered off the stage" was not just a reference to the undesirability of black migration. It can also be read as an endorsement of plans, popularized by the ACS, for the mass expulsion of the domestic black population.

Ulysses S. Grant catered to this body of opinion during his Presidency when he explored the possibility of a mass-scale resettlement of freed blacks in Haiti. The reasoning behind this project is summed up by Horne, who cites a document which states that

President Grant desired to see the "valuable timbers" of the Dominican Republic in U.S. hands. Moreover it was the gate to the "Caribbean Sea" and most importantly, "capable of supporting the entire colored population of the United States"; since "the present difficulty in bringing all parts of the United States to a happy unity and love of country grows out of the prejudice to color," he was eager to see *the mass deportation of the newly freed to Hispaniola*.[132] (Emphasis added)

Horne explains that the then president of the Dominican Republic was open to annexation by the United States.[133] It bears emphasizing, however, that Grant White House's language about the "mass deportation" of the "newly freed to Hispaniola" is a reference to the government-sponsored migration of the black US citizen population to the Republic of Haiti. The Haitian government stubbornly resisted this plan and although many black Americans had reason to flee to Haiti, the tide of black opinion also turned against the annexation and relocation proposal.[134]

The fact that this proposal failed is not as important as what it reveals about how US elites were thinking about the "black problem" in the 1870s. In a nutshell, the federal government was much more interested in exporting blacks from the United States than importing more blacks, as migrant workers. This context helps to explain why the Yick Wo decision was of no more practical relevance to the black population of the postbellum era than were the alien property rights decisions of the early 1800s. All of these decisions protected the rights of a migrant and noncitizen population that was closed off to blacks, much like the whites-only lunch counters that had been made possible by Jim Crow laws.

Meanwhile, Yick Wo became the starting point for a genealogy of progressive precedents on immigrant rights that were exclusively defined by the grievances of European and Asian noncitizens (see table 2.2). Like Yick Wo, all of these cases deployed constitutional rights and federal supremacy arguments to protect noncitizens from restrictive local laws. The first Supreme Court decision in this case history, that cites Yick Wo as a precedent, is *Truax v. Raich* (1915),[135] which involved an Austrian national who challenged an Arizona law that imposed a quota on the percentage of immigrants that were allowed in the workforce of local employers. Three more decisions follow Truax, that were issued between 1941 and 1948, which cited Yick Wo and set progressive precedents for noncitizen rights. One of these cases involved a pair of European naturalized citizens who contested Pennsylvania alien voters registration law,[136] and the other two involved challenges California laws that targeted Asian noncitizens.[137]

I have chosen 1948 as the end date for this series because it marks the last time that a Supreme Court case in the Yick Wo genealogy was decided in the Jim Crow era. The point I want to underline is that the Fourteenth Amendment was being used to protect noncitizen rights during the same period of time that the Supreme Court was faithfully defending the legality of Jim Crow laws. So although the Fourteenth Amendment had been crafted with black former slaves in mind, it was used much more effectively to protect the rights of nonblack noncitizens, in the late nineteenth century, than to protect the rights of the "newly freed" black American population. These disparities in the treatment of black and nonblack populations are amply illustrated by a comparison of Yick Wo and the 1896 *Plessy v. Ferguson*[138] decision.

The Supreme Court's decision in Plessy was the culmination of a dispute that began with an attempt to challenge the legality of the 1890 *Louisiana Separate Car Act*, which mandated "equal but separate" train car accommodations for blacks and whites.[139] The Supreme Court's decision enshrined the legality of racial segregation within constitutional law—a situation that lasted over fifty years until the issuance of the *Brown v. Board of Education* decision in 1954.[140]

The remarkable thing about the Plessy and Yick Wo decisions is how similar they were—in terms of the core issues at stake in each case—and how differently the Supreme Court ruled on them. Both of these cases revolved around exclusionary laws, enacted by local governments that had been motivated by racial animus. The arguments raised in both cases also carried implications for the validity of the "police powers" argument, used by local governments to justify their sovereign authority, and for the viability of the Fourteenth Amendment as a way of protecting racialized minorities and pushing back against these "police powers."

In Plessy, the Supreme Court made an argument that was diametrically opposed to the one it issued in Yick Wo. It also bears noting that Plessy was decided ten years after Yick Wo. The Supreme Court could easily have drawn on the progressive interpretation of Fourteenth Amendment rights that it introduced in Yick Wo and used it as a basis for protecting black rights in Plessy. But of course, the court did not do this. Yick Wo was allowed to recede into the background as if it pertained to an entirely different legal history (and to an entirely different category of person) despite the fact that both cases revolved around similar legal principles.

The Plessy court justified Jim Crow laws on the basis of the very same police powers argument that the Supreme Court had struck down in most of the cases it heard on port-of-call fees throughout the nineteenth century (which was also used by the defenders of the local ordinance in Yick Wo).[141] In Yick Wo, the Supreme Court insisted that it was not necessary for an ordinance to explicitly name Chinese migrants as its targets in order for it to be considered racist, arguing that "though the law itself be fair on its face and impartial in appearance ... it is applied and administered by public authority with an evil eye and an unequal hand..."[142] But when confronted with Jim Crow laws that explicitly demarcated areas for "whites only" and "coloreds only" or "Negros only" the Plessy court found no violation of the Fourteenth Amendment.

If one leaves aside the question of race, it could be argued that the Supreme Court was powerless to use the supremacy argument to block the spread of Jim Crow laws because these laws did not concern noncitizens, treaty powers, or questions of international commerce. But contemporary legal observers have not treated the Plessy decision as a begrudging accommodation to the racist sentiments of its day. Instead, Plessy has been criticized for the role it played in establishing the racist architecture of the Jim Crow era.[143] One of these critiques is provided by Saidiya Hartman who argues that "the police power of the state, as invoked in Plessy, basically created 'biologized internal enemies'"[144] and that rather than describing a departure from liberal values, Plessy epitomized the liberal response to the "problem" posed by of black freedom.[145]

As I noted previously, the way Plessy rationalized racial inequality was similar to the arguments used by the Supreme Court's 1985 *Jean v. Nelson* decision. In Jean, the Supreme Court insisted that INS detention policies that targeted Haitian refugees were actually being implemented in a race-neutral matter.[146] In Plessy the Supreme Court argued that Jim Crow laws that may have looked discriminatory on their face were actually in conformity with the equal protection clause, so long as it could be shown that the separate facilities provided to blacks were equal to those for whites.[147] Both of these legal arguments corroborate Calvin Warren's theory about the distortion that allows the Law of Being to communicate its judgments, in refracted ways, through the being of the law.[148]

On one hand, there is a racist ontology that excludes blackness from the Human family. But this judgment on blackness is not codified into the language of the law because doing so would require the law to grant blackness some legal standing, no matter how precarious. Hence, the judgment on blackness is ventriloquized through other discourses—even ones that profess fidelity to the principle of nondiscriminatory treatment—which produce black rightlessness without having to explicitly say that they are doing so.

These judgments underscore the continuing significance of the black/nonblack binary which is incessantly referenced and effaced by the law. But the story I have told, in which nonblack migrants are privileged by the law over black populations, becomes more complicated in the early twentieth century. At this point in time, the Supreme Court begins to use the federal supremacy argument in a different way, to restrict the rights of nonblack migrants. I briefly review this legal history in the next section.

WHITE NATIONALISM AND DE JURE DISCRIMINATION

The nativist and white supremacist movements of the late nineteenth and early twentieth century were organized around concerns about "race suicide" which extended far beyond concerns about Chinese immigrants.[149] As many scholars have explained, Jewish, Irish, as well as Southern and Eastern European immigrant populations all came under suspicion as the new faces of a racial and cultural threat to Anglo-American society.[150] One of the most impactful legal outcomes of these anti-immigrant sentiments was the enactment of the 1921 and 1924 Immigration Acts which put an end to the immigration boom of the early 1900s and imposed nation origin quotas that were designed to limit the migration of "racially undesirable" types.[151]

This was a time of continuity and change for the federal supremacy argument and its relationship to the black/nonblack binary. Nativistic racism that mainly targeted nonblack migrants made new inroads into established political institutions, including the federal courts. During this time, the Supreme

Court began using the federal supremacy argument to attend to the concerns of local governments and their citizen constituencies, rather than to protect noncitizens. Between 1914 and 1934, it issued a string of ten decisions that sided with local laws that restricted noncitizen rights.

Similar to the progressive string of decisions that followed from Yick Wo, these restrictive uses of the federal supremacy argument were exclusively focused on cases involving nonblack noncitizens. Four of the ten decisions involved laws that restricted access to employment or public licenses for all noncitizens, and the aggrieved parties in all of these cases were European immigrants.[152] The remaining six of these cases concerned Alien Land Laws that excluded foreign-born Asians from property ownership.[153]

But despite these setbacks, the progressive genealogy of Supreme Court decisions, that begins with Yick Wo, winds its way through this era. The 1915 *Truax v. Raich* decision that was discussed earlier falls in this era. This decision did not involve an Asian noncitizen plaintiff, but it used case law concerning the rights of Chinese noncitizens (citing Yick Wo) to make a constitutional argument on behalf of all noncitizens.[154] There was also the 1924 *Asakura v. Seattle* decision, which affirmed the legality of a business license held by a Japanese immigrant.[155]

Starting in 1941, the Supreme Court began to change course again, issuing a string of decisions that reflected the earlier tradition of the federal supremacy argument. The majority of these decisions, which were issued between the 1940s and the early 1980s, were used to protect noncitizen rights (see table 2.3). The *Oyama v. California*[156] and *Takahashi v. Fish and Game Commission*[157] decisions are especially significant because they used the "Yick Wo formula" (a federal supremacy argument buttressed by an argument for constitutional rights) to strike down the same kinds of anti-Asian laws that the Supreme Court had defended several decades earlier. These two decisions mark the end of the anti-Asian era of the federal supremacy argument. But it is important to remember that this was still the Jim Crow era. Although the Supreme Court's defense of noncitizen rights became weak and unreliable in this era, its position on Jim Crow was more absolute.

The US black population would have to wait for almost a decade after the Oyama and Takahashi decisions, before the Supreme Court used similar constitutional rights arguments to strike down local laws that targeted blacks—with its historic decision on *Brown v. Board of Education*.[158] This is another instance in which the Fourteenth Amendment was put in the service of nonblack migrants more readily than for the black population.

I am not using this observation to suggest that the suffering caused by anti-Asian racism is of less significance than that of antiblack racism. But it is also important to try one's best to accurately explain how these experiences of suffering are perpetuated by established institutions and the dominant culture. As several critical race theorists have explained, there are racisms that differ in kind and not just by degree.[159] Although one can identify points of intersection between them, the "race problem" that the Asian migrant posed

Table 2.3 Decisions on Local Laws Restricting Noncitizen Rights in the Late Jim Crow and Post-Civil Rights Era

Struck Down Restrictive Local Laws				Upheld Restrictive Local Laws			
Year	Case	Nationality of Noncitizen Plaintiffs	Local Law	Year	Case	Nationality of Noncitizen Plaintiffs	Local Law
1941	Hines v. Davidoff	Italian and unspecified European	Alien registration	1976	De Canas v. Bica	Mexican	Employment of unauthorized migrants
1948	Oyama v. California	Japanese	Land law				
1948	Takahashi v. Fish & Game Comm'n	Japanese	Gaming licensing				
1973	In re Griffiths	Netherlander	Professional certification	1978	Foley v. Connelie	Irish	Public employment (Police)
1973	Sugarman v. Dougall	Guyanese, Dominican El Salvadorian	Public sector employment (Civil Service)	1979	Ambach v. Norwick	Scottish Finnish	Public employment (K-12 Teachers)
1976	Examining Board v. Flores de Otero	Mexican, Spanish	Professional certification	1982	Cabell v. Chavez-Salido	Unspecified Latin American	Public employment (Probation Officer)
1977	Nyquist v. Mauclet	French	In-state tuition for resident aliens				
1982	Toll v. Moreno	Paraguayan Bolivian	In-state tuition for work visa dependents				
1982	Plyler v. Doe	Mexican	Public education for unauthorized migrant children	2011	Chamber of Commerce v. Whiting	Latin American and Misc. Unspecified	Employment of unauthorized migrants
2012	Arizona, et al. v. US	Mexican and unspecified Latin American*	Unauthorized entry and presence; employment of unauthorized migrants				

Source: Table generated by author. Data or cases from Federal Register and justia.com.

for the US white establishment was rooted in different histories of regulation, prerogatives, and imaginaries than the "black race problem." These differences are reflected in the way that de jure discrimination against Asians has unfolded compared to black populations.

Anti-Asian land laws, for example, did not simply target persons of Asian descent or "Asian appearance" but Asian noncitizens. This does not mean that Asians who happened to be citizens were spared from the machinery of anti-Asian racism. Rather, it shows that US anti-Asian racism is intimately connected to the history of immigration and nationality law and ideas about racialized foreignness.[160] Antiblack racism, in contrast, cannot be adequately explained by this history. Jim Crow laws, for example, were indifferent to the citizen or immigrant status of blacks. I have tried to bring this antiblack context into view by calling attention to the timing of the Oyama and Brown decisions, and through my earlier contrast between the Plessy and Yick Wo decisions. This antiblack context is also reflected in the stubborn refusal of US policy-makers to cultivate flows of free, black migrant labor, which is a pattern that continued well into the twentieth century.

Black populations were eventually incorporated into the postbellum migration regime, but more slowly and in lower numbers than Asian and Latinx populations. Some of the earliest recorded patterns of postbellum-era black migration to the United States can be dated to the early 1900s, mainly involving black Caribbean migrants, traveling to the east coast of the United States (and primarily, New York City).[161] However, the systemic recruitment of black Caribbean migrant labor does not take off in earnest until the 1940s.[162]

Vilna Bashi has shown that, even during this period of expansion, the attitudes of US policy-makers toward black migrants were still being shaped by a strong current of antiblack racism, which was shared by policy-making elites in Canada and the UK.[163] Much of the evidence that Bashi provides of these antiblack sentiments comes from the publicly expressed racist opinions of policy-making elites, which are relevant to the use of their discretionary authority (including treaty making powers that could be used to cultivate flows of migrant labor).[164] She also describes the tactics that were used to manipulate immigrant screening processes and quotas, which informed the implementation of the law but were not reflected in the language of the law. Bashi explains, for example, that the 1924 National Origins Act, which played a pivotal role in ending the early twentieth-century immigration boom, was publicly advertised as a strategy to preserve a white majority US population, and that it was hailed as a major victory by the Ku Klux Klan.[165] Furthermore, the Congressional research that informed the drafting of the act had drawn on eighteenth-century scientific racist treatises that ranked "Negroids" lowest on the global hierarchy race groups.[166]

Bashi also explains that scientific racist ideologies "were used to deny entry to all 'inferior races' on grounds that 'immigrants' poor performance [was attributable] to Negroid strains inherent in their biological character."[167] Even so, the language of the act did not explicitly prohibit black migration. Rather than treating blacks as a distinct national origin group, the antiblack sentiments and ideologies that informed the National Origins Act treated blackness as an "undesirable" strain that could be present, to varying degrees, in almost any national origin group. In this way, the prohibition on blackness pervaded the immigrant screening process without being a hyper-visible feature of the national origin exclusions that had been authorized by the law.

THE POST-CIVIL RIGHTS ERA

The quiet and amorphous qualities of the prohibition on black migration in the twentieth century help to explain why it has been overlooked as a defining feature of US immigration policy. The challenge of exposing this prohibition was further compounded by the legal precedents of the civil rights era. As Derrick Bell and many other critical race theorists have pointed out, these progressive developments were hailed, by conservatives and liberals, as signs of a new post-racial US culture.[168] So the problem of black rightlessness transitioned from one kind of invisibility to another. In the Jim Crow era, black people were rendered invisible by being systematically excluded from public life. And in the post-civil rights era, this history of black exclusion was rendered invisible by a public discourse that celebrated the end of racism.

In this new era, constitutional rights arguments became an even more prominent feature of Supreme Court jurisprudence on local laws and noncitizen rights (see table 2.3). An important turning point is the 1971 *Graham v. Richardson* decision.[169] Graham was the first Supreme Court decision in the post-civil rights era to continue the Yick Wo tradition—blending a federal supremacy and a constitutional rights argument to protect noncitizens from restrictive local laws.[170] It is also the first Supreme Court decision to expand on the constitutional rights argument that had been introduced by Yick Wo.

In Graham, the Supreme Court argued that aliens are a "discrete and insular minority."[171] This language formalized an understanding of the noncitizen as a minoritized category in-itself that had always been implied by Yick Wo. The Graham court went on to argue that laws that potentially discriminate against immigrants should be subject to "close judicial scrutiny."[172] This legal test of "close scrutiny" introduced a more exacting standard than Yick Wo. It did not only insist that noncitizens were entitled to constitutional protections, but that the courts must carefully consider whether these protections are comparable to the ones afforded to citizens and other protected groups.

The federal supremacy argument still makes an appearance in Graham, but the ascendant theme is the fortified constitutional rights argument. This argument relied on an analogous reasoning, in which the noncitizen category is likened to a racial-ethnic minority. The Graham court did not explicitly state that a "discrete and insular minority" is necessarily a racial-ethnic minority. Nevertheless, the idea of the minority as a protected category had been established by laws, court decisions, and legislation that had been developed in response to the black civil rights movement. It is also important to keep in mind that Graham's constitutional rights argument, which is traceable to Yick Wo, is grounded in an interpretation of the Fourteenth Amendment which has been applied to cases involving racial discrimination.[173] Hence, Graham can be read as saying that noncitizens are not necessarily racial-ethnic minorities, but due to their noncitizen status, they are entitled to the same protections as racial-ethnic minorities.

The odd thing about this reasoning is that the immigrant/noncitizen can be analogized to a racial minority while remaining a nonracial category. But as I have shown, this is not actually the case. If you situate the immigrant/noncitizen in the context of US political culture, government policy, and jurisprudence, it becomes more apparent that the immigrant/noncitizen is a de facto nonblack category. When the immigrant/noncitizen is described in race-neutral terms, the nonblack (and antiblack) history of this category can be hidden behind a veil of ignorance. The courts can behave as if the immigrant/noncitizen category is racially inclusive while turning a blind eye to the sentiments, policies, and practices that have historically excluded blacks from the US migration flow.

In the post-civil rights era, however, the prohibition on black migration, which had already began to soften in the early twentieth century, became even more pliable. From the 1960s onward, blacks began to enter the United States in unprecedented numbers. Between 1960 and 1980 the black foreign-born population increased seven fold and tripled between 1980 and 2005[174] (and doubled again between 2000 and 2016[175]). But it bears noting that the relative size of the black immigrant population has remained very small; never amounting to more than a fraction of 1 percent of the entire US population, and accounting for no more than 9 percent of the US foreign-born population.[176]

This change in the black composition of the US migration flow was also reflected in the racial spectrum of noncitizen plaintiffs who appear in progressive Supreme Court decisions. Although challenges to anti-immigrant laws in this era are still defined by the grievances of nonblack noncitizens, black immigrants do, finally, make an appearance in *Sugarman v. Dougall* (1973).[177] It bears noting, however, that Sugarman marks their first and last appearance in this case history (as of the time of this writing).

Sugarman is also significant for being the second Supreme Court decision to apply the Graham standard of "close scrutiny" to challenge restrictions on noncitizen rights. In this case, the issue of contention was a state law that restricted civil service positions to citizens. The lead plaintiffs in the case had been fired from competitive civil service jobs because of their noncitizen status. This group included an Afro-Guyanese national and two Dominican nationals.[178]

The Guyanese national hailed from a population that has been historically identified as black or Afro-Caribbean.[179] The blackness of the Dominican plaintiffs, however, is more difficult to determine due to the Dominican Republic's history of antiblack racism[180] and the divergent ways that Dominicans have been racialized (and racially identified) in the United States.[181] All of these complexities provide an apt entry point into the racial context for the reception of black immigrants in the post-civil rights era.

Immigration scholars have explained that the 1965 Immigration Act produced a major change in the racial composition of the US migration flow, much of which was unanticipated.[182] Lawmakers built mechanisms into the act that were designed to control the size of the non-European migrant flow.[183] Nevertheless, the dismantling of the racist national origin restrictions and the new avenues for family reunification that were made possible by the 1965 Act set the stage for an era of US immigration that was increasingly defined by Asian and Latinx migrant flows.[184] This change in the racial-ethnic composition of the migration flow has met by a more cautious and concerned attitude toward immigration on the part of the general public.[185] These changes in popular attitudes were also accompanied by a discourse, produced by scholars, policy-makers, and the media, which emphasized the nonblack qualities of the new immigrants.

The discourse on the Asian model minority[186] was constructed in the late 1960s, to praise migrants who were able to overcome social obstacles (including racism) without succumbing to destructive, anti-social patterns of behavior—the point of reference for these comparisons being the restiveness of the US black population. The paradigm of ethnicity theory, which crystallized in the mid-twentieth century and rose to ascendency in the post-civil rights era, circulated a more nuanced version of these narratives.[187] Critical race theorists have faulted ethnicity theory for understating the power of institutional racism and promoting a model of immigrant integration that puts a collectivist spin on the same rugged individualism that is typical of conservative discourses about individual achievement and the free market.[188] Ethnicity theory has also been criticized for making pointed attacks on black politics and culture.[189]

These discourses were not concerned, primarily, with keeping black bodies out of the migration flow. Instead, they treat blackness as a pathological orientation toward US society which is reflected in self-defeating attitudes and behaviors that can be abstracted from the "racially apparent" body. These discourses were used to warn nonwhite immigrants (including black immigrants) against becoming like the US "black underclass."[190] As a result, Jamaican, Dominican, and Nigerian migrants could be constructed as "black ethnics" who could achieve success in the United States by adopting the mindset of the "white ethnics" of generations past rather than the confrontational politics of the black native-born population. As Tekle Woldemikael has shown, it was also possible for some Haitian migrants to integrate this way, by accentuating cultural identities, a work ethic, and cultivating social networks that were clearly distanced from the US black population.[191]

The Haitian refugee crisis unfolded against the backdrop of this discourse on (anti)blackness and immigration. But the crisis also drew attention to a very different kind of "race problem." The coded racism of the post-civil rights era was very effective in using the end of de jure discrimination to shift focus on the failings of the black population. According to these discourses, the problem was no longer state-sanctioned racism but blacks themselves, who were blamed for not taking advantage of the opportunities now available to them.[192]

Haitian refugees, however, could not be inserted, so easily, into these narratives. The government's treatment of Haitian refugees called attention to an overt kind of racism that was supposed to be over, even according to the colorblind ideologies of the post-civil rights era, political establishment. It certainly appeared to many sympathetic observers that the "undesirability" of Haitian refugees lay in the mere fact of their blackness.[193] This was not a coded attack on black pathology that could be abstracted from the racialized body; it had everything to do with racialized bodies.

The public outrage about the government's treatment of Haitian refugees was of little consequence for federal court opinion. The Nelson and Civiletti cases presented an opportunity for the federal courts to demonstrate that the arguments innovated by Yick Wo could apply to black aliens, but as I showed at the beginning of this chapter, all of these arguments failed.

In 1980, Judge King cited Yick Wo to support his decision in *HRC v. Civiletti*.[194] The constitutional rights argument he advanced was discounted by the Fifth Circuit Court, and it is completely absent from the Nelson case history. In *Nelson v. Jean*, Judge Spellman considered but ultimately dismissed the viability of a constitutional rights argument and the higher courts that heard the appeal of the case steadfastly defended the government's detention policy.[195] The end result is that Yick Wo provided no help for the Haitian plaintiffs of the Civiletti and Nelson cases. But it so happens that the years immediately preceding the Civiletti decision (between 1973 and 1979) were a peak period for the influence of the progressive federal supremacy argument. This is the period in which Yick Wo and its predecessors, like Graham, were being cited most consistently by the Supreme Court in decisions that strengthened noncitizen rights and as table 2.3 shows, this case history was defined, overwhelmingly, by plaintiffs from nonblack migrant populations.

The 1982 *Plyler v. Doe*[196] decision, which struck down a California law barring public school access to undocumented migrant children, is the last in this series of progressive precedents. I want to emphasize that Plyler is a good decision that provided a much needed corrective to a rising tide of anti-Mexican and anti-immigrant racism. But it is still necessary to come to grips with the disparities of the law and the way they align with the black/nonblack binary. Plyler is the apex of Yick Wo's influence—it is a point at which the combination of federal supremacy and constitutional rights arguments that was inaugurated by Yick Wo is finally extended to undocumented migrants. But in the background of this legal victory, there is the Haitian program, the INS policy of mandatory detention for Haitians, and the maritime interdictions targeting Haitians that began just one year before Plyler was decided. The arguments of Yick Wo were also marshalled by the advocates of Haitian refugees but with very different results.

The failure of Yick Wo to protect Haitian refugees says something very important about the singularity of the black refugee experience. Meanwhile, from the 1990s onward, the US government's treatment of Haitian refugees began to define the new normal for its treatment of all noncitizens. Mark Dow, Carl Lindskoog, Naomi Paik, and Kristina Shull have all made important contributions to this argument and I make my own contribution in the closing chapters of this book.[197] This is not just a matter of Haitian refugee policy setting precedents that influence and eclipse other trajectories of immigration and refugee law. The more progressive currents of this body of law also became weaker of their own accord.

In the years after Plyler, the federal supremacy argument was still used to protect noncitizens, but this argument became more distanced from the constitutional rights argument that distinguished Yick Wo. The turning point is *Toll v. Moreno*,[198] which was decided by the Supreme Court just a few months before Plyler. Like Plyler, this case concerned access to education for noncitizens. The plaintiffs were the dependents of a work visa holder who were challenging a state policy that restricted in-state university tuition to citizens (and LPRs). Also like Plyler, the Supreme Court found in favor of the noncitizen plaintiffs, but it did so using a very different argument which relied exclusively on the federal supremacy of the US government.

The justices of the Toll court acknowledged that an earlier District Court decision[199] had found in favor of the plaintiffs, using a Fifth Amendment due process argument and the equal protection clause of the Fourteenth Amendment. The Toll court did not flatly reject this argument but found that they had "no occasion to consider whether the [in-state tuition] policy violates the Due Process or Equal Protection Clauses."[200] Instead, the justices relied exclusively on the supremacy clause from Article IV of the Constitution to ground their argument.[201] For further support, they cited a list of prior decisions that had used the Yick Wo constitutional rights argument to protect noncitizens (including Graham, Takahashi, Hines, and Truax, see table 2.2). But the justices only found these cases significant for the federal supremacy argument that was contained in each of these decisions.[202]

With this argument, the Toll court made it clear that the federal supremacy argument had always accompanied the constitutional rights argument that had been innovated by Yick Wo, and that the supremacy argument was, in its view, the dominant jurisprudence. Effectively, the Toll decision returned the federal supremacy argument to a much earlier tradition that began in the early 1800s, with cases involving the property rights of white immigrants. The beneficiaries of the Toll decision were not constructed as the members of vulnerable minority group that was entitled to the protections of constitutional law, but as "good investments" who were living in the United States at the pleasure of the federal government.

Almost thirty years would pass, after the Plyler and Toll decisions, before the Supreme Court heard another case that involved a dispute between local and federal authorities over immigrant rights. The most significant case of this era was *Arizona v. US* (2012),[203] which was, on balance, a positive decision for immigrant rights. Like Plyler, it is also a case that revolves around the treatment of Latinx unauthorized migrants.[204] Even so, the Plyler decision is peripheral to its argument. The Supreme Court began its opinion in *Arizona v. US* using the Toll decision to frame its discussion of local immigration laws and produced a similar argument that relied exclusively on federal supremacy to rest its case.[205] At the time of this writing, the Supreme Court has heard only one case on the subject of local immigration laws since it decided Arizona, and this case follows the same pattern—relying exclusively on a federal supremacy argument to protect noncitizen rights.[206]

THE FAILINGS OF THE LAW

The Haitian refugees who challenged the Haitian program and the mandatory detention policies of the INS had no success in using *Yick Wo v. Hopkins*, or any of its predecessors, to protect their rights. My goal in this chapter has been to surface the legacies of antiblack racism that explain why this is so. My discussion has been extensive and complex because there is no single factor that explains why the Supreme Court used Yick Wo to support its decision in Plyler, but stubbornly rejected the arguments used by the advocates of Haitian refugees (including arguments that are traceable to Yick Wo). Instead of a magic bullet, there is an accretion of policy decisions and informal but institutionalized bodies of "racial opinion" that inform these decisions, disparate interpretations of the law, and sovereign desires protected by the law, which take shape over a century and half. The cumulative effect is a situation in which Haitian refugees are subjected to unprecedented measures and are left without the protection of the laws and a progressive jurisprudence that has been extended to other migrant and refugee populations.

In order to surface this context I have had to tell a different kind of story about the relationship between immigration law and sovereign power. The US government's treatment of Haitian refugees in the 1980s was justified, in part, by the Plenary Power doctrine. But I have also shown that the exclusion of Haitian refugees can be situated within a history of prohibitive attitudes toward black migration that date to the period of the Haitian revolution. These antiblack sentiments are also reflected, indirectly, in the jurisprudence on federal supremacy that has been used, since the early 1800s, to protect the rights of nonblack immigrants.

On one hand, there is the Plenary Power doctrine which has been used to restrict migration flows in the name of, or in response to, the concerns of a white citizenry. And on the other hand, there is the federal supremacy argument that has been used to protect the rights of a predominantly, nonblack migrant population which has been targeted by restrictive laws. The stories that migration scholars tell about the history of anti-immigrant racism in the United States are usually confined to the contentious history of these two social bodies: the white citizenry and racialized immigrants.

I have made a point of showing how black populations—whether immigrant or native born—have been excluded from both of these social bodies. Haitian refugees were targeted by the Plenary Power doctrine and also stranded by the federal supremacy argument. Their predicament was aggravated by the former kind of sovereign power and ignored by the latter.

The Yick Wo decision, for example, used a federal supremacy argument to push back against the police powers of local governments. So this could be seen as a decision in which the US government was prepared to protect racial minorities against the extremes that can result from arguments that appeal to the sovereignty of local governments. But when it came to the Plessy decision, which was issued ten years later, the Supreme Court was willing to let the states' rights argument carry the day. In this case, there was no contradiction between the "public happiness" of local communities and the sovereign prerogatives of the US government.[207] A similar sentiment crops up in the language that President Grant used to describe his mass deportation plans for the black population,[208] as well as the Reagan administration's concerns about the threat that Haitian refugees posed for the security and well-being of the general public.[209]

One lesson to take from all of these sensibilities is that antiblackness cannot be contained within a political cartography that is divided along the lines of local versus federal sovereignty. For the same reason, blackness does not describe a predicament that is specific to the native or the immigrant, nor either to the citizen or the alien: it describes an otherness that is banished to the fringes of all of these categories.

Throughout the chapter, I have also tried to show how antiblack sentiments congeal into exclusionary practices that operate outside of the law, or at least, with minimal legal oversight. For example, the Carter-era Haitian program and Reagan-era detention policy were both products of the discretionary authority of INS administrators who were operating, in turn, under the discretionary authority of the executive office. The interdiction operations, which began in 1981, allowed the government to expand on this discretionary authority in unprecedented ways. This discretionary authority has been justified through reference to the Plenary Power doctrine, as illustrated by the Eleventh Circuit's argument in *Jean v. Nelson.*[210] But I have also tried to show how the alienation of Haitian refugees from the law can be located within a history of power that dates to the "mass deportation" strategies of the ACS. For all practical purposes, the exclusionary objectives of this kind of power are indistinguishable from those of the Plenary Power doctrine, with the important exception that they predate Plenary Power and they have rarely been reconciled to the law. As Justice Taney explained, in his dicta from the Dred Scott decision, belief in the inferiority of blacks was so deeply engrained in US (elite) culture that the imperative of excluding blacks required no expressly formulated policy or legal justification.[211] The imperatives of controlled mobility can be read in light of this antiblack commonsense.

Control over black mobility—which is necessary for the organization of a racially segregated world—can be indulged, most completely, in a space that operates outside of the strictures of the law and other kinds of binding regulations. This is why it is important to read a theory of power into the conspicuous absence of blacks from US migration flow throughout the nineteenth and much of the twentieth century, and the absence of black plaintiffs from progressive legal decisions on immigrant rights, during this same period of time. As I have tried to show, these twin absences are not evidence that the US government had simply overlooked the possible benefits of black migration. These absences are symptomatic of an amorphous, but well-established and pervasive body of discourse that opposed black migration. This is also why my efforts to trace the exclusion of blacks from the US migration flow have taken the form of a ghostly context that I have tried to weave through my historical treatment of federal supremacy argument.

This history of black exclusion does not take away from the histories of nativism that have targeted other racialized populations. But it is important to note that black populations are more peripheral to the US immigration story than Asian and Latinx populations because blacks have been historically viewed as the antithesis of the ideal immigrant. Whereas nonblacks have been racialized as undesirable, or useful but disposable immigrants, blacks have been constructed as both anti-citizens and anti-immigrants.[212]

All of these examples underscore the point that it is necessary to take antiblackness more seriously, as a persistent undercurrent of US immigration law. As it concerns the argument I have made in this chapter, this means that you have to come to terms with the racialized social body that underlies the law. This social body, and the ways of seeing that sustain it, should be understood as a durable feature of the modern world which precedes and exceeds the determinations of the law. Instead of relying on constitutional law to enforce egalitarian principles that, presumably, transcend race, it is more important to expose the actually existing currents of antiblack racism that flow through the law, and the social bodies that are protected, exploited, and controlled by these currents. I provide another example of this analysis in the next chapter.

NOTES

1. *HRC v. Civiletti*, 503 F. Supp. 442 (S.D. Fla. 1980), 450.

2. Michael Posner, *Violations of Human Rights in Haiti*, A Report of the Lawyers Committee for International Human Rights to the Organization of American States, November 1980, accessed September 25, 2021, https://ufdc.ufl.edu/AA00001006/00001/2j, 14.

3. Ibid., 6.

4. *Civiletti*, 503 F. Supp. 442 at 451, 516–517.

5. Bayard Rustin, "Prepared Statement of Bayard Rustin, Chairman, A. Philip Randolph Institute," Hearing Before the Subcommittee on Immigration Refugees, and International Law of Committee of the Judiciary, House of Representatives, Ninety-Eighth Congress, Second Session on H.R. 4853 Cuban/Haitian Adjustment, Serial No, 64 May 9, 1984, 70–75.

6. Ibid., 72.

7. Hearing Before the Subcommittee on Immigration Refugees, and International Law of Committee of the Judiciary, House of Representatives, Ninety-Eighth Congress, Second Session on H.R. 4853 Cuban/Haitian Adjustment, Serial No, 64 May 9, 1984, III-IV.

8. Jerome Audige, "Prepared Statement of Jerome Audige, Executive Director, New Jersey Haitian/American Cultural Foundation," Hearing Before the Subcommittee on Immigration Refugees, and International Law of Committee of the Judiciary, House of Representatives, Ninety-Eighth Congress, Second Session on H.R. 4853 Cuban/Haitian Adjustment, Serial No, 64 May 9, 1984, 143.

9. Ibid., 144.

10. One of the first places in which the term appears is in the opening pages of Frank Wilderson, *Red, White and Black: Cinema and the Structure of US Antagonisms* (Durham, NC: Duke University Press, 2010), 8.

11. Hiroshi Motomura, "Immigration Law after a Century of Plenary Power: Phantom Constitutional Norms and Statutory Interpretation," *Yale Law Journal* 100, no. 3 (1990): 546–613.

12. *Chae Chan Ping v. United States*, 130 U.S. 581 (1889) (The Chinese Exclusion Case) and the Chinese Exclusion Act Pub.L. 47–126, 22 Stat. 58, Chap. 126 (1882).

13. Motomura, "Immigration Law after a Century of Plenary Power," 560–565.

14. Ibid., 592–593 and 600–613. Motomura's analysis of phantom norms and his recommendations for change extend beyond the Plenary Power doctrine. I have paraphrased the elements of his argument that pertain to Plenary Power.

15. Giorgio Agamben, *State of Exception* (Chicago: University of Chicago Press, 2005), 11–24.

16. Motomura, "Immigration Law after a Century of Plenary Power," 550–554 and 580–593.

17. *Civiletti*, 503 F. Supp. 442.

18. *Haitian Refugee Center v. Smith* 676 F.2d 1023 (5th Cir. 1982).

19. The District Court issued a pair of decisions, *Louis v. Nelson*, 544 F. Supp. 973 (S.D. Fla. 1982); *Louis v. Nelson*, 544 F. Supp. 1004 (S.D. Fla. 1982)—followed by: *Jean v. Nelson*, 727 F.2d 957, 967 (11th Cir. 1984); *Jean v. Nelson* 472 U.S. 846 (1985).

20. Kathleen Hawk et al., *Florida and the Mariel Boatlift of 1980* (Tuscaloosa: University of Alabama, 2014), 31–38.

21. *Civiletti*, 503 F. Supp. 442 at 510.

22. *Civiletti* at 511–512.

23. *Civiletti* at 511–513.

24. *Civiletti* at 523–526; Carl Lindskoog, *Detain and Punish* (Gainesville, FL: University of South Florida Press, 2017), 26–32.

25. *Civiletti* at 516.

26. Michelle Alexander, *The New Jim Crow: Mass Incarceration in the Age of Colorblindness* (New York: The New Press, 2012), 59–89.

27. *Civiletti* at 452–456; 526–529.

28. Kristina Shull, "Nobody Wants These People: Reagan's Immigration Crisis and America's First Private Prisons" (PhD Diss., University of California-Irvine, 2014), 58–59.

29. *Civiletti* at 517.

30. *Civiletti* at 514–516.

31. Shull, "Nobody Wants These People," 44–45, 62–63.

32. Mark Dow, "Unchecked Power Against Undesirables," in *Keeping Out the Other*, eds. David Brotherton and Philip Kretsedemas (New York: Columbia University Press, 2008), 29–43 at 30–31.

33. *Civiletti* at 515–516.

34. For a summary and critique of bias theory, see Eduardo Bonilla-Silva, "Rethinking Racism: A Structural Interpretation," *American Sociological Review* 62, no. 3 (1997): 465–480.

35. *Civiletti* at 450–452.

36. *Civiletti* at 510–519.

37. *Civiletti* at 457 and 468, citing *Yick Wo v. Hopkins* (118 U.S. 356 [1886]) which established that noncitizens are entitled to constitutional rights because they fall under the territorial jurisdiction of US law (and not due to legal status). The Yick Wo decision will be discussed in more detail later in this chapter.

38. Motomura, "Immigration Law after a Century of Plenary Power," 565–568. Motomura acknowledges that Yick Wo made a straightforward constitutional argument on behalf of immigrant rights, but he also argues that it defined the scope of these rights in a way that was never reconciled to the Plenary Power doctrine, and that the precedent it established contributed to a history of phantom norm decisions within US immigration law.

39. King cites *Brown v. Board of Education* (347 U.S. 483, 74 S. Ct. 686, 98 L. Ed. 873 [1954]) in the same note in which he cites *Yick Wo v. Hopkins*, along with several other watershed decisions that strengthened constitutional rights for women, racial minorities, and noncitizens, including *Loving v. Virginia* (388 U.S. 1, 87 S. Ct. 1817, 18 L. Ed. 2d 1010 [1967]); *Graham v. Richardson* (403 U.S. 365, 91 S. Ct. 1848, 29 L. Ed. 2d 534 [1971]); *Roe v. Wade* (410 U.S. 113, 93 S. Ct. 705, 35 L. Ed. 2d 147 [1973]). *Civiletti* at 457.

40. King sums up and rebuts this argument in his discussion of the excludable status of Haitian refugees. *Civiletti* at 461–462. This jurisprudence on excludability is discussed in more detail in chapter 3.

41. *Haitian Refugee Center v. Smith*, 676 F.2d 1023 (5th Cir. 1982).

42. *Smith*, 676 F.2d 1023 at 42–46.

43. In its argument the court fortified its due process argument by referencing the US government's obligations, as signatory to the 1967 UN Protocol Relating to the Status of Refugees. *Smith* at 46–48.

44. Referring to Judge King's criticism of the US government's violation of the international legal principle of nonrefoulement, by insisting on returning asylum seekers to Haiti, given the evidence of oppressive country conditions that King recited in his decision. *Smith* at 60.

45. As noted earlier the district court issued a pair of decisions (by the same judge), see n10. The review in this section draws from the second decision; *Louis v. Nelson*, 544 F. Supp. 1004 (S.D. Fla. 1982).

46. *Louis*, 544 F. Supp. 1004 at 979–980.

47. *Louis* at 982.

48. *Louis* at 1001–1004.

49. *Louis* at 1003–1004.

50. *Louis* at 1004.

51. *Jean v. Nelson*, 727 F.2d 957 (11th Cir. 1984) at 957–959.

52. *Jean*, 727 F.2d 957 at 959–960.

53. *Louis*, 544 F. Supp. 1004 at 998–999.

54. *Jean*, 727 F.2d 957 at 960–965.

55. *Jean v. Nelson*, 472 U.S. 846 (1985) at 848.

56. *Jean*, 472 U.S. 846 at 855–857.

57. *Jean*, 472 U.S. 846 at 859–864.

58. *Jean*, at 868–870. Right-to-be-racist is my own turn of phrase. Marshall communicates the same idea, but using different language in the decision itself.

59. *Jean*, 544 F. Supp. 1004 at 965–967.

60. *Plessy v. Ferguson*, 163 U.S. 537 (1896).

61. *Plessy*, 163 U.S. 537 at 542–545; *Dred Scott v. Sandford*, 60 U.S. 393 (1856). See chapter 1 and 4 for a more detailed discussion of the Scott decision.

62. *Jean v. Nelson*, 472 U.S. 846 at 859–870. Also see Motomura, "Immigration Law After a Century of Plenary Power."

63. *Yick Wo*, 118 U.S. 356.

64. *Yick Wo*, 118 U.S. 356 at 357–365.

65. *Yick Wo* at 356.

66. *Civiletti*, 503 F. Supp. 442 at 457 and 468.

67. *Jean*, 472 U.S. 846 at 874–875.

68. Motomura, "Immigration Law after a Century of Plenary Power"; David Ralph, "Haitian Interdiction on the High Seas: The Continuing Saga of the Rights of Aliens Outside United States Territory," *Maryland. J. Int'l L. & Trade* 17 (1993): 227; Maria Sepulveda, "Barring Extraterritorial Protection for Haitian Refugees Interdicted on the High Seas," *Catholic University Law Review* 44, no. 1 (1994): 321–362.

69. U.S. Const. art. 4, § 2.

70. For a discussion of preemption, pertaining to immigration law, see Patrick Reagin, "Arizona v. United States: Unstitching the Patchwork of Reactionary

State-enacted Immigration Legislation through Federal Preemption," *Loyola Law Review* 58, no. 4 (2012): 1035.

71. Gerald Neuman, "The Lost Century of American Immigration Law (1776–1875)," *Columbia Law Review* 93, no. 8 (1993): 1833–1901.

72. *Martin v. Hunter's Lessee*, 14 U.S. 304 (1816).

73. *Yick Wo*, 118 U.S. 356 at 368–369.

74. *Jean*, 727 F.2d 957 at 860.

75. Ibid.

76. *Knauft v. Shaughnessy*, 338 U.S. 537 (1950) at 337.

77. For a more extensive review, see Philip Kretsedemas, "The Controlled Expansion of Local Immigration Laws," in *Immigration Policy in the Age of Punishment*, eds. David Brotherton and Philip Kretsedemas (New York: Columbia University Press, 2018), 140–164.

78. I selected these cases starting with a 2012 precedent decision that applied the federal supremacy argument to a dispute concerning the authority of local governments to enact their own immigration laws: *Arizona v. US*, 567 U.S. 387 (2012), see Table 3.3. Using a process similar to snowball sampling, I identified other Supreme Court cases, cited in this decision, that had taken up the question of federal versus local authority on matters of immigration law or noncitizen rights. I performed the same operation on this new group of cases, identifying all of the relevant Supreme Court decisions they cited and repeated this process until the sampling method turned up no new cases.

79. Daniel Kanstroom, *Deportation Nation* (Cambridge, MA: Harvard University Press, 2007), 77–83.

80. Although the anti-miscegenation laws intensified throughout the 1700s, the earliest anti-miscegenation laws can be traced to the late 1600s. Erica Cooper, "One 'Speck' of Imperfection—Invisible Blackness and the One-Drop Rule: An Interdisciplinary Approach to Examining *Plessy v. Ferguson* and *Jane Doe v. State of Louisiana*" (PhD diss., Indiana University, 2008), 15–20; Frank Sweet, *Legal History of the Color Line* (Palm Coast, FL: Backintyme, 2005).

81. Cooper, "One 'Speck' of Imperfection," 68–70.

82. Ibid., 68–78.

83. Neuman, "The Lost Century of American Immigration Law (1776–1875)."

84. *Fairfax's Devisee v. Hunter's Lessee*, 11 U.S. 603 (1812); *Martin*, 14 U.S. 304.

85. *Martin*, 14 U.S. 304 at 327–328.

86. *Martin* at 356–357 and 360–363.

87. *Martin* at 325.

88. *Martin* at 324–325.

89. *Martin* at 334.

90. *Martin* at 313.

91. *Blythe v. Hinckley*, 180 U.S. 333 (1901).

92. Jefferson served as governor of Virginia 1779–1781. The Martin decision dates the beginning of the local court's record of the property dispute to 1791—at that time, Jefferson was beginning his term in the US Senate.

93. US Presidents affiliated with the Democratic-Republican party held office in an unbroken chain of succession for a quarter century, beginning with Jefferson in 1801, continuing with James Madison and ending with James Monroe, whose term ended in 1825. The 1813 Fairfax and 1816 Martin decisions both occurred under Madison's presidency.

94. Fred Kaplan, *Lincoln and the Abolitionists* (New York: HarperCollins, 2017), 102–104.

95. Kanstroom, *Deportation Nation*, 23–45.

96. Kaplan, *Lincoln and the Abolitionists*, 99–102.

97. Ibid., 102–104.

98. Julius Scott, *The Common Wind: Afro-American Currents in the Age of the Haitian Revolution* (New York: Verso, 2018), 203.

99. Ibid., 190–192.

100. Gerald Horne, *Confronting Black Jacobins: The US, the Haitian Revolution, and the Origins of the Dominican Republic* (New York: Monthly Review Press, 2015), 30–34, 9–80; Kaplan, *Lincoln and the Abolitionists*, 99–102.

101. Ladelle McWhorter, *Racism and Sexual Oppression in Anglo-America* (Bloomington, IN: University of Indiana Press, 2009), 77–88.

102. Ibid., 87–95.

103. Kaplan, *Lincoln and the Abolitionists*, 157, 280.

104. Eric Burin, *Slavery and the Peculiar Solution: A History of the American Colonization Society* (Gainesville, FL: University Press of Florida, 2003); Horne, *Confronting Black Jacobins*, 154; Kanstroom, *Deportation Nation*, 85–86; Kaplan, *Lincoln and the Abolitionists*, 132–33.

105. Burin, *Slavery and the Peculiar Solution*, 15–18.

106. Ibid., 6–33.

107. Ibid., 34–56; Kaplan, *Lincoln and the Abolitionists*, 169, 172.

108. Burin, *Slavery and the Peculiar Solution*, 90.

109. Kaplan, *Lincoln and the Abolitionists*, 160.

110. Burin, *Slavery and the Peculiar Solution*, 13, 20; Kaplan, *Lincoln and the Abolitionists*, 99–102, 160–61.

111. The end of Jefferson's first term as president (1801–1804) coincides with the signing of the Haitian Declaration of Independence (in January 1804) that formally ended the thirteen-year revolutionary war.

112. Scott, *The Common Wind*, 30 and 58; Horne, *Confronting Black Jacobins*, 30–53.

113. Leon Pamphile, "The Haitian Response to the John Brown Tragedy," *Journal of Haitian Studies* 12, no. 2 (2006): 135–142.

114. The understanding that the Fourteenth Amendment (along with the Thirteenth and Fifteenth Amendment) was intended for blacks is best described as an informal jurisprudence and body of elite opinion that informed the interpretation of the law. This body of opinion explains why the protections of the Fourteenth Amendment were not extended to Asian minorities and Mexican Americans until more than a decade after its adoption. See Juan Perea, "A Brief History of Race and the US-Mexico Border," *UCLA Law Review* 51 (2003): 283. As I show in this chapter, however, through the late nineteenth and up to the mid-twentieth century, the "equal protection" argument was

used much more consistently, to challenge local laws targeting nonblack noncitizens than it was to protect black citizens who were targeted by similar kinds of local laws.

115. *Yick Wo*, 118 U.S. 356.

116. In *Chy Lung v. Freeman*, the Supreme Court recounted local complaints against Chinese steamship passengers, which include pointed references to Chinese women as "lewd and debauched." *Chy Lung v. Freeman* 92 U.S. 275 (1875) at 276.

117. *New York v. Miln*, 36 U.S, 102 (1837).

118. *Miln*, 36 U.S. 102 at 142–143.

119. For a more involved discussion of the history of sovereign authority from which the "police powers" argument descends, see Michel Foucault, *Society Must Be Defended, Lectures at the College de France, 1977–1978* (NY: Palgrave-MacMillan, 2007) 313–362.

120. *Miln*, 36 U.S. 102 at 142–143.

121. *Chy Lung*, 92 U.S. 275 at 276; *Henderson et.al. v. Mayor of NY,* 92 U.S. 259 (1875), 2–5; *Passenger Cases*, 48 U.S. 283 (1849), 393–394.

122. *Chy Lung* at 276.

123. *Henderson*, 92 U.S. 259; *Passenger Cases*, 48U.S. 283; *People v. Compagnie Generale Transatlantique*, 107 U.S. 59 (1883).

124. *Chy Lung*, 92 U.S. 275 at 276.

125. *Yick Wo*, 118 U.S. 356 at 356.

126. *Yick Wo*, 118 U.S. 356 at 374; citing *Henderson* 92 U.S. 259, and *Chy Lung*, 92 U.S. 275.

127. *Yick Wo* at 369.

128. The government's position on this matter is recounted by the 1893 *Fong Yue Ting v. US* decision, which is discussed in more detail in chapter 3. *Fong Yue Ting v. United States*, 149 U.S. 698 (1893).

129. Cindy Hahamovitch, *No Man's Land: Jamaican Guestworkers in America and the Global History of Deportable Labor* (Princeton: Princeton University Press, 2011), 12–13. The interest that US elites showed in Asian labor in the postbellum era recalls the labor recruitment strategies that were used by the British Colonial office in the Caribbean a few decades earlier, after the British empire ended slavery in the 1830s.

130. Hahamovitch, *No Man's Land*, 12–15. During this period, the US government recruited black Caribbean labor for projects it was coordinating in Central and South America but avoided importing these workers to the United States.

131. Correspondence of R. J. Lackland to Judge David Irvin, July 30, 1869, quoted in Horne, *Confronting Black Jacobins*, 307.

132. Horne, *Confronting Black Jacobins*, 288.

133. Ibid., 291.

134. Ibid., 295–310.

135. *Truax v. Raich*, 239 U.S. 33 (1915).

136. *Hines v. Davidowitz*, 312 U.S. 52 (1941). The national origins of the plaintiffs in this case are described in the District Court case that precedes the Supreme Court decision (but not in the Supreme Court decision itself). Mr. Davidowitz is only vaguely described as a naturalized US citizen, whereas his co-plaintiff Mr. Travaglini is identified as an "Italian alien." *Davidowitz v. Hines*, 30 F. Supp. 470 (M.D. Pa. 1939).

137. *Oyama et.al. v. California* 332 U.S. 633 (1948); *Takahashi v. Fish & Game Comm'n* 334 U.S. 410 (1948).

138. *Plessy v. Ferguson*, 163 U.S. 537 (1896).

139. *Plessy*, 163 U.S. 537 at 540, cited as *Louisiana Separate Act*, c.111 (1890).

140. *Brown v. Board of Education*, 347 U.S. 483 (1954).

141. *Plessy*, 163 U.S. 537 at 544–545. Also see *Henderson*, 92 U.S. 259 at 2–5; *Passenger Cases*, 48 U.S. 283 at 393–394; *Yick Wo*, 118 U.S. 356 at 367.

142. *Yick Wo*, 118 U.S. at 373.

143. Akhil Amar, "Plessy v. Ferguson and the Anti-canon.(Supreme Mistakes)," *Pepperdine Law Review* 39, no. 1 (2011): 75–89; Richard Maidment, "Plessy v. Ferguson Re-Examined," *Journal of American Studies* 7, no. 2 (1973): 125–32.

144. Saidiya Hartman, *Scenes of Subjection* (Oxford: Oxford University Press, 1997), 199.

145. Ibid., 189–206.

146. *Jean*, 472 U.S. 846 at 850–852.

147. *Plessy*, 163 U.S. 537 at 546–548.

148. Warren, *Ontological Terror*, 64–67.

149. John Jackson and Nadine Weidman, *Race, Racism, and Science Social Impact and Interaction* (Santa Barbara, CA: ABC-CLIO, 2004), 109–119.

150. Karen Brodkin, *How Jews Became White Folks and What That Says about Race in America* (Brunswick, NJ: Rutgers UP, 1998); Noel Ignatief, *How the Irish Became White* (New York: Routledge, 1995); David Roediger, *The Wages of Whiteness: Race and the Making of the American Working Class* (London; New York: Verso, 1999).

151. *The Emergency Immigration Act*, Pub.L. 67–5, 42 Stat. 5 (1921); *The Immigration Act of 1924*, Pub.L. 68–139, 43 Stat. 153 (1924); discussed in, Bill Ong Hing, *Defining America Through Immigration Policy* (Philadelphia: Temple University Press, 2003), 62–72.

152. *Patsone v. Pennsylvania*, 232 U.S. 138 (1914); *Heim v. McCall*, 239 U.S. 175 (1915); *Crane v. New York*, 239 U.S. 195 (1915); *Ohio ex Rel. Clarke v. Deckebach*, 274 U.S. 392 (1927).

153. *Terrace v. Thompson*, 263 U.S. 197 (1923); *Frick v. Webb*, 263 U.S. 326 (1923); *Webb v. O'Brien*, 263 U.S. 313 (1923); *Porterfield v. Webb*, 263 U.S. 225 (1923); *Cockrill v. California*, 268 U.S. 258 (1925); *Morrison v. California*, 291 U.S. 82 (1934).

154. *Truax*, 239 U.S. 33 at 239.

155. *Asakura v. Seattle*, 265 U.S. 332 (1924). This case relied exclusively on a federal supremacy argument.

156. *Oyama et.al. v. California*, 332 U.S. 633 (1948).

157. *Takahashi v. Fish & Game Comm'n*, 334 U.S. 410 (1948).

158. *Brown*, 347 U.S. 483.

159. Katrina Quisumbing King, "Recentering U.S. Empire: A Structural Perspective on the Color Line," *Sociology of Race and Ethnicity* 5, no. 1 (2019): 11–25 at 15; Moon Kie-Jung, "The Enslaved, the Worker, and Du Bois's Black Reconstruction: Toward an Underdiscipline of Antisociology," *Sociology of Race and Ethnicity* 5, no. 2 (2019): 157–168 at 163; P. Khalil Saucier and Tryon Woods, "Introduction: Racial

Optimism and the Drag of Thymotics," in *Conceptual Aphasia in Black*, eds. P. Khalil Saucier and Tryon Woods (Lanham, MD: Lexington Press, 2016), 1–34.

160. Robert Chang, *Disoriented: Asian Americans, Law and the Nation-State* (New York: NYU Press, 1999); Lisa Lowe, *Immigrant Acts: On Asian American Cultural Politics* (Durham, NC: Duke University Press, 1996).

161. Ira Reid, *The Negro Immigrant* (New York: Columbia University Press, 1939). Vilna Bashi also notes that black migration from the West Indies to the United States ranged between approximately 900 and 1,500 persons per year between 1908 and 1922. Vilna Bashi, "Globalized Antiblackness: Transnationalizing Western Immigration Law, Policy, and Practice," *Ethnic and Racial Studies* 27, no. 4 (2004): 584–606 at 603n7. There is also a more sparse history of episodic, black migration events that date to the early nineteenth and eighteenth centuries. The existence of local laws designed to curb black migration in the late eighteenth century is one testament to these migrations. See Scott, *The Common Wind*, 58 and 66; Harvey Whitfield, "The Development of Black Refugee Identity in Nova Scotia, 1813–1850," *Left History* 10, no. 2 (2005): 9–31.

162. Hahamovitch, *No Mans Land*, 12–21. The US Bracero Program of the early 1940s, which is more famously known for the recruitment of Mexican migrant laborers, also opened the door for tens of thousands of black, West Indian migrant workers (who composed approximately 17 percent of the total Bracero workforce). Vilna Bashi, "Globalized Anti-blackness," 590.

163. Bashi, "Globalized Antiblackness." At the beginning of this article, Bashi observes that attitudes toward black migration have been shaped by racial hierarchies that have existed for centuries. But she also speculates that blacks simply were not "on the radar" of US policy-making elites, as candidates for mass migration, prior to the nineteenth century—and observes that the history of racist exclusions in US immigration law starts with late nineteenth-century policies on Asian migration (588). Although these statements are not wholly inaccurate, my argument in this chapter underscores the intentionality of US elites in avoiding the recruitment of black migrants in the decades prior to the Chinese Exclusion Act. This is an argument that Bashi makes in her review of early nineteenth-century Canadian immigration policy (dating to 1818), but she provides no supporting evidence for comparable attitudes among US elites of that era (585–587).

164. Ibid.

165. Bashi, "Globalized Antiblackness," 590.

166. Ibid. Bashi notes that these treatises ranked "Caucasians" as the most advanced of the "races." I have emphasized the place that blacks (categorized as "Negroes" or "Negroid") were accorded by these same treatises because it is more theoretically relevant to the argument I'm making in this chapter.

167. Ibid, citing from: Peter Wang, *Legislating Normalcy: The Immigration Act of 1924* (San Francisco: R & E Research Associates, 1975), 61.

168. Derrick Bell, "Brown v Board of Education and the Interest-Convergence Dilemma," in *The Derrick Bell Reader*, eds. Richard Delgado and JeanStefancic, (New York: NYU Press, 2005), 27–32; Eduardo Bonilla-Silva, *Racism Without Racists: Color-blind Racism and the Persistence of Racial Inequality in the United States* (Lanham, MD: Rowman & Littlefield, 2003); Paul Gilroy, *There Ain't No Black in the Union Jack: The Cultural Politics of Race and Nation* (New York: Routledge Classics, 2002).

169. *Graham v. Richardson*, 403 U.S. 365 (1971).

170. I am defining "post-civil rights" era as post *Brown v. Board of Education*, 347 U.S. 483 (1954) and post 1965 *Civil Rights Voting Act*, Pub.L. 89–110, 79 Stat. 43 (1965). The case which immediately precedes Graham (using the same combination of federal supremacy and constitutional rights arguments to strike down a local law) is *Takahashi v. Gaming Commission*, 334 U.S. 410 (1948): (See Table 3.3).

171. *Graham*, 403 U.S. 365 at 372.

172. *Graham* at 372–376.

173. *Ex parte Virginia*, 100 U.S. 339 (1879); *Neal v. Delaware*, 103 U.S. 370 (1880); *Loving v. Virginia*, 388 U.S. 1 (1967).

174. Mary Kent, "Immigration and America's Black Population," Population Reference Bureau, last modified, December 10, 2007, https://www.prb.org/blackimmigration/.

175. Monica Anderson and Gustavo Lopez, "Key Facts about Black Immigrants in the U.S," Pew Research Center, last modified, January 24, 2018, https://www.pewresearch.org/fact-tank/2018/01/24/key-facts-about-black-immigrants-in-the-u-s/.

176. These proportions are derived from total black foreign-born population figures presented in Anderson and Lopez "Key Facts About Black Immigrants," and US foreign-born population figures from the "Data Hub: Number and Share of Total U.S. Population, 1850–2017," Migration Policy Institute, accessed December 3, 2020, https://www.migrationpolicy.org/programs/data-hub/us-immigration-trends.

177. *Sugarman v. Dougall*, 413 U.S. 634 (1973).

178. *Sugarman*, 413 U.S. 634 at 857.

179. The primary populations in Guyana are of African and South Asian descent, and the Guyanese political sphere has been historically divided along these racial-ethnic lines. Perry Mars, "Ethnic Conflict and Political Control: The Guyana Case," *Social and Economic Studies* 39, no. 3 (1990): 65–94.

180. Ryan Mann-Hamilton, "What Rise from the Ashes: Nation and Race in the African American Enclave of Samana," in *Migrant Marginality: A Transnational Perspective*, eds., Philip Kretsedemas, Jorge Capetillo and Glenn Jacobs (New York: Routledge, 2013), 222–238.

181. Silvio Torres-Saillant, "The Tribulations of Blackness: Stages in Dominican Racial Identity," *Latin American Perspectives* 25, no. 3 (1998):126–146.

182. Douglas Massey and Karen Pren, "Unintended Consequences of US Immigration Policy: Explaining the Post-1965 Surge from Latin America," *Population and Development Review* 38, no. 1 (2012): 1–29.

183. Bashi, "Globalized Antiblackness," 593 and 599; Mae Ngai, *Impossible Subjects: Illegal Aliens and the Making of Modern America* (Princeton: Princeton University Press, 2014), 256–257 and 288; Bill Ong Hing, *Defining America Through Immigration Policy*, 93–114.

184. Massey and Pren, "Unintended Consequences of US Immigration Policy."

185. These trends in public opinion apply to the United States but also extend to many other nations. See Timothy Hatton and Jeffrey Williamson, *Global Migration and the World Economy: Two Centuries of Policy and Performance* (Cambridge, MA: MIT Press, 2005), 307–311 and 377–391.

186. Ellen Wu, *The Color of Success: Asian Americans and the Origins of the Model Minority* (Princeton: Princeton University Press, 2013). Claire Jean Kim has provided a complementary analysis of the competitive framing of Asians and blacks in US racial discourse which situates the model minority (and the discourses that preceded and informed it) in a broader historical perspective, dating to the mid-nineteenth century. Claire Jean Kim, "The Racial Triangulation of Asian Americans," *Politics & Society* 27, no. 1 (1999): 105–138.

187. *Beyond the Melting Pot* is widely regarded as a seminal text. Nathan Glazer and Daniel Moynihan, *Beyond the Melting Pot the Negroes, Puerto Ricans, Jews, Italians, and Irish of New York City*, 2nd ed. (Cambridge, MA: MIT, 1970). Ethnicity theory also builds on an earlier body of writing on cultural pluralism (that had, historically, focused on cultural differences among European migrant populations). See Richard Bernstein et al., "Cultural Pluralism," *Philosophy & Social Criticism* 41, no. 4–5 (2015): 347–356.

188. Michael Omi and Howard Winant, *Racial Formation in the United States*, 3rd ed. (New York: Routledge, 2014), 21–52.

189. Ibid. This criticism, which has not been exclusively produced by critical race theorists, has spilled over to the 1965 Moynihan Report (considering that Moynihan was also coauthor of *Beyond the Melting Pot*, see n186). See Lawrence Bobo and Camille Zubrinsky, "Race in the American Mind: From the Moynihan Report to the Obama Candidacy," *The Annals of the American Academy of Political and Social Science* 621, no. 1 (2009): 243–259; Herbert Gans, "The Moynihan Report and its Aftermaths: A Critical Analysis," *Du Bois Review* 8, no. 2 (2011): 315–327.

190. The culture of poverty thesis is a principal example. Andrew Maxwell, "The Underclass, 'Social Isolation' and 'Concentration Effects' 'The Culture of Poverty' Revisited," *Critique of Anthropology* 13, no. 3 (1993): 231–245. More nuanced versions of these arguments surfaced in the segmented assimilation thesis, which warned about a downwardly mobile pathway to integration, in which nonwhite immigrant youth share the same outcomes as native-born black and brown criminalized youth. Alejandro Portes and Min Zhou, "The New Second Generation: Segmented Assimilation and Its Variants," *The Annals of the American Academy of Political and Social Science* 530, no. 1 (1993): 74–96. Mary Water's research on black Caribbean migrants (which borrows from ethnicity theory) also makes the argument that black self-identification can be a contributing factor to downward mobility. Mary Waters, *Black Identities: West Indian Immigrant Dreams and American Realities* (Cambridge, MA, 1999).

191. Tekle Woldemikael, "A Case Study of Race Consciousness among Haitian Immigrants," *Journal of Black Studies* 20 (1989): 224–239.

192. See n171.

193. As evidenced by Judge King's decision in *HRC v. Civiletti* (503 F. Supp. 442) and the civil rights and social justice groups that mobilized to protect the government's Haitian refugee policies. Shull, "Nobody Wants These People," 59–62.

194. *Civiletti*, 503 F. Supp. 442 at 457 and 468; *Louis*, 544 F. Supp. 1004 at 999.

195. *Louis*, 544 F. Supp. 1004 at 979–981; *Smith*, 676 F.2d 1023 at 42–46.

196. *Plyler v. Doe*, 457 U.S. 202 (1982).

197. Dow, "Unchecked Power Against Undesirables"; *American Gulag, Inside US Immigration Prisons* (Berkeley, CA: University of California Press, 2005); Naomi

Paik, "Carceral Quarantine at Guantanamo Legacies of US Imprisonment of Haitian Refugees, 1991–1994," *Radical History Review* 115 (2013):142–168; Lindskoog, *Detain and Punish*; Shull, "Nobody Wants These People."

198. *Toll v. Moreno*, 458 U.S. 1 (1982). This decision was the culmination of a series of cases, involving two prior Supreme Court decisions. *Toll* v. *Moreno*, 441 U.S. 458, 461 (1979); *Elkins v. Moreno*, 435 U.S. 647 (1978).

199. *Toll*, 458 U.S. 1 at 9, citing *Moreno v. Toll*, 489 F.Supp. 658 (D.Md. 1980).

200. *Toll at* 9–10.

201. *Toll* at 10.

202. Ibid.

203. *Arizona v. US*, 567 U.S. 387 (2012), Table 2.3 shows that the first decision after this almost thirty-year hiatus was actually the *Chamber of Commerce v. Whiting* decision [563 U.S. 582 (2011)]. Whiting addressed employer sanctions measures that were enacted as part of the Arizona Legal Workers Act (SB 1070) and found that these measures were not preempted by federal law. *Arizona v. US*, on the other hand, addressed a more broadly framed law, the Support Our Law Enforcement and Safe Neighborhoods Act (SB 1070) which introduced several screening and enforcement practices that targeted undocumented migrants. In addition to stirring up more public controversy, the Supreme Court's decision on SB 1070 provided a more revealing insight into its varying positions on different aspects of immigration law. See Kevin Johnson, "Immigration in the Supreme Court 2009–2013," *Oklahoma Law Review* 68, no. 57 (2015): 87–91.

204. In this case, the Supreme Court issued a mixed decision which struck down three of the four features of an Arizona state law that targeted unauthorized migrants as well as employers and other persons who were alleged to provide material support to these migrants, *Arizona*, 567 U.S. 387, 20–47.

205. *Arizona* at 2.

206. *Arizona v. Inter Tribal Council of Arizona, Inc.*, 570 U.S. 1 (2013).

207. Hartman notes that this discourse on "happiness" emerges in Plessy as a criticism of its practical objectives, but in the language of the decision itself, the spirit of this desire surfaces in the appeal to "natural affinities." Hartman, *Scenes of Subjection*, 193 and 205; *Plessy*, 163 U.S. 537 at 551.

208. Referring to the "happy unity" that will be enabled by the mass deportation of the black population. Horne, *Confronting Black Jacobins*, 288.

209. Shull, "Nobody Wants These People," 44–45; 62–63.

210. *Jean*, 733 F.2d 908 at 860.

211. *Dred Scott v. Sanford*, 407–408.

212. This statement sums up an argument I have made throughout this chapter, which is informed by Afropessimist and critical race theory. But it also bears noting that, even in the mainstreams of early twentieth-century sociology, there was a frank understanding that blacks faced social barriers to "assimilation" that were unlike those faced by other minoritized groups. See Robert Park, "Racial Assimilation in Secondary Groups with Particular Reference to the Negro," *American Journal of Sociology* 19, no. 5 (1914): 606–623.

Chapter 3

Radical Exclusion

All of INS' efforts are designed to ferret out aliens who for one reason or another are inadmissible, thereby keeping the number and character of immigrants entering the United States in line with congressional policy. Inadmissible aliens are either deportable or excludable; the former being persons who have effected an "entry," the latter being persons deemed not to have entered the United States. The irony of this distinction is that deportable aliens, many of whom entered the country surreptitiously, are given more rights under the law than excludable aliens who present themselves to immigration. The practical effect of this is to encourage those who attempt to sneak across the border because they are rewarded with greater rights than those aliens who attempt to comply with our laws. *Introduction to Louis v. Nelson*[1]

JUDGE SPELLMAN'S LAMENT

Critical studies of immigration enforcement have focused almost exclusively on the predicament of deportable people.[2] But in his opening statement from *Louis v. Nelson*, Judge Spellman calls attention to a different kind of problem. Haitian refugees were not exposed to the unmitigated power of the US government because they were deportable aliens. If Haitians refugees were merely deportable they would have had a stronger legal foothold to defend themselves from being removed. Spellman goes on to observe that Haitian refugees were being categorically distinguished from deportable subjects. In order to understand their predicament, the condition of excludability has to take center stage.

In this chapter, I am going to engage in acts of legal storytelling that recenter and add more theoretical depth to the predicament of the "excludable alien." Before getting into the details, it is important to note that the legal distinction between deportable and excludable aliens was eliminated by the 1996 Illegal Immigration Reform and Immigrant Responsibility Act (IIRIRA).[3] Since IIRIRA was enacted, enforcement actions that used to be categorized as "deportations" and "exclusions" have been folded into the catch-all category of "removals." So it would appear that the excludable/deportable distinction is of little relevance for immigration law today.

I am going to show, on the other hand, that the excludable/deportable distinction that was described by Judge Spellman in 1982 is still salient today, as a sociopolitical reality, even if it is no longer recognized by the law. This distinction also provides an insight into the continuing relevance of the de facto, black/nonblack binary that reverberates through the US migration regime. Excludability is not a problem that uniformly and exclusively effects black noncitizens, but as the Haitian refugee experience shows, there is a special relationship between antiblackness and the desire to exclude. In the pages ahead, I am going to introduce the concept of radical exclusion to describe the racist undercurrents of excludability and to explain how they act as conduits for antiblack racism.

RECONCEIVING EXCLUDABILITY

My analysis is going to focus on the same era of Haitian refugee policy that I reviewed in chapter 2. But instead of situating these policies and legal battles in light of a history that dates to the eighteenth and nineteenth centuries, I am going to pay more attention to a jurisprudence that comes to maturity in the twentieth century. I aim to show that excludability was not just an outcome produced by the government's Haitian refugee policies; it was an axiomatic feature of these policies and the legal arguments that were used to defend them.

Before Haitians could be excluded "in fact" they, first, had to be constituted as excludable aliens. This condition of excludability is the connecting thread that runs between the Haitian program and the interdiction operations that began just a few years later. Before I get deeper into this analysis, I want to return to Judge Spellman's exegesis on inadmissibility, to make another point.

The reader may have noticed that the judge couches the distinction between deportable and excludable aliens in a rather divisive, moralistic language. According to Spellman it is ironic that people who announce their intentions to enter the United States (and in this case, he is referring specifically to Haitian asylum seekers) can end up with less rights under US law than migrants who entered the United States by "sneaking across" the border.

But what he really seems to be implying is that this distinction is arbitrary and unjust.

The end result is that Haitian refugees are constructed as morally deserving through a point of contrast with another, less-than-deserving kind of alien. In Spellman's statement, this effect is created through allusions to honesty and dishonesty. The refugee who arrives unannounced at the borders of the United States and petitions for asylum can be commended for their honest intentions to submit themselves to the law, as opposed to the migrant who crosses the border, with no intentions of notifying the government about their presence. The distinction between these legal types also lends itself to a racial-ethnic shorthand, in which the dishonest deportable alien gets associated with Cuban, Mexican, and other Latinx populations[4] while, for Spellman's purposes, Haitians are cast in the role of the honest excludable alien.

It is important to keep in mind that the case Spellman was deciding did not concern undocumented migrants, so the aspersions he was casting on this group (and indirectly on all Latinx populations) carried no practical implications for US immigration law. Nevertheless, his commentary provides a good example of how arguments that were used to defend the Haitian refugees became tragically contorted as they struggled to find some footing within established legal precedent. As I explained in the last chapter, Spellman was sympathetic to the plight of the Haitian refugees and tried his best to protect them from the discriminatory practices of the government's Haitian program. He weighed the merits of the equal protection and due process arguments that had been advanced by the Haitian plaintiffs but reasoned that their chance of prevailing on these grounds was very slim due to their status as excludable aliens. As a result, Spellman's efforts to render a sympathetic decision were caught in the grips of a contradiction, between the moral purpose of the law and the limits of its jurisdiction. His explanation of the distinction between the deportable subject and excludable alien can be read as a commentary on this contradiction.

No matter how unfairly the Haitian refugees had been treated, the moral purpose of the law did not extend to excludable aliens. Spellman did not necessarily agree with this proposition but he accepted its authority as the established legal precedent. Although he insinuated that there is something inherently unfair about the way US law has defined the rightfulness of deportable subjects and excludable aliens, he did not launch into an argument against the higher court decisions that had established this distinction. Instead, his frustrations were channeled into his comments on "dishonest" undocumented migrants. The resulting effect is a moral revaluation of the deportable/excludable distinction, which did nothing to change the inferior legal standing of the excludable alien and, on top of that, catered to resentments against undocumented migrants and Latinx populations.

The process I have just described plays out in many ways in the legal challenge to the government's Haitian refugee policies. Judges, attorneys, and legal advocates bravely exposed gross inequities in the government's treatment of Haitian asylum seekers. But their arguments rarely got to the bottom of the discrimination they were trying to contest. In the last chapter, for example, I explained how Judge King's trenchant criticism of the government's Haitian refugee policies[5] was hamstrung by his presumption that racism was a matter of individual bias that was clearly prohibited by the law. Judge Spellman, on the other hand, was more wary about whether excludable aliens could rely on the protections of the law. Nevertheless, his decision betrayed a desire for a standard of equal treatment that was indifferent to the distinction between excludables and deportables.

This presumption, that the law is necessarily opposed to discrimination (or at least that it should tend in that direction), contrasts with the explanations of antiblackness and the law that I introduced in chapter 1. In that discussion, I drew attention to the contrast between the formal language of the law and a supra-legal sovereign authority that defines its scope and when blackness becomes salient as a way of framing social problems, it is typically subordinated to the dictates of sovereign authority. The Plenary Power doctrine describes how this sovereign authority has been established within US immigration law,[6] but there is a relationship between (anti)blackness and this sovereign authority which predates the Plenary Power doctrine.[7] Moreover, as some scholars have argued, (anti)blackness can be understood as a habitus that is oriented toward policing the ontological boundaries of the law, marking the distinction between those for whom the law is intended and other social types whose predicaments are rendered completely unintelligible.[8]

So on one hand, language prohibiting discriminatory treatment can make its way into constitutional law, in a way that is vaguely applicable to all racial minorities as well as many other protected categories. But the sovereign authority of federal and local governments can be given leeway to decide exactly how "far" these protections are extended and to whom. This is one reason why the US courts were able to reconcile the equal protection of the clause of the Fourteenth Amendment to the social and legal fact of Jim Crow segregation for well over half a century.[9]

In order to explain how this kind of exclusion works, it is necessary to situate the law in light of a context that exceeds it. Judge Spellman, for example, was trying to raise questions about the unequal treatment of Haitian refugees. He proceeds on the assumption that the inferior legal standing of the Haitian plaintiffs could be explained by the distinction between deportable and excludable aliens, as defined by the letter of the law. But he was also well aware, from his recitation of the facts of the case, that the plaintiffs were not contesting how they were being treated compared to deportable migrants.

They were contesting how they were being treated compared to other non-black, foreigners who were excludable aliens, just like themselves.[10]

RADICAL EXCLUSION

As excludable aliens, Haitian asylum seekers were more beholden to the sovereign dictates of the government than any other legal category of noncitizen. But the bare facts of their legal situation do not explain how this sovereign authority was used. In order to explain how Haitian refugees were actually treated, compared to other excludable aliens, a distinction has to be made between the excludable alien as a legal category and a desire to exclude particular social types that is enabled by sovereign power. This latter kind of exclusion also relies on categorical distinctions, but these distinctions are not necessarily written into the law.

Even so, the concept of exclusion still offers a helpful starting point for bringing this subtext into view. It calls attention to a distinction between tolerable, exploitable others and intolerable others who poses an existential threat to the social order. As Etienne Balibar has explained, the Marxist concept of the "reserve army of labor" is insufficient to explain this latter kind of otherness.[11] These are not people whose exclusion can be explained by a ruthless cost-benefit analysis, whereby the cultivation of an excessive supply of workers, which swells the ranks of the unemployed or partly employed, exerts a downward pressure on wages.

Balibar calls attention to a kind of exclusion that makes people radically superfluous to the modern economy. These are populations whose lives "do not matter," not even as a means of generating profit for others. This kind of exclusion is not unique to black populations, but it also cannot be abstracted from a history of violence that is predicated on the control of black bodies. Saucier and Woods have traced the connections between this history of anti-blackness and the interdiction practices that are responsible for the deaths of African refugees in the contemporary Mediterranean. They assert

the violence that seized Africans, subjected them to the Middle Passage, and in so doing transmogrified their humanity into blackness, was purely gratuitous. It was unconnected to any behaviors or transgressive acts. In the world slavery makes, violence against the black body is gratuitous, not contingent, instrumental or incidental: it is punishment for being. Gratuitous violence is the mark of the sub-human, of objectified human existence par excellence. The suffering of the Lampedusa affair, then, cannot be quantified through a political economic analysis; nor can the violence of the Mediterranean borderlands be analogized to the U.S.–Mexico border. The Lampedusa victims are held, in memoriam, in the Mediterranean's abyss of blackness, a plane of nonexistence connoting the structural antagonism of blackness, a position of subjection in excess of the empirical registers of exploitation and oppression.[12]

Saucier and Woods's analysis complements Balibar's explanation of extreme violence. Like Saucier and Woods, Balibar traces this violence to the histories of European colonial predation that "made" the modern world.[13] But going a step further, Saucier and Woods emphasize that this process is umbilically connected to the violence that converts African people into black bodies.

The history of the Middle Passage speaks to the violence of forced displacement that produces the black slave. The drowning of African refugees in the Mediterranean Sea appears to belong to a different order of domination, which is focused on arresting black population movements rather than the importation of black bodies. But the connecting thread between both of these histories is a tactics of controlled mobility reserved for radically different, racial others. Although dominion over the black body may have laid the foundation for the modern economy, the imperative of dominion always superseded a pragmatic interest in profit and exploitation. Dominion must come first, creating a social ontology that establishes an order of rank between all of the biopolitical entities that constitute the modern order.[14] Before the dark skinned African can be "economically incorporated" they must be made a slave. And once chattel slavery is dismantled, the modern world order finds other ways of perpetuating this condition of racialized nonhumanity.

In making this argument, Saucier and Woods find it necessary to point out the limitations of Nicholas De Genova's deportability theory.[15] They explain that deportability theory follows in the footsteps of the Marxist critique of political economy, by emphasizing how the removability of the migrant intensifies their exploitability as a contingently useful worker.[16] They go on to produce a critical re-reading of De Genova's theory of how illegality and immigration controls function as a kind of "inclusion through exclusion."[17]

De Genova has argued that the primary subject of deportability is not the migrant who is actually targeted for deportation but the much larger population of migrants who remain "inside" the global North, living under the constant threat of removal.[18] Deportability conditions the behaviors of these migrants, who are incorporated into the social and economic life of the global North by an immigration regime that is constantly reminding of them how easily they can be removed. This condition of precarity can be connected, in turn, to the Marxist critique of neoliberalism, which has produced a comparable condition of insecurity for the native-born worker (through the scaling back of worker rights, the gutting of the social safety net, and the disappearance of benefited, full-time work[19]).

The issue here is not that De Genova's explanation of deportability is incorrect but that it does not suffice as an explanation for the exclusion suffered by the interdicted refugee. Saucier and Woods insist that De Genova's theory of deportability does not capture the absolute character of this kind of exclusion. They go on to argue that interdicted African refugees are victims of a process that is better described as "preclusion" rather than "exclusion."[20]

These acts of preclusion work in the opposite direction of deportability. According to De Genova, the machineries of power that create the social fact of deportability coalesce around the person who is potentially deportable (and precariously included) rather than the person who is actually deported (and definitively excluded). Preclusion, on the other hand, is geared toward producing exclusion as its primary intended effect. It does not coercively include migrants, using tactics of exclusion. It is animated by a much less sophisticated imperative, to exclude for the purpose of exclusion. Preclusion routes undesirable bodies back to where they came from on pain of death.

From here on out, I use the term "radical exclusion" to describe this imperative, to emphasize that it is a more extreme form of exclusion than described, historically, by US law, but that it is exclusion nonetheless. I am also going to use radical exclusion to set up a point of comparison and critical engagement with the legal discourse on excludability. For the purpose of my analysis, radical exclusion is the inevitable product of antiblack animus. It is what follows when antiblack sentiments are allowed free reign to shape immigration and refugee policies. For this same reason, radical exclusion operates in excess of the formal, legal meaning of excludability and is rarely made plain in the letter of the law.

Formally defined, the excludable alien is somebody who has "not yet entered" the territory of the nation or is not regarded as having been admitted even if they happen to be physically present. But contingent on the outcome of their hearing before the immigration courts, the excludable alien may be admitted. They may end up being granted a secure legal status or they may just get "upgraded" to deportable status (this being someone who is not admitted as a permanent resident, but is allowed to stay under an indefinitely suspended order of removal). The radically excluded alien, on the other hand, has no chance of being admitted. US interdiction operations, for example, have been conducted under the premise that Haitian refugees are not even entitled to an exclusion hearing, which could determine whether or not they are admissible.[21] These interdicted refugees are not just potentially excludable aliens; they are already presumed-to-be-excluded in advance of being apprehended.

Radical exclusion describes the most thoroughly excluded substratum of the excludable alien category. The black people who are overconcentrated in this stratum are not representative in any conventional, statistical sense, of the broader population of excludable aliens. But I also aim to show that the predicament of the excluded, black refugee epitomizes the condition shared by all of the people who find themselves trapped in the excludable category. Radical excludability distills all of the essential features of excludability, as a technique of control, and amplifies them to their highest level of intensity.

In the rest of the chapter I use this concept of radical exclusion to trace connections between different phases in the history of the Haitian interdictions. But before I begin this analysis I am going to provide more context on the legal history of excludability and its complicated relationship to the black/nonblack binary.

THE LEGAL JURISPRUDENCE ON EXCLUDABILITY AND ITS LOOSE ENDS

In its 1950 decision on *Knauff v. Shaughnessy*, the Supreme Court offered a succinct statement on the rights of excludable aliens, stating that "any procedure authorized by Congress for the exclusion of aliens is due process, so far as an alien denied entry is concerned."[22] This statement does not go as far as saying that excludable aliens have absolutely no due process rights. It insists that the US government is not obligated to grant them any more rights than it deems are warranted by the circumstances at hand. Although the federal courts have disagreed about the scope of these rights, and taken issue with the government's interpretation of them, the overarching tendency of US jurisprudence on this matter, over the last seventy years, operates within the framework of this statement articulated by the Knauff decision.

Furthermore, most of the legal history of excludable category is not concerned with the rights of excludable aliens, but whether an alien is excludable or not. In other words, the rightlessness of the excludable alien is a foregone conclusion for most of these court decisions. It also bears noting that the *Yick Wo v. Hopkins* decision has been evoked by this jurisprudence, for the purpose of affirming the legitimacy of the excludable/deportable distinction.[23] The argument famously advanced by the Yick Wo court, that all people residing on US soil are entitled to the full protections of the US Constitution regardless of their legal status, underscores the point that these rights are territorially bounded and that they do not apply to people who are not "here." In this regard, the statement by the Knauff court was really just a clarification of the legal argument that is intrinsic to the concept of excludability. Excludability marks the geopolitical limits of the US Constitution: the point at which the government's obligation to uphold the Constitution gives way to a zone of pure sovereign authority.

The *Johnson v. Eisentrager* decision, which was also decided by the Supreme Court in 1950, provides another important point of clarification. It states that "the alien, to whom the United States has been traditionally hospitable, has been accorded a generous and ascending scale of rights as he increases his identity with our society."[24] It is a foregone conclusion that the people, referenced, by this statement are "already here" residing in the United States. But the statement also insists that the alien's claim on these rights strengthens with the duration of their residence. The Eisentrager court limited its commentary to lawfully residing aliens, and it presumed that length of residence went hand in hand with the acquisition of citizenship. But later federal court decisions gave credence to the fact of residence, separate and apart from legal status. Regardless of whether the migrant is a lawful resident or undocumented, any history of residence will suffice to exempt them from the excludable category.

Once the fact of residence has been separated from legal status, the distinction between the excludable and the deportable alien becomes much fuzzier and open to interpretation, which is the point that Judge Spellman makes at the beginning of *Louis v. Nelson*. Why is the refugee, who enters US waters without authorization and is being held on US soil, awaiting the outcome of their asylum case treated as if they are "not here"? Meanwhile, other migrants who also entered without authorization and have not announced their presence to the US government are treated as if they are "here"? To stir up the pot a little more, we should keep in mind that the Haitian interdictions were rationalized by the Reagan administration as a program to control "illegal immigration."[25] But, for Haitian refugees, "illegality" had nothing to do with deportability. The discourse on illegality only redoubled their excludability, widening the distance between the rightlessness of the Haitian refugee and the precarious inclusion of the resident, undocumented migrant population.

The US jurisprudence on excludability offers no clear guidelines for resolving the dilemma I have just raised. The one thing that the courts have agreed on is that people who have "entered" the United States are entitled to rights which are inaccessible to those who have "not entered." But the question of what it means, exactly, to "have entered" has been defined and qualified in a number of ways. It is also important to consider how the ambiguity surrounding the question of entry has been shaped by histories of racism and race-making.

Orlando Patterson's writing on natal alienation offers an insightful perspective on these questions of excludability.[26] According to Patterson, natal alienation is a defining feature of black slavery. It does not just describe the violence that tears Africans from their homeland, but a condition that permeates their alienated existence in the "new land."

Like the excludable alien, the exterritorial status of the black slave disqualifies them as a legal person. But it is also important to emphasize that this condition of rightlessness is not rooted in a geopolitical imaginary the same way it is for the excludable alien. The excludable alien can be refused entry at the will of any sovereign government, but this refusal is premised on the assumption that the alien hales from somewhere else that recognizes them as citizen or at least, more informally, as a member of society. The black slave, on the other hand, is radically divorced from any concept of a homeland that could recognize them as a rights-bearing subject, which is what Patterson is getting at with the concept of "natal alienation." The slave is the property of others: not a person who can make claims about their rights or their territorial belonging.

One of the premises established by the modern system of racial slavery is that the slave remains a slave no matter where they go.[27] They are excluded from the law on the basis of an ascribed status that is rationalized by the legal distinction between slave and free, but which is also informed by a racist social ontology. Hence, the blackness of the African slave overdetermines their rightlessness, which is why the problem of black rightlessness was shared by the freed black population of the antebellum era, and why it persists as a problem for black people after the dismantling of chattel slavery (and after the dismantling of Jim Crow).

When reflecting on this problem, I also think it helps to underscore an obvious point, which is that all black bodies do not experience this condition of black rightlessness in the same way. All black refugees, for example, have not had the same experience as Haitian refugees, and this is because black rightlessness is not innate to the black body. This condition of rightlessness is the product of power practices that rely on a racist ontology to render problems and possibilities visible to itself. This is why I find the concept of radical exclusion useful, because it focuses attention on (anti) blackness as an attribute of the law, government policy, and state power rather than as an innate attribute of the bodies that are targeted by these institutions.

If antiblackness is to be accorded any significance in the treatment of Haitian refugees, you have to account for the interplay of formal, institutional practices (the letter of the law) and the racist sentiments that guide the application and interpretation of the law. This also means that the matter of excludability cannot be explained only by the legal question of "entry." It is also important to consider how decisions about entry can be overdetermined by distinctions between bodies that are deemed worthy of entry, and others that are deemed inherently undesirable and have no claim on the law.

There are at least three overlapping processes at play in this question of entry, which are summarized in table 3.1. First, there is the matter of entry as

Table 3.1 Permutations of Entry and Excludability

Has the noncitizen entered?	Which noncitizens should be allowed to enter?	Which noncitizens are the most desirable entrants?
The Legal Fact of Entry (Realist Paradigm) A legal determination based on the noncitizen's intentions and authorization to enter.	*Sociopolitical Construction of the Border* Laws, policies, diplomatic agreements, enforcement practices that make the border more permeable for some noncitizen populations than others.	*Social Ontology (Racialized Metaphysics)* A social ontology that hierarchically organizes noncitizen populations by their desirability, and which informs the policy response to each population.

Source: Table and data created by author.

a basic, legal fact. According to the law, has the refugee "entered" and if so how, and do the terms of their entry need to be qualified in any way? Second, going beyond the law, there is the way that policies and enforcement practices make the border more permeable for some populations than others. The legal fact of entry is mainly concerning the intentionality of the migrant. This second factor, on the other hand, pays more attention to the intentionality of the government.

It has been well documented that enforcement practices can be used to make the border selectively permeable at different points in time or for different populations. This selective permeability corroborates De Genova's theory of deportability. It describes a process whereby some migrant populations are allowed to enter the United States, either as "candidates for citizenship" who are granted legal status or as undocumented residents who have to live with the imminent possibility of deportation (as well as a great many people whose situation straddles both of these conditions[28]). But there is another predicament that deportability theory does not address, which is faced by migrant populations who are not even "allowed" to become deportable subjects. These are the radically excluded populations that encounter a border which is stubbornly impermeable.

These starkly different experiences with border enforcement lead to a third consideration. We have to account for the hierarchy of social desirability that helps to explain why the state responds in such vastly different ways to different migrant and refugee populations. As a point of contrast, De Genova's theory does not admit to there being any significant differences in the way migrant populations are valued by the state, which also means that there are no significant differences in the way these populations are racialized and regulated. Deportability may be concentrated among Latinx populations, but it is not explained in light of factors that are specific to a Latin American history of racialization and imperial conquest as has been discussed, for example, by

Juan Perea.[29] There is ultimately no difference between the black, Asian, and Latinx deportable migrant, and migrant populations that are systematically denied entry are of no great significance to the theory.

Put another way, deportability theory has produced an explanation of migrant exploitation and precarity that takes the fact of entry for granted. Deportability theory is not concerned with "who is let in" but with "who gets to stay" and how the threat of removal conditions the socioeconomic life of migrants who are "already here." Consequently, it never gets around to theorizing the third dimension of entry and excludability that is described in table 3.1 (on the far right). If we view the permeability of the border in light of the populations that have been refused entry, we have to consider how enforcement practices and other government policies operate as public statements about the desirability and deservingness of different alien populations. So the question of who "has actually entered" is always bleeding into another set of considerations about the kinds of populations that US policy makers think are "suitable" to enter the United States. As a result, the receptivity of the government toward the alien—and the racist sentiments that condition this receptivity—can influence the practical, legal determination about whether the alien has, in fact, "entered."

If one considers the "racial demographics" of contemporary migration, it should be apparent why the white/nonwhite distinction is of little value for explaining these distinctions between precariously included and absolutely intolerable foreigners, since the majority of newcomers to the United States today are nonwhite.[30] The rise of migration from non-European and postcolonial nations has been met, by a corresponding tendency in public opinion, to racialize the entire immigration flow as nonwhite.[31] But there are also patterns of racial stratification, operating through this large, nonwhite immigrant population, which privilege lighter skinned migrants who identify as "nonblack," at the expense of darker skinned migrants who are more likely to identify as "black."[32]

Keeping this all in mind, the statement on excludability from the *Johnson v. Eisentrager* decision takes on new significance. In that statement, the court did not actually say that rights are acquired on the condition of entry. The court's precise wording was that rights are accorded to aliens to whom "the US has been traditionally hospitable" and that for the beneficiaries of this "hospitability," rights grow stronger the longer the alien resides in the United States. Although the court was probably not intending to make a statement about race,[33] there is ample evidence of how this "traditional hospitality" toward migrants, refugees, and other aliens has been shaped by racist sentiments, and how blacks have been viewed as uniquely undesirable candidates for immigration.[34]

PLENARY POWER, RADICAL EXCLUSION, AND CHINESE IMMIGRANTS

The prior section focused on the relationship between antiblackness and excludability. In this section, I am going to shift focus to the history of anti-Chinese laws and anti-Asian racism in the United States. Chinese immigrants may not have been the first racialized population to be radically excluded by the US government. They were, however, the first population to be excluded as "undesirable aliens" by constitutional law. The Supreme Court's decision in the 1889 *Chinese Exclusion Case*[35] figures prominently in this history. In this decision the court produced a jurisprudence that affirmed the constitutionality of a series of federal laws, beginning with the 1882 *Chinese Exclusion Act*.[36]

The 1882 Act barred the entry of Chinese migrants to the United States for a period of ten years, starting ninety days after the ratification of the Act.[37] The petitioner in the Chinese Exclusion Case had entered the United States prior to the ratification of the Act and established a twelve-year history of lawful residence in the United States.[38] According to the 1882 Act, he belonged to a category of Chinese migrants who could continue to reside in the United States and who could also leave and return, so long as he received travel authorization from the US government. The petitioner acquired this authorization, went to China, and attempted to re-enter the US approximately one year later, in the fall of 1888. He was denied entry by custom officers at the port of San Francisco on the grounds that his certificate to re-enter was invalid.[39] The reason given was that his travel certificate was now invalid, according to the new rules authorized by a new amendment to the 1882 Chinese Exclusion Act, which had been ratified just eight days before his return to the United States.

Simply put, this is a case in which the US government changed the rules of entry for Chinese migrants. The end result is that people who had, at one time, been regarded as lawful residents who had "entered" the United States were now regarded as excludables who had no right to (re)enter. The authority to exclude Chinese migrants rested on the Plenary Power doctrine that had been articulated in the 1882 Chinese Exclusion Act. In its decision, the Supreme Court also provided a more detailed account of the strained diplomatic relations between China and the United States, which explained why the US government had decided to bar the entry of Chinese immigrants. The court also made a point of describing Chinese immigrants as the source of a new "race problem." The following is an excerpt from this discussion.

> If, therefore, the government of the United States, through its legislative department, considers the presence of foreigners of a different race in this country,

who will not assimilate with us, to be dangerous to its peace and security, their exclusion is not to be stayed because at the time there are no actual hostilities with the nation of which the foreigners are subjects. The existence of war would render the necessity of the proceeding only more obvious and pressing. The same necessity, in a less pressing degree, may arise when war does not exist, and the same authority which adjudges the necessity in one case must also determine it in the other.[40]

In this statement the court analogized the Chinese "race problem" to the threat of war, and it used this analogy to smooth over some apparent contradictions in its argument. It acknowledged that the Chinese Exclusion Acts had imposed restrictions on the rights of Chinese migrants that ran counter to treaty agreements that the US government had signed with the Emperor of China.[41] It also acknowledged that, despite a recent history of political tensions between China and the United States, that there were no actual hostilities between these nations which would lead Chinese migrants to be considered "enemy aliens."[42] But as I just noted, the court went on to argue that the "race problem" posed by a growing population of Chinese laborers was equivalent to the threat of war. So although Chinese immigrants were not, factually speaking, enemy aliens, they could still be treated "as if" they were enemy aliens (i.e., as the progenitors of an analogous kind of threat).

Michel Foucault's analysis of race supremacy and the modern art of governance provides some helpful insights into the subtext for the Supreme Court's reasoning on this matter.[43] Foucault explains that war is one of the foundational schemas for the modern idea of race, which begins its history as an oppositional discourse, but is eventually converted into a tactical and ideological arm of state power. Race, as a vector of war, is intimately related to the modern state's agenda for societal transformation.

Siniša Malešević's writing on war and social theory is also very instructive.[44] He has shown that most of the social and political theory produced in the nineteenth century (and earlier) operated within this framework, as a discourse on state power (consistent with the Machiavellian tradition in which intellectual treatises are devised as instructions on ruling for the political elite). According to this body of sociological theory, the relationship between state and society is necessarily antagonistic and steeped in war-like metaphors. In a similar vein, Foucault explains that the modern state's interest in securing its territory and population leads it into a permanent state of undeclared war with the social body that it is charged with governing, as it seeks to root out all sorts of deviant tendencies and internal enemies that are thwarting its agenda.[45] Viewed through the lens of these discourses, the racial other poses an existential threat to the authority of the state and its capacity to govern. So when a population is singled out by the state as the source of a "race problem," it is signaling its intentions to deal with that population in an exceptional way. The Supreme Court's 1893 decision in *Fong Yue Ting v. US*[46] provides a striking illustration of exactly how exceptional these measures would become.

The Chinese Exclusion Case described an increasingly draconian series of exclusions, in which the bar on migration from China was expanded to include a bar on re-entry to the United States for lawfully residing Chinese migrants. The enforcement practices that were contested in Fong Yue Ting took things a step further, making it possible for Chinese migrants, who were already residing in the territory of the United States, to be treated no differently than excludable aliens.

The case revolved around an 1892 Congressional act—exclusively targeting Chinese people—that made it possible for Chinese migrants to be deported if they could not furnish proof of residence in the United States.[47] The means of securing this proof of residence was a certificate issued by the local collector of internal revenue. If the Chinese migrant could not furnish a certificate on request, they would have to secure the testimony of at least one "credible white witness" to vouch for their history of residence.[48]

The enforcement actions that were used to remove Chinese migrants who could not comply with this residency-check requirement were described as "deportations."[49] But it is notable that the Supreme Court began its decision by citing the constitutional and sovereign authority of the US government to exclude alien populations. At one point in the decision, the court explicitly addressed this murky ground, in which the deportability of these migrants bled into a condition of excludability, noting that

> for the reasons stated in the earlier part of this opinion, Congress, under the power to *exclude or expel aliens,* might have directed any Chinese laborer found in the United States without a certificate of residence to be removed out of the country by executive officers, *without judicial trial or examination, just as it might have authorized such officers absolutely to prevent his entrance into the country.* But Congress has not undertaken to do this. (Emphasis added)[50]

In this statement, the court was basically arguing that the US government was not obligated to grant Chinese residents any more rights than it would to an excludable alien who had never entered the United States. As a recurring theme of this decision, the court referred to the expulsion and exclusion of aliens as interchangeable features of the government's authority.[51] By repeatedly framing expulsion and exclusion in this way, the court emphasized that the deportable and excludable aliens were "here" by permission of the government and that the government exerted a comparable degree of discretionary authority over its treatment of both kinds of aliens. Hence, it could argue that Chinese migrants who could not furnish proof of residence were not entitled to the same due process as citizens, but that Congress had decided, nonetheless, to grant them a modicum of procedural rights.[52]

The court went on to explain that the Chinese migrant who is unable to furnish proof of residence is not automatically deported. The government must still abide by a process whereby they are brought before a judge, who is presented with the charges against them and will make a final decision based on the facts presented.[53] To bolster its argument the court introduced an infamous rationalization that has been heavily criticized by many immigration and legal scholars—that deportation is not punishment, but a value-neutral administrative procedure.[54] The practical effect of this argument is to lower the bar for what counts as due process. If deportation is not punishment, then it does not constitute a significant deprivation of liberty, and the government is not obligated to ensure that the rights of the alien are protected, as it would in a criminal trial.

THE FONG YUE TING DISSENT: AFFIRMING THE NONBLACKNESS OF THE RACIALIZED MIGRANT

The majority opinion for Fong Yue Ting was used to justify an exclusionary treatment that was unprecedented for Chinese migrants. Several Supreme Court justices took issue with the majority opinion. The dissenters were especially concerned about the blurring of the distinction between deportable subjects and excludable aliens. Most of their concerns turned on this question: How could people who are clearly long-term residents be treated as if they were excludable aliens who had never been granted legal entry to the United States?

These dissenting opinions also provide an early example of a problem that has plagued immigrant rights advocacy throughout the twentieth century and into the new millennium. They attempted to protect Chinese migrants with arguments that implicitly affirmed their nonblack status.[55] These arguments were ultimately used to exempt Chinese migrants from the hazards of radical exclusion rather than to directly challenge the racist undercurrents of these exclusions.

The dissent issued by Justice Brewer provides a nuanced introduction to this problem. Brewer's dissent pushed back on two key issues that deportation was not punishment and that the due process rights of Chinese migrants were not being violated by these enforcement practices.[56] Brewer argued that deportation clearly was punishment and deportation procedures had to meet a higher bar of due process rights. He pointed out that the plaintiffs in Fong Yue Ting were not granted a formal trial, that the decision to deport was made by a single magistrate who was also the official determining the facts of the case, and that the evidence required (the furnishing of a sympathetic white witness) was nearly impossible for most Chinese migrants to acquire.[57]

Justice Brewer also raised an alarm about how these enforcement practices were hopelessly blurring the lines between deportable and excludable aliens. In making this point, Brewer made a comparison between the predicament of the Chinese alien and the black slave. Quoting a speech made by Ohio senator John Sherman, he observed that these enforcement practices "inaugurate in our system of Government a new departure—one, I believe, never before practiced, *although it was suggested in conference that some such rules had been adopted in slavery times to secure the peace of society*" (emphasis added).[58]

There are two divergent themes at work in this statement. Residency-check requirements for Chinese migrants are likened to history of controlled mobility, associated with the black slave, that predates Chinese migration by over two centuries. But they are also described as a "new departure . . . never before practiced." This odd chronology begs the question of exactly why the residency-check requirements constitute a "new departure" and for whom. They are not a new departure as it concerned treatment of the black slave or the controls imposed on free blacks, who were also targeted by local laws that required them to carry "papers" authorizing travel across state and municipal borders.[59]

The implication of Senator Sherman's statement (as quoted by Brewer) is that the residency-check requirements are a "new departure" because they were being extended to populations that had never been treated this way before. Using his own words, Brewer goes on to argue, "It is true this statute is directed only against the obnoxious Chinese, but, if the power exists, who shall say it will not be exercised tomorrow against other classes and other people? If the guaranties of these amendments can be thus ignored in order to get rid of this distasteful class, what security have others that a like disregard of its provisions may not be resorted to?"[60]

Here we have another very telling and racially complex statement. With his casual reference to the "obnoxious Chinese," Brewer normalizes the anti-Asian racism of his day—underscoring the otherness of the Chinese immigrant. But in the same breath, he acknowledges that a line has been crossed, and that the crossing of this line threatens a much larger population that is even more deserving of having their rights protected than the "obnoxious Chinese." Operating in the shadows of Brewer's language is a black/nonblack binary. The Chinese resident is clearly not white, but incursions on the rights of this racial other set a dangerous precedent that pose a more eminent threat to the white population than the controls that had been routinely imposed on black slaves.

These troublesome tendencies in the dissenting opinions for Fong Yue Ting become even more explicit in the statement by Justice Field. Field began his dissent by noting that he was "honored" to be a member of the court that affirmed the legality of the Chinese Exclusion Acts. On this point, it bears emphasizing that Justice Field delivered the majority opinion in that case. But he had serious misgivings about the residency-check requirements that were being contested by Fong Yue Ting. A linchpin of Field's argument is that the Chinese were friendly and not enemy aliens and that even the Aliens and Seditions Acts had not gone so far as to restrict the rights of friendly aliens.[61]

In his attempt to protect Chinese immigrants, Field provides an early example of a tendency that shows up in arguments that were levied against the US government's Haitian refugee policy. Field introduces a race-neutral interpretation of a racially charged legal construct and proceeds on the assumption that his race-neutral interpretation is the established norm.

The majority opinion in the Chinese Exclusion Case (which was led by Field) made a very explicit argument about how the "race problem" posed by Chinese immigrants justified treating them like enemy aliens, even if they were not "actually" enemy aliens.[62] But in Fong Yue Ting, Field departs from this body of opinion which he helped to create. He insists that immigrants should only be categorized as enemy aliens if formal hostilities have been declared between their home nation and their current host nation. By implication, he is arguing that race should not factor into the government's assessment of the threat posed by Chinese residents, but he does not directly challenge the racist underpinnings of the Chinese exclusion laws (and he raises no questions about the Plenary Power doctrine that authorized these exclusions). Instead, Field sidesteps the race question and produces an argument that attempts to exempt Chinese residents from the same racist rationale for exclusion that he had endorsed in the Chinese Exclusion Case.

Field's dissent could be read as a pragmatic attempt to protect Chinese residents that operated within the confines of established jurisprudence. But this leads him to adopt a strategy that cannot face up to the racist animus driving these exclusions. He does not confront the fact that the Chinese were being targeted because they were Chinese, and not because they were returning migrants, or new entrants, or because there were (or were not) formal hostilities between the United States and China.

Field's argument rests on the premise that the US government cannot, in good conscience, treat long-term residents as if they were rightless, excludable aliens. But in order to take this position he has to hold to a double standard, which allows the government to be racist when it comes to excluding new entrants but assumes that this racism can be reigned-in by constitutional law when it comes to residents. The result of the Fong Yue Ting decision shows that Field had guessed wrong. The racist rationale for the Chinese

Exclusion Act, and the Supreme Court's endorsement of this rationale in the Chinese Exclusion Case, established a precedent that it made it that much easier for Chinese residents to be treated like excludable aliens. And although Field may have been outraged by the majority opinion in Fong Yue Ting, he was blind to the way that US law, at that very same moment in time, was tolerating a similar condition of rightlessness for black ex-slaves who had recently been granted citizenship.[63]

Like Justice Brewer, Field tries to insert Chinese residents into a category of rights-bearing subjects that is presumably race-neutral, but is more practically speaking, nonblack. This black/nonblack binary becomes most apparent when Field cites James Madison's and Thomas Jefferson's denunciation of the Aliens and Seditions Acts as "unconstitutional and barbarous."[64] Field uses their arguments to underscore his point that deportation is, in fact, punishment. But Madison and Jefferson's race politics call attention to another distinction. They may have opposed laws that expanded the deportation powers of the federal government, but the aliens whose rights they championed were white Europeans.[65] Meanwhile, as I explained in the last chapter, Madison and Jefferson were also prominent members of the American Colonization Society, which advocated for a mass deportation program that exclusively targeted blacks.[66]

Field, like immigration scholars of the present day, reads the arguments levied against the Aliens and Seditions Acts in the most generous light possible.[67] The antiblack subtext of these arguments is ignored because it is not, presumably, an essential component of the principles that Madison and Jefferson were espousing. This reasoning sets the stage for a curious dilemma in which racism—and antiblack racism especially—must not be accorded any explanatory power as a driver of law and policy, so that the egalitarian potential of the alien rights argument can be salvaged. But this oversight leads Field, and many contemporary scholars, to misjudge the racist animus that powers anti-immigrant laws.

The Chinese Exclusion Acts and the Fong Yue Ting decision show how this racist animus is always working to expand the scope of excludability. The end result is a condition of radical exclusion which is not concerned with who "actually" entered the United States, but with redefining the meaning of "entry" to ensure that the "wrong types" cannot enter (as well making it easier to retroactively exclude the "wrong types" who are already "here"). In Fong Yue Ting, this desire to exclude threatened to collapse the legal distinction between the deportable subject and the excludable alien. Like the *Plessy v. Ferguson* decision, which was decided a few years later, the Supreme Court insisted that laws that made unprecedented incursions on the rights of racialized populations actually operated in conformity with constitutional law.[68]

Justice Brewer's dissent in Fong Yue Ting hinted at the possibility of thinking about these two forms of racial marginality in relation to each other:

that the extremes of anti-Chinese exclusion could not be properly explained without understanding the rightlessness of the US black population. But as I explained above, Brewer's overture to the history of slavery was confined to a single statement loaded with ambiguous implications.

The overriding tendency of the dissents that were issued by the Fong Yue Ting court was to downplay the salience of race. The dissenting justices tried to exempt Chinese residents from racist exclusions (effectively arguing that they deserved the same treatment as white aliens) rather than taking issue with the government's authority to racially discriminate in the first place, or with the racism of the general public.

In the decades that followed, the Chinese exclusions withered away. The exclusions that had been originally authorized by the 1882 Chinese Exclusion Act expired after a period of ten years.[69] On expiration, the exclusions were renewed, but by the early twentieth century the scope and severity of the exclusions became incrementally weaker, until they were finally repealed in December 1943.[70] During this same period of time, the federal courts continued to set new precedents on matters of excludability that were defined by cases involving white, Asian, and Latin American petitioners. Race, gender, and able-bodied status were an important feature of the subtext for many of these decisions, but they all revolved around matters of individualized suspicion.[71] None of these cases involved arguments that were used, categorically, to exclude an entire racial group.

So it could be argued that the strategy of the dissenters in Fong Yue Ting did, eventually, prevail. The dangerous moment, in which Chinese rightlessness became almost indistinguishable from black rightlessness, was avoided, without having to directly challenge the racist desires that animate radical exclusion. The Chinese exclusions were dismantled as the political times changed and a different zeitgeist gripped the mood of the nation. But the jurisprudence and constitutional precedents that provided legal cover for the racist exclusion of Chinese migrants were never overturned. The next group of "undesirables" to feel the full brunt of these exclusions were Haitian refugees. This is one of the main reasons why some scholars have treated the Chinese exclusions as the legal prehistory for the US government's policies on Haitian refugees.[72] Although this history does not adequately explain the antiblack undercurrents of US immigration law, it still provides an important point of reference for my analysis.

The Chinese exclusions are important, firstly, for establishing race as a criterion that can be legitimately factored into the government's decisions about excludability and entry. Secondly, legal deliberations over these exclusions were quietly informed by a black/nonblack binary that influenced the way that Supreme Court justices framed their arguments. I have also shown that this racial binary was evoked by the *defenders* of

Chinese migrants more so than their detractors, in an effort to shore up their deservingness for inclusion. This second problem is the more important of the two. It underscores a point I make throughout this book, which is that arguments on behalf of migrant rights—and critical theories of migrant marginality—take the nonblack migrant as their de facto starting point, but without explicitly acknowledging they are doing so. This silence, about the salience of the black/nonblack binary, is usually predicated on the idea that these arguments and theories are inclusive for all migrants and refugees. I'm arguing, on the other hand, that in order to be more genuinely inclusive, it is necessary to account for the singularity of antiblack racism. I pursue this argument in the next section by showing how the problem of black rightlessness intersects with, but also differs from the jurisprudence on excludability that took shape throughout the twentieth century, and which set the stage for the government's Haitian refugee policies in the late 1970s and 1980s.

A DIFFERENT KIND OF EXCLUDABILITY

The legal construct of excludability has always occupied a central place in the US government's justifications for its treatment of Haitian refugees. *Pierre v. US*[73] is one of the first cases to contest this treatment, which involved a group of Haitian refugees who had petitioned for asylum several years before the creation of the Haitian program. The legal justification for the Haitian program continued to rely on this jurisprudence on excludability through the late 1970s. After the government initiated its first interdiction program, in the fall of 1981, the federal courts produced arguments that expanded the scope and meaning of excludability in unprecedented ways.[74] Throughout this case history, the Supreme Court's 1958 decision, in *Leng May Ma v. Barber*,[75] surfaces as an important touchstone for defining the legal meaning of excludability.

The Ma decision was a contemporary of the Eisentrager and Knauff decisions that were discussed earlier in this chapter. In all of these decisions, the courts agreed that excludable aliens are not guaranteed the same constitutionally protected rights as US residents. These decisions were also informed by the security concerns of the Cold War era.[76] The Ma decision stood apart from the others, in that it was concerned with the veracity of her claim to citizenship, more so than her political loyalties.[77] Nevertheless, it was issued during a time when the Cold War-era politics had exacerbated the US government's preexisting concerns about Chinese migration, giving rise to enforcement operations that were geared toward weeding out immigration fraud in the Chinese population.[78]

Leng May Ma had attempted to enter the United States, insisting that she was a citizen. The government could not verify her citizenship and Ma, eventually, abandoned her claim. But she went on to argue that she would be persecuted by China's communist government if she was returned there by the United States, which is why she should be granted a stay of deportation.[79] Effectively, Ma was no longer appealing to her rights as a citizen but for something like refugee relief, even though she did not formally apply for asylum.[80] The Supreme Court denied her request. The court argued that she was not entitled to a stay of deportation because she had never been formally admitted to the United States—making her an excludable alien and not a deportable subject.[81] As a result, her removal from the United States was not "deportation" but a denial of entry. The court acknowledged that Ma had been allowed to live in the United States while her case was being heard, but it emphasized that she had only been admitted on parole. According to the law, she had still not been granted entry to the United States, and she was not entitled to the same legal considerations as an alien who had "actually entered."

One of the basic points that the government and the federal courts make when they cite the Ma case is that Haitian refugees are in the same situation.[82] They have not "entered" the United States, and because they have not entered, they are not entitled to same procedural and constitutional rights as does someone who is regarded as "being here." But there are also significant differences in the issues at stake in these cases. In Ma's case, there was a steady retrogression of legal statuses. She begins by claiming citizenship, she ends up struggling to claim the rights of a deportable subject, but is eventually found to be excludable. Hence, the main problem for Ma is that she ends up being trapped in the excludable category. In contrast, the Haitian refugees who raised legal challenges to the Carter-era "Haitian program" were not contesting the fact of their excludability, they were complaining about the starkly different way they were being treated, compared to other excludable aliens.[83]

Ma, for example, was paroled into the United States while her case was being decided. Haitian refugees, on the other hand, have struggled to receive even this consideration. While other excludable asylum seekers have been allowed to live in US communities while their cases were pending, Haitians have been forced into detention facilities. Complaints about these Haitian-specific mandatory detention policies were the driving force behind the *Louis v. Nelson* decision that was issued by Judge Spellman in 1982.[84] These same complaints fueled a parallel set of cases, which were contested in New York, which took issue with the way Haitian refugees were treated during the era of the Haitian program. All of these cases centered on allegations of racially biased parole decisions, made by Charles Sava, the INS director for the New York District.[85]

Like the Nelson and Civiletti cases, the District Court decisions in this case were sympathetic to the plight of the Haitian refugees. Robert Carter was the New York District Court judge who issued both of these sympathetic decisions in March and April of 1982.[86] He called attention to a pattern of decision-making that appeared to target Haitian refugees just because they were Haitian.

According to Sava, Haitian refugees were unsuitable candidates for parole because they posed a higher risk of absconding into the US population, and also posed a higher risk of becoming a public charge, even if they were admitted to the United States. Some of the criteria he used to support this analysis included the undocumented status of most of the Haitian refugees, their skill level (he deemed most of them to be "illiterate farmers"), the unlikelihood of their asylum petitions being granted by the immigration courts, and also that, if they were paroled, they would be cared for by church organizations and nonprofits, rather than family and friends.[87]

On review, Judge Carter found all of these criteria implausible. He based his decision on a detailed comparative case study of the non-Haitian refugees that Sava had paroled. He noted that all ninety of the non-Haitian aliens, who were processed at the same time as the Haitian plaintiffs, had been granted parole while they waited to hear the final outcome of their case.[88] He also took note of a smaller subgroup of twelve non-Haitian asylum seekers that exhibited many of the traits that Sava had used to deny parole to Haitians. Like the larger group of non-Haitian asylum seekers, the racial-ethnic composition of this group would be more accurately described as "nonblack" than "nonwhite." It included six Iraqis, three Iranians, one Dominican, one Lebanese, and one Polish national.[89]

According to the records supplied by the INS, several of the aliens in this non-Haitian/nonblack group did not have family or friends in the United States, did not have any better legal documentation than the Haitian petitioners, and did not end up being granted asylum—but Sava paroled them anyway.[90] Meanwhile, several of the Haitian refugees who were denied parole actually had friends and family in the United States and were skilled workers who did not fit the "illiterate farmer" generalization that Sava used to categorize this entire group of refugees.[91] Judge Carter concluded that Sava had abused his discretionary authority.[92] There was little evidence that Sava had considered the individual merits of each Haitian's case, as he had for other asylum seekers; instead he seemed to be following a practice of categorically denying parole to Haitian refugees.

All of this evidence calls attention to a radical exclusion that was operating through the excludable alien category and stratifying it along the lines of a black/nonblack binary. This seemed to be a clear case of the US border being rendered more permeable for some excludable aliens compared to others, and it seemed that the blackness of the Haitian refugees had a lot to do with the way the US government was making its decisions over who to parole and who to grant asylum. This is not the same kind of problem that is described by the Ma decision. In fact, there is no equivalent to this complaint—of an entire national origin group being categorically denied parole or entry on the basis of race—in any of the precedent decisions on excludability that were issued in the post-war era.[93]

The government's position, however, was that irrespective of the facts of the complaint, the Haitian refugees had no more legal footing to press their claim than did Ma. The excludable alien's demand for equity does not carry the same weight as it would if they had actually entered the United States. In a nutshell, this was the argument advanced by the Second Circuit Court that heard Sava's appeal.[94] The Second Circuit Court overturned the District Court decisions issued by Judge Carter and argued that, despite its possible flaws, Sava had reasonably exercised his discretion and that his authority to make these decisions was fully authorized by the law.

The Second Circuit Court's argument in this case was similar to the Eleventh Circuit Court argument in *Jean v. Nelson* (which had also over-turned a sympathetic lower court decision, see chapter 2). The court did not go as far as the Eleventh Circuit, in citing *The Chinese Exclusion Case* and *Fong Yue Ting v. US*[95] for support but it still observed (citing Judge's Carter's own language) that "no one disputes 'Congress may employ race or national origin as criteria in determining which aliens to exclude from the country.'"[96]

The Circuit Court also argued that Sava's decisions did not constitute "invidious discrimination" against Haitian refugees.[97] On its face, this argu-ment appears to be gripped by a painful contradiction. The court acknowl-edged that the US government had the authority to racially discriminate in its treatment of excludable aliens, but that the INS director's treatment of Haitian refugees was not discriminatory.[98]

To shed a little more light on this quandary, the Second Circuit Court had been caught in a trap of sorts. It had to contend with the argument about invidi-ous discrimination because this was a product of its own jurisprudence, stem-ming from a 1966 decision on *Wong Wing Hang v. INS*.[99] Carter observed that though government officials have been granted broad discretionary authority over the treatment of excludable aliens, they can still be held accountable for the abuse of their discretion, which includes decisions made, "'without a ratio-nal explanation,' in marked, unexplained contradiction of established policy," also including, "invidious discrimination against a particular race or group."[100]

The Second Circuit responded to this challenge by reminding Carter that, in his own decision, he had acknowledged that the US government had the authority to deny entry to excludable aliens for any reason, including race.[101]

But the judges of the Second Circuit did not push the argument any further. They used the remainder of their decision to provide counterfactuals to the District Court's argument, to show that Sava's decisions did not constitute racial discrimination and that Judge Carter had illegitimately substituted his own subjective judgment for Sava's equally legitimate judgment on how to decide the fate of the Haitian refugees.[102]

Like the Supreme Court's decision in *Jean v. Nelson*, it seemed that the Second Circuit did not want to lean too heavily on the Plenary Power doctrine, but it also did not want to undermine its status as established doxa. The end result was a curious argument that affirmed the government's right to discriminate in principle, while insisting that it was not doing so in practice. Although this could be explained as a flaw in the reasoning of the Second Circuit Court, it can also be understood as a conceptual aphasia shared by many court decisions, which pervades US immigration law.

The crux of the problem is that US law has a long history of applying the same legal standards in different ways, to different racially categorized populations. But the federal courts have rarely attempted to justify this unequal treatment with a formal legal argument. When the courts have rationalized inequality—especially from the late nineteenth century onward—they typically follow the lead of the Plessy decision, by insisting that these inequalities do not violate the egalitarian foundations of the law.[103] As a result, the difference between acts of discrimination is tolerated by the law, and others that are deemed unlawful are obfuscated by arguments which insist that the former kind of discrimination is not "really discriminatory." This problem is compounded by the Kantian underpinnings of the modern system of law, which insists that all legal constructs are universally applicable to all persons who are governed by the law.[104] The practical upshot of this Kantian reasoning is that, however, the courts define "unlawful discrimination" at any given point in time, is taken be universally applicable to all potential victims of racial discrimination. But as I have shown over the last several chapters, the US legal discourse on race and discrimination has done a poor job of mitigating the effects of antiblack racism. Despite its universalist ambitions, this discourse always has always been constructed at a distance from the problem of black rightlessness.

I drew attention to this problem in my earlier discussion of the Fong Yue Ting decision. The dissenting justices in that case produced arguments which took for granted that black rightlessness and anti-Chinese exclusions were rooted in separate legal histories. Hence, "alien rights" could be affirmed with little concern for the antiblack subtext for these rights arguments. Complaints could also be raised about "unprecedented" restrictions on migrant rights, while acknowledging, in the same breath, that US law had a long history of treating blacks in a similar way.

In the Sava cases this distance crops up as a distinction between problems that differ in scale. The Second Circuit Court's decision in Wong Wing Hang, which introduced the construct of invidious discrimination, concerned the fate of a noncitizen who was suspected of entering the United States with a fraudulent legal status.[105] In this case, the issue of contention had to do with whether an individual petitioner had been treated in a biased way. Sava, on the other hand, was following a policy that was identical to the practice of mandatory detention that had been used by South Florida INS officials during the years of the Haitian program.[106] Barring a few exceptions, this policy was standard practice for all Haitian refugees.[107] In this case, Haitians were being categorically excluded by a policy authorized by the INS, and Sava was also known to be one of the INS officials who had a hand in creating this program.[108]

According to the Second Circuit's jurisprudence on invidious discrimination, Sava's policy of mandatory detention could not be discriminatory precisely because it was not a biased interpretation of government policy—it was a faithful translation of the government's policy on Haitian refugees. Or at least, this is one way that you could interpret the (non)applicability of the invidious discrimination argument. As I've already noted, the Second Circuit declined to advance this argument. Instead, the court insisted that Sava had used his discretionary authority in a reasonable way which did not rise to the level of invidious discrimination—and this argument leads to an intractable conundrum.

In the years to come, the Haitian program and the Haitian interdictions would be widely criticized by the scholarly community.[109] This well-established body of opinion begs the question: If the Second Circuit's standard of invidious discrimination could not be applied to the government's treatment of Haitian refugees, then of what use is it? This is, admittedly, a rhetorical question, but it underscores the argument that I have been making over the last several pages.

The jurisprudence on invidious discrimination, as it was interpreted by the Second Circuit Court, did not actually protect Haitian refugees from discriminatory treatment; it only bolstered an argument about the race-neutrality of the law and the reasonableness of Sava's use of his discretionary authority. The Second Circuit was not prepared to plainly argue that the government's constitutional authority to "employ race or national origin as criteria in determining which aliens to exclude from the country" was the foundation of Sava's policy of mandatory detention for Haitians.[110] Judge Carter was also reticent to broach this issue.

There is just one mention of the Haitian program in the two decisions that were issued by Carter. Even though he acknowledged that Sava was one of the architects of this program,[111] Carter goes on to observe that

Petitioners attempted to show ...some newspaper reports concerning the administration's policy towards Haiti, and some specific conduct of INS trial attorney Michael DiRaimondo, that there exists a national policy of detention for Haitians which applies to no other ethnic group. *The court is not persuaded by the scanty evidence presented on this matter.*[112] (emphasis added)

In this passage, Judge Carter is admitting that the existence of a "national policy of detention" for Haitians would have posed a problem for his argument. If it could be established that Sava was following a policy endorsed by the federal government, then he was not abusing his discretionary authority; he was acting in consort with the US government's sovereign authority over immigration which had been affirmed by Plenary Power doctrine. So in order for Judge Carter to argue that Sava had abused his discretion, it was necessary to portray him as a rogue official, who was distorting the government's policies.

It bears emphasizing, once more, that this line of argument follows from Carter's reliance on the construct of invidious discrimination. This construct proved ineffective, because it affirms the race-neutrality of the law and it is unable to raise questions about the discriminatory nature of the sovereign authority that can be channeled through the law. So although Judge Carter disagreed with the Second Circuit over the legitimacy of Sava's decisions, both courts made arguments that were averse to seeing how antiblack racism could operate as a deeply engrained and institutionalized feature of the law.

Consequently, both courts remained stubbornly blind to the racist implications of the sovereign authority that they had both affirmed in their decisions. Judge Carter was not prepared to challenge the scope of this sovereign authority, and the Second Circuit was not prepared to connect the dots between its affirmation of Plenary Power and the construct of invidious discrimination. The most straightforward way to do this was *not* the path it took, which was to provide alternative rationalizations for all of Sava's decisions, to show they were all motivated by "reasonably nonracist" considerations.

The most straightforward argument to make was that Sava *had* racially discriminated against Haitian refugees and that these acts of discrimination were lawful. These acts of discrimination were not "invidious" because they did not distort the intentions of the government's refugee policy; they were faithful interpretations of a policy which had been issued by the government for the explicit purpose of preventing the entry of Haitian refugees because they were racially undesirable (or a "racial threat").

This, however, would have been an indelicate argument to make, and one that has been rarely advanced by any federal court. It is not just an argument that contradicted the egalitarian, sensibilities of the post-civil rights era. It also would have posed a problem for a regimen of controlled mobility, dating to the days of the transatlantic slave trade, that has been shielded from legal scrutiny.

The Haitian interdiction program, that was launched by the Reagan administration while the Sava cases were making their way through the court system, was both a new development and more of the same. It relied on a tactics that allowed the government to avoid binding legalities, plunging Haitian refugees into a condition of abject rightlessness. This outcome, tragically, was nothing new. But the interdictions also relied on a territorial imaginary that made it possible to rationalize the rightlessness of Haitian refugees in a new way, and which relieved the federal courts of having to make indelicate arguments about the government's right to be racist. I discuss this history of legal argumentation in the next chapter.

NOTES

1. *Louis v. Nelson*, 544 F. Supp. 973 (S.D. Fla., 1982) at 977.

2. This tendency in the academic literature parallels the focus of the public and policy debate on immigration across the Western industrialized world around issues of illegality: whether this entails debates over enforcement practices that target "illegals" or reforms that extend legal status to undocumented migrants. Deportability figures into these debates as a condition effecting people who are already residing in the host nation and face the risk of removal due to their precarious status. Nicholas De Genova's theory of deportability, which is discussed later in this chapter, is a cornerstone for much of this critical scholarship (see n15–19). The literature on this subject is so voluminous that it is difficult to adequately represent with a few citations. Nevertheless, it is worth noting that books and special journal issues devoted to the immigration issues of the day usually revolve around these issues (I have also made some contributions to this literature). Some examples include David Brotherton and Philip Kretsedemas, eds., *Keeping Out the Other: A Critical Introduction to Immigration Enforcement Today* (New York: Columbia University Press, 2008); Julie Dowling and Jonathan Xavier Inda, eds., *Governing Immigration Through Crime: A Reader* (Stanford, CA: Stanford University Press, 2013); Tanya Golash-Boza, *Deported: Immigrant policing, Disposable Labor and Global Capitalism* (NYU Press, 2015); James Hollifield, Philip Martin, and Pia Orrenius, eds., *Controlling Immigration: A Global Perspective* (Stanford, CA: Stanford University Press, 2014).

3. Gary Palmer, "Guarding the Coast: Alien Migrant Interdiction Operations at Sea," *International Law Studies* 72, no. 1 (1998): 157–179 at 173.

4. Although undocumented migration has been stereotypically associated with Mexican immigrants, tensions between Cuban and black populations in South Florida are, arguably, a more salient feature of the racial-ethnic subtext for Spellman's comments. For a brief history of these tensions, which can be traced to group competition over federal resources dating to the 1960s, see Alejandro Portes and Alex Stepick,

City on the Edge: The Transformation of Miami (Berkeley, CA: University of California Press, 1993).

5. In *Haitian Refugee Center (HRC) v. Civiletti*, 503 F. Supp. 442 (S.D. Fla. 1980). This decision was issued two years before Judge Spellman's decision in *Louis v. Nelson*, involving a group of Haitian plaintiffs who were contesting the same government policies.

6. The Plenary Power doctrine was first articulated, as a matter of federal law, in the Chinese Exclusion Act of 1882 (Pub.L. 47–126, 22 Stat. 58, Chap. 126). The Supreme Court jurisprudence that affirmed the constitutionality of these exclusions (and of the Plenary Power doctrine) is discussed later in this chapter.

7. See chapter 2 for a discussion of this history.

8. For a summation of this arguments, see Calvin Warren, *Ontological Terror: Blackness, Nihilism and Emancipation* (Durham, NC: Duke University Press, 2018), 62–110. Warren's theory of the law is discussed in more detail in chapter 1.

9. See my comparative discussion from chapter 2 of the Supreme Court decisions for *Yick Wo v. Hopkins*, 118 U.S. 356 (1886); *Plessy v. Ferguson*, 163 U.S. 537 (1896); and *Brown v. Board of Education*, 347 U.S. 483 (1954).

10. See chapter 2 for a more thorough discussion. The crux of the matter is that other (nonblack) excludable aliens were being routinely paroled into the United States, while they waited for their asylum claims to be decided, whereas Haitians were routed into detention. Later in this chapter, I review data presented in courtroom proceedings that sheds some more light on these kinds of disparities. This data comes for a series of cases that were heard by the New York District Courts, contemporaneous to *Louis v. Nelson* and addressing the same issues.

11. Etienne Balibar, *Violence and Civility: On the Limits of Political Philosophy* (New York: Columbia University Press, 2015), 63–92.

12. P. Khalil Saucier and Tryon Woods, "Ex Aqua The Mediterranean Basin, Africans on the Move and the Politics of Policing," *Theoria* 141:61, no. 4 (2014): 55–75 at 60–61.

13. Balibar, *Violence and Civility*, 81–91.

14. Saucier and Tryon Woods, "Ex Aqua," 60–62. Although my use of the term "biopolitical" is a nod to Foucault, it bears emphasizing that Saucier and Woods' argument is informed by Frank Wilderson's theory of antiblackness and modern society. Frank Wilderson, *Red, White & Black: Cinema and the Structure of U.S. Antagonisms* (Durham, NC: Duke University Press, 2010).

15. Based mainly on a reading of this highly influential essay. Nicholas De Genova, "Migrant 'Illegality' and Deportability in Everyday Life," *Annual Review of Anthropology* 31, no. 1 (2002): 419–447.

16. Saucier and Woods, "Ex Aqua," 58–59.

17. De Genova, "Migrant 'Illegality' and Deportability in Everyday Life," 429; Saucier and Woods, "Ex Aqua," 59.

18. Ibid., 438–439.

19. David Harvey, *A Brief History of Neoliberalism* (London: Oxford University Press, 2007); Guy Standing, "The Precariat: From Denizens to Citizens?" *Polity* 44, no. 4 (2012): 588–608. I have also produced a variant of this argument in Philip

Kretsedemas, *The Immigration Crucible: Transforming Race, Nation and the Limits of the Law* (New York: Columbia University Press, 2012), 13–44.

20. Saucier and Woods, "Ex Aqua," 59.

21. This argument was first articulated in District Court opinions that provided a legal justification for the Reagan-era interdictions: *Haitian Refugee Center, Inc. v. Gracey*, 600 F. Supp. 1396 (D.D.C. 1985); *Haitian Refugee Center v. Gracey*, 809 F.2d 794 (D.C. Cir. 1987) Both of these decisions are discussed in the next chapter.

22. *Knauff v. Shaughnessy*, 338 U.S. 537 (1950) at 338.

23. *Yick Wo v. Hopkins*, 118 U.S. 356 (1886), cited by *Johnson v. Eisentrager*, 339 U.S. 763 (1950) at 771; *United States v. Verdugo-Urquidez*, 494 U.S. 259 (1990) at 271.

24. *Johnson*, 339 U.S. 763 at 770–771.

25. Carl Lindskoog, *Detain and Punish: Haitian Refugees and the Rise of the World's Largest Immigration Detention System* (Gainesville, FL: University of Florida Press, 2018), 50–57.

26. Orlando Patterson, *Slavery and Social Death: A Comparative Study* (Cambridge, MA: Harvard University Press, 2018 [1982]).

27. This premise was legally contested but was affirmed by antebellum-era constitutional law via the Fugitive Slave Act, Pub.L. 31–60, 9 Stat. 462 (1850), and *Dred Scott v. Sandford*, 60 U.S. 393 (1856). It also bears noting that this premise, that race determines rightlessness, extends to the contradictory position of the "free black," especially in the antebellum era. See Daniel Kanstroom, *Deportation Nation* (Cambridge, MA: Harvard University Press, 2007), 63–90; Warren, *Ontological Terror*.

28. A good example is temporary visa holders, many of whom are admitted with a legal status that gives them the right to apply for legal permanent residence, but without guaranteeing the outcome of the application process. This population is not a primary target of immigration enforcement, but visa holders can become "undocumented" or "irregular" migrants if their visa expires or is revoked. See Kretsedemas, *The Immigration Crucible*, 23–46.

29. Juan Perea, "A Brief History of Race and the US-Mexican Border," *UCLA Law Review* 51 (2003): 283.

30. It is well known that the migration to the United States from the late twentieth century onward has been driven primarily by Latinx and Asian populations (and a small but growing number of African and AfroCaribbean migrants) while the share of European migrants has decreased precipitously. Hatton and Williamson have shown that this is a global phenomenon which is not specific to the United States. Timothy Hatton and Jeffrey Williamson, *Global Migration and the World Economy: Two Centuries of Policy and Performance* (Cambridge, MA: MIT Press, 2005), 203–224.

31. Hatton and Williamson, *Global Migration and the World Economy*, 341–366.

32. For some examples of the role that black/white and black/nonblack distinctions have played in the stratification of the US migrant population, see Eduardo Bonilla-Silva, "We are all Americans!: The Latin Americanization of racial Stratification in the USA," *Race and Society* 5, no. 1 (2002): 3–16; Arlene Dávila, *Latino Spin: Public Image and the Whitewashing of Race* (New York: NYU Press,

2008); Joni Hersch, "Profiling the New Immigrant Worker: The Effects of Skin Color and Height," *Journal of Labor Economics* 26, no. 2 (2008): 345–386; Stacey Lee, *Unraveling the "Model Minority" Stereotype: Listening to Asian American Youth* (New York: Teachers College Press, 2015); Matthew Painter, Malcolm Holmes, and Jenna Bateman, "Skin Tone, Race/Ethnicity, and Wealth Inequality Among New Immigrants," *Social Forces* 94, no. 3 (2016): 1153–1185; Mary Waters, *Black Identities* (Cambridge, MA: Harvard University Press, 2009).

33. *Johnson*, 339 U.S. 763. The plaintiffs in this case were described as "nonresident enemy aliens," were captured in China by the United rights, because they had no status under US law (having never "entered") and had been apprehended and tried outside of the territorial jurisdiction of the United States.

34. See chapter 2 for a more detailed discussion of this history. Although the scholarship on US immigration has not devoted much of its attentions to antiblackness, it is well established that US immigration law and policy has been crafted with an eye for the "racial preferences" and enhancing the traditional "racial composition" of the US citizen population. Bill Ong Hing, *Defining America Through Immigration Policy* (Philadelphia: Temple University Press, 2004); Kanstroom, *Deportation Nation*; Mae Ngai, *Impossible Subjects: Illegal Aliens and the Making of Modern America* (Princeton, NJ: Princeton University Press, 2004).

35. *Chinese Exclusion Case*, 130 U.S. 581 (1889).

36. *Chinese Exclusion Act*, Pub.L. 47–126, 22 Stat. 58, Chap. 126 (1882).

37. *Chinese Exclusion Act*, Pub.L. 47–126, 22 Stat. 58, Chap. 126 (1882). See also *Chinese Exclusion Case*, 130 U.S. 581 at 597.

38. *Chinese Exclusion Case*, 130 U.S. 581 at 581–582.

39. *Chinese Exclusion Case* at 582.

40. *Chinese Exclusion Case* at 606.

41. *Chinese Exclusion Case* at 591–594.

42. *Chinese Exclusion Case* at 591.

43. Michel Foucault, *Society Must Be Defended: Lectures at the Collège de France, 1975–1976* (New York: Macmillan, 2003).

44. Siniša Malešević, *The Sociology of War and Violence* (London: Cambridge University Press, 2010), 28–49.

45. Foucault. *Society Must Be Defended*, 1–22 and 43–64.

46. *Fong Yue Ting v. US*, 149 U.S. 698 (1893).

47. *Fong Yue Ting*, 149 U.S. 698 at 699–705.

48. *Fong Yue Ting* at 699.

49. *Fong Yue Ting* at 729.

50. *Fong Yue Ting* at 755.

51. *Fong Yue Ting* at 698, 705–707, 708–709, 722, 730.

52. *Fong Yue Ting* at 728–729.

53. Ibid.

54. *Fong Yue Ting* at 730.

55. A recurring theme of the contemporary scholarship on this issue has to do with the way that immigrant criminality and downward mobility is racialized and is either directly or indirectly associated with blackness and with problems

associated with poor, black urban communities. For varied perspectives, see Tamara Nopper, "Why Black Immigrants Matter: Refocusing the Discussion on Racism and Immigration Enforcement," in *Keeping Out the Other: A Critical Introduction to Immigration Enforcement Today*, eds. David Brotherton and Philip Kretsedemas (New York: Columbia University Press, 2008), 204–240; Aihwa Ong, *Buddha is Hiding: Refugees, Citizenship, the New America* (Berkeley, CA: University of California Press, 2003); Herbert Gans, "Second-Generation Decline: Scenarios for the Economic and Ethnic futures of the Post-1965 American Immigrants," *Ethnic and Racial Studies* 15, no. 2 (1992): 173–192. Also see n32.

56. *Fong Yue Ting*, 149 U.S. 698 at 732–745.

57. *Fong Yue Ting* at 741–742.

58. *Fong Yue Ting* at 733. In this excerpt Sherman also compares the residency-check requirements to the policies used to control the mobility of Australian convict-laborers. Viewed in this light, he was not necessarily likening the treatment of Chinese immigrants to that of black slaves, but calling attention to a worrisome system of social control that "transcended" both race and slavery. In the next chapter, I advance a theory of (anti)blackness and criminality that accounts for these different facets of controlled mobility.

59. Kanstroom, *Deportation Nation*, 63–90.

60. *Fong Yue Ting*, 149 U.S. 698 at 743.

61. *Fong Yue Ting* at 746–749.

62. *Chinese Exclusion Case*, 130 U.S. 581 at 606.

63. As evidenced by the spread of Jim Crow laws, the use of lynchings to terrorize black populations, and the various forms of labor trafficking and early experiments in using criminal codes to track blacks into systems of forced labor. Edward Baptist, *The Half Has Never Been Told: Slavery and the Making of American Capitalism* (New York: Basic Books, 2016); Douglas Blackmon, *Slavery by Another Name: The Reenslavement of Black Americans from the Civil War to WWII* (New York: Anchor Books, 2008); Warren, *Ontological Terror*.

64. *Fong Yue Ting*, 149 U.S. 698 at 747–748.

65. As discussed in chapter 2. Also see Kanstroom, *Deportation Nation*, 24 and 33.

66. Also see Kanstroom, *Deportation Nation*, 85–86; Fred Kaplan. *Lincoln and the Abolitionists.* (New York: HarperCollins, 2017), 132–33.

67. For two examples, see David Cole, "Enemy Aliens." *Stanford Law Review* 54, no. 5 (2002): 953–1004; Kanstroom, *Deportation Nation*, 63.

68. *Plessy v. Ferguson*, 163 U.S. 537 (1896).

69. *Chinese Exclusion Case*, 130 U.S. 581 at 597.

70. Being repealed by the *Magnuson Act*, Pub.L. 47–126, 57 Stat. 600 (1943). For an overview, see Kenneth Holland, "A History of Chinese Immigration in the United States and Canada," *American Review of Canadian Studies* 37, no. 2 (2007): 150–160.

71. Some examples include *Knauff v. Shaughnessy*, 338 U.S. 537 (1950), which concerned the excludability of the German, alien wife of a German naturalized US citizen and former military officer; *Kaplan v. Tod*, 267 U.S. 228 (1925), which

concerned the excludability of the mentally disabled child of naturalized, US immigrant parents; *Delgadillo v. Carmichael*, 332 U.S. 388 (1947), which concerned the excludability of a Latin American resident alien with criminal convictions who was attempting to re-enter the United States; and *Kwong Hai Chew v. Colding*, 344 U.S. 590 (1953), which concerned the excludability of a resident Chinese alien, attempting to re-enter the United States.

72. For an example, see Hiroshi Motomura, "Immigration Law after a Century of Plenary Power: Phantom Constitutional Norms and Statutory Interpretation," *Yale Law Journal* 100, no. 3 (1990): 546–613.

73. *Pierre v. United States*, 547 F.2d 1281 (5th Cir. 1977). There may be cases that predate Pierre, since the unauthorized entry of Haitian refugees to the eastern seaboard of the United States has been dated to 1962, but Pierre is the earliest case, of its type, to be cited in the case history of the legal challenge to the Haitian program and the interdictions. A contemporary of Pierre is *Sannon v. United States*, 427 F. Supp. 1270 (S.D. Fla. 1977), which is distinguished for being the only case in which Haitian refugees attempted to challenge their status as excludable aliens. In *Pierre v. US*, Haitian refugees admitted their excludability but challenged the denial of parole, similar to the complaints raised in *Louis*, 544 F. Supp. 973 (under Judge Spellman) and the New York District Court cases that I discuss in this section (see n85).

74. The first federal court decision to significantly expand on the meaning of excludability, as it concerned Haitian refugees, was *Haitian Refugee Center, Inc. v. Gracey*, 600 F. Supp. 1396 (D.D.C. 1985), which argued that Haitian refugees occupied a category of excludability that ranked below even that of aliens who are put through exclusion hearings. I discuss this history of interdiction-era legal justifications in more depth in chapter 4.

75. *Leng May Ma v. Barber*, 357 U.S. 185 (1958).

76. *Knauff*, 338 U.S. 537, denied entry to a German alien on the grounds "confidential information, the disclosure of which, in his judgment, would endanger the public security," but which, judging from the context of the decision, had something to do with the petitioner's status as a former enemy alien (being a German citizen during the era of the Third Reich, though she did attempt to flee Germany after Hitler came to power). The excludable aliens in *Johnson*, 339 U.S. 763 were German military officers who had served in the German military during World War II. In other cases of this era, the concerns about the alien admissibility were tinged with security concerns about aliens hailing from Soviet bloc nations. *Paktorovics v. Murf*, 260 F.2d 610 (2nd Cir. 1958); *Shaughnessy v. Mezei*, 345 U.S. 206 (1953).

77. *Leng May May*, 357 U.S. 185 at 187. Though it bears noting that Ma was attempting to flee the Chinese Communist government, which at the time was under the chairmanship of Mao Zedong.

78. Ngai, *Impossible Subjects*, 202–225.

79. *Leng May Ma*, 357 U.S. 185 at 186–188.

80. Ma did not apply for asylum but her appeal was similar to that of many defensive asylum cases, in which petitioners request a stay of deportation (or withholding of removal) on the grounds of feared persecution. The majority opinion referenced this clause in the Immigration and Nationality Act (which was adopted in accordance

with the 1951 Refugee Convention) at the beginning of the decision, noting that "this is a habeas corpus case involving § 243(h) of the Immigration and Nationality Act, which authorizes the Attorney General to withhold deportation of any alien within the United States to any country in which in his opinion the alien would be subject to physical persecution." *Leng May Ma*, 1357 U.S. 185 at 85.

81. *Leng May Ma*, 188–190.

82. For some examples, see *Bertrand v. Sava*, 684 F.2d 204 (2d Cir. 1982) at 684; *Jean v. Nelson*, 727 F.2d 957 (11th Cir. 1984) at 727; *Sale v. Haitian Centers Council, Inc.*, 509 U.S. 155 (1993) at 156.

83. *Louis*, 544 F. Supp. 973; *Jean*, 727 F.2d 957; *HRC v. Civiletti*, 503 F. Supp. 442 (S.D. Fla. 1980).

84. *Louis*, 544 F. Supp. 973.

85. These cases include *Vigile v. Sava* 535 F. Supp. 1020 (S.D.N.Y. Mar. 5, 1982); *Bertrand v. Sava*, Nos. 81 Civ. 7371, 81 Civ. 7372 (S.D.N.Y. April 5, 1982); *Bertrand v. Sava*, 684 F.2d 204.

86. For *Vigile*, 535 F. Supp. 1020 and *Bertrand v. Sava*, Nos. 81 Civ. 7371, 81 Civ. 7372.

87. *Vigile*, 535 F. Supp. 1020 at 1007–1014.

88. *Vigile* at 1011.

89. *Vigile* at 1011–1012.

90. *Vigil* at 1012–1014.

91. Ibid.

92. *Vigile*, 535 F. Supp. 1002 at 1020.

93. See n23, 71, 76, 77 and 99.

94. *Bertrand v. Sava*, 684 F.2d 204 (2d Cir. 1982).

95. *Jean v. Nelson*. 727 F.2d 957, at 964.

96. *Bertrand*, 684 F.2d 204 at 213, citing *Vigile*, 535 F. Supp. 1002 at 1016.

97. *Bertrand*, 684 F.2d 204 at 212–214.

98. This argument is reminiscent of the Supreme Court's decision in *Jean v. Nelson*, 472 U.S. 846 (1985), which criticized the Eleventh Circuit for making a constitutional argument (supported by the Plenary Power doctrine) about the government's authority to exclude immigrants on racial grounds (or any other reason), while insisting that this authority was, nonetheless, legitimate—and then went on to argue that the government's Haitian Refugee policy was not actually discriminatory. This case is treated in more depth in chapter 2.

99. *Wong Wing Hang v. INS*, 360 F.2d 715 (2d Cir. 1966).

100. *Vigile*, 535 F. Supp. 1002 at 1007.

101. *Bertrand*, 684 F.2d 204 at 213, citing *Vigile*, 535 F. Supp. 1002 at 1016.

102. *Bertrand*, 684 F.2d 204 at 213–218.

103. These kinds of legal arguments are consistent with colorblind racism theory, which has explained how race-neutral and even, facially, antiracist language can be deployed in ways that perpetuate racial inequality. See Eduardo Bonilla-Silva and David Dietrich, "The Sweet Enchantment of Color-Blind Racism in Obamerica," *The Annals of the American Academy of Political and Social Science* 634, no. 1 (2011): 190–206. But whereas colorblind racism has been treated as a phenomenon that is

specific to the post-civil rights era, the history of federal court decisions show that these dynamics were alive and well in the antebellum and early postbellum era—as demonstrated by my reading of Plessy in chapter 2. Also see David Cole, *No Equal Justice* (New York: New Press, 1999), 78–194. According to Afropessimist theory, this process in which race and racism is "erased" by the law, is intrinsic to the way that antiblack animus has been reconciled to the law. Warren, *Ontological Terror*, 62–109.

104. For a sympathetic overview of this Kantian perspective on ethics and the law, see Joseph Carens, "Realistic and Idealistic Approaches to the Ethics of Migration," *The International Migration Review* 30, no. 1 (1996): 156–170; Nicholas Tampio, "Rawls and the Kantian Ethos," *Polity* 39, no. 1 (2007): 79–102; and for a critical assessment, see Bruno Latour, *We Have Never Been Modern* (Cambridge, MA: Harvard University Press, 1993).

105. *Wong Wing Hang*, 360 F.2d 715 at 715.

106. As described in *Louis*, 544 F. Supp. 973.

107. The only exception that Sava made was for pregnant Haitian women: *Vigile*, 535 F. Supp. 1002 at 1014–1018. Also see *Civiletti*, 503 F. Supp. 442 at 510–518.

108. *Vigile*, 535 F. Supp. 1002 at 1017–1018.

109. Thomas Jones, "*Haitian Refugee Center, Inc. v. James Baker, III*: The Dred Scott Case of Immigration Law," *Dickenson Journal of International Law* 11 (1992): 1; Harold Koh, "The Human Face of the Interdiction Program," *Virginia Journal of International Law* 33 (1993) 483; Jenna Loyd and Alison Mountz, "The Caribbean Roots of US Migration Policy," *NACLA Report on the Americas* 51, no. 1 (2019): 78–84; Hiroshi Motomura, "Haitian Asylum Seekers: Interdiction and Immigrant Rights," *Cornell International Law Journal* 26 (1993): 695; David Ralph, "Haitian Interdiction on the High Aeas," *Maryland Journal of International Law and Trade* 17 (1993) 227; Maria Luisa Sepulveda, "Barring Extraterritorial Protection for Haitian Refugees Interdicted on the High Seas: *Sale v. Haitian Centers Council, Inc.*," *Catholic U. Law Review* 44 (1994): 321; Cheryl Tompkin, "Criminal at the Gate: A Case for the Haitian Refugee," *Black Law Journal* 7 (1981): 387.

110. *Bertrand*, 684 F.2d 204 at 212–214.

111. *Vigile*, 535 F. Supp. 1002 at 1017–1018.

112. Ibid.

Chapter 4

Challenging the Interdictions

They were organizers before and they were fighting for democracy. And it was because of their organization that's why they end up at Guantanamo because the military was chasing them, because they were being beaten, their wives or children were being raped. They brought that skill with them in organizing the camp. They had a camp president, they had lieutenants, they had people who could come up with slogans. They feel militant, like hey listen I shouldn't be treated that way, I have my rights too as a human being.—*Ronald Aubourg, Guantanamo Public Memory Project*[1]

RONALD AUBOURG'S REFLECTIONS ON GUANTANAMO

Ronald Aubourg visited the US naval base at Guantanamo Bay, Cuba, several times in the early 1990s. He is one of the Haitian American professionals who provided language interpretation services for the Haitian refugees who were being held there by the US government. Aubourg had much to say about the squalid conditions of the camp.[2] He remembers how the refugees were left exposed to hurricane force winds. They were fed canned food that was past its expiration date. The base did not even provide cribs for the babies and after Aubourg and other camp workers complained about this, the refugees were only given cardboard for the babies to sleep on. But what most distinguishes Aubourg's reflections is not this litany of suffering. He also points out that many of the refugees were seasoned organizers who had experience creating grassroots resistance networks under the shadow of the Duvalier regime, and that they put these organizing skills to work in protesting conditions at the camp. Harold Koh, the attorney who argued several of the cases

147

that challenged the interdictions, has made similar observations about the advocacy networks that formed between refugees, legal counsel, and service workers.[3]

These accounts shine a light on the political savvy of the Haitian refugees which, in the official record, is usually buried under layers upon layers of legal argumentation. What we see in the court records are judicial interpretations of the arguments that have been made on the refugees behalf. What is less obvious, from perusing these records, is the determination of the refugees to get these cases heard by the US courts in the first place—underscoring Patricia Tuitt's observation about how the law is propelled by the "reluctant labor of repressed, subjugated individuals."[4]

Unfortunately, though, this is not a story of subjugated people prevailing against the odds and forcing the law to live up to its egalitarian principles. It is a story about how the US government successfully evaded the commitments it made to international refugee law, so it could pursue an enforcement operation that was even more exclusionary than the Haitian program of the late 1970s. Even so, it is important to keep in mind that federal officials would not have gone to these lengths were it not for the insistence of the refugees on demanding rights that the government refused to recognize. This stubborn insistence is summed up by Aubourg's interpretation of the refugees' plea, when he says, "I have my rights too as a human being." This simple statement can be read as a distillation of the refugees' political philosophy. It can also be read as an audacious challenge to the underlying premise of the interdiction policy: an assertion of rights by a rightless people. And if it is read in light of the histories of antiblack racism that I have traced in the prior chapters, this statement turns into a provocative and unsettling series of questions: "Who has the right to have rights?" "Who is included in the human family?" And whispering alongside these two questions there is a third, "Who is the law intended for?" Even though the Haitian refugees, and their allies, were not successful in changing the government's policies, they forced the US judicial system to make unprecedented arguments which invested these questions with a new relevance.

THE BEGINNINGS OF THE INTERDICTION ERA

The US government's interdiction program for Haitian refugees began a decade before Aubourg first stepped foot in Guantanamo Bay. On September 29, 1981, President Reagan issued Executive Order 12324,[5] which was drafted by the same immigration taskforce that helped craft the 1986 IRCA.[6] Like IRCA, the executive order was framed as a strategy for controlling "illegal immigration" but unlike IRCA, it contained no mechanisms for adjusting the legal status of the Haitian refugees who had been branded with the stigma of illegality.[7] It is also ironic that, two years earlier, President Carter endorsed a piece of legislation, with unanimous support from the Senate, that was intended to bring US law in closer alignment with international refugee law.[8] But this law was written for refugees and, as far as the government was concerned, it was an open question as to whether fleeing Haitians were authentic refugees.[9] There was nothing especially new about these discursive maneuverings. The government had been casting aspersions about the authenticity of Haitian asylum seekers since the days of the Haitian program, when it first began classifying them as "economic migrants."[10]

The newest thing about the interdictions was their exterritorial rationale, which made it possible for the executive office to enlist the US Coast Guard in a border enforcement operation that could be executed outside the legal jurisdiction of the United States. This operation was justified through reference to sections of the Immigration and Nationality Act that authorized the Coast Guard to enforce violations of US laws on the high seas.[11] INS officers were also stationed on Coast Guard cutters, for the purpose of assessing the asylum claims of all refugees intercepted at sea. After the legal challenge to the interdictions got underway, this asylum screening process became a point of contention, with the government and defenders of the interdicted Haitians arguing over whether these screenings were controlled by international refugee law.[12]

This debate became even more heated after the George Bush administration issued its Executive Order 12807 on May 24, 1992 (typically referred to as the "Kennebunkport Order").[13] The asylum screenings that had been authorized by the Reagan-era executive order were criticized for being a thinly veiled rationale for exclusion, considering that only eleven of 22,940 Haitians who were interdicted during the Reagan era were granted asylum.[14] The Kennebunkport Order went a step further and completely eliminated the asylum screenings.[15]

Several months before the Kennebunkport Order was issued Haitian president Jean Bertrand Aristide was ousted by a military coup.[16] Immediately after the coup, the US government halted its interdiction operations and paroled over 10,000 Haitians into the United States from the military base at Guantanamo Bay, Cuba.[17] The Kennebunkport Order ended this brief spell of granting Haitians access to the US immigration courts. So, beginning in May 1992, the United States begun returning tens of thousands of fleeing Haitians to a dictatorship that had recently ousted a democratically elected government by force of arms, without bothering to determine whether any of their fears of persecution were valid.

These actions were met with widespread criticism across the international community and sparked more protests on behalf of the Haitian refugees in the United States. In one of its statements on the interdictions, the UNHCR observed that the United States' treatment of Haitian refugees was not just unprecedented for US law and policy; it had no precedent in the entire history of modern refugee law.[18] According to Harold Koh, the government had created the equivalent of a "floating Berlin wall" around Haiti.[19]

Although the roster of foreign nationals who were apprehended by the United States' interdiction operations expanded steadily through the 1980s and 1990s, no other group was treated to such a repressive enforcement strategy.[20] The US government, for example, did not attempt to create a "floating Berlin wall" around the Dominican Republic (though it shared the same island as Haiti) or China or India or Cuba, though aliens from all of these nations appear in the government's interdiction statistics.[21]

This commitment, to treating Haitians in a categorically different way than all other refugees, was also reflected in the treatment of Haitians who were deemed to have credible asylum claims. Prior to the Kennebunkport Order, interdicted Haitians who were found to have a plausible fear of persecution were detained on the US naval base in Guantanamo Bay.[22] These were the refugees that Ronald Aubourg got to know through his work as an interpreter. One of these refugees was Estella Fleury. Her troubles in Haiti began with the death of her six-month-old son, who was killed by a stray bullet that she believes was fired from the gun of a Tonton Macoute who was terrorizing her neighborhood.[23] In the years that followed, Estella was brutalized on several occasions by people affiliated with the Macoutes, because of her support for pro-democracy forces. The worst of these beatings occurred in the fall of 1991, around the same time as the military coup against Aristide. At the time, Estella was three months pregnant with her second child. She fled Haiti immediately after this beating. Her boat was interdicted by the Coast Guard and when she was transferred to Guantanamo she spent eight days in the hospital to be treated for pregnancy complications that were connected to the attack. Luckily she was still able to give birth to a healthy baby girl and she was also, eventually, granted asylum and transferred to the US mainland.

One detail that is conspicuously absent from Estella's story is advice she may have received from legal counsel and this is because she, very likely, had no lawyer to help her.[24] According to court testimony, Haitians were the only refugee group at Guantanamo to be denied access to legal representation.[25] Refugees like Estella belonged to a small minority of fortunate ones who were spared the terror of repatriation, but they were still not treated as rights-bearing subjects.

The interdictions also began during the same period of time in which the HIV/AIDS epidemic was becoming a focal point of media attention, and Haitians figured prominently among the stigmatized minority groups who became associated with the HIV virus.[26] In 1987, the US Congress enacted a law that allowed the government to bar the entry of aliens with communicable diseases.[27] This law provided a rationale for denying medical care to interdicted

Haitians who were HIV positive, because they would have to be admitted to the US mainland to receive this care. Once again, Haitians were the only national origin group to be systematically denied entry to the United States on these grounds.[28] Meanwhile, on Guantanamo, the United States created the world's first camp just for HIV-positive detainees, which was also exclusively composed of interdicted Haitians.[29] This camp, like so many other aspects of the government's Haitian refugee policy, raised questions about the nature of the threat it was being used to contain. Was it the threat of communicable disease? Or was this public health concern being overdetermined by the fear of another kind of contamination that was rooted in a racist phobia of the black body?

These sorts of questions circle back to a point I have made in the prior chapters. The interdictions may have been unprecedented within the context of US immigration law, but they can also be understood as an eruption, within the law, of an antiblack animus that predates the history of the modern refugee. I develop this argument in the rest of the chapter, which is organized into three sections. The first section explains how the courts justified the legality of the interdictions in their early years, before the coup against the Aristide administration. The second section reviews the more contentious series of challenges that emerged after the 1991 coup and explains how the higher courts dealt with these challenges. The third section reviews the final series of federal court cases that deliberated on the interdictions, which addressed the treatment of HIV-positive Haitians at Guantanamo and the challenge to the legality of the Kennebunkport Executive Order.

In each of these sections I explain how legal arguments were used to put distance between the rightless predicament of the Haitian refugees and their blackness. For the judges that defended the government's position, it was important to frame this condition of rightlessness as a question of territorial jurisdiction which had nothing to do with race. The argument against the interdictions, on the other hand, exposed the contradictions of the government's position but without directing attention to the racist ontology that was operating through these territorial arguments. Even when the question of racial discrimination entered into the picture, it was reliant on legal arguments that could not acknowledge the ontological dilemma of black rightlessness. In the closing section of the chapter, I explore this problem in more depth by discussing Harold Koh's account of the legal challenge and its implications for refugee rights advocacy.

RATIONALIZING THE INTERDICTIONS: THE EXTERRITORIAL ARGUMENT

When the interdictions are understood as an exercise in radical exclusion, the relationship between the government's legal argument and its enforcement goals is easy enough to explain. The executive office wanted to prevent an unsolicited migration of black bodies from entering the United States and the legal argument for the interdictions was used to eliminate any barrier that stood in the way of the government's efforts to meet this goal. But taken at face value, these legal arguments were embarrassingly incoherent, because they placed the government in the awkward position of claiming that its actions did not violate international or constitutional law and that they operated in perfect continuity with its prior history of refugee law and policy.

For example, the government argued that it had the authority to enforce US laws outside of the territorial jurisdiction of the United States, but that interdicted Haitians had no due process rights, because US law did not apply outside the territorial jurisdiction of the United States.[30] The interdictions were also carried out under the mantle of an immigration control agenda which described Haitians as "illegal aliens" and not refugees.[31] Nevertheless, throughout the 1980s, the government adhered to a written policy of asylum screenings for Haitians interdicted on the high seas, while insisting, at the same time, that interdicted Haitians had no rights under international refugee law.[32] When legal advocates for the Haitian refugees pushed the government on this matter, it argued that the language in its interdiction protocols concerning the asylum interviews, which appeared to reference standards from international refugee law, was not legally binding and did not actually commit the government to honor any of these standards.[33]

The apparent absurdities of these arguments fade away if you give credence to the exterritorial rationale that informed them. This shift in the framing of the government's Haitian refugee policies became immediately apparent in the first pair of federal cases that contested the legality of the Reagan-era interdictions. Both of these cases, which were titled *Haitian Refugee Center vs. Gracey*, were decided by the District of Columbia federal court, between 1985 and 1987.[34]

Unlike the prior disputes over the Haitian program, no Haitian refugees were included in the plaintiff group, because they were being intercepted, detained, and repatriated miles away from the US mainland. As a result, the suit was led by a US-based Haitian-run, nonprofit that advocated on behalf of the refugees.[35] The complaints they raised established a template that was carried on by many of the later challenges to the interdiction program.

The Haitian Refugee Center (HRC) argued that the refugees had been unlawfully denied access to a great number of rights, including the rights articulated in the United Nations Conventions and Protocols (of which the United States was a cosigner), the procedural rights guaranteed by the United States' 1980 Refugee Act and the Immigration and Nationality Act, as well as due process rights, guaranteed by the Fifth Amendment to the Constitution.[36]

The legal challenges that the HRC raised against the Haitian program, a decade earlier, had begun with a strong show of support from the District Courts.[37] But in the Gracey cases, the District Court issued an unambiguous endorsement of the interdiction program. The tenor of the court's opinion is reflected in this closing statement from the first Gracey decision.

> The plaintiffs contend that "the Executive cannot free itself of its procedural obligations merely by reaching out to sea and changing the locale of its process."
> . . . However, *because the statutory obligations do not exist until an alien comes within the United States, plainly the Executive can avoid those obligations by interdicting the Haitians on the high seas.* As long as interdiction is within the power of the President, which it is . . . there can be no claim that it violates the statutory "rights" of aliens in other respects merely because it frustrates the efforts of the illegal aliens to reach the point where those rights attach. Until a person has a right, there can be no denial of that right. (Emphasis added)[38]

The court's argument in this decision relied on precedents set by prior cases that had affirmed the legality of the Haitian program, including the Eleventh Circuit Court's opinion in *Jean v. Nelson* and the Second Circuit Court's decision in *Bertrand v. Sava.*[39] But the court also made a point of explaining why interdicted Haitians were different from the excludable aliens who had been targeted by these programs.[40]

Even though excludable aliens have a fragile claim on the law they are at least entitled to an exclusion hearing which determines whether they will be granted entry to the United States. Most of the jurisprudence on excludability, from the post-war era through the late twentieth century, has centered on these kinds of cases, in which there is a dispute over whether an alien qualifies for admission to the United States which has to be settled by an exclusion hearing.[41] The 1950 Leng May Ma decision that I discussed in chapter 3 is a good example.[42] Another example is provided by *Landon v. Plasencia* (1982)[43] which was decided just a few months after the Reagan administration began the Haitian interdiction program. In this case, a Mexican noncitizen who had been legally residing in the United States for many years was charged, shortly after returning from a trip to Mexico, with attempting to smuggle several undocumented migrants into the country. One of the main questions raised in this case was whether her violation of US laws against smuggling changed the nature of her departure and put her in the category of an excludable alien rather than a returning resident. The important point, however, is that it was necessary for her to be put through an exclusion hearing before the immigration courts could make this determination.

The Gracey court, on the other hand, argued that interdicted Haitians belonged to a category of excludables who were not even entitled to an exclusion hearing.

The bitter irony is that Haitian refugees had always been treated as if they were on the lowest tier of the excludable alien category, going back to the Haitian program. In those days, the treatment of Haitian refugees was justified by arguments which insisted that Haitians were being treated no different than other excludable aliens (or at least that this treatment did not rise to the level of "invidious discrimination").[44] The Gracey court took an entirely different approach. Instead of turning a blind eye to the blatantly inequitable treatment of Haitian asylum seekers, it supplied a legal rationalization for this unequal treatment. Haitians could be categorically distinguished from other excludable aliens, not because they were black, or because they were Haitian but because they had been intercepted on the high seas.[45] The troubling ramifications of this argument became even more apparent in the District Court's second Gracey decision.

Both of the law suits against the US government that were evaluated by the Gracey decisions were filed by the HRC. In its first decision, the Gracey court acknowledged that the HRC had the right to issue a complaint on behalf of the interdicted refugees.[46] But in its second decision, the court argued that the HRC had no such right.[47] Once again, the court relied on the exterritorial nature of the interdictions to press its argument. It observed that the HRC could not claim interdicted refugees as part of its "client group" because they had not yet entered the United States, and thus were not yet apart of this constituency.[48] This decision dragged the rightlessness of the refugees down to a new low. It was not enough to argue that interdicted Haitians had no right to an exclusion hearing. The court also argued that legal advocates in the United States had no right to communicate with these refugees.

There was one qualified dissent issued at the end of the second Gracey decision, which took issue with the majority opinion.[49] The dissenting judge argued that the HRC clearly had legal standing to represent the interdicted refugees, as the court had agreed in its first decision. He also sympathized with the plight of the refugees and speculated that their claims of persecution could all be valid and compelling. Even so, this was his conclusion:

> This case presents a painfully common situation in which desperate people, convinced that they can no longer remain in their homeland, take desperate measures to escape. Although the human crisis is compelling, there is no solution to be found in a judicial remedy. The stark reality here is that, pursuant to the allegations of the amended complaint, this court is constrained to conclude that the HRC has not alleged a claim upon which relief can be granted.[50]

So despite appearing to sympathize with the refugees, the judge's overarching argument was in complete accord with the opinion advanced in the first Gracey decision. The Haitian Resource Center had a right to file a suit, but the suit was ultimately without merit. Haitian refugees may well have suffered persecution and excludable aliens may have very limited and precarious access to constitutional rights, but these matters were all beside the point. All of these possibilities would become relevant only if the refugees fell under the territorial jurisdiction of the US government, but interdicted Haitians were not "that kind" of excludable alien.

The "stark reality" to which the judge refers, in the quote above, is this exterritorial space. It could be described, paradoxically, as a territorially bounded exterritorial space. It lies outside of all legal jurisdictions but it can still be plotted on a map. Once you cross into this space, laws, ethical considerations, and any other obligation that might hold anywhere else in the world no longer applies, and there is nothing that any US judge can do about it. According to this judge's argument, even if the government openly admitted that it was targeting Haitians refugees for racist reasons, there would still be no grounds to pursue a claim, because the refugees have been apprehended in this nowhere land.

There is a quality to this dissent that recalls Saidiya Hartman's analysis of white abolitionist discourse. Hartman explains that the effort of white abolitionists to identify with the plight of the black slave only replicated the social distance between black and white, and affirmed whiteness as the only possible epistemic vantage point through which black pain could be rendered legible.[51] In a similar vein, the dissenting judge in the second Gracey decision expresses sympathy for Haitian refugees, but from the other side of an unbridgeable, moral and legal chasm. Whereas the abolitionist may have been unable to interrogate their own white, racial habitus, they were still making an effort to challenge the institution of slavery. In contrast, the dissent in the Gracey decision is complicit in crafting the legal architecture for the "stark reality" that it claims it is unable to change. Under the grips of this argument, one can acquiesce to the rightlessness of the refugees because of "where" they are and not "what" they are. But this way of seeing elides another stark reality: the question of "where" the Haitians were intercepted was overdetermined by the question of "what" they were. So, Haitians were the "wrong" kind of refugees in a double sense, as people who were apprehended outside of the territorial borders of the United States, and as members of a stigmatized, poor, black population—with the former kind of "wrongness" being latently informed by the latter.[52]

CHALLENGING THE INTERDICTIONS
AFTER THE 1991 COUP

In February 1991, Jean Bertrand Aristide became Haiti's first democratically elected president in recent history, taking over from the Duvalier regime which had been in power since 1957.[53] Within a matter of months, the Aristide administration was toppled by a coup, organized by military forces allied with the former Duvalier regime. Not surprisingly this event triggered a new mass flow of thousands of refugees from Haiti.[54] In the eyes of many US citizens and the international community, the plight of these refugees conformed, in every significant way, to the criteria for political persecution established by international refugee law.[55]

These events set the stage for a new series of legal challenges. The first of these challenges was conveyed by a December 1991 Florida District Court decision for *Haitian Refugee Center Inc. v. Baker.*[56] The complaints raised by the plaintiffs were similar to those raised in the Gracey decisions, but they made several improvements to their legal strategy. The HRC made connections with a group of interdicted refugees who joined them as plaintiffs in the case. Unlike Gracey, HRC was not filing suit on behalf of an "abstract"[57] group of refugees with which it had never interacted. The HRC also claimed that the interdiction operations were interfering with its own First Amendment rights, as a registered US nonprofit, to provide legal counsel to these refugees, many of whom were being detained at the US naval base in Guantanamo.[58] Ironically, the HRC was able to find support for this argument in the Eleventh Circuit's *Jean v. Nelson* decision, which had made a strong argument in favor of mandatory detention for Haitian asylum seekers.[59] As a result, the legal significance of this decision was dramatically transformed. Just a few years earlier, in the Gracey decisions, *Jean v. Nelson* was still being used to affirm the government's sovereign authority over immigration law.[60] But for *HRC v. Baker*, it was re-purposed as a decision that affirmed the First Amendment rights of legal service organizations and their clients to associate and communicate with each other.

The District Court judge, Carl Atkins, found the HRC's case persuasive, though he did not affirm all of its arguments. Atkins found that the interdicted refugees could not claim the protections of the 1980 Refugee Act and the Fifth Amendment.[61] He agreed with the HRC that the asylum screening procedures outlined by the Reagan-era executive order that established the interdiction program were misleading and contradicted the government's own argument—but that the refugees had no legal grounds to hold the government accountable for the confusion it created with this language.[62] Nevertheless, Atkins agreed with the plaintiffs that the interdictions did not free the United States of its obligation to the UN Convention on Refugees, especially Article 33, which stipulated that refugees cannot be delivered back into the hands of their persecutors (a.k.a. the nonrefoulement principle).[63] On this point, he emphasized that the refugees were not asking to be admitted to the United States. They were only asking not to be returned to a military regime that was persecuting supporters of a government that it had just violently overthrown.

Even if the refugees had no rights under US law, the US government was still obligated to respect this maxim of international refugee law.

Atkins's argument was an important intervention on the exclusionary commonsense that was being used to justify the interdictions. Even so, he never got to the point of questioning the antiblack sentiments that were woven through this commonsense. His argument, like that of many other critics of the government's policies, was organized around the idea that it was clearly wrong that Haitian refugees were being treated in such a different way from other refugee populations—and that this treatment was a clear violation of international refugee law. But the demand which follows from this argument—which insists that Haitians should be treated "just like other refugees"—declines to address the reasons why they are being treated so differently.

For example, Atkins was the first federal judge to make the important distinction between the question of admittance to the United States and the nonrefoulement principle. He pointed out that the US government could not call upon its sovereign powers over immigration (epitomized by the Plenary Power doctrine) to justify its actions.[64] Plenary Power only affirmed the government's authority to refuse admission—even for blatantly racist reasons— but it still did not give the government the right to return Haitian refugees into the hands of their persecutors. The practical problem with this argument, however, is that few other nations were willing to take the refugees in. Most nearby nations in the Caribbean and parts of Latin America followed the United States' example.

In the aftermath of the coup, an intergovernmental commission of Caribbean and Latin American nations was formed, which operated under the auspices of the UNHCR. Of the over 30,000 refugees that had fled Haiti, this commission only recognized 1,300 as qualifying for asylum under international law, and only granted asylum to thirty-five of them.[65] As the Haitian refugee crisis worsened throughout the 1990s the leaders of many nearby nations expressed an interest in repatriating large numbers of Haitians, including Jamaica, The Bahamas, the Turks and Caicos, Martinique, Guadeloupe, St. Martin and French Guiana, as well as the Dominican Republican which had been openly supportive of the military regime that toppled Aristide.[66] The combined total of Haitians that were repatriated by these nations in the mid-1990s is also on par with the number of Haitian Guantanamo detainees that were repatriated by the United States during the same period of time.[67]

On first glance, this pattern of exclusion decenters the significance of US racism, in explaining the handling of the crisis. Most of these nearby nations were black majority societies that were governed by a political class that was either mostly black or "multiracial" with a few prominent black public figures. From a pragmatic perspective, these nations did not have the resources or the infrastructure to manage a large influx of refugees and, at the time, they also were not in a position—or did not have an interest—in challenging the US government's handling of the crisis.[68]

The response of these Caribbean nations to the Haitian crisis underscores a point made by Black Studies scholars about the alienation of the black masses from the postcolonial and post-civil rights-era political class that, purportedly, represent them.[69] The institutional culture in which this political class is embedded is riven with the same antagonisms, and the same vexing questions about the relationship of blackness to the law, that characterize the US federal court system. These black and nonwhite elites preside over systems that perpetuate black marginality and black otherness in a disturbingly routine way.

As many scholars have argued, it is important to read a theory of race and racism into the structural inequalities that plague black populations, regardless of what the people, who sit on top of these structures, "look like." This uncompromising approach to the study of racial inequality can be used to explain the mechanisms of black incarceration in the Obama era,[70] the huge overrepresentation of black migrants in the caseload of criminal deportations during this same period of time[71] and, as it concerns this book, the reasons why Haitian refugees were turned away by so many Caribbean nations. The fact that so many nearby nations imitated the stance of the US underscores the transnational and world historical nature of the black predicament. Atkins's appeal to nonrefoulement, as a reasonable point of objection to the US government's insistence on its sovereign right to exclude failed to account for the scope of this problem. It is also important to note that Atkins's arguments, and the sympathetic decisions reached by other District Courts, fell on deaf ears when they made their way to the higher courts.

In his account of the legal challenge to the interdictions, Harold Koh explains that it is widely understood that there was little chance of winning these cases in the courts. The point of the legal challenges, according to Koh, was to win at least one or two cases. Even if these cases were overturned later on, the progressive norms and framing strategies that were generated by sympathetic decisions could be translated for other politics arenas—especially the public sphere and the Congress—to build support for a political solution that could be implemented by the president.[72] This is also why Koh insists that the main goal of legal advocates, for *HRC v. Baker*, was to keep the cause of the Haitian refugees alive until Bill Clinton assumed the Presidential office.[73] Koh's strategy was vindicated. But as I explain later on, this political victory did not address the problem of antiblack racism and had no significant impact on the government's reliance on interdictions as a strategy for managing Haitian refugee flows.[74]

All of these problems notwithstanding, Judge Atkins's decision for *HRC v. Baker* was still of great practical significance for Haitian refugees who were on the brink of being repatriated. Atkins issued a Temporary Restraining Order, which prevented the government from repatriating any of the refugees in the plaintiff group, and which also required the government to grant HRC access to the Haitian refugees being held at Guantanamo.[75] This decision was followed by a series of appeals that sent the case bouncing back and forth between the District Court and the appellate courts over a period of months and was finally ended by a ruling from the Supreme Court.[76]

Atkins's initial decision was immediately appealed by the government. Within a matter of days, the Eleventh Circuit Court issued a brief statement that remanded the case to the District Court with guidance on how to re-decide the case. The Eleventh Circuit did not agree that the UN Convention on Refugees applied to interdicted refugees, and though it did not challenge the First Amendment argument, it insisted that this argument did not justify the imposition of the restraining order.[77] The Eleventh Circuit claimed that the HRC's First Amendment argument only gave it access to provide legal counsel to the refugees, but it could not prevent the government from returning the refugees to Haiti.[78]

The response of the District Court to this ruling was to find a new way to justify the restraining order. Judge Atkins did this by rehabilitating an argument he had originally rejected, concerning the APA.[79] This APA argument had been used by Judge Spellman in *Louis v. Nelson*, to stall the repatriation of Haitian refugees under the Haitian program.[80] In that case, Spellman insisted that the government had not abided by its own policies and procedures in its handling of Haitian asylum claims and that, before it processed any more cases (and return any more Haitian refugees), it had to provide a more coherent explanation of these policies and procedures. For all practical purposes, this was a due process argument, but because it was focused on enforcing administrative standards it did not have to rely on an appeal to Fifth Amendment rights, which the courts agreed the refugees did not have.

For Atkins, the APA argument was more important as a means of distinguishing between the legitimate and illegitimate use of the government's discretionary authority. Similar to the jurisprudence on "invidious discrimination" that was used by Judge Carter in *Vigile v. Sava*,[81] this argument hinged on a distinction between the legitimate sovereign powers of the federal government and overreaching interpretations of these powers by lower-level government functionaries.[82]

Atkins's reappraisal of the APA argument forced the defenders of the Haitian refugees into a corner. This argument was used to, at least temporarily, stall the repatriation of Haitian refugees and lay the groundwork for the political strategy described by Koh. But it also continued a pattern whereby progressive currents of legal opinion shied away from questioning the sovereign powers of the government. All the APA argument allowed the refugees to do was to complain about the improper implementation of government policy, but not to question the content and goals of the policies themselves. As a result, racial discrimination could only be conceptualized as an abuse of power on the part of frontline workers, which had to be clearly distinguished from the government's legitimate authority to exclude aliens for any reason that it saw fit to do. The fact that the plaintiffs in *HRC v. Baker* did not even bother to raise a complaint about racism is a testament to how effective the courts were in establishing this argument.[83]

This silence operated on both sides of the legal deliberations. Judicial decisions that were sympathetic to the refugees paid lip service to the government's sovereign authority over immigration law. But as Hiroshi Motomura has explained, they attempted to maneuver around this authority by crafting phantom norms based on constitutional rights that were applied analogously to immigration law.[84] This strategy relied on subconstitutional arguments which usually focused on matters of procedural rights. The APA argument used by Judge Atkins in *HRC v. Baker* (like the argument used by Judge Spellman in *Louis v. Nelson*) was a variation on this phantom norm strategy. Atkins used a question of subconstitutional law (concerning the implementation of policies and statutes) to produce an effect that is roughly equivalent to that of a constitutional argument (over due process rights and equal protection). Motomura explains that on close inspection, there was no precedent in US immigration law for these arguments, and that they were all foreclosed by the Plenary Power doctrine.[85]

Meanwhile, the judges that supported the government's position also seemed reluctant to make the Plenary Power doctrine a centerpiece of their arguments, though they paid deference to it.[86] The exterritorial rationale for the interdictions provided a convenient way of evading this issue. Both sides could present their arguments about the territorial scope of US and international refugee law without directly referencing or confronting the Plenary Power doctrine. But as a result, the entire field of debate catered to a premise that had been introduced by the interdiction operations—which is that the rightfulness of the Haitian refugees hinged on how you interpreted the territorial scope of the law. On closer inspection, however, this territorial schema can be understood as a spatialized translation of antiblack sentiment. The sovereign desire that animated the interdictions was not fundamentally territorial, it was directed at preventing the entry of a "particularly undesirable" refugee population.

Arguments about the territorial scope of the law never got to the bottom of the sovereign desire that the interdictions had been designed to satisfy. As a consequence, they never attempted to question the institutional racism that had been authorized by the Plenary Power doctrine or the nihilistic morality of antiblack racism. The fact that these issues could not be directly broached in the courtroom is indicative of how well protected they were by legal precedent. These issues were the ghostly presence that explained the public outrage over the interdictions but, legally speaking, they were beside the point.

Thomas Jones has produced one of the few legal analyses of the interdictions that has engaged this repressed antiblack subtext.[87] Jones's discussion is organized around the premise that the arguments used in *HRC v. Baker* to justify the interdictions bear a striking resemblance to those of the *Dred Scott v. Sandford*[88] decision. He points out that, in both cases, there is a relationship between rightlessness and efforts to the control the mobility of black populations.

In *HRC v. Baker* (and in the earlier Gracey decisions) the federal courts constructed a new kind of excludable alien: the interdicted migrant. The rightlessness of this alien made it possible for the government to flout international refugee law and deliver them back into the hands of their persecutors. Similarly, in Dred Scott, the Supreme Court affirmed the legality of fugitive slave laws which mandated that escaped slaves be returned to their masters.[89]

The differences between the cases, however, are just as significant as their similarities. In Dred Scott the spatial organization of the racial order is described and supported by a discourse on black inferiority.[90] This decision is also significant for the argument it made about the exterritorial scope of black subjugation. In its opinion, the Supreme Court took issue with an earlier jurisprudence which insisted that slaves automatically became free on entering a jurisdiction that did not recognize the institution of slavery.[91] In this case, the sovereignty of state and local governments, which was typically championed by the slaveholding classes, became problematic.[92] To "fix" this problem, the Supreme Court argued that the rightlessness of the slave could not be modified by these localized bodies of law. The property claim of the master on the body of the slave was vaulted above all matters of territorial jurisdiction. The slave was always a slave, no matter where they happened to be, until such time that the master decided to forfeit their ownership and manumit the slave.[93]

But the courts took a very different approach when it came to the interdictions. They insisted that where people happen to be make all the difference when it comes to their rightfulness. Consequently, Haitian refugees were deemed to have no rights because they were apprehended outside of the territorial jurisdiction of US law. This kind of territorial reasoning is indicative of a shift in the public organization of the US racial order—which was already apparent in the Plessy decision. The constitutional amendments of the reconstruction era cemented race-neutrality and antidiscrimination into the normative foundations of US law.[94]

In this era it was no longer plausible to argue, as in Dred Scott, that black movement could be subsumed under a system of control that transcended territorial boundaries and be rationalized by a racist belief in the innate inferiority of black people. Instead, the spatial organization of the racial order was rationalized by a discourse that facially conforms to a "post-racist" public culture. One consequence of this change is that the regimen of black rightlessness becomes more reliant on territorial distinctions. Jim Crow segregation, for example, is premised on the idea that black and white self-interests were equally well served by a spatial order which ensured that both racial groups kept "to their own space."[95] The interdictions, on the other hand, are premised on the idea that all refugees (black or nonblack) had equal access to the same rights, so long as they were in the "right space" (within the territorial jurisdiction of the United States). So instead of affirming an exterritorial authority to control black bodies wherever they are located, a more sophisticated stratagem emerges that limits black rightlessness to certain "designated spaces" and then goes about maneuvering black bodies into these spaces. Viewed in this light, the leveraging of the high seas by the government's interdiction program is not very different from the way that mass incarceration, within the United States, has produced similar spaces of rightlessness for the black population.[96]

Jones's analysis of *HRC v. Baker* invites these sorts of comparisons between criminal law and immigration law, and between the antebellum and postbellum era.[97] He calls attention to tactics of control that are traceable to the institution of slavery and which are still being replicated by present-day enforcement practices. But this history was not referenced by any of the courtroom deliberations over the interdictions. Haitians were constructed as objects of administration for a body of immigration law that was positioned at a great distance from the antebellum era, from US criminal law or any other set of institutional arrangements that could center (anti)blackness as an explanatory framework for their predicament. To illustrate further, I will turn to the series of cases that challenged the interdiction operations of the Bush and Clinton administrations.

CHALLENGING THE INTERDICTIONS AFTER THE REES MEMO AND THE KENNEBUNKPORT ORDER

On February 24, 1992, the Supreme Court denied any further appeals of *HRC v. Baker*.[98] As a result, the Eleventh Circuit Court's decision, which was issued earlier that month, ended up becoming the last word on the subject.[99] The Eleventh Circuit's final decision concluded that the government had full authority to conduct the interdictions in the way that had been outlined by the Reagan administration executive order, and that Haitians who had been categorized as "economic migrants" had no choice but to accept repatriation to

Haiti.[100] According to the language of the interdiction protocol, these people had been "screened-out" by the INS officers who had been conducting asylum interviews on US Coast Guard cutters.

There was, however, a much smaller group of Haitians that INS officers had determined to be legitimate refugees. These people had been "screened-in" and were being detained at the US camp in Guantanamo. When the Supreme Court blocked any further appeals of *HRC v. Baker*, it did so with the understanding that the government would allow these screened-in Haitians to be treated like "regular" excludable aliens.[101] These Haitian refugees would be allowed to travel to the US mainland so they could be put through an exclusion hearing to evaluate the merits of their asylum claims.

But five days after the Supreme Court issued its decision, the INS issued new procedures for handling the asylum claims of the Haitians that had been screened-in. Instead of being transferred, automatically, to the US mainland, screened-in Haitians would be screened one more time, by INS officers stationed on Guantanamo. The guidelines for this re-screening process were outlined in a document that came to known as the Rees memo.[102] The memo directed INS officers to reevaluate the refugee status of people who had been "determined to have a communicable disease that is not curable."[103] Although Haitians were not mentioned directly in this memo, and "communicable disease" framed the government's concerns very broadly, the target population for these new procedures was HIV-positive Haitians.

The new screening process raised many concerns for the detained Haitian refugees. The Rees memo did not state that people who had been previously screened-in would be reclassified as "illegal aliens" just because they were HIV positive.[104] Even so, it appeared that HIV-positive status was a red flag that would lead INS officers to reevaluate the initial decision to classify them as refugees, the overarching goal being to prevent all HIV-positive Haitians from being paroled into the United States.

HIV-positive Haitians were held in a "humanitarian camp" designed only for Haitians.[105] Haitians were also the only detainee group to be medically tested for HIV, and whereas the government allowed other HIV-positive foreign nationals to enter the United States, it refused to allow entry to all HIV-positive Haitians.[106] Furthermore, the "re-screenings" that were conducted under the auspices of the Rees memo denied HIV-positive Haitians procedural rights that were guaranteed by the 1980 Refugee Act.[107] The Haitian detainees at Guantanamo also claimed that the re-screening process initiated by the Rees memo was not just focusing on HIV-positive Haitians and that all detainees, regardless of their HIV status, were being denied access to legal counsel.[108]

These complaints set the stage for a new legal challenge. This time, the legal challenge was led by the Haitian Centers Council (HCC) which filed a lawsuit in collaboration with many of the screened-in Haitians. The plaintiffs argued that the Rees memo contradicted the original protocol for processing interdicted refugees which the government said it would honor in its testimony before the Supreme Court.[109] Their complaints were evaluated by a New York District Court in *HCC v. McNary*.[110] The court's decision, which was delivered by Judge Sterling Johnson, was sympathetic to the refugees. He issued a restraining order that prevented the government from continuing the re-screenings until it had responded to all of the concerns raised by the plaintiffs.[111] This decision launched a series of appeals that led the case to be heard thirteen times by the appellate courts (including the Supreme Court) before coming to rest in June 1993.[112]

The case became more complex as it made its way to the higher courts. Several months after the first District Court decision, the Bush administration issued the Kennebunkport Executive Order.[113] As I explained at the beginning of the chapter, this executive order introduced a momentous change to the workings of the interdiction program. It eliminated the screening process that had been required by the original, Reagan-era executive order and mandated the Coast Guard to return all interdicted Haitians to the charge of the Haitian government. The "no-screen" procedures authorized by the order made it very clear that the US government was not concerned with the fate of the interdicted Haitians after they were returned to Haiti.

The language of the Kennebunkport Order also appeared to have been crafted with an eye for the legal challenges that had been raised by *HRC v. Baker*. Section 3 of the order stated that none of the procedures described by the order should be construed as creating a substantive or procedural right for any party, including any attempt to hold the government accountable for alleged violations of the Administrative Procedure Act.[114] This was not a new argument. It reiterated the position that the Eleventh Circuit had arrived at in its final decision on *HRC v. Baker*.[115] But this language also indicated that the government was both expecting a legal challenge and attempting to preemptively disqualify any argument that would be raised against the order.

The prohibitive intentions of Section 3 did not appear to have much effect. The legal challenge to the Kennebunkport Order ended up appealing to the very same substantive and procedural rights that had been referenced in Section 3. The charge of racial discrimination, which had been absent in *HRC v. Baker*, made its way back on the list of complaints, along with a more robust critique of the government's violation of international refugee law.[116] These arguments did not rely on the same kind of strategic sophistry that occurred in *HRC v. Baker*, in which sympathetic courts turned to administrative law as a substitute for legal protections that had been denied to the refugees due to the exterritorial nature of the interdictions. It appeared that the boldness of the government's actions had emboldened the defenders of the refugees to challenge the legality of the interdictions on more substantive grounds.

By the fall of 1992 the original complaint about the re-screening process authorized by the Rees memo was joined by a complaint about the Kennebunkport Order. The plaintiff group was now composed of (a) people who had been returned to Haiti after having been re-screened, (b) people who had been screened-in but were being indefinitely detained, (c) other Haitians being held on Guantanamo who were unscreened but who might have been screened-in before the Kennebunkport Order had taken effect, and (d) Haitians with credible asylum claims who had been returned to Haiti without being screened. Some court decisions addressed the complaints of all of these groups, while others focused on the complaints of a specific subgroup.[117]

The focal point of these complaints also evolved over time. For example, the challenge to the "no-screen" policy of the Kennebunkport Order and indefinite detention—which became important issues for the final decisions in this case history—began as a dispute over access to legal counsel.[118] There was also some overlap in the people who were included in the plaintiff groups that were making these complaints.[119] I will not attempt to trace the connections between all of these aspects of the legal challenge as they made their way through the courts. Instead, I am going to focus on how the courts tried to challenge or affirm the exterritorial rationale for the interdictions, and how the problem of black rightlessness was peripheral to this entire field of debate.

AN (EX)TERRITORIAL RATIONALE
FOR RADICAL EXCLUSION

The New York District Court decisions on *HCC v. McNary*, which had been mostly sympathetic to the Haitian plaintiffs, were appealed by the government to the higher courts.[120] In July 1992, the Second Circuit Court issued its decision on the case, which agreed with the District Court.[121] This decision signaled that the legal challenge over the Kennebunkport Order was going to be more contentious than the Reagan-era interdiction operations.

The Second Circuit is the same court that had the final word in the challenge to INS director Charles Sava's detention policies for Haitian refugees (see chapter 3). In that case, the Second Circuit found that the complaints of the detained Haitians were without merit and that the District Court was in the wrong for challenging the way that Sava had used his discretionary authority.[122] Even more significant, the court argued that Sava's discretionary authority was not controlled by the 1967 United Nations Protocol on refugees, because it was not a "self-executing" agreement.[123] The gist of this argument was that the protections of the Protocol had to be explicitly affirmed by constitutional law before they could take effect.

The position that the Second Circuit took in *HCC v. McNary* was very different. The court issued a robust challenge to the government's territorial rationalization for Haitian rightlessness. It insisted that the government was not exempted from its obligations to international refugee law just because it was intercepting Haitians on the high seas.[124] The court also observed that the US Congress had crafted legislation in the past which was used to regulate conduct on the high seas, which meant that the interdictions did not lie completely beyond the scope of US law.[125] The premise of this argument is similar to the "functional equivalent of the border" which legal scholars have used to explain how legal rights and jurisdictions can be applied to the high seas.[126] The court's position on this matter is summed up by its proposition that "only when the United States itself acts extraterritorially does [US law] have extraterritorial application."[127]

The court used this proposition to explain how US law could apply exterritorialy while being reasonably delimited. Because Haitians were being targeted by US enforcement practices, they should be afforded some modicum of due process and procedural rights. But this did not mean that noncitizens in any corner of the world could file suit for entry to the United States and enlist the protections of the US Constitution to support their case. The court went on to argue that the US government was violating a cornerstone of international refugee law which had no territorial limitation: the nonrefoulement principle described in Article 33 of the United Nations Convention on Refugees.[128]

The government, not surprisingly, had devised its own territorial interpretation of Article 33, which claimed that the article only prohibited the return of refugees who had entered the territory of the receiving nation. According to this argument, Haitian refugees were not really being returned because they had not yet entered the United States. In making this argument, the government insisted that the French word "refouler" had acquired a specific territorial meaning, in the context of the United Nations deliberations, which is not captured by the English word "return."[129]

The Second Circuit Court challenged this argument. It insisted that the meaning of nonrefoulement did not hinge on where the refugee was being removed-from, but where they were being removed-to.[130] The court also noted that the 1980 Refugee Act included language that clearly forbade the attorney general from violating the nonrefoulement principle, and that the Congress had revised this language to emphasize that it did not just apply to refugees who were physically present in the United States.[131] One implication of this argument is that the nonrefoulement principle had been executed, within US law by the 1980 Refugee Act.

The Second Circuit went on to argue that the law defines its own territorial configuration. To properly interpret the territorial scope of the law, one has to decipher the intentions of the law and how these intentions align with established legal precedent. This is why the Second Circuit could argue, as it did in *Bertrand v. Sava*, that there were articles of the UN Protocol on refugee rights that did not apply to refugees on who were present on US soil and also why it could argue, in *HCC v. McNary*, that Article 33 on nonrefoulement could apply to refugees who were interdicted on the high seas. This distinction was not guided by a hard and fast interpretation of the territorial scope of the law, which treats territorial jurisdiction as a construct that exists independently of the law. Instead, the determining factor has to do with the way that aspects of international law are executed within US law.

Sava, for example, implemented his policy of mandatory detention before the passing of the 1980 Refugee Act. At that time, according to the Second Circuit, the UN Protocol had not been fully executed within US law and it was also not clear that Sava's policy violated any of its articles. In contrast, the violations of Article 33 that were alleged in *HCC v. McNary* had occurred long after the UN Protocol had been executed in US law, and there was no ambiguity about the US government's violation of this article. The Second Circuit also decided that the language used by the 1980 Refugee Act did not limit Article 33's application to refugees within the territorial jurisdiction of the United States, so it followed that the nonrefoulement principle applied exterritorialy.[132]

The interpretation I have just provided focuses on continuities in the reasoning used by the Second Circuit in *Bertrand v. Sava* and *HCC v. McNary*. But this appearance of continuity melts away if you focus on the final outcome for both cases.

Keeping the above in mind, here is a different reading of the Second Circuit Court's decisions. When the court argued in *Bertrand v. Sava* that Haitian refugees who were within the legal jurisdiction of the United States had no grounds to appeal to international refugee law, this decision was allowed to stand by the higher courts.[133] But when the Second Circuit argued that interdicted Haitians were protected by the nonrefoulement principle from Article 33 of the UN Protocol, this argument was eventually overturned by the Supreme Court[134] (to be discussed shortly). The reason the Supreme Court gave for overturning the Second Circuit's decision in McNary was a very familiar one—that the law, which includes both national and international law, does not apply to the high seas.[135] But the Haitian refugees who challenged Sava's parole decisions were being held in detention centers on the US mainland and not on the high seas, these refugees were still denied access to international law, and the government saw no reason to contest the Second Circuit's decision in this case.

If you view the outcome of both cases from the vantage point of black rightlessness a very simple and brutal set of imperatives comes into view. Haitian refugees were going to be maneuvered into a condition of rightlessness whether they were intercepted at sea or being held on the US mainland. Regardless of where they were located, the government was prepared to deny Haitian refugees access to whatever aspects of international or national law it needed to deny them access to in order to prevent their entry to the United States.

There were also some glaring contradictions in the government's (ex)territorial argument, which I referenced at the beginning of this chapter. The Second Circuit Court picked on these contradictions when it wryly noted that "according to the government, the Haitians are somehow violating the [Immigration and Nationality Act's] prohibition on illegal entry while afloat on the international waters of the Windward Passage."[136]

The court used this observation to underscore the point that *HCC v. McNary* was not about the government's sovereign right to secure its borders. The court did not take this argument any further, but it begs the question of why the US government could evoke a sovereign authority without territorial limits, meanwhile fleeing Haitians were only allowed rights that operated within narrow, territorial limits (and which could never be accessed when they were needed most). If you strip away the territorial gloss from these arguments you are left with an authority whose power is unconstrained by the law, and bodies that are exposed to the force of the law but which have no rights under the law. This situation recalls Agamben's explanation of the absolute power that the sovereign wields over bare life.[137] Afropessimist scholars have evoked this same power dynamic in their account of the racist ontology that spans the era of antebellum slavery and the present day.[138]

The Second Circuit Court, on the other hand, produced an argument that was just as mute in the face of this power dynamic as the government's rationale for the interdictions. The court was able to poke holes in the government's position, but it still took the territorial premise of the government's argument at face value. As a result, it spent its energies on explaining why the government's territorial interpretation of the law was baseless. But it was not prepared to see that the territorial rationale for the Kennebunkport-era interdictions (of which it was very critical) was a logical extension of the same desire-to-exclude that it had tolerated, years earlier, from Sava.

Not surprisingly, the court did not have a serious analysis of antiblack racism as an engrained feature of US politics which relies on power practices that have been historically enabled by the law. This is the kind of analysis that is suggested by Jones's discussion of *HRC v. Baker* and has been stated more forcefully by scholars such as Calvin Warren, Saidiya Hartman, Dorothy Roberts, and Derrick Bell.[139] From this perspective, antiblack racism can be understood as a collective and institutional process that helps to explain the law. The Second Circuit, on the other hand, remained stuck in a paradigm that treated racism as a matter of individual bias.[140] As a result, it kept on pointing out contradictions in the government's argument, without being able to produce a coherent explanation of the exclusionary sentiments that lay behind them.

The Second Circuit's attempt to reign in the government's sovereign authority ultimately failed. But it is important not to lose sight of the fact that the Second Circuit's decision for *HCC v. McNary* was an unprecedented show of support for the interdicted Haitians. For the first time in the history of the US government's Haitian refugee policy, an appellate court had reviewed a lower court decision that had been sympathetic to the refugees and produced an even stronger argument on their behalf. This intervention had a major impact on the way the District Court ruled on the case.

When Judge Johnson, of the New York District Court, first decided *HCC v. McNary*, he found that interdicted refugees could not appeal to the protections against nonrefoulement that were included in the 1980 Refugee Act.[141] Although Johnson issued a restraining order against the government, and expressed his deep misgivings about the interdictions, he deferred to the Eleventh Circuit Court's argument about the territorial limits of constitutional law which had been established in the litigation of *HRC v. Baker*.[142] A few weeks later, Johnson issued a second decision on this case that dealt specifically with the complaints of HIV-positive Haitians who were being denied legal counsel at Guantanamo.[143] In this decision Johnson argued, regretfully, that the due process clause of the Fifth Amendment did not apply to interdicted Haitians, though he did also argue that the HCC had a First Amendment right to give legal counsel to the refugees, and imposed an order that temporarily stopped the government against re-screening or repatriating refugees, regardless of HIV status that had already been "screened-in."[144] Later that summer, Judge Johnson issued a memorandum that dealt with the applicability of Article 33 (on nonrefoulement) from the UN Convention on Refugees and took a similar position. He called Article 33 "a cruel hoax and not worth the paper it was written on" but ceded that his hands were tied.[145]

Johnson's choice of words resonates with a long history of black rightlessness; they are evocative of the language that Calvin Warren cites from the *African Repository* which describes the "freedom" of emancipated blacks in the 1850s as a "cruel mockery." The author of this passage goes on to observe that "in some respects [free blacks] are even worse off than the slaves."[146] Warren uses this bleak observation to call attention to a condition of abject rightlessness that cannot be corrected by the law. It is a condition that is overdetermined by a structure of social relations and a social ontology which ensures that black bodies are unable to make use of their rights, even after they are granted.

The exterritorial rationale for the interdictions produced a similar outcome, by converting the nonrefoulement principle into a "cruel hoax" for Haitian refugees. By insisting that international refugee law operates within territorial limits, it was possible to advance an argument that paid lip service to the universality (and race-neutrality) of the law, while delimiting these universal rights in a way that specifically excluded black, Haitian bodies. Judge Johnson pushed back against this argument, but like so many sympathetic judges before him, he did not know how to go about exposing the problem of black rightlessness.

The Second Circuit's final decision for *HCC v. McNary*[147] gave Judge Johnson a much stronger ground for using constitutional law to decide the case. When Johnson issued his next decision on the case in November 1992, he did so by citing the 1980 Refugee Act, Article 33 of the UN Convention on Refugees as well as the due process clause of the Fifth Amendment.[148] He found the interdiction operations to be in violation of all of these laws, holding that the INS officers had abused their discretion in arbitrary and capricious ways, that the Coast Guard had clearly violated the nonrefoulement principle, and that the government had "created a separate and unequal asylum track for Haitians only."[149]

This was a remarkable outcome which strengthened the rights of all segments of the plaintiff group, including screened-in Haitians at Guantanamo (including those who were HIV positive) and Haitians who had been targeted by the no-screen procedures of the Kennebunkport Order. Perhaps the most remarkable thing about this outcome is that Johnson applied rights arguments that had been unable to survive the review of appellate courts in the days of the Haitian program. Judge King's endorsement of the Fifth and Fourteenth Amendment rights of Haitian refugees (from *HRC v. Civiletti*) was watered down considerably by the Fifth Circuit on final review.[150] Judge Spellman did not even bother appealing to constitutional law in *Jean v. Nelson* (opting instead for an APA argument).[151] Meanwhile, in *Bertrand v. Sava* the Second Circuit eviscerated the sympathetic decision that the plaintiffs in the Sava cases originally received from the District Court.[152]

This high point in the legal advocacy for Haitian refugees did not last long. The government appealed the decision and most of the progressive precedents established by Judge Johnson and the Second Circuit's decision were overturned several months later when the Supreme Court heard the case, which was now named *Sale v. HCC*.[153] It also bears noting that Judge Johnson issued his final decision for *HCC v. McNary* on November 12, several days after Bill Clinton's victory in the 1992 Presidential election.[154]

On the campaign trail Clinton had appealed to public outrage over the treatment of Haitian refugees and had publicly praised the Second Circuit

Court's decision on *HCC v. McNary*.[155] So when Judge Johnson issued his decision, he may have assumed that the days of the interdiction program were numbered. But before assuming office, Clinton reversed his position.[156] The opinion delivered by the Supreme Court in *HCC v. Sale* was in line with Clinton's new stance on interdictions. For the Supreme Court, of course, this was not a new position. Its decision was consistent with its unwavering support for the government's Haitian refugee policies, dating to the days of the Haitian program.

The Supreme Court's argument in *HCC v. Sale* was a faithful recitation of the position the government had taken throughout the case history of *HCC v. McNary*.[157] In the Second Circuit decision, almost a year earlier, these arguments were raised by a lone dissenting judge.[158] In *HCC v. Sale*, they were the majority opinion. All of these arguments relied on territorial reasoning that could be traced to the Gracey decisions.

The Supreme Court reintroduced the government's argument about the territorially delimited meaning of "refouler" that had been dismissed by the Second Circuit. Supreme Court justices provided more detail on the original deliberations over Article 33 in UN Convention, using the statements of the delegate from the Netherlands to support their interpretation.[159] They produced a similar interpretation of the language on nonrefoulement in the 1980 Refugee Act, claiming that—despite appearances—this language only applied to refugees who were under the legal jurisdiction of the United States.[160] According to this argument, it was irrelevant whether or not the UN Conventions were self-executing or whether they had been "already executed" by US law. The key point was that the territorial scope of nonrefoulement did not include the high seas. The court also argued that the repatriation of Haitian refugees, being carried out by the interdictions, did not fall under the direct authority of the attorney general in any case (since the attorney general is the government official who is held accountable to the nonrefoulement principle in the 1980 Refugee Act). It observed that the interdictions were carried out by the Coast Guard, and that the Coast Guard's authority to enforce US laws exterritorialy was not controlled by the attorney general.[161]

In his dissenting opinion, Justice Blackmun famously observed that the government's argument "rested on three implausible assertions: that 'the word "return" does not mean return . . . [that] the opposite of "within the United States" is not outside the United States, and . . . [that] the official charged with controlling immigration has no role in enforcing an order to control immigration.'"[162] Justice Blackmun's legal clerk summed things up even more succinctly, noting that, "The longer I work on this case, the more convinced I become that the Government's . . . argument may not even pass the 'straight face test.'"[163]

But criticism or ridicule of the government's position does not substitute for an explanation. The Second Circuit Court did not express its dismay as baldly as Justice Blackmun, but it followed the same cue when it decided *HCC v. McNary*, by repeatedly calling attention to the incoherency of the government's argument.[164] As I have argued, on the other hand, the government's actions only appeared incoherent because it relied on a racist ontology which could not be openly expressed within the law. As a result, it used legal arguments, which operated on the premise that black rightlessness did not exist, to rationalize tactics that had been used for centuries to control the movements of black bodies.

The territorial rationale for the interdictions helped to smooth over these contradictions—by creating a space that was exempt from the rule of law, which made it possible to transform the problem of blackness rightlessness into a question of administrative jurisdiction. This rationale for exclusion also produced some counterintuitive outcomes which provide some telling insights into the racist subtext of its guiding imperatives.

For example, if the government's argument is taken at face value, there should have been a difference in the rights granted to Haitians who were processed through the Haitian program compared to the Haitians who were targeted by the interdictions. The former group was composed of "regular" excludable aliens who were present on the US mainland and who fell under the jurisdiction of US law. Although their access to constitutional law was very marginal, according to the Gracey decisions, they were still in a categorically better position than Haitians who were intercepted on the high seas. The Eleventh Circuit Court that affirmed the legality of the Haitian program also acknowledged that these excludable aliens had a First Amendment right to legal counsel.[165]

But none of the rights that were attributed to the refugees who were put through the Haitian program translated into protections that made any significant difference in the outcome of their asylum claims. The overwhelming majority of asylum seekers who were processed through the Haitian program were returned to Haiti.[166] So although these refugees were categorically distinguished from interdictees, for the purpose of the government's argument, there was no practical difference in the rightlessness of both groups. Haitian program refugees were denied the protections of the UN Protocol on refugee rights, denied the protections of the Fifth and Fourteenth Amendment, as well as the 1980 Refugee Act.[167] Interdicted refugees were also routinely denied these protections.

There is, however, one important exception. Judge Johnson's final decision in *HCC v. McNary* (with help from the Second Circuit Court) resuscitated most of these rights arguments on behalf of interdicted Haitians.[168] Although this was a welcome decision, it underscores the arbitrary nature of the distinctions that were made between the rightlessness of both groups. This arbitrariness was further underscored by Judge Johnson's decision in *HCC v. Sale*.[169]

Johnson issued this decision approximately two weeks before the Supreme Court decided *Sale. v. HCC*.[170] This decision was made in the same spirit as Johnson's final decision in *HCC v. McNary*. The Supreme Court decision in *Sale v. HCC* was focused on Haitians who had been interdicted at sea under the no-screen policy established by the Kennebunkport Order.[171] Johnson's decision on *HCC v. Sale*, on the other hand, was concerned with HIV-positive Haitian detainees who had been screened-in (before the issuance of the Kennebunkport Order) and were being held at Guantanamo.[172] These Haitians belonged to the plaintiff group that had originally challenged the Rees memo in the early phase of the deliberations over *HCC v. McNary*.

The core issues of contention in this case took the legal battle, full circle, back to *Bertrand v. Sava*, from the days of the Haitian program in the late 1970s and early 1980s.[173] The plaintiffs were asking the government to grant them access to legal counsel and parole them to the US mainland, where they could wait until the immigration courts decided the fate of their asylum claims.[174] Their medical condition added to the poignancy of their demands, since access to the US mainland would also give them access to health care services that were unavailable on Guantanamo.[175] The demand for dignified treatment and human rights that was burning at the heart of these complaints was not lost on Judge Johnson. His decision for *HCC v. Sale* was a radical about-face from his April 1992 decision for *HCC v. McNary*,[176] when he expounded on the "cruel hoax" of international refugee law and denied the requests of the HIV-positive Haitian detainees.

Johnson's argument in *HCC v. Sale* was presaged by a long list of injustices suffered by the plaintiffs.[177] The US government's practice of testing refugees for the HIV virus had exclusively focused on Haitians. Its ban on allowing HIV-positive noncitizens to enter the United States had, also, been exclusively enforced for Haitians. The open-air camp in which HIV-positive Haitians had been sequestered was squalid, surrounded by barbed wire and regularly subjected to military sweeps. To sum up the government's attitude toward the detained Haitians, Johnson used the words of an INS representative to the director of Congressional and Public Affairs, who had reportedly said, "They're going to die anyway aren't they?"[178]

Johnson concluded by ruling that the US naval base at Guantanamo was not exempt from US Constitutional law and that the Rees memo, that had denied the HIV-positive detainees access to an exclusionary hearing, was unlawful.[179] He ordered that all of the plaintiffs be paroled to the US mainland where they could receive appropriate medical care and be allowed to state their asylum claims before the immigration courts.[180] Unlike all of the prior District Court rulings that had challenged the parole decisions of the INS, Johnson's decision was not overturned by a higher court. It was the only unequivocal victory in the history of the legal challenge to the interdictions.

The HIV-positive detainees whose cause Johnson had championed included single and married adults, pregnant mothers, and children. They had all received what is, possibly, the most dehumanizing treatment of any of the Haitian interdictees. But Johnson's decision begs a very important question. His decision was allowed to stand. Meanwhile, on the same day that the plaintiffs from Johnson's case were released from Guantanamo, the Supreme Court issued its decision for *HCC v. Sale*, which justified the repatriation of the vast majority of interdicted Haitians to an oppressive government.[181] Why? And why were the refugees who had contested the parole practices of the Haitian program years earlier—who were supposed to have a stronger claim on the law—treated with much less consideration? None of these refugees, who had filed suit in the Nelson or Sava cases, were successful in getting the INS to change its practice of mandatory detention for Haitians. So how were the most stigmatized group of Haitian refugees able to prevail where all others had failed?

PROGRESSIVE LEGAL STRATEGY AND THE PERSISTING PROBLEM OF BLACK RIGHTLESSNESS

Harold Koh has provided many important insights into the backstory for the unlikely outcome that I have just described. Koh explains that HIV-positive Guantanamo detainees fared better than the "boat people" who were trying to avoid repatriation, because the detainees had more opportunity to build relationships with US citizen supporters (despite the denial of legal counsel), which contributed to the strength of their case.[182]

These reflections recall the interview excerpt from Ronald Aubourg that I used to open this chapter; they underscore the agency and political savvy of the refugees. But Koh goes on to explain how the fate of the refugees was ultimately determined by networks of political authority that were concentrated in the US government.

Koh observes that, prior to Judge Johnson's momentous decision, President Clinton had been facing mounting pressure from the Congressional Black Caucus on the treatment of interdicted Haitians at Guantanamo—and especially those being held in the "HIV camp." During this same time, Clinton had decided to withdraw his nomination for Lani Guinier, a prominent critical race theorist and black feminist legal scholar, for the position of assistant attorney general of the Civil Rights Division. Clinton met with members of the CBC shortly after he made this decision and after Judge Johnson decided *HCC v. Sale*. At this meeting Clinton was urged to support Johnson's ruling. Koh speculates that Clinton probably followed their guidance because he did not want to risk alienating the CBC any further, given his recent decision about Guinier.

Koh also notes that the federal courts tended to look for cues from the president's office, especially when it came to making decisions on Haitian refugee policy.[183] Johnson's decision for *Sale v. HCC*, for example, could have been appealed by the government all the way to the Supreme Court, which would have very likely decided to deny the parole that was requested by the HIV-positive Haitian detainees. So the practical impact of Johnson's decision was heavily reliant on how President Clinton chose to use his discretionary authority. Koh uses this analysis to explain the political context for the Supreme Court's decision in *Sale v. HCC*.

> Once the Clinton administration played the "presidential card" before the Supreme Court, adopting the Bush policy as well as its briefs, the handwriting was on the wall. After President Clinton changed his position, Justices Kennedy, O'Connor, Souter, and Stevens-the potential swing votes- were left to wonder, "If two presidents can live with refoulement (including one who had once condemned it), why can't we?"[184]

Koh uses this context to explain why such a large majority of Supreme Court justices were prepared to support the US government's flagrant violation of the nonrefoulement principle. He also points out that the Congress failed to act for similar reasons, which were reinforced by the unfortunate timing of the Haitian exodus, during an economic recession.[185] In this same reflection, Koh contrasts Haitians to Cuban and Russian asylum seekers "who enjoy significant legislative support." Here, and elsewhere in his analysis, Koh acknowledges the salience of race, observing that "black, poor Haitians afflicted with the HIV virus constitute the archetypal 'discrete and insular minority,' for whom such support was not forthcoming."[186] Even so, Koh offers no analysis of the antiblack racism that could be driving this Haitian-specific animus.

This aporia in Koh's reasoning offers yet another example of the awkward silences that inhibit the analysis of black rightlessness. Even in the most insightful and well-meaning accounts, one can run up against these silences. As I noted at the beginning of this chapter, Haitians were not excluded just because they were refugees. They were excluded because they were something other than refugees, in the eyes of the government. Koh acknowledges this racist subtext as well, but he does not use it as the starting point for an analysis of antiblack racism as an institutionalized feature of the law. If it is understood, as I argued in chapter 2, that US immigration law evolved as a nonblack institution, then it follows that there is an inherent tension between blackness and the idea of the noncitizen—whether immigrant or refugee. This tension is a reflection of the ontological crisis that Warren has exposed through the paradigm of the "free black."[187]

Warren explains that the legal transition produced by emancipation does not alter the structural position that blackness has been assigned by a racist ontology that relegates blackness to nothingness.[188] Consequently, the problem of blackness and the violence of antiblackness are reorganized by emancipation without being fundamentally transformed. Legal distinctions between deportables and excludables and between excludable aliens and interdicted aliens produce a similar confusion as the promise of emancipation. These distinctions describe a political field in which legal status determines rightfulness, independent of any other social status.

The excludable Haitian who is present on the US mainland should be in a better position than the interdicted Haitian, just as the antebellum emancipated black (and the postbellum black citizen) should be "more free" than the slave. But as I noted above, the practical outcomes of the legal challenge to the interdictions complicate these tidy distinctions. Some of the Haitians who were targeted by the interdictions became the beneficiaries of rights that were routinely denied to Haitians asylum seekers in the years of the Haitian program. And for the vast majority of Haitian refugees, the Haitian program and the interdictions produced the same effect—compulsory repatriation to Haiti.

So how does one explain these disparities and continuities? My answer is that the radical exclusion that was being produced by the government's Haitian refugee policies was not strictly determined by legal status, but by racist sensibilities that overdetermined the interpretation of legal status. In a similar vein, the decision of Judge Johnson to "free" over 300 HIV-positive Haitians from the detention camps at Guantanamo was an important legal victory that did not fundamentally change the social ontology that informed the interdictions. Like the manumission of the antebellum slave, Johnson's decision exempted the Guantanamo detainees from a dehumanizing condition that was still being suffered by a much larger population.

Johnson insisted that the naval base at Guantanamo fell under the jurisdiction of US law and of the government.[189] Citing the Second Circuit decision for *HCC v. McNary*, he observed that "interdicted Haitians are not 'some undefined, limitless class of noncitizens who are beyond our territory,' they are instead an identifiable group of people who were interdicted by Americans in international waters pursuant to a binding agreement between the United States of America and Haiti, and who have been detained on territory that is subject to the exclusive control of the United States."[190]

Johnson used this argument to protect a group of Guantanamo detainees who had been "screened-in" by the INS officers prior to the issuance of the Kennebunkport Order. But his argument about the reach of the law could just as easily have been applied to the tens of thousands of Haitian refugees who were returned to Haiti with no screening process whatsoever, after the issuance of this same executive order. And although the dire health condition of the HIV-positive detainees made their case deserving of special humanitarian consideration, the Haitian refugees in this group had the benefit of being screened-in before the asylum interview process had been terminated by the Kennebunkport Order. There were, undoubtedly, many other HIV-positive Haitians with plausible asylum claims who had been returned to Haiti after the order's no-screen protocol took effect.

The difference between the few hundred plaintiffs who benefited from Judge Johnson's decision and the tens of thousands who were excluded by the Supreme Court's decision was, on its face, a matter of administrative discretion and jurisdiction. It was a matter of the screening practices being used by the INS, at a given point in time, which had constituted each plaintiff group. It was also a matter of how the legal jurisdiction of US law had been defined by the deciding judge. Perhaps most important, it was a matter of which court got to have the final say on which case.

These matters of administrative jurisdiction explain why some Haitians were spared from the worst outcomes of the interdictions but they also distract attention from antiblackness as the overarching and constant imperative that had been animating US Haitian refugee policy since its earliest days. Legal deliberations over the government's Haitian refugee policies were used to determine how a condition of radical exclusion would be distributed across a black population—but not to question the "necessity" for the exclusion, and the antiblackness informing this necessity.

Even the most progressive decisions participated in this aphasia, which treated the interdictions as a problem of legal interpretation rather than as an interdiction on blackness. Reduced to a legal argument and government policy, the interdictions could be remedied by judicial decisions. But if the evisceration of blackness is a founding element of the law, then it is necessary for the law to confront the antiblack subtext that informs its idea of justice. This confrontation is also about coming to terms with paradigmatically different understandings of time and temporality.

There is a black experience of time which challenges an amnesiac present to confront its investment in a future that has not come to terms with the traumas of a violent and racist past. This understanding of time is not necessarily opposed to the idea of a future, but it cultivates a healthy, critical suspicion of narratives that are invested in futures premised on the elimination of blackness. This is an experience of time that interrogates the possibilities of a future from the vantage point of a problematic present. On the other hand, there is a liberal-modernist experience of time that is invested in the idea of a continuously unfolding sequence of victories over obstacles to progress. This experience of time is not white so much as it is nonblack, or put another way, it is constructed at a distance from a black existential perspective.

This kind of future-oriented time is reflected in Harold Koh's writing on refugee rights advocacy. For example, in his post hoc analysis of the legal challenge to the interdictions, Koh acknowledges that the US government prevailed for the moment. But he also argues that the government's territorial rationale for the interdictions will eventually have to give way to a transnational sphere of progressive legal advocacy. He goes on to propose the following: "This reasoning predicts that in time, the United States will comply with the norm of 'extraterritorial nonrefoulement,' in much the same way as it ultimately bowed to the demand for anti-kidnapping rules in its extradition treaty with Mexico."[191]

Koh's optimism may have seemed plausible at the time, but much of what has happened over the past two decades has contradicted his predictions for change. Although the movement to strengthen the exterritorial application of international law continues, with some success, the US experiment with exterritorial law enforcement has clearly been more influential than Koh expected. Instead of the United States bowing to the influence of a progressive international consensus, the European Union, along with many individual Western industrialized nations, has begun to imitate the United States' example.[192] For these reasons, I argue that it would be more instructive to use the Haitian interdictions to explain the US government's treatment of Latinx migrants and refugees, rather than the reverse.

Koh, on the other hand, suggests that US treaties with Mexico could set a precedent for exterritorial rights arguments which, by implication, could be used to reign in the US government's interdiction program. With this proposition, Koh treats the predicament of the black interdictee and the racially nondescript Latinx noncitizen as if they are interchangeable. But the unquestioned legal and normative framework for this common ground is that of the nonblack alien. To be more specific, nonblackness ends up being the default normative framework (in the same way that white privilege rarely has to declare itself), because black rightlessness is not surfaced as a problem.

In contrast, when I use the Haitian interdictions as a starting point for explaining US-Mexico border policy in the Trump era (as I do in chapter 6), the analysis has to begin by foregrounding the durability and explanatory salience of the black/nonblack binary. Antiblackness has to be conceptually centered before I can explain how policies and enforcement practices that were first designed for blacks can migrate to the other side of the binary. Toward this end, I am going to show that policies, enforcement practices, and court rulings devised to control blacks can establish precedents for the treatment of non-blacks, and that they are never entirely severed from their black beginnings.

This proposition underscores a point I have made over the last several chapters. Antiblack desire is inherently excessive. It operates through the law, but it is always seeking to exceed the legal codifications that give it form and teeth. This tension plays out in many ways, in the relationship between the jurisprudence excludability and the imperatives of radical excludability. It is reflected in the dismay of federal judges who tolerated or even endorsed the racist prerogatives of the sovereign decision at one point in time, but are unable to contain its excesses when it encroaches on legal precedents and principles that they held to be sacrosanct.[193] It may seem redundant to say that antiblackness is always excessive in relation to blacks. But this is precisely what liberal-minded judges and jurists refuse to acknowledge when they attempt to reconcile racist prerogatives to the egalitarian aspirations of the law, in the hopes that antiblack animus can be reasonably contained. This same excessive quality helps to explain why antiblack animus can establish precedents that are extended beyond the boundaries of blackness.

Antiblack racism is premised on the idea of an unbridgeable distance between the human and the subhuman, which it also fears is constantly in jeopardy of collapsing on itself. At the same time, it uses the space of blackness as an incubator for new cruelties which it proliferates across the "unbridgeable" distance between black and nonblack. In the next chapter, I will explain how this process unfolded in the interdiction practices of the mid-1990s and will situate it within the broader trend toward the criminalization of migrants and refugees.

NOTES

1. Guantanamo Public Memory Project, "Ronald Auborg Interview, 1991," New York: Columbia University's Institute for the Study of Human Rights, Accessed September 24, 2021, https://gitmomemory.org/stories/ronald-aubourg/.

2. Ibid.

3. Harold Koh, "The 'Haiti Paradigm' in United States," *Yale Law Review* 103 (1993): 2391–2455.

4. Patricia Tuitt, *Race, Law, Resistance* (New York: Taylor & Francis Group, 2004), 2.

5. Exec. Order No. 12324, 3 C.F.R. 46 FR 48109 (1981). See also Proclamation No. 4865, 46 Fed.Reg. 48107 (October 1, 1981).

6. *Immigration Reform and Control Act*, Pub.L. 99–603, 100 Stat. 3359 (1986). Kristina Shull, "Nobody Wants These People: Reagan's Immigration Crisis and America's First Private Prisons" (PhD diss, University of California-Irvine, 2014), 49–58.

7. Referring to the "amnesty" provisions that allowed almost 3 million undocumented Mexican migrants to adjust to legal permanent resident status in the late 1980s, via IRCA. See Pia Orrenius and Madeline Zavodny, "Do Amnesty Programs Reduce Undocumented Immigration? Evidence from IRCA," *Demography* 40, no. 3 (2003): 437–450.

8. This legislation was designed with the Indo-Chinese refugee crisis in mind Refugee Act of 1980, Pub. L. 96–212, 94 Stat. 102. (1979). National Archives Foundation, "Refugee Act of 1980," accessed September 24, 2021, https://www .archivesfoundation.org/documents/refugee-act-1980/.

9. See the discussion of the Haitian program in chapter 2. Also see *Haitian Refugee Center v. Civiletti*, 503 F. Supp. 442 (S.D. Fla. 1980).

10. Shull, "Nobody Wants These People," 58–59.

11. 8 U.S.C. §§ 1182(f) and 1185(a) (1). See *Haitian Refugee Center v. Gracey*, 600 F. Supp. 1396 (D.D.C. 1985) at 1399–1400.

12. *Haitian Refugee Center v. Baker*, 953 F.2d 1498 (11th Cir. 1992).

13. Executive Order No. 12,807, 57 Fed. Reg. 23,133 (1992).

14. These statistics span 1981–1990. They do not account for the last two years of this operation (1991–1992) before the Kennebunkport Order was issued. Ruth Wasem, *US Immigration Policy on Haitian Migrants* (Washington, DC: Congressional Research Service, 2011), 4.

15. Executive Order No. 12,807.

16. Caribbean National Weekly, "This Day in History: The 1991 Coup d'Etat in Haiti Took Place," September 29, 2016, https://www.caribbeannationalweekly.com/ caribbean-breaking-news-featured/day-history-1991-coup-detat-haiti-took-place/.

17. Wasem, *US Immigration Policy on Haitian Migrants*, 4.

18. Brief No: 92-344 for the UNHCR as Amicus Curiae, 13–16, *Haitian Centers Council, Inc. v. McNary*, 969 F.2d 1350 (2d Cir. 1992) at 1365–1366.

19. Harold Koh, "The Human Face of the Haitian Interdiction Program," *Virginia Journal of International Law* 33 (1993): 487.

20. See the beginning of the introduction for a review of the statistics that support this claim. Sources include Bureau of Transportation Statistics. "Table 5.1 U.S. Coast Guard Migrant Interdictions at Sea, Calendar Years 1991–2001"; US Department of Homeland Security, USCG Migrant Interdiction Statistics "Table 534. Coast Guard Migrant Interdictions by Nationality of Alien." Originally accessed May 2011: http://www.uscg.mil/hq/cg5/cg531/AMIO/ FlowStats/currentstats.asp/ Reposted at this link and accessed November 21, 2020: https://view.officeapps.live.com/op/view.aspx?src=http%3A%2F%2Fwww2.census.gov%2Flibrary%2Fpublications%2F2011%2Fcompendia%2Fstatab%2F131ed %2Ftables%2F12s0534.xls.

21. The policy of categorically denying an entire national origin group access to asylum screenings and returning them to their "home nation" was unique to Haitian refugees. Koh, "The Human Face of the Haitian Interdiction Program"; Hiroshi Motomura, "Haitian Asylum Seekers: Interdiction and Immigrant Rights," *Cornell International Law Journal* 26 (1993): 695.

22. *Sale*, 823 F. Supp. 1028 at 1036–1040.

23. Fleury's story was not discussed by Aubourg but she arrived at Guantanamo Bay in 1992, during the same time that Aubourg was serving as an interpreter. See Lucille Renwick, "Haiti Memories: Searching for a New Life, Hundreds of Refugees Have Arrived in L.A. With Their Stories of Despair and Brutal Treatment Back Home," *LA Times*, August 21, 1994, accessed September 24, 2021, https://www.latimes.com/archives/la-xpm-1994-08-21-ci-29766-story.html.

24. In her account of Fleury's story, Renwick does not provide any information about whether she did or did not have legal counsel on Guantanamo, but court transcripts indicate that Haitian refugees who arrived at Gitmo in the early 1990s were denied legal counsel. *Sale v. HCC*, 509 U.S. 155 (1993), 823 F. Supp. 1028 at 1036–1040. Renwick explains that Fleury received help from Catholic Charities (which could have included legal counsel) to resettle in the Los Angeles area after the government decided to grant her asylum but there is no indication in Renwick's account that independent legal counsel played a role in swaying the government's decision. Renwick, "Haiti Memories."

25. *Sale*, 509 U.S. 155, 1036–1040.

26. Koh, "The Human Face of the Haitian Interdiction Program," 487; Naomi Paik, "Carceral Quarantine at Guantánamo: Legacies of US Imprisonment of Haitian Refugees, 1991–1994," *Radical History Review* 115 (2013): 142–168 at 152–156.

27. The 1987 immigration ban for people with HIV/AIDS was added to a list of travel ban criteria that were already included in the 1952 Immigration and Nationality Act. Paik, "Carceral Quarantine at Guantanamo," 155. The ban was lifted in 2010. Centers for Disease Control and Prevention (CDC), U.S. Department of Health and Human Services (HHS) Medical examination of aliens—Removal of human immunodeficiency virus (HIV) infection from definition of communicable disease of public health significance. Final rule. Fed Regist. 2009; 74: 56547–56562. Cited from Susanna Winston and Curt Beckwith, "The Impact of Removing the Immigration Ban on HIV-Infected Persons," *AIDS Patient Care and STDs* 25, no. 12 (2011): 709–711 at n2.

28. Paik, "Carceral Quarantine at Guantanamo," 155.

29. Koh, "The Human Face of the Haitian Interdiction Program," 486–488; Paik, "Carceral Quarantine at Guantánamo," 152–156.

30. This is an argument that Justice Blackmun advanced in his criticism of the majority opinion in *Sale v. Haitian Centers Council, Inc.*, 509 U.S. 155 (1993) at 188–193.

31. This being the main premise of the Reagan-era executive order, titled *The Interdiction of Illegal Aliens*, which inaugurated the US government's Haitian interdiction operations. Exec. Order No. 12324.

32. *Baker*, 789 F. Supp. 1552 at 1555–1557.

33. As argued by the majority opinion in *Sale*, 509 U.S. 155.

34. *Haitian Refugee Center, Inc. v. Gracey*, 600 F. Supp. 1396 (D.D.C. 1985); *Haitian Refugee Center v. Gracey*, 809 F.2d 794 (D.C. Cir. 1987).

35. The District Court described the plaintiff group as the HRC, a nonprofit membership corporation located in Miami, Florida, and two of its members. *Gracey*, 600 F. Supp. 1396 at 1397.

36. *Gracey*, 600 F. Supp. 1396 at 1401.

37. *Civiletti*, 503 F. Supp. 442; *Bertrand v. Sava*, Nos. 81 Civ. 7371, 81 Civ. 7372 (S.D.N.Y. April 5, 1982); *Louis v. Nelson*, 544 F. Supp. 973 (S.D. Fla. 1982).

38. *Gracey*, 600 F. Supp. 1396 at 1404.

39. Using *Bertrand v. Sava* to argue that the UN Protocol on refugee rights is not self-executing under US law and using *Jean v. Nelson* to underscore the legal distinction between excludable and deportable aliens. *Bertrand v. Sava* 684 F.2d 204 (2d Cir. 1982); *Jean v. Nelson* 727 F.2d 957 (11th Cir. 1984); *Gracey*, 600 F. Supp. 1396 at 1405–1406.

40. Ibid.

41. For examples, see *Delgadillo v. Carmichael*, 332 U.S. 388 (1947); *Johnson v. Eisentrager*, 339 U.S. 763 (1950); *Paktorovics v. Murf*, 260 F.2d 610 (2nd Cir. 1958); *Shaughnessy v. Mezei*, 345 U.S. 206 (1953).

42. *Leng May Ma v. Barber*, 357 U.S. 185 (1958).

43. *Landon v. Plasencia*, 459 U.S. 21 (1982).

44. According to the jurisprudence established by the Second Circuit Court, which focused on flagrantly biased interpretations of the law by government officials. *Wong Wing Hang v. INS*, 360 F.2d 715 (2d Cir. 1966).

45. *Gracey*, 600 F. Supp. 1396.

46. Ibid.

47. *Gracey*, 809 F.2d 794.

48. Ibid.

49. Judge Edwards, concurring and dissenting in part. Ibid.

50. Ibid.

51. Saidiya Hartman, *Scenes of Subjection: Terror, Slavery, and Self-Making in Nineteenth-Century America* (New York: Oxford University Press, 2007), 17–23.

52. Consistent with Warren's explanation of how antiblack racism takes form as a distortion within the law, whereby the existential-ontological judgment on blackness (the Law of Being) is facilitated by a cooler, race-neutral discourse that is steeped in the codifications of the law (the being of the law). See chapter 1. Calvin Warren, *Ontological Terror: Blackness, Nihilism and Emancipation* (Durham: Duke University Press, 2018), 62–109.

53. Maureen Taft-Morales and Clare Ribando, *Haiti: Developments and U.S. Policy Since 1991 and Current Congressional Concerns* (Washington, DC: Congressional Research Service), 1.

54. Koh, "The Haiti Paradigm," 2393–2394.

55. One of the main sources of outrage, which is summarized by attorney Harold Koh in his account of the litigations (and which made its way into the arguments of sympathetic judges: *Baker*, 789 F. Supp. 1552 at 1554), is that the US government was not obligated to take in Haitian refugees but that it could not deliberately return them to the government that they claimed was persecuting them. These actions, on the part of the government, appeared to be a flagrant violation of the nonrefoulement principle that is a cornerstone of international refugee law. This issue is discussed in more detail later in this chapter. See Koh, "The Human Face of the Haitian Interdiction Program," 484–486. For an overview of the opinion of the international

community on this matter, see Brief No: 92-344 for the UNHCR as Amicus Curiae, *McNary*, 969 F.2d 1350 at 1365–1366.

56. *Baker*, 789 F. Supp. 1552.

57. This language comes directly from the decision in which Judge Atkins insisted that HRC's claim differed from the "abstract social interest" in the plight of the Haitian refugees that formed the basis for the complaints that drove the Gracey decisions. *Baker*, 789 F. Supp. 1552 at 1559.

58. This argument can be taken as a response to an observation made by the Gracey District Court, which was referenced by Atkins in his sympathetic decision, noting that "in contrast to Gracey, where the court noted that HRC, 'rather curiously, [did] not make the claim that the interdiction program violate[d] their first amendment rights,' HRC has made such a claim in this case." *Baker*, 789 F. Supp. 1552 at 1559–1560. Citing: *Gracey*, 809 F.2d at 800.

59. *Jean*, 727 F.2d 957, 983 at 983–984.

60. *Gracey*, 600 F. Supp. 1396 at 1405; *Gracey*, 809 F.2d 794 at n126.

61. *Baker*, 789 F. Supp. 1552 at 1574–1576.

62. Ibid.

63. *Baker*, 789 F. Supp. 1552 at 1579–1582.

64. *Baker*, 789 F. Supp. 1552 at 1567–1568.

65. Patrick Gavigan, "Migration Emergencies and Human Rights in Haiti," Paper prepared for the Conference on Regional Responses to Forced Migration in Central America and the Caribbean, September 30–October 1, 1997, accessed September 24, 2021, https://www.oas.org/juridico/english/gavigane.html, 1–2.

66. Gavigan, "Migration Emergencies and Human Rights in Haiti," 3–4.

67. The United States repatriated 20,000 Haitians between 1994 and 1995, whereas Caribbean governments repatriated over 30,000 during this same period of time (including 20,000 by the Domincan Republic, 8,000 by the Bahamas, 3,000 by Turks and Caicos; not counting the smaller repatriation case loads of other Caribbean nations). Gavigan, "Migration Emergencies and Human Rights in Haiti," 4.

68. Gavigan, "Migration Emergencies and Human Rights in Haiti."

69. Roy Bryce-Laporte, "Black Immigrants: The Experience of Invisibility and Inequality," *Journal of Black Studies* 3, no. 1 (1972): 29–56; Julian Go, ed., *Rethinking Obama* (Bingley, UK: Emerald Group Publishing, 2011); Jared Sexton, "Proprieties of Coalition: Blacks, Asians, and the Politics of Policing," *Critical Sociology* 36, no. 1 (2010): 87–108.

70. Ian Haney Lopez, "Post-Racial Racism: Racial Stratification and Mass Incarceration in the Age of Obama," *California Law Review* 98, no. 3 (2010): 1023–1074.

71. Tamara Nopper, "Why Black Immigrants Matter: Refocusing the Discussion on Racism and Immigration Enforcement," in *Keeping Out the Other: A Critical Introduction to Immigration Enforcement Today*, eds. David Brotherton and Philip Kretsedemas (New York: Columbia University Press, 2008), 204–240.

72. Koh, "The Haiti Paradigm," 2400–2401.

73. Ibid. The first District Court decision on *HRC v. Baker* (789 F. Supp. 1552) was decided on December 3, 1991, almost one month after Bill Clinton's electoral victory over former president George Bush.

74. This context is examined in more depth in chapter 5. The highpoint of the US government's Haitian interdiction operations (exceeding over 37,000 interdicted Haitians in a single year) occurred in 1992, as the deliberations over Baker were finalized by the appellate courts. The second highest annual peak (over 25,000 interdictions) occurred in 1994, under the auspices of Operation Sea Signal, which was implemented by the Clinton administration. Although Haitian interdictions have not, to this date, exceeded these highs, Haitians still figure prominently among the targets of interdiction operations, from the 1990s to the present. Wasem, *US Immigration Policy on Haitian Migrants*, 2 and 5–7.

75. *Baker*, 789 F. Supp. 1552 at 1578–1579. This TRO was actually the continuation of an order issued by District Judge Donald Graham on November 19, 1991, prior to the hearing of the case. *Baker*, 789 F. Supp. 1552 at 1557.

76. Including two District Court decisions and two decisions by the Eleventh Circuit Court of Appeals. *Baker*, 789 F. Supp. 1552; *Haitian Refugee Center v. Baker*, 789 F. Supp. 1579 (S.D. Fla. 1991); *Haitian Refugee Center v. Baker*, 949 F.2d 1109 (11th Cir. 1991); *Haitian Refugee Center v. Baker*, 953 F.2d 1498 (11th Cir. 1992). The Supreme Court ended the legal dispute with a ruling that denied a final appeal by the plaintiffs, but the most decisive argument in this case history was made by the Eleventh Circuit. *Haitian Refugee Center v. Baker*, 112 S. Ct. 1245 (1992); Thomas Jones, "Haitian Refugee Center, Inc. v. James Baker, III: The Dred Scott Case of Immigration Law," *Penn State International Law Review* 11, no.1 (1992): 1–48 at 23.

77. *Baker*, 949 F.2d 1109.

78. Ibid.

79. In the first hearing, Atkins determined that the APA did not apply because the "actions in question" fell under the discretionary authority of the government. *Baker*, 789 F. Supp. 1552 at 1575. In the second hearing, Atkins held that on closer review, a distinction could be made between the president's discretionary authority to create and implement the interdiction operation and the discretionary authority used by subordinates who were charged with carrying out the program The APA argument recognized the former kind of discretionary authority as legitimate but took issue with the latter. *Baker*, 789 F. Supp. 1579 at 1582.

80. *Louis v. Nelson*, 544 F. Supp. 973 (S.D. Fla. 1982) at 988–989.

81. *Vigile v. Sava* 535 F. Supp. 1020 (S.D.N.Y. March 5, 1982) at 1007.

82. *Baker*, 789 F. Supp. 1579 at 1582. Also see n75.

83. *Baker*, 789 F. Supp. 1579 at 1557. The roster of complaints that were introduced in the first District Court decision—which excluded complaints about racial discrimination—did not change as the case made its way to the higher courts.

84. Hiroshi Motomura, "Immigration Law After a Century of Plenary Power: Phantom Constitutional Norms and Statutory Interpretation," *Yale Law Journal* 100, no. 3 (1990): 546–613.

85. Ibid., 564–575.

86. *Jean v. Nelson*, 472 U.S. 846 (1985); *Bertrand v. Sava*, 684 F.2d 204 (2d Cir. 1982). See discussions of these cases in chapters 2 and 3.

87. Jones, "Haitian Refugee Center, Inc. v. James Baker, III."

88. Ibid., 24–28; *Dred Scott v. Sandford*, 60 U.S. 393 (1854).

89. *Dred Scott*, 60 U.S. 393 at 496 and 593–594.

90. *Dred Scott*, 60 U.S. 393 at 407–408.

91. *Dred Scott*, 60 U.S. 393 at 394–396.

92. A good example being the opposition of slaveholding elites to the 1789 Alien and Sedition Acts, which was not simply a show of support for "alien rights" but a reaction to the consolidation of federal power and a defense of the rights of private (white, male) property holders. Fred Kaplan, *Lincoln and the Abolitionists* (New York: HarperCollins, 2017), 102–104 (discussed in chapter 2). This concern for protecting private individuals from the overreaching powers of the government is also reflected in the "states rights" arguments used by white citizenries to fortify social distances from black populations, as evidenced by the majority opinion for *Plessy v. Ferguson*, 163 U.S. 537 (1896) (also discussed in chapter 2).

93. *Dred Scott*, 60 U.S. 393 at 418, 479–480, 555 and 573.

94. This shift can be regarded as precursors for the colorblind and "post-racial" discourses on race that usually attributed to the post-civil rights era (post Jim Crow). Michelle Alexander, *The New Jim Crow: Mass Incarceration in the Age of Colorblindness* (New York: The New Press, 2012); Eduardo Bonilla-Silva and David Dietrich, "The Sweet Enchantment of Color-Blind Racism in Obamerica," *The Annals of the American Academy of Political and Social Science* 634, no. 1 (2011): 190–206.

95. John Cell, *The Highest Stage of White Supremacy: The Origins of Segregation in South Africa and the American South* (Cambridge, UK: Cambridge University Press, 1982), 82–102.

96. Alexander, *The New Jim Crow*, 20–58; Lisa Marie Cacho, *Social Death: Racialized Rightlessness and the Criminalization of the Unprotected* (New York: NYU Press, 2012), 35–60.

97. Jones, "Haitian Refugee Center, Inc. v. James Baker, III," 24–28.

98. *Haitian Refugee Center v. Baker*, 112 S. Ct. 1245 (1992). Also see Harold Koh and Michael Wishnie, "The Story of *Sale v. Haitian Centers Council*: Guantanamo and Refoulement," in *Human Rights Advocacy Stories*, eds. Margaret Satterthwaite and Deena Hurwitz (Eagan, MN: Westlaw and Foundations Press, 2008), 385–432 at 391.

99. *Baker*, 789 F. Supp. 15.

100. *Baker*, 789 F. Supp. 1579.

101. *Haitian Centers Council v. McNary*, 789 F. Supp. 541 (E.D.N.Y. 1992) at 544; Koh and Wishnie, "The Story of *Sale v. Haitian Centers Council*," 392–393.

102. The memo was prepared by General Counsel of the INS, Grover Joseph Rees. *McNary*, 789 F. Supp. 541 at 544–545.

103. Ibid.

104. Ibid.

105. *Haitian Centers Council v. Sale*, 823 F. Supp. 1028 (E.D.N.Y. 1993) at 1038–1039.

106. *Sale*, 823 F. Supp. 1028 at 1035.

107. *Sale*, 823 F. Supp. 1028 at 1046–1047.

108. *Sale*, 823 F. Supp. 1028 at 1040–1041.

109. *Sale*, 823 F. Supp. 1028 at 1045–1046; *Haitian Centers Council v. McNary*, 789 F. Supp. 541 (E.D.N.Y. 1992) at 544–545.

110. *McNary*, 789 F. Supp. 541.

111. *McNary*, 789 F. Supp. 541 at 546–548.

112. The case was heard by the Second Circuit Court five times and eight times by the Supreme Court, in addition to three hearings by a New York District Court (Eastern District of New York City). Koh and Wishnie, "The Story of *Sale v. Haitian Centers Council*," 393.

113. Executive Order No. 12,807, 57 Fed. Reg. 23,133 (1992); Koh and Wishnie, "The Story of *Sale v. Haitian Centers Council*," 394–395.

114. *Haitian Centers Council v. McNary*, 969 F.2d 1350 (2d Cir. 1992) at 1353.

115. *Baker*, 953 F.2d 1498 at 1508–1509.

116. *Haitian Centers Council v. McNary*, 807 F. Supp. 928 (E.D.N.Y. 1992) at 929–930.

117. For example, the first two District Court decisions and final Second Circuit Court decision for *HCC v. McNary* addressed the complaints of all of these plaintiff groups: *McNary*, 789 F. Supp. 541; *McNary*, 807 F. Supp. 928; *McNary*, 969 F.2d 1350. The District Court's final decision in *HCC v. Sale* focused on HIV-positive plaintiffs (*Sale*, 823 F. Supp. 1028), whereas the Supreme Court decision for *Sale v. HCC* focused on Haitian interdictees who were being returned to Haiti, without being screened, under the Kennebunkport Order (*Sale v. Haitian Centers Council*, 509 U.S. 155 (1993)).

118. Koh and Wishnie, "The Story of *Sale v. Haitian Centers Council*," 385–387 and 393.

119. The Second Circuit Court described the plaintiff groups in this way: "(1) some 150 Haitians who have been repatriated even though previously screened-in; (2) thousands of Haitians with credible fears of persecution who are being or will be interdicted, but should have been screened-in; and (3) those Haitians on Guantanamo Naval Base who are now unscreened and would be screened-in but for the summary repatriation which the government may seek." *McNary*, 969 F.2d 1350 at 1354–1355.

120. *McNary*, 789 F. Supp. 541; *McNary*, 969 F.2d 1350.

121. *McNary*, 969 F.2d 1350.

122. *Bertrand*, 684 F.2d 204 at 212–214.

123. *Bertrand*, 684 F.2d 204 at 218–219.

124. *McNary*, 969 F.2d 1350 at 1361–1363.

125. *McNary*, 969 F.2d 1350 at 1358.

126. Tom de Boer, "Closing Legal Black Holes: The Role of Extraterritorial Jurisdiction in Refugee Rights Protection," *Journal of Refugee Studies* 28, no. 1 (2014): 118–134.

127. *McNary*, 969 F.2d 1350 at 1358.

128. *McNary*, 969 F.2d 1350 at 1361–1366.

129. *McNary*, 969 F.2d 1350 at 1365–1366.

130. Ibid.

131. *McNary*, 969 F.2d 1350 at 1361.

132. *McNary*, 969 F.2d 1350 at 1361.

133. The Second Circuit's opinion for *Bertrand*, 684 F.2d 204 was allowed to be the final word for that case history. The plaintiffs undoubtedly tried to appeal the decision to the Supreme Court, but it did not take up the case.

134. *Sale*, 509 U.S. 155.

135. This was the argument advanced by the Supreme Court in *Sale*, 509 U.S. 155.

136. *McNary*, 969 F.2d 1350 at 1367.

137. Giorgio Agamben, *Homo Sacer: Sovereign Power and Bare Life* (Stanford, CA: Stanford University Press, 1998), 71–74, 91–103.

138. Warren, *Ontological Terror*, 19–20, 51 and 89; Frank Wilderson, *Red, White & Black Cinema and the Structure of US Antagonisms* (Durham, NC: Duke University Press, 2010), 38–49.

139. Derrick Bell, *Faces at the Bottom of the Well: The Permanence of Racism* (New York: Basic Books, 1992); Hartman, *Scenes of Subjection*; Dorothy Roberts, *Killing the Black Body: Race, Reproduction, and the Meaning of Liberty* (New York: Vintage, 1998); Warren, *Ontological Terror*.

140. Typified by its jurisprudence on invidious discrimination, *Wong Wing Hang*, 360 F.2d 715.

141. This position is stated most clearly in Johnson's summary of the case history in his second hearing of the case, *McNary*, 807 F. Supp. 928 at 933.

142. *McNary*, 789 F. Supp. 541 at 543–545.

143. *HCC v. McNary*, WL 155853, No. 2, CV 1258 (E.D.N.Y. 1992: April 6 Decision, April 15 Order on Clarification, June 5 Memorandum and Order).

144. *McNary*, WL 155853 at 5–6 and 8.

145. *McNary*, WL 155853 at 8.

146. Warren, *Ontological Terror*, 87.

147. *McNary*, 969 F.2d 1350 at 1361–1366.

148. *McNary*, 807 F. Supp. 928 at 929–930.

149. *McNary*, 807 F. Supp. 928 at 930.

150. *Civiletti*, 503 F. Supp. 442 at 462–463 and 514; *HRC v. Smith*, 676 F.2d 1023 (5th Cir., 1982).

151. *Louis*, 544 F. Supp. 973.

152. *Bertrand*, 684 F.2d 204.

153. *Sale*, 509 U.S. 155.

154. The 1992 US Presidential election was held on Tuesday, November 3. Judge Johnson issued his second and final decision for *HCC v. McNary* on November 12, 1992.

155. Koh, "The Haiti Paradigm," 2403.

156. Ibid.

157. As recited in the two District Court decisions and the decision issued by the Second Circuit Court. *McNary*, 789 F. Supp. 541; *McNary*, 807 F. Supp. 928; *McNary*, 969 F.2d 1350.

158. *McNary*, 969 F.2d 1350 at 1369–1381.

159. *Sale*, 509 U.S. 155 at 179–182.

160. *Sale*, 509 U.S. 155 at 156.

161. *Sale*, 509 U.S. 155 at 171–175.

162. *Sale*, 509 U.S. 155 at 188–189.

163. Koh and Wishnie, "The Story of *Sale v. Haitian Centers Council*," 406.

164. As evidenced by its "Windward passage" commentary, see n135 and the accompanying discussion in the body of the chapter.

165. *Jean*, 727 F.2d 957 at 983–984.

166. *Civiletti*, 503 F. Supp. 442 at 450–452 and 523–530.

167. *Louis*, 544 F. Supp. 973; *Jean* 727 F.2d 957; *Jean*, 472 U.S. 846.

168. *McNary*, 807 F. Supp. 928.

169. *Sale*, 823 F. Supp. 1028.

170. The District Court decision was issued June 8, 1993, and the Supreme Court decision on June 21, 1993.

171. Koh and Wishnie, "The Story of *Sale v. Haitian Centers Council*," 394–398.

172. *Sale*, 823 F. Supp. 1028 at 1032–1033.

173. *Bertrand*, 684 F.2d 204.

174. *Sale*, 823 F. Supp. 1028 at 1042–1045.

175. *Sale*, 823 F. Supp. 1028 at 1043–1044.

176. *McNary*, WL 155853 at 8.

177. *Sale*, 823 F. Supp. 1028 at 1036–1039.

178. *Sale*, 823 F. Supp. 1028 at 1039.

179. *Sale*, 823 F. Supp. 1028 at 1042–1043 and 1046–1050.

180. *Sale*, 823 F. Supp. 1028 at 1049–1050.

181. Koh, "The Haiti Paradigm," 2397.

182. Koh and Wishnie, "The Story of *Sale v. Haitian Centers Council*," 413–416.

183. Koh, "The Haiti Paradigm," 2413–2415.

184. Ibid., 2414.

185. Ibid., 2411–2413.

186. Ibid., 2413.

187. Warren, *Ontological Terror*, 1–25.

188. Ibid.

189. *Sale*, 823 F. Supp. 1028 at 1042–1043.

190. *Sale*, 823 F. Supp. 1028 at 1042, citing *McNary*, 969 F.2d at 1343.

191. Koh, "The Haiti Paradigm," 2408.

192. Jeffrey Kahn, "The Caribbean Roots of European Maritime Interdiction." *Society for Cultural Anthropology: Refugees and the Crisis of Europe*, June 28, 2016: https://culanth.org/fieldsights/the-caribbean-roots-of-european-maritime-interdiction.

193. As evidenced by Justice Field's dismay at the exclusionary extremes of the Fong Yue Ting decision—*Fong Yue Ting*, 149 U.S. 698 (1893) at 746–749—despite his support for the exclusionary outcomes of the *Chinese Exclusion Case*, 130 U.S. 581 (1889). A contemporary example is the Second Circuit Court's criticism of the violations of international refugee law that were promulgated by the Kennebunkport Order (*McNary*, 969 F.2d 1350) despite its tolerance of similar violations of refugee rights under the Haitian program (*Bertrand*, 684 F.2d 204).

Chapter 5

Reconfiguring the Black/ Nonblack Binary

The Radical Exclusion of Haitian and Cuban Refugees in the Era of Operation Sea Signal

HUMANITARIANISM AS ANTIBLACKNESS

Under the Clinton Presidency, the US government's interdiction operations became, paradoxically, more humanitarian and more exclusionary. The largest number of Haitian and Cuban refugees interdicted in a single year occurred in this era, the US government spent unprecedented sums of money to house and feed these people outside of the legal-territorial jurisdiction of the United States and involved humanitarian relief organizations in the vetting of their asylum claims (while insisting all the while that these interdicted people were not actually refugees and could not claim the protections of US or international law).[1] This is also the era in which the US government began to subject Cuban asylum seekers to restrictive policies that bore a striking resemblance to the ones it had been using to control the movements of Haitian asylum seekers.[2] Even so, this change in policy for Cubans did not, ultimately, change the US government's singularly exclusionary treatment of Haitians.

In the pages ahead, I am going to use this policy history to shine a light on the hierarchical relationship between blackness and nonblackness that echoes through the law. I aim to show that the black/nonblack binary can undergo many permutations, and that it is possible for peoples' relationship to this binary to change over time, but without changing the fundamental attributes of the binary. I am also going to attend to the complications produced by the silences of the law, which pronounce a judgment on blackness by refusing to name it as such—denying it any standing—while at same time, producing singularly exclusionary outcomes that agree with antiblack sentiment.

The narratives of Haitian asylum seekers and the social justice constituencies that have tried to protect their rights provide an important corrective to these silences by making antiblackness salient as a way of explaining the law. This is one reason why the charge of racism has been voiced, most loudly, by civic and social movement organizations in the public sphere rather than in the court rooms of the political establishment.[3] The stories of fiction writers can perform similar work. A good example is Edwidge Danticat's short story, *Children of the Sea*,[4] which is one of the most well known literary meditations on the Haitian refugee experience.

Children of the Sea threads together the aspirations and desperate conditions that have driven Haitian asylum seekers to the high seas in search of a freer life. It also offers a commentary on the racial consciousness of Haitian refugees and their awareness of the racist subtext of US policy. Danticat communicates all of this simply enough by having one of the refugees in her story notice that everyone is getting sunburned, and observing "Now we'll never be mistaken for Cubans."[5] With this brief statement, there is an acknowledgment that Cuban refugees get treated differently than Haitians under US refugee policy and that the blackness of Haitians (who tan darker than Cubans, at least in the imagination of Danticat's characters) has something to do with the way these groups have been categorically distinguished by the US government.

As soon as Danticat confronts the reader with this antiblack reality she complicates it by noting, almost as an afterthought, "Even though some of the Cubans are black too." But the Haitian refugees in Danticat's story also know that Cubans, regardless of skin color, do not receive the same inhospitable treatment as Haitians. She underscores this point by having the same character, who observes that "some of the Cubans are black too," recount a story of fleeing to the United States on a boat filled with Cubans, but was singled out by the Coast Guard when the boat was interdicted and repatriated to Haiti, while the Cubans were admitted to Miami. This story is probably a commentary on the open arms policy that was embedded in the law by the *1966 Cuban Adjustment Act* that was in effect during the same time that the US government embarked on its Haitian-focused interdictions of the early 1980s.[6] It could also be read as a commentary on the double standards of US refugee policy that continued through the wet foot/dry foot policy of the 1990s and well into the new millennium with border enforcement and public health policies that have been carried out by the Trump and Biden administrations.[7] But if you take the antiblack subtext seriously, you also have to contend with an ontological imaginary that predates modern refugee law.

As I have explained in the prior chapters, (anti)blackness is better understood as a space of otherness that defines the outer limits of the law, rather than a subjectivity that describes a person's standing before the law. So how does this extra-legal otherness operate through the refugee policies of the post-civil rights era? And how reliant is it on the immanent corporality of dark-skinned bodies? For example, could it be that Cubans who are often described as "black" are still lighter skinned than most Haitians—which is why they tend to get better treatment? Or is there more to their racial privilege than the simple fact of their skin color? Even if some of these Cubans are as dark as some Haitians, could it be that they get better treatment because they belong to the same national origin group as lighter skinned Cubans? If this is the case, then maybe racial privilege is not just a matter of skin color, it also about categorical distinctions—backed up by the force of law—that are applied to populations, with ruthless indifference to the morphological diversity of these populations. Even after acknowledging all of this, however, it is still possible to distinguish Haitian from Cuban bodies, which is why it is easy enough to "pick out" a Haitian refugee in a boat of Cubans, or why Danticat insists that Haitians tan darker than Cubans. Even if antiblackness is never just about bodies it cannot be untethered, completely, from racialized interpretations of the body.

I am going to explore these permutations of (anti)blackness in the rest of the chapter and trace the role they play in reconfiguring the black/nonblack binary, but without undermining the categorical distinctions on which it relies. As I have already noted, I am going to focus on a period in US refugee policy in which the exclusionary treatment that had once been reserved for Haitians is extended to Cubans and begins to set the tone for the way the US government treats most migrants and refugees. This can also be described as a period of time in which mechanisms of control that had been originally designed with black bodies in mind begin to permeate the nonblack side of the black/nonblack binary.

I am going to show that there are ways in which black/nonblack distinctions attach to categories of people and not just to bodies. But I am also going to show bodies still matter, and even when people who are normally categorized as nonblack are treated like black people, they do not entirely lose their nonblack privilege. Even as things get worse for all migrants and refugees, the black/nonblack binary can still be recalibrated in ways that signal the privilege—no matter how fragile—that nonblack persons enjoy over black bodies.

I am going to substantiate this theory of the black/nonblack binary with a close reading of the last major legal challenge, to date, that was levied against the US government's interdiction operations. This challenge begins shortly after the Supreme Court decides *Sale v. Haitian Centers Council* in 1993. This time, the class action suit was initiated by Cuban refugees and was later joined by nonprofits and legal advocates who were allied with Haitian refugees. The Eleventh Circuit Court's decision for *Cuban American Bar Association (CABA) v. Christopher*,[8] which was issued in January 1995, sits at the center of this legal dispute. But it is important to note that CABA was just one manifestation of a much broader process which transformed the relationship between immigration, refugee, and criminal law. Before I get into the details of the CABA suit, I am going to spend some time discussing this broader context.

REFUGEES, IMMIGRANTS, AND THE "NEW" CRIMINALITY

In the last chapter, I explained how the Supreme Court went to great lengths—bordering on the absurd—to defend its position that the US Constitution and international refugee law did not apply to interdicted Haitians.[9] The argument the court advanced in *Sale v. HCC* (which was radically different from the District Court decision in *HCC v Sale*, see chapter 4) epitomized this commitment to alienating Haitian refugees from the protections of the law. In this decision, it argued that the nonrefoulement principle only applied to people who were living under the territorial jurisdiction of the nations who had signed on to the 1951 Refugee Convention.[10] To hold its position, the court was prepared to break with the consensus opinion of the international community and contest the UNHCR's interpretation of the foundational documents of modern refugee law that it had been charged to uphold.[11]

"The Supreme Court's opinion in *Sale v. HCC* was an ominous precursor for the direction that US immigration law would take in the decades to come. Thomas Gammeltoft-Hansen and Nikolas Tan have gone a step further, to argue that the Haitian interdictions are one of the precursors for a global paradigm of immigration enforcement and refugee policy that has taken shape in the new millennium—the deterrence paradigm.[12] One feature of this paradigm, which is epitomized by interdiction operations, involves strategies that divert migrant and refugee flows before they reach their intended destinations. The aims of these deterrence tactics are served by a diverse array of laws and policies that make it easier for migrants and refugees to be removed after they have already entered a nation, or which create disincentives that are designed to encourage their voluntary departure. Some examples cited by Gammeltoft-Hansen and Tan include limitations on "family reunification and cuts to social benefits" as well as the issuance of "more temporary or subsidiary forms of protection," which is illustrated by the government's increasing reliance on Temporary Protected Status (TPS) as an alternative to asylum.[13]

The goals of the deterrence paradigm are also reflected in the use of criminality as a broad framework for justifying more aggressive kinds of immigration enforcement practices.[14] In the late 1980s, for example, the INS began to create enforcement programs that streamlined the deportation of immigrants after they served sentences for criminal convictions.[15] Patricia Macías-Rojas has explained that funding for these programs increased significantly between 1987 and 1989, but this was only the beginning of a massive expansion of crime-themed deportation programs that grew at an even faster rate throughout the 1990s.[16]

The Anti-Drug Abuse Acts of 1986 and 1988 were an important feature of the legislative agenda of the War on Drugs, which massively expanded the size of the black, native-born incarcerated population.[17] These laws also introduced the category of the "aggravated felony" to immigration law, which increased the range of offenses that could trigger deportation proceedings for immigrants—which were typically minor, nonviolent offenses.[18] The aggravated felony quickly became a controversial feature of immigration law, because it included a broad range of minor, nonviolent offenses that were not treated as "aggravated felonies" under criminal law. The variety of offenses that were categorized as aggravated felonies, for the purposes of immigration law, was steadily expanded throughout the 1990s.[19]

The year that *Sale v. HCC* was decided, was another important turning point in this movement toward the criminalization of immigrants. Beginning in 1993, Democratic politicians played an important role in pushing for tougher sanctions on crimes committed by unauthorized migrants and also calling for restrictions on the constitutional rights of noncitizens in deportation proceedings.[20] These maneuvers helped to establish the new discourse on criminal aliens and the criminalization of illegality as a bipartisan phenomenon, and contributed to what many activists and scholars have called the good/bad immigrant dichotomy.[21] This good/bad dichotomy allowed lawmakers to reconcile the discourse on immigrant criminality with the romanticized idea of the United States as a land built by hardworking immigrants. Instead of demonizing the social category of the immigrant, like the nativist ideologies of the late nineteenth century,[22] the public image of the immigrant was bifurcated into two radically different social types—law abiding workers and community members, and dangerous deviants.

Legislation like the 1996 Antiterrorism and Effective Death Penalty Act and the 1996 IIRIRA introduced new definitions of immigrant criminality (along with expanding the aggravated felony category) that cemented the good/bad immigrant distinction into law.[23] Although this distinction is premised on the idea that bad immigrants deserve to be deported because they do bad things, it also can be understood as a strategy for regulating a growing immigrant population, which creates new definitions of crime that intensify the vulnerability and removability of most noncitizens.

Similar developments were playing out in refugee law and policy, with the US government's Haitian refugee policies being a pivotal aspect of this process. The Reagan-era interdictions, beginning in 1981, served as a rough template for the immigration control strategy that was introduced by the

1986 *IRCA*.[24] Meanwhile, the 1990 *Immigration Act* and the 1996 *Illegal Immigration and Immigrant Responsibility Act* introduced measures to immigration law that had once been a unique feature of the government's Haitian refugee policies including the practice of mandatory detention, restrictions on the ability of immigrants to question the terms of their detention, and changes to the legal definition and implementation of enforcement practices that blurred the lines between excludability and deportability.[25]

HUMANITARIANISM AND SOCIAL CONTROL

Another related feature of the deterrence paradigm is the phenomenon of carceral humanitarianism. Kelly Oliver, who coined this term, has explained how it combines techniques from the world of criminal law enforcement with a mandate to protect vulnerable populations that is patterned after the mandates of refugee relief operations.[26] Under the aegis of carceral humanitarianism, the movements of displaced populations can be criminalized—by discourses on anti-smuggling or the goal of preventing unauthorized migration—but individual refugees can still be constructed as victims who are being rescued by border enforcement. As a result, interdiction operations can be framed as efforts to save the lives of people trying to make dangerous crossings in leaky and overcrowded boats.[27] This appeal to humanitarian values was also used to justify the treatment of HIV-positive Haitian detainees at Guantanamo. Judge Johnson took issue with this language in his landmark decision for *HCC v. Sale*, when he observed that what the government was calling a program of "humanitarian assistance" was better described as the world's first "HIV prison camp" that had been designed for Haitian refugees.[28]

Luca Mavelli has made a similar observation about the humanitarian language that has been used to justify European interdiction operations. Mavelli sums up the darkly ironic goals of these operations which claim "to save lives by not saving lives in order to discourage 'irregular' migrants from undertaking dangerous sea voyages."[29] The humanitarian aid provided by these operations is delivered in tandem with a strategy for tightening borders, which contributes to the growing number of refugee deaths at sea even as it rescues a minority of them from these very same perilous conditions. This is one reason why carceral humanitarianism can be understood as yet another manifestation of the deterrence paradigm.

But Gammeltoft-Hansen and Tan's theory of the deterrence paradigm has its limitations, which are shared by carceral humanitarianism, and many of the other concepts that have been used to explain other worrisome developments in the treatment of migrants and refugees. All of these concepts emphasize the novelty and recency of the problems they are describing. I am going to situate these concepts within a different reading of historical time.

As I have explained in the prior chapters, draconian measures that appear unprecedented in the sphere of immigrant and refugee law can be traced to other histories of law (as well as histories of power that operate outside the law) that revolve around the control of black mobility. This is why it is difficult to situate "new" trends in criminalization within a history of criminal or immigration law that applies to all people. There is a more complex chronology at work, which involves the relationship between separate but relationally defined trajectories of law and power that have been differentially applied to black and nonblack bodies. What appears to be "new" for one population (and one type of body) is often just the eruption within a relatively new field of law and policy, of a type of power that has been imposed on other bodies for quite some time. To better understand this process, it is necessary to read a theory of antiblackness into the analysis of criminality and statelessness.

ON CRIMINALITY, STATELESSNESS, AND ANTIBLACKNESS

Hannah Arendt's writing provides an important starting point for theorizing the criminalization of refugees.[30] Arendt's discussion of this issue revolves around the contrast between criminality and statelessness. She explains that the concept of criminality rests on a more secure foundation of rights than that of statelessness, and this is despite the fact that the refugee's only offense is the mere fact of their displacement. Arendt goes on to observe that criminality would be a step up for the stateless refugee in this hierarchy of rights.[31] By violating criminal law, they are at least recognized as having some kind of standing under the justice system, which grants the criminal suspect access to constitutional and civil rights.

Juliet Stumpf makes a similar point in her influential discussion of the growing intersections of criminal and immigration law, or crimmigration.[32] She describes criminal law as an institution that is used to govern rights-bearing subjects who are at risk of being deprived of these rights. Immigration law operates the other way round. It starts with a rightless subject who might be granted a more secure legal status, depending on the outcome of their immigration case. This starting premise may be less punitive than that of criminal law, but the immigrant petitioner also begins at a greater distance from the protections of the law.

Criminal law, on the other hand, affords the accused a more secure foundation of rights precisely because it is punitive, and because it is typically administered to people who are regarded as "members" (or at least residents) of the society whose laws they are accused of violating. But as Stumpf has explained, the criminalization of immigration law has blurred these distinctions.[33] Criminal violations can take on different meanings and carry more severe consequences within immigration law than they do in criminal law. Furthermore, the noncitizens who suffer these consequences are not afforded the same procedural and due process rights as the subjects of the criminal justice system, and the end result of this process is usually expulsion from the United States.

Criminality can also function as a meta-conceptual framework for immigration law and policy. To borrow from Malcolm Feeley and Jonathan Simon, this meta-conceptual framework is geared toward managing populations that are always-already criminalized, rather than punishing individual criminal acts.[34]

In their theory of the new penology, Feeley and Simon explain how criminality has been converted into a calculation of "dangerous probabilities" that are endemic to particular kinds of populations.[35] Irrespective of whether individual members of these populations have committed a criminal act, they are exposed to forms of surveillance and social control that are informed by calculations of the risk this population poses to the wider society. There is ample evidence of how this population management approach toward crime has been used to police poor, black, urban communities.[36] Although this understanding of criminality does not rely on the same kind of neo-Darwinian reasoning as the eugenicist policies of the early twentieth century, it reinforces similar associations between race and social problems.[37] The discourse on carceral humanitarianism, which I discussed at the beginning of the chapter, provides another example.

Lisa Cacho describes a similar chain of associations when she insists that "the law is dependent upon the permanence of certain groups' criminalization."[38] Feeley and Simon arrive at the same conclusion, using a different line of argument, when they insist that the new penology is a variation on systems theory more so than criminology.[39] In other words, criminal behavior is not treated as a correctable problem that could manifest, potentially, within any individual member of a society. Crime is an indicator of the troubled relations between populations that are conceptualized as mutually exclusive social systems; it is the threat that an inherently criminal population (system A) poses to an inherently noncriminal/law abiding population (system B).

As a result, group membership overdetermines assessments of criminality. If an individual belongs to a criminalized population, they will be targeted by surveillance and enforcement practices that are designed to deter and mitigate the "criminal threat" they pose to society, irrespective of whether they have or have not actually committed a criminal act.

Under this population management model, the main goal of crime control is to minimize the statistical probability that a population which has been categorically defined as "criminal" or "crime-prone" poses to the wider society. This is one reason why the US government could categorize Haitian refugees as "illegal aliens," interdict them, and detain them before they had actually committed an act of unlawful border crossing. Haitian illegality was overdetermined by the population problem they posed for the US government and this problem, in turn, was informed by an institutionalized body of opinion which viewed Haitians as "undesirables" and unsuitable for incorporation into US society. These sentiments can be traced to the prohibition on black migration that was described in chapter 2. They are also amply illustrated by the insistence of federal government officials on describing Haitians as a threat to the US public, rather than as genuine refugees.[40] Going back to the language of the *Johnson v. Eisentrager* decision, black, poor, Haitian refugees were the antithesis of the kind of populations to whom the United States has been "traditionally hospitable."[41]

This new kind of criminality complicates the distinction that Arendt has made between criminality and statelessness. It is not so easy, in the present day, to distinguish the problem of the criminalized person from that of the stateless refugee. There still are people charged with crimes who benefit from the system of rights, described by Arendt, which is restricted to members of a given society. But criminality is also being used to rationalize the preemptive exclusion of migrants and refugees and to streamline their removal from the United States. This kind of criminality is better understood as a route into statelessness rather than a predicament that can be categorically distinguished from statelessness.

It is also important to keep in mind that statelessness is not a predicament that is unique to the noncitizen. As I explained in chapter 2, with help from Jared Sexton, blackness can also be experienced as a kind of de facto statelessness.[42] The rise in mass incarceration, for example, has been accompanied by policies and practices that have restricted social membership for all criminalized populations (but keeping in mind that this population is still disproportionately black). The due process and procedural rights that criminal suspects have access to, in principle, have been eroded by the practice of plea bargaining, the massive expansion of fines for noncriminal violations (which can result in a criminal conviction if the fees are not paid), and a host of policies, fines, and other kinds of institutional barriers that make it difficult for people to re-enter the community of rights-bearing subjects after they have served time.[43] These are just a few examples of how the bright line separating the rights-bearing criminal convict from the stateless refugee, described by Arendt, has become a lot fuzzier over the last few decades.

The relationship between race and criminality can also play out in different ways. When the problem of criminality is discussed in relation to migrants and refugees, it is often to suggest that these populations have "become criminalized." In this case, it would appear that criminality is experienced as a degradation of social status. People who had once been categorically distinguished from criminals—as future citizens, hard-workers, or deserving victims—are now being treated as "dangerous types." On the other hand, as Cacho has explained there are racialized populations whose social existence informs the meaning of criminality, and as Frank Wilderson has explained, the black body lies at the center of all of these ideas about criminality.[44] These are not bodies that possess a social status that can be degraded by criminality. The spectacular difference of these bodies defines the immanent and practical meaning of criminality. Blackness supplies the chain of signification that is used to decipher the meaning of criminality, whether it is through reference to particular kinds of bodies, the organization of social spaces or social situations.

This relationship between blackness and criminality sets up another vexing question when it comes to explaining the criminalization of migrants and refugees. If nonblack migrants are subjected to policies and enforcement practices that were originally used to control blacks, does this mean that they have been "blackened"? And if this is the case, then what remains of the black/nonblack binary? How is it possible for the stigma of blackness to effect people on the nonblack side of the binary without hopelessly blurring the distinction between black and nonblack? I began to explore this question at the beginning of the chapter, with my reflections on Danticat's writing. I am now going to treat it in more detail.

PERMUTATIONS OF THE BLACK/NONBLACK BINARY

Haitians, like many other black migrants and refugees, have a complex relationship to the stigma of blackness. In the context of the interdictions, Haitians epitomized the threat of black otherness. But in different contexts, Haitians have been spared this kind of treatment. For example, many Haitian immigrants have been inserted in narratives that distinguish them from US-born blacks. Tekle Woldemikael and Mary Waters have both shown how Haitians, and other Caribbean migrants, deployed their ethnic identities as a way of distancing themselves from the stigma of blackness, and were able to portray themselves, with varying degrees of success as "exceptional blacks" or "model minority blacks."[45] Alejandros Portes and Alex Stepick have also shown how some Haitian immigrant populations in South Florida tried to distance their politics from the "confrontational" stance associated with the native-born black population—opting instead for a more pragmatic, ethnic enclave model.[46] These radically different experiences beg the question: when and why does antiblackness matter as determinant of black social existence?

This is not the same thing as asking what blackness *is*, or what is antiblack racism. These sorts of questions are focused on explaining the predicament of blackness, once antiblackness has become salient as the dominant framework for an encounter. The question of "when and why" has more to do with the way that the predicament of blackness gets distributed across social contexts and populations.

The US government's interdiction operations were primarily focused on Haitian refugees, but all Haitians have not been treated in this manner. Black people are disproportionally targeted by aggressive policing practices and mass incarceration, but all black people are not targeted, all of the time, by all of these practices. Even if we start with the premise that all black people are exposed to some form of antiblack racism on a regular basis, there can still be significant differences in how this problem surfaces in peoples' lives and in the way it is experienced.

In chapter 1, I introduced one way of thinking about this diversity of black experience when I made a distinction between (anti)blackness as an apparatus of power and the sociological construct of the black population. The idea I wanted to get across is that black people can experience the predicament of blackness in different ways, because they are being exposed to antiblack sentiments that are being channeled through different circuitries of power. Viewed in this light, blackness is not a cultural attribute of a population that has been defined in advance "as black," it is an effect produced by a structural and discursive apparatus that operates at a higher level of abstraction than that of the "black population." I am going to develop this theoretical perspective on blackness a little further with some help from Michel Foucault's writing on modern racism.

Although Foucault does not discuss the black/white or black/nonblack binary, it is significant that his concept of modern racism is binarized.[47] According to Foucault, modern racism emanates from a biopolitical stratagem of governance that is geared toward defining and managing the relationship between superior and inferior races. There can be many different permutations of these superior/inferior distinctions, but there are only two racial types—and ultimately, just one "true" race: the superior-normal type which can be distinguished from all of the deviant strains that must be "cleansed" from it. It is also important to emphasize that the superior/inferior binary is a product of state discourse rather than a property that is intrinsic to these populations. Consequently, the racial binary can be understood as an inevitable product of the modern state's need to create an autopoietic discourse on power.

The binary is a parsimonious, meta-conceptual framework that can be applied to any population and adapted to any contingency. The abstract structure of the binary does not require that it be racist (it can also operate through

discourses on sexuality, gender, and class, though as some Foucauldian scholars have argued, all of these features of the binary are inextricably related and
inform each other[48]). Nevertheless, there is a genealogical relationship between
the racist binary, the dichotomous underpinnings of modern systems of knowledge (as illustrated by Cartesian dualism), and the emergence of a system of
biological knowledge about human populations that is informed by an evolutionary teleology (as illustrated by Social Darwinism and Spencerian theory).[49]

Viewed in this light, blackness cannot be reduced to a shared experience
that is rooted in the culture and history of populations that are traditionally
categorized as black. Instead, (anti)blackness is the means through which the
organizational imperatives of established structures of power are translated
into a field of racial visibility. For a Saussurean semiotics this ordering logic
could be described as paradigmatic rather than syntagmatic.[50] It does not
describe the historical permutation of things, as they change across time and
space, but the autopoietic logic that allows them to cohere across time and
space.

Of course, no paradigmatic sign-system is completely impervious to the
winds of history. The cosmological imaginary on which antiblack racism
relies can be explained by the unique conjunction of a stratagem of state
power and ideologies about race and societal progress that took shape during the super-exploitation of Africa and the Americas.[51] The important point,
from an Afropessimist perspective, is that this conjuncture of forces establishes antiblackness as a foundational element of modern capitalist society.
So it is not enough to say that these societies are racist and that antiblackness
is one of the historical permutations that this racism can take, which implies
that while modern capitalism is inherently racist, it is not necessarily or
always antiblack. To the contrary, the Afropessimist argument insists antiblackness is foundational to modern racism and to the ordering logics of the
modern state.

Foucault's explanation of modern racism does not contradict this explanation of blackness, it simply declines to address it. Scholars who have used
Foucault's race theory to explain the fluidity of race have arrived at con-
clusions that are not very different from Jared Sexton's explanation of the
relational quality of blackness and nonblackness.[52] The distinction between
blackness and nonblackness (like the distinction between the racially "superior" and "inferior") is adaptable, but the fundamental attributes of the binary
do not change. Nonblackness is always defined according to its distance
from blackness. This understanding of the relational quality of blackness and
nonblackness is very similar to the differentialist explanation of race that has
been attributed to Foucault.[53]

It is also possible to read this understanding of antiblackness into theory
on the new penology and of carceral humanitarianism. The new penology

relies on a discourse on crime that operates at the same meta-conceptual level as the racist ontology that anchors the black/nonblack binary. Criminogenic populations end up being transposed versions of the genetically determined criminal types of early twentieth-century eugenicist theory.[54] Irrespective of whether criminality is understood to be biologically determined, culturally determined, or a statistically inevitable risk factor determined by the social circumstances of a given population, the function of the criminogenic label remains the same. The condition of radical exclusion that had once been rationalized by very transparent arguments about black inferiority is now a racialized structural location in a field of power that can be perpetuated by a more plastic and racially complex kind of discourse. In both cases, the same kinds of bodies end up being excluded. This could be described as a discourse that relies on past iterations of blackness as its frame of reference, even as it branches out in new ways.

Carceral humanitarianism is an even more nuanced discourse. The interdicted refugee can be constructed as the victim who is being rescued from a dangerous and "illegal" migration scheme. But these enforcement operations are still used to police a biopolitical divide, between a refugee population that is predominantly composed of nonwhite, nonwesterners and the predominantly white citizen populations of the Western industrialized world. Mavelli also explains that the humanitarian agenda of these operations creates biopolitical distinctions that cut through the interdicted refugee population. Since these operations were not designed to "rescue" every refugee on the high seas, decisions have to be made that require

"selecting those that have priority for being saved (for example, when drug supplies are insufficient)," or in the case of the Mediterranean refugee crisis, deciding which "worthy lives" must be saved (even risking other lives to this end) in the name of the humanitarian imperative, and which "unworthy lives" can be left to drown in the name of security.[55]

The distinction Mavelli makes between refugees who deserve to be saved and those who are left to drown is extremely important for a theory of (anti) blackness. As many scholars have explained, blackness describes this very same threshold point—between life that is deserving of being preserved and cultivated and other forms of life that will be allowed to die.[56]

As it concerns my analysis, I also want to emphasize that every black/nonblack distinction takes its meaning from a specific kind of institutional discourse, which can be understood as a circuitry of power. The fact that some bodies are recognizable as black and others are not is the product of a circuitry of power, which can be traced to the racist typologies of the eighteenth century that established the black body as a distinct ocular phenomenon and invested it with a particular meaning.[57] The concept of the black population is the product of another relatively distinct circuitry of power, which is more abstract than a strictly morphological definition of blackness. Census statistics and social science research all play an important role in the production of this demographic feature of blackness. The more important point is that blackness is not an attribute that is intrinsic to a particular kind of body or population; it is the effect produced by a circuitry of power. (Anti)blackness is the prism of intelligibility that these circuitries use to order the social terrain, marking distinctions between what belongs and what does not and between lives that must be nurtured and those that can be allowed to let die.

The immanent parameters of black rightlessness can change, in response to new contingencies, without changing the hierarchical structure of the racist binary itself. Even though the precise configuration of the black/nonblack distinction may change, the end result is still a condition of rightlessness that relies on (anti)blackness as an immanent and discursive anchor point for all of these oppressive practices. This understanding of the black/nonblack binary sets the stage for my analysis of the CABA decision.

US POLICIES FOR CUBAN AND HAITIAN REFUGEES IN THE 1990S

Here is one way of summing up the theory of the black/nonblack binary that I presented in the last section. People with nonblack bodies can be exposed to exclusions that emanate from a history of antiblackness without "becoming black." The proliferation of these exclusions does not erase the distinction between black and nonblack, because they rely on the black/nonblack binary to produce their effects. So things can get worse for growing numbers of people who are not usually (or ever) viewed as black, but these desperate conditions can still be stratified in a way that conforms to the black/nonblack binary.

In the remainder of the chapter I am going to provide a detailed illustration of this process by taking a close look at the Eleventh Circuit Court of Appeals decision for *Cuban American Bar Association (CABA) v. Christopher.*[58] This case took up the complaints of Cuban-Mariel and Haitian detainees who had been interdicted at sea and were being held at US military bases in Guantanamo Bay, Cuba, and in Panama.

The starting point for these issues of contention can be traced to the summer of 1994, when a new mass exodus of refugees from Cuba began appearing on the shores of South Florida.[59] This exodus was not as large as the one that occurred in the late 1970s, which was controlled by the Carter-era Mariel boatlift operation. Nevertheless, it was the most dramatic increase that the US government had seen in recent years, numbering in the tens of thousands.[60] The concerns of US lawmakers were also piqued by Fidel Castro's announcement, in August of that year, that his government would no longer take steps to prevent the unauthorized emigration of Cuban citizens to the United States.[61] Approximately 8,000 Cuban refugees made the travel across the Caribbean Sea and landed on the shores of South Florida, before the United States changed its policy on Cuban refugees.[62]

The participants of the 1994 Cuban exodus had counted on being granted asylum under the open arms policy, which had been in place for almost three decades. The policy had been formalized by the 1966 *Cuban Adjustment Act*, which expedited the asylum process for Cubans and virtually guaranteed that they would be granted legal permanent residence.[63] Under the new policy, Cuban-Mariel refugees were interdicted by Coast Guard cutters and military vessels and detained at US military bases at Guantanamo and Panama.[64] Although Cuban refugees had shown up in the government's interdiction statistics throughout the late 1980s and early 1990s, this was the first time in which Cuban refugees were being categorically treated in a similar way as Haitians.[65]

Perhaps the most important change, as it concerned the US government's new Cuban refugee policy, is that fleeing Cubans had lost the privilege of being paroled into the United States. Effectively, they had been demoted to the status of the Haitian plaintiffs from *Jean v. Nelson* and *Sale v. HCC*.[66] An agreement reached by the Clinton and Castro administrations in September 1994 outlined the terms of the new policy.[67]

The US government agreed to allow the entry of up to 20,000 Cubans per year—either as refugees or visa holders—but these people would have to apply for admission in advance, using formal legal channels. Cubans who took to the sea, with the intention of entering the United States without authorization, would not be granted entry. After being interdicted and detained, the only options afforded to these people would be repatriation to Cuba, to remain indefinitely detained at a US military base or to apply for asylum to another nation. It is also important to note that this upsurge in Cuban refugee flows was occurring in the midst of a continuing mass exodus from Haiti that had been triggered by the ousting of the Aristide administration in 1991.[68]

Over the course of 1994, the Clinton administration had been devising a political solution to the Haitian refugee crisis which revolved around the goal of restoring the Aristide Presidency.[69] The expectation was that the restoration of Aristide would end, or at least significantly decrease, the mass exodus of Haitians to the United States, and the Clinton administration gambled correctly in its judgment.[70] Viewed in a cynical light, this was a pro-democracy initiative that was really informed by the security interests of the US government. But it was still a rare and welcome development for a great many

Haitians. It had been 200 years since the US executive office had deployed military forces in the service of Haitian democracy—the only other incident being the decision of the Adams administration to send warships to defend revolutionary-era Haiti from the British and the French.[71]

Meanwhile, the US government was still making policy decisions that set Haitian detainees apart from Cubans and exposed them to harsher treatment. Although the government initially announced, under the Clinton-Castro accord, that no Cuban detainees would be paroled into the United States, it later modified this policy. In October 1994, Attorney General Reno announced that the US government would consider parole for Cuban refugees held at the camps in Panama and Guantanamo who were over the age of seventy, chronically ill, unaccompanied minors, and for other children and their immediate families who would "adversely affected" by long-term detainment in the camps.[72] This policy effected little more than 500 detainees. So it is important to emphasize that the "no-parole" policy had not changed for well over 99 percent of the Cuban detainee population, which numbered approximately 33,000 people in the fall of 1994.[73] But it also bears noting that this policy was not extended to Haitian refugees.[74] The most concerning thing about this change in policy is not that the United States was being exceptionally generous to the Cuban-Mariel detainees but that it refused to extend this same gesture to an equally miniscule number of Haitians.

This new policy was also distinguished by its concern for the humanitarian treatment of Cuban detainees, which revolved around concerns about their personal sufferings in the camps.[75] But when this policy was later contested, by Haitian detainees, the government justified its decision by an assessment of the political situation in Cuba versus Haiti.[76] By this time, Aristide had been returned to power and the government made this turn of events a central feature of its argument. Because democracy had been restored in Haiti, and the Haitian government was, at least officially speaking, on friendlier terms with the United States than the Castro administration, it stood to reason that Haitians had a less compelling reason to seek shelter in the United States than Cubans. Although this is a plausible explanation, it revolves around an argument about "country conditions" that derives from asylum law[77]—and it is undercut by the fact that, as a matter of policy, the US government refused to categorize any of the Cuban-Mariel or Haitian detainees as refugees.[78]

If the government was to be consistent in its treatment of Haitian detainees as nonrefugees, the only conditions that should have mattered for its decision to issue humanitarian parole were living conditions in the camps not the political situation in Haiti. But this is not what happened. The squalid conditions in the camps provided a sufficient rationale for granting parole to Cuban detainees, but not to Haitians, who presumably were not "suffering" the same way. This argument about the different country conditions at play in Cuba and Haiti was also undercut by the fact that Cuban and Haitian detainees were both encouraged to repatriate to their home nations. The legal contest that gave rise to *CABA v. Christopher* begins with Cuban litigators and other immigrant rights advocates challenging the government's attempt to repatriate a group of twenty-three Cubans.[79]

I am going to examine this case in more detail in the next section. The point I wanted to make with this opening discussion is that the government's policy on Haitians was marked by a severity that could not be entirely explained by the arguments that were used to justify it. These arguments can be described as the trace effects of a distortion which, as Calvin Warren has explained, obfuscates and enables a judgment on blackness.[80] But in this case, the judgment on blackness was multilayered.

Mariel-Cuban detainees were exposed to policies that had first been used to control black mobility. But Mariel-Cuban detainees were also selectively exempted from some of the exclusions imposed on Haitians. Meanwhile, the overarching justification for the government's policies for both populations was anchored in the logic of carceral humanitarianism, which treated Cuban and Haitian detainees as different features of the same "population problem." The next section takes a closer look at how all of these racialized processes played out in the arguments of the federal courts.

CABA V. CHRISTOPHER AND THE RACIST SUBTEXT OF CARCERAL HUMANITARIANISM

By the time the Clinton administration's policies on Cuban and Haitian refugees entered litigation, the mass exodus from both nations had been largely contained. The flow of Haitian refugees was slowed to a trickle after the reinstatement of Aristide.[81] At the peak of the Haitian crisis in 1995, over 16,800 Haitians were being held at Guantanamo but by the end of the year there were only approximately 8,000 Haitian detainees.[82] This decrease in the Haitian detainee population was driven, mainly, by voluntary repatriations and there was no significant increase in the size of this population by the time the federal courts began their deliberations.

The Clinton-Castro accord produced a similar effect for the Mariel-Cuban exodus. In the summer and early fall of 1994, over 33,000 Cubans had taken to the high seas.[83] By the time the federal courts started their deliberations, the Cuban exodus had slowed to almost zero and there were approximately 20,000 Cuban detainees who were being held in the camps at Guantanamo and Panama.[84]

As in most of the case histories surrounding the government's interdiction policies, the District Court decision was favorable to the refugees. By the time Judge Atkins of the Southern District Court of Florida heard the case in November 1994, the complaints of litigators for the Cuban detainees had been joined by those of the HRC.[85] Atkins issued a temporary restraining order which granted attorneys access to both groups of detainees to inform them of their rights and options, blocked the repatriation of all Cuban and Haitian detainees if they had not been granted a consultation with a lawyer, directed Attorney General Reno to extend the same parole policy she had fashioned for Cuban detainees to Haitians as well, and also required the government to release names of all the Haitian detainees to the HRC.[86]

The government appealed this decision, which was sent to the Eleventh Circuit Court of Appeals for review. When the Eleventh Circuit issued its decision in January 1995 it significantly amended but did not completely override the District Court's initial decision. The Eleventh Circuit agreed that the government should allow Cuban Legal Organizations "reasonable access" to clients who had requested legal counsel in writing.[87] Although this was, on its face, a considerate ruling, it barred these legal organizations from accessing the larger majority of Cuban detainees who had not requested legal counsel (and probably were not aware that this counsel was available). The Eleventh Circuit also overrode the District Court's order that prevented the repatriation of Cuban detainees who had agreed to be repatriated.[88] But the court also prohibited the government from repatriating Cuban detainees who had not provided a written declaration of their desire to be returned to Cuba.[89]

The Eleventh Circuit's decision on the legal rights of the detainees, however, was a more stalwart in its defense of the government's position. The court struck down all of the claims on statutory, constitutional, and international law that were levied by the detainees and their legal counsel. It denied Cuban and Haitian detainees access to the Immigration and Nationality Act, including sections pertaining to Article 33 of the 1951 Refugee Convention; denied Cuban plaintiffs the protections of the 1966 Cuban Refugee Adjustment Act; and denied Cuban and Haitian detainees the protections of the Fifth Amendment, which included both "due process and equal protection of laws."[90]

The Eleventh Circuit's decision was forecasted by the legal precedents it chose to frame its argument. At the beginning of its opinion, the court made a point of highlighting three cases from the history of litigations over the government's Haitian refugee policies. These cases included the Supreme Court's decision in *Sale v. HCC* (1993), and two of its prior decisions: for *HRC v. Baker* (1992) and *Jean v. Nelson* (1984).[91]

In all of these cases, the majority opinion issued a staunch defense of the government's policies, so the litigants should not have been surprised with the argument that followed. With this choice of cases, the Eleventh Circuit confirmed that the Haitian refugee policies of the Reagan-Bush and late

Carter era had established the legal foundations for the policies that were being contested by CABA. Hence, the Eleventh Circuit was basically admitting that there was a causal relationship between this prior history of Haitian refugee policies and the recent change in policy for Cuban-Mariel refugees. This was not just a matter of the government treating Haitian and Cuban refugees in a comparable way; the government's prior treatment of Haitians was directly informing its treatment of Cubans.

The Eleventh Circuit argued that the high seas, and the military bases where the detainees were being held, did not fall under the jurisdiction of US or international law.[92] These arguments were patterned after ones that can be traced to *HCC v. Sale*, *HRC v. Baker*, and *HRC v. Gracey*.[93] The CABA decision, however, was distinguished by an emphasis on the humanitarian intentions of the government's policies.

The majority opinion observed that interdiction operations had been guided by the goal of saving rafters lives and to deter unsolicited migration flows that were dangerous to the refugees themselves; it described the refugees as beneficiaries of an "American tradition of humanitarian concern and conduct," and referenced the "humanitarian groups" that were allowed to visit migrants at the base (including the UNHCR, Amnesty International, Inc., the US Committee for Refugees, and Church World Service).[94]

All of these activities occurred under the auspices of Operation Sea Signal, which had been initiated by the Clinton administration in August 1994.[95] The operation was guided by policies that were patterned after the "no-screen" policy which had been introduced by the Bush administration's 1991 Kennebunkport Order.[96] Consequently, no attempt was made to hear the asylum petitions of the interdicted Cubans and Haitians that were being detained at Guantanamo. Cubans were given the opportunity to file for an immigration visa or refugee relief, on the condition that they repatriate to Cuba and file an application through the US Embassy in Havana.[97] But the US government was adamant that no one would be considered for asylum if they attempted to enter the United States without prior authorization.[98]

Sea Signal also differed from prior interdiction operations in the way it handled repatriations. Cuban and Haitian detainees were not repatriated without their consent, which meant that the US government was prepared to house them on Guantanamo indefinitely.[99] The US government spent upward of half a billion dollars on the housing structures used to shelter the detainees and to keep the bases supplied with living essentials, but the camps still served a carceral function—to confine a population that was being prevented from entering the United States.[100] Plus according to many reports, conditions for many detainees were squalid and unsanitary.[101] Attorney General Reno's policy of selective parole for the aged, infirm, and certain families with children can be read as an implicit acknowledgment of the hardships of camp life.[102]

The humanitarian mandate of Sea Signal also played an important role in the Eleventh Circuit's argument for why the detainees had no access to the law. One of the arguments advanced by the plaintiffs is that the detainees' First Amendment rights had been violated because they were being deprived of access to independent legal counsel—and that this was a matter of special concern for detainees who had agreed to be repatriated.[103] The court argued that because the repatriated detainees had not requested legal counsel, they could not be legitimately considered part of the class on whose behalf the suit was being filed.[104] But its more substantive argument was that the detainees had no First Amendment "liberty interest" to defend because they did not have the right to have rights.

One of the anchoring themes of this argument was that the detainees were the beneficiaries of a "gratuitous humanitarian act."[105] The gratuitousness of the act underscored its extra-legal nature. To borrow from Agamben, the detainees were bare life; people who deserved only to have their basic living needs attended to.[106] So the government had no obligation to these people of the sort that a rights-bearing subject could demand of it. This point was underscored by the government's insistence on categorizing all of the detainees as migrants, rather than refugees, and denying them access to screening procedures to determine the legitimacy of their asylum petitions. The connections between all of these points were summed up by the court in the following way:

> "Screening" is a preliminary process during which a determination may be made that the migrant has a well-founded fear of persecution if repatriated. . . . The individual Cuban and Haitian plaintiffs have argued that the processing which occurs when migrants are brought into safe haven is similar to the screening procedure which takes place when the government attempts to discern if a migrant is a refugee. However, providing safe haven residency is a gratuitous humanitarian act which does not in any way create even the putative liberty interest in securing asylum processing that the Second Circuit found that initial screening creates.[107]

In the context of this argument, the concept of the "gratuitous humanitarian act" functioned as a way of normalizing the rightlessness of the detainees. There are parallels between this argument and antebellum-era jurisprudence that governed the conduct of masters and slaves.

Saidiya Hartman has explained that the courts of the antebellum era sometimes took a dim view of white property owners who violently abused their slaves, but they rarely imposed legal sanctions on the master for their behavior. Instead the courts usually counseled both slaves and masters to value the sentimental attachments that, presumably, governed daily life on the plantation.[108] Like the "gratuitous humanitarian act," these sentimental attachments could be described as an extra-legal ethical sensibility: something one understands they ought to do, but they are not obligated to do by force of law. The master was not obligated to treat the slave with care and consideration but they were counseled that it would be wise of them to do so. In a similar vein, the Eleventh Circuit observed that the US government could have repatriated all of the Guantanamo detainees without seeking their permission, but through an act of generosity it established procedures for securing their consent.[109] The Eleventh Circuit also implied that the government was not legally obligated to protect the lives of Cuban and Haitian boatpeople and that it did not have to invest its resources in constructing housing structures on Guantanamo for them or invite international humanitarian organizations to monitor the way they were being treated.[110]

In the context of this argument, the "humanitarian gesture" takes on a meaning which is radically different from the "human right." The court made it clear that the detainees did not have an inherent right to be treated in a fair and dignified manner. Instead they were the objects of a bureaucratic administration that was predicated on their rightlessness. Humanitarianism provided a discursive gloss for these administrative practices which were used to manage the movements of an unwanted population through techniques of interdiction, confinement, and repatriation.

THE CONTINUING SIGNIFICANCE
OF HAITIAN BLACKNESS

The Eleventh Circuit was very consistent in arguing that the government's policy on Haitian refugees was now the controlling precedent for its treatment of all of the detainees who were being held at Guantanamo. I have argued that this is a matter of policies that were first designed to control black mobility, being extended to a more diverse population of blacks and nonblacks. The arguments of the plaintiffs, however, never exposed this racist subtext and, when they questioned the government's policies, they did so in ways that ignored the salience of the black/nonblack binary. A good example is the challenge that the Cuban American Bar Association and the HRC levied against the Eleventh Circuit's final decision in *HRC v. Baker*[111] (which the Eleventh Circuit had used to frame its decision for CABA). This decision is important because it established arguments about the territorial limits of the law that were used to justify the "no-screen" procedures of the Kennebunkport Executive Order which ended up becoming standard practice for the government's interdiction operations from 1992 onward.

Lawyers for the plaintiffs argued that *HRC v. Baker* only applied to people interdicted on the high seas, who were repatriated directly to their home nation, and that it did not apply to interdictees—like those in CABA—who were being detained at Guantanamo.[112] The Eleventh Circuit responded to this argument by reminding the plaintiffs that in, in its final decision for *HRC v. Baker*, it had also addressed the situation of "screened-in" Haitians who were being held at Guantanamo, and reached a similar conclusion, that they had no access to US or international law.[113] The court concluded by insisting that the precedent it established about the rightlessness of Guantanamo detainees for *HRC v. Baker* also held for the detainees whose complaints were addressed in the CABA decision.

The lawyers for the Cuban detainees could have made another argument about the inapplicability of *HRC v. Baker* that called attention to the anti-black history of these interdiction operations. Simply stated, *HRC v. Baker* had been designed for Haitians not Cubans. When the Eleventh Circuit issued this decision, the "no-screen" practices that had been authorized by the Kennebunkport Executive Order were being administered, exclusively, for Haitian refugees. Cuban refugees, during this same period of time, were still benefiting from the "open arms" policy that originated in the mid-1960s.[114]

This would, admittedly, have been a prickly argument to make, for at least two reasons. Instead of uniting Cuban and Haitians under a shared complaint, it would have exposed a racial fault-line running between these two popula-tions. This argument would also have left lawyers for the Cuban detainees open to the charge that they were attempting to capitalize on the racial privilege that Cuban refugees had enjoyed, for a great many decades, over Haitians. But this argument would also have forced the Eleventh Circuit to directly address the racist subtext of the government's interdiction operations and to offer some kind of explanation for the sudden shift in the government's exercise of its sovereign authority over Cuban refugee policy. Why was a policy that had once been administered exclusively for Haitians now being administered to Cubans as well? Why had Cubans been exempt from these radically exclusionary Haitian refugee policies in the first place? And could legal precedents like *HRC v. Baker* be retroactively applicable to a national origin group that had been originally exempted from them?

It is difficult to say how the Eleventh Circuit would have responded to these sorts of questions. At the very least, these questions would have forced the court to provide an explanation for the government's differential and unequal treatment of Haitian and Cuban refugees. As I have argued throughout this chapter, this line of questioning calls attention to the continuing significance of a black/nonblack binary that has always been a feature of US immigration and refugee policy.

But these arguments were not raised. Consequently, the Eleventh Circuit was given free reign to justify the radical exclusion of Cuban and Haitian detainees with an argument that mimicked the colorblind premise of the plaintiff's complaints. The plaintiffs tried to devise an inclusive argument for why *HRC v. Baker* did not hold for "all" Guantanamo detainees. The Eleventh Circuit responded by arguing that the government's policies on Haitian refugees (including but also extending beyond *HRC v. Baker*) now applied to "all" people who were interdicted on the high seas and detained in offshore facilities. But neither side in this debate had any interest in calling attention to the racist historiography of the Eleventh Circuit's argument, which is that these policies and enforcement practices that were now being applied to "all" people had originated as a deterrence strategy that was exclusively used to control black mobility.

It also bears noting that the suppression of antiblackness, as a topic of deliberation, did not create a level playing field for the treatment of Cuban and Haitian detainees. Although it avoided couching its arguments in racial terms, the Eleventh Circuit continued to reinscribe the black/nonblack binary in ways that singled out Haitians. An important example is the reasoning used by the court to defend Attorney General Reno's policy on selective parole for Cuban detainees.[115] As I explained earlier, this policy allowed a relatively small number of Cuban detainees with special family or health conditions to be transferred to the US mainland. In its complaint, which was integrated into the law suit, the HRC insisted that this policy should be extended to Haitian unaccompanied minors.[116]

In its response to this complaint, the Eleventh Circuit drew on the precedent it had established with its decision for *Jean v. Nelson*.[117] In chapter 2, I explained that this argument was controversial for the Supreme Court because of the Eleventh Circuit's reliance on the Plenary Power doctrine. The Supreme Court insisted that it was not necessary for the Eleventh Circuit to make a constitutional argument on behalf of the government's authority to exclude migrants and refugees due to race, national origin, or any other reason.[118] The Supreme Court also argued that Haitian detainees had no claim on the law but that the government's parole decisions were being conducted in a fair and impartial manner (i.e., they were not racially biased).[119]

Given this history of contention, it is significant that the Eleventh Circuit was allowed to decide CABA and that the Supreme Court refused to hear the appeal that was requested by the detainees' lawyers. The practical result of this decision is that, for CABA, the Supreme Court deferred to the Eleventh Circuit's opinion on the government's constitutionally protected right to discriminate on the basis of race. The Eleventh Circuit returned to this argument in its discussion of Attorney General Reno's parole policy.

Citing its own language from *Jean v. Nelson*, the court insisted that parole is "an act of extraordinary sovereign generosity."[120] Like the "gratuitous humanitarian act" this "extraordinary generosity" is not regulated by the law and is buttressed by the government's sovereign power, "to draw distinctions among aliens based on nationality."[121] The argument the Supreme Court made in the *Chinese Exclusion Case*, which affirmed the legality of the Plenary Power doctrine, illustrates how these sovereign decisions can be informed by racist sensibilities.[122] Although the Eleventh Circuit did not directly cite this case in CABA, the *Chinese Exclusion Case* was an important precedent that was cited in the argument it made for *Jean v. Nelson*; and *Jean v. Nelson*, in turn, was very important for the argument it advanced in CABA.[123] In this way, the argument about the government's authority to make racist decisions was reduced to a ghostly presence that operated at a distance from the court's argument, while remaining an important part of its legal foundations.

On the other hand, the practical examples that the court used to justify Attorney General Reno's exclusion of Haitians had to do with the different political conditions of Haiti compared to Cuba.[124] One implication of this argument is that the exclusion of Haitians from Attorney General Reno's parole policy was not based on race or national origin, but on different conditions in Haiti that would make it easier for Haitians to repatriate than Cubans (namely, Aristide's return to power and Haiti's status as a "friendly nation" vis-à-vis the United States). As I explained earlier, this argument conflated the humanitarian reasons for parole—that were based on the health, age, and family status of detainees—with country conditions criteria that were more relevant to asylum law. But it also calls attention to a distortion that always seems to surface when the federal courts make arguments that defend racially exclusionary policies. On one hand, the Eleventh Circuit's defense of the government's authority to discriminate relied on legal precedents that contain explicitly racist arguments. But on the other hand, when the court had to give a more precise explanation of the reasoning behind Attorney General Reno's decisions, it resorted to arguments that used a race-neutral rationale.

This pattern of Haitian-specific exclusions continued after CABA was decided. Several months after the Eleventh Circuit issued its decision, the Clinton administration released an accord that allowed the approximately 20,000 Cuban detainees who were still being housed in the camps to be paroled to the United States.[125] This invitation was not extended to Haitians for the same reasons that they were excluded from AG Reno's parole policy. This accord also introduced the wet foot/dry foot policy which established a controversial double standard for the treatment of Cuban and Haitian asylum seekers.[126]

The wet foot/dry foot policy replicated the same multilayered pattern of inequalities as the CABA decision. The policy was, on one hand, more restrictive than the one it replaced and it used a standard for granting asylum to Cubans that had been influenced by the government's policy on Haitian refugees. Unlike the prior open arms policy, Cubans who were interdicted at sea would be granted no claim on the law and would be returned to Cuba.[127] These Cuban refugees were now going to be exposed to the same deterrence policy that the government had devised for Haitian refugees in the early 1980s. But the wet foot/dry foot policy also granted Cubans a preferential treatment that was denied to Haitians. Cuban refugees who managed to touch ground on US soil would be granted an expedited pathway to asylum, similar to what they had enjoyed under the former, open arms policy.[128] In contrast, Haitians who reached US soil were treated to a policy of mandatory detention, denied any screening of their asylum claims and tracked into deportation proceedings.[129]

THE PERMUTATIONS OF
ANTIBLACKNESS, REVISITED

I have used this chapter to explore several inter-related arguments about the relationship between blackness, statelessness, and criminality; about how the black/nonblack binary is enabled by US law and policy; and why carceral humanitarianism was an important feature of the deterrence strategies of the Clinton era. In this closing discussion I want to thread the connections between these arguments.

I began by observing that the growing intersections of criminal and immigration law are just one manifestation of the deterrence paradigm that has been theorized by Gammeltoft-Hansen and Tan.[130] When immigrants are criminalized, they are usually being set up for removal, but the deterrence paradigm is geared, more broadly, toward managing the mobility of "undesirables." This can involve new techniques of removal, interdiction, and reparation, and sophisticated combinations of incentives and coercions that are used to preemptively avert mass exodus scenarios before they even start. Mark Duffield has explained how all of these techniques of deterrence can be connected to a global theory of racism, in which racist imaginaries become encoded in the territorial organization of a world-scale political and economic system.[131] Whereas investment capital and securitized flows of precarious, highly skilled labor migrants experience a kind of hyper-mobility, huge investments are made to ensure that poor, nonwhite populations "stay in their place" in the poor and nonwhite corners of the world. This is, effectively, what the US government was trying to do to the Haitian and Cuban refugees who raised their complaints in *CABA v. Christopher*.

Feeley and Simon's theory of the new penology provides more helpful insights into this dilemma.[132] When the US government categorized these detainees as migrants rather than refugees, it was also, by default, construct-ing them as "illegal" migrants. People who cross national borders without authorization, and are understood to be "refugees," are entitled to a hearing about their claims of persecution, which could result in them being granted a permanent legal status. People who do the same thing, but are categorized as "migrants," are nothing more than lawbreakers in the eyes of the government.

This is why the "population problem" posed by the CABA detainees could be described as a body of ideas that was informed by notions of illegality-as-criminality, even though it was not concretely anchored in criminal or immigration law. The CABA detainees could not be formally charged with breaking any US laws, because they had been apprehended in a space that lay outside rule of law. If these detainees were formally charged with an immi-gration or criminal violation, they would also have to be granted access to the rights that the federal courts refused to bestow on them. So it would appear that this was a population of lawbreakers who were radically alienated from the very same body of law that they were accused of violating: they were stateless criminals.

The humanitarian discourse that pervaded the Eleventh Circuit's decision, and which also appears in the mandate for Operation Sea Signal, adds another level of nuance to this kind of criminality. Although Cuban and Haitian detainees were, effectively, treated like incarcerated persons, their incarcera-tion was abstracted from the legal question of their criminality. They were described as people who had been saved from drowning by the government's interdiction operations and their detainment at Guantanamo was framed as a gratuitous humanitarian act. As I explained previously, this humanitarian discourse was accompanied by arguments that justified their rightlessness.

This emphasis on the government's humanitarian motives underscored the point that it was not acting out of legal obligation and that the detainees had no grounds to make claims about their rights under US or international law. In this regard, the CABA detainees were very different from the criminal-ized populations on the US mainland whose incarceration was understood to be a form of punishment. But this is also why Feeley and Simon's writing on the new penology is so prescient, because it describes the rise of a meta-conceptual paradigm of criminality that has been applied to both of these populations.[133]

Both groups are defined in light of a problem that they pose on a popula-tion scale. The concept of lawbreaking is converted into a potential that is immanent to these populations, regardless of whether it has been manifested in any particular situation. As a result, these populations are exposed to forms of surveillance and control that are premised on the assumption that they are always-already predisposed to causing these "problems." In the case of racial others on the US mainland, this problem usually has something to do with the violation of personal property. In the case of the CABA detainees, the problem is the violation of US immigration laws (i.e., entering without authorization). But in both cases, there is a subtext which has more to do with the violation of racialized social distances.

The "crime" of black populations in the United States has always been intimately associated with socioeconomic, political, and sexualized anxieties about the collapsing of boundaries that separate white from black.[134] There was a similar anxiety at play in the treatment of CABA detainees, which had to do with the fear of uncontrolled flows of racially suspect populations pouring into the US mainland. But if we are prepared to take these propositions seriously, then we also have to reflect a little more carefully on what's "new" about the new penology.

The new penology can be described as a mutation in the way systems of law and criminological theory rationalize the management of "undesirable" populations. But the targets of the new penology and practical outcomes of the practices that are implemented under its aegis are not very new at all. The mass incarceration that has been rationalized by the new penology can be understood as a new iteration of the same controls on black mobility that are reflected in political culture of the Jim Crow era, and before that, the chattel slavery of the antebellum era.

In each era, there is both a rupture and an intimate communication between questions of jurisdiction and the unasked question about the predicament of the black other. In the antebellum era, jurisdictional questions about legal status were used to ventriloquize a judgment on blackness. In the Jim Crow era, the discourse on "states rights" produces a similar effect, and in CABA this role is played by an argument about the territorial limits of the law. The connecting thread for all of these questions of legal jurisdiction is not a particular jurisprudence or discourse on race, but a racialized effect. In each era, the same kinds of racialized bodies and populations end up with the short end of the stick—and this problem underscores the salience of the black/nonblack binary.

Foucault's theory of modern racism has underscored its binarized and relational structure: there are superior types who are always defined though a point of contrast with inferiors.[135] Scholars in the field of Black Studies have pointed out that this binarized structure is both ontologically and historically antiblack.[136] Although the binary has given form to a multiplicity of racial distinctions, antiblackness is a recurring theme across its genealogical permutations, which can be traced to its beginnings. This is one reason why the black experience of racism is so often used as a point of reference for other racisms. Patterns of de facto segregation and systemic racism targeting Latinx populations are tagged the new "Juan Crow,"[137] criticism of "immigrant apartheid" references South African racial apartheid[138] and there are also the ubiquitous references to new forms of slavery, or oppressive conditions that are analogous to slavery, which evoke the specter of antebellum-era chattel slavery.[139] In a similar vein, antiblackness can be understood as the reservoir of collective anxieties that gives meaning to the concept of criminality in the postbellum era. Blackness is not criminalized. Criminality relies on blackness to anchor the idea of the "criminal type."

If you trace this relationship between antiblackness and criminality far enough, it leads to a seemingly intractable dilemma. Because antiblackness anchors the racist binary, it has an explanatory power that is not equaled by the nonblack category. But it has been denied this explanatory power as a matter of ontologically necessity (from the vantage point of antiblack racism) precisely because of the role it has played as the threshold of the knowable and the limit point of the human. This is another way of restating a problem I introduced in chapter 1 concerning the institutionally conditioned collective amnesia around the questions of slavery and blackness in the Western canon. The insistence of so many scholars in treating black and nonblack categories as analogous features of the same kind of racism is another reflection of this problem.

I have used my analysis of *CABA v. Christopher* to underscore this point: that blackness is not interchangeable with nonblackness. Blackness describes a more extreme kind of exclusion and it can be used to explain worsening conditions for people who are usually positioned on the nonblack side of the binary.

There is evidence, for example, that Cuban-Mariel and Haitian refugees were viewed as interchangeable versions of the same racial threat by local white populations.[140] Even so, the US government has a long history of treating Cuban refugees in a "better" and categorically different way than Haitians—and the policy history recounted by the CABA decision testifies to this fact. The treatment of Haitians cannot be explained by policies of unprecedented severity that are first hatched to control Cubans, which gradually proliferate to Haitians. If the standards established by the US treatment of Cuban refugees had extended to Haitians, the result would have been a more lenient and open policy for Haitians. It is also not the case that policies for Cuban and Haitian refugees got worse, at the same time, as if these were parallel developments. The Eleventh Circuit's decision for CABA made it very clear that the elimination of the open arms policy, and its replacement by a more draconian policy, rests on legal precedents that were established by the US government's policy on Haitian refugees.[141] So, the arrow of causation flies from blackness to nonblackness, but not the other way.

It is also important to emphasize that the government's policy on Haitian refugees has its own precursors. As I explained in chapter 2, the Haitian inter-dictions can be situated within a genealogy of controls on black mobility (or, what I have called the prohibition on black migration) that is traceable to the late seventeenth century. It is this history, more so than the Haitian refugee policies of the 1970s–1990s, which establish the antiblack foundations of the exclusionary sentiments that explain the new policy on Cuban refugees that takes shape in the mid-1990s. But I also tried to show that antiblackness was not just a feature of the historic context for the CABA decision, it is also reflected in its practical outcomes.

Although the Eleventh Circuit's opinion extended the government's Haitian policies to Cubans, it continued to justify policy decisions that, inexplicably, extended small mercies and special considerations for Cuban detainees that were denied to Haitians. The Clinton administration put an exclamation point on these inequities when it decided to parole all of the remaining Cuban detainees into the United States months after the Eleventh Circuit decided CABA, while declining to do the same for Haitians.[142]

These outcomes underscore a point I made in my explanation of how conditions, hatched on the "black" side of the black/nonblack binary, can effect people on the "nonblack" side but without eliminating the racist binary that privileges the latter group at the expense of the former. I have shown, for example, that the US government's Haitian refugee policies were an important precursor for its change in policy on Cuban-Mariel refugees. The "population problem" posed by Cuban refugees in the mid-1990s was translated through a set of concerns that can be connected to a history of (anti)blackness, but the problem itself was not specifically concerned with the control of black mobility. Instead, fears of black uncontrolled black mobility could be described as the starting template for a broader set of concerns, about "undesirables" from the postcolonial, global South spilling over into the global North. Meanwhile the US government's treatment of Haitian detainees underscores an experience of radical exclusion that is specific to bodies and populations that are coded as black. Antiblackness continued to be salient in the government's unequal treatment of Haitians from Cubans—indicating that the extension of "black policies" to "nonblack" Cubans still required the radical exclusion of black bodies as an anchoring sensibility.

These permutations of black rightlessness can be complicated even more, but in a productive way, by Kevin Johnson's research on racism and immigration law. Johnson has explained that, around the same time that the Eleventh Circuit was deciding CABA, the Supreme Court issued a series of decisions that granted relief to black and nonblack immigrants who were on the verge of being deported for drug offenses.[143] Johnson notes that the court viewed these plaintiffs, sympathetically, as "small time immigrant drug offenders (black and brown) caught up in war on drugs."[144] The Supreme Court's decisions in these cases could be taken as a signal that it thought the war on drugs and its confluence with crimmigration law had gone too far in eviscerating immigrant rights.

These decisions offer more corroboration for Arendt's explanation of the distinguishing features of criminality and statelessness.[145] The intersections of criminal and immigration law may have made it easier for criminal convictions to become a pathway to statelessness for a growing number of noncitizens. Even so, black and nonblack immigrants who were being put through deportation proceedings in the mid-1990s still had more rights than the Cuban and Haitian detainees who were the focus of the CABA decision. Of course, this does not mean that antiblack racism is not an issue in the US deportation system. Although blacks make up a relatively small minority of the overall deportation caseload, they are hugely overrepresented in the subpopulation of migrants that are deported for criminal convictions.[146] Nevertheless, the black immigrant convicted of a drug offense is not in the same condition of abject rightlessness as that of the Cuban or Haitian Guantanamo detainee population.

There is something more at play, in these experiences of exclusion than an animus which indiscriminately exposes all black bodies to the same kind of exclusion. There are also the circuitries of power, that I discussed earlier in this chapter, which explain how the racist binary becomes salient for a given body or population at a given place or point in time. All of these propositions set up the analysis I am going to provide in the next chapter, about how the Haitian interdictions set the stage for the US-Mexico border enforcement policies of the Trump era.

NOTES

1. For an introduction to these Clinton-era enforcement practices see n95–100 and the accompanying discussion in the text. Statistics on peak years of Haitian (and Cuban) interdictions were discussed in the introductory chapter. Over 60,000 Haitian and Cuban refugees were interdicted in 1994, under Operation Sea Signal, topping the previous peak of over 33,000 Haitian and Cuban refugees under the G. W Bush-era Kennebunkport policy. See Bureau of Transportation Statistics, "Table 5.1 U.S. Coast Guard Migrant Interdictions at Sea, Calendar Years 1991–2001," https://www.bts.gov/archive/publications/maritime_trade_and_transportation/2002/table_05_01; Ruth Ellen Wasem, *US Immigration Policy on Haitian Migrants* (Washington, DC: Congressional Research Service, 2011).

2. This change in policy is discussed later in this chapter. See n63–67 and accompanying discussion in the text.

3. I reference this public sphere activism throughout the book. For one of the most detailed examples, see n5–9 in chapter 2 and the discussion in the accompanying text.

4. Edwidge Danticat, "Children of the Sea," in *Krik? Krak!* (New York: Soho Press, 1995), 1–29.

5. Ibid., 8.

6. *Cuban Adjustment Act*, Pub. L. 89–732, 80 Stat. 1161 (1966). See also n63 and the accompanying discussion in the text.

7. For a discussion of the wet foot/dry foot policy, see n126–129 and the accompanying discussion in the text. The border enforcement polices of the Trump and Biden administrations are discussed in chapter 6. The policy of most relevance for Haitian asylum seekers is "Title 42" which grants the government broad discretion to deny entry on the grounds of public health concerns. See Nicole Phillips and Tom Ricker, *The Invisible Wall: Title 42 and its Impact on Haitian Migrants*, Haitian Bridge Alliance, Quixote Center and UndocuBlack Network, March 25, 2021, accessed September 19, 2021, file:///C:/Users/pkret/OneDrive/Documents/Writing%20&%20Research/Black%20Interdictions/Chapter%20Drafts/Completed%20Drafts/The-Invisible-Wall.pdf.

8. *Cuban American Bar Association v. Christopher*, 43 F.3d 1412, 1419 (11th Cir. 1995).

9. *Sale v. Haitian Centers Council*, 509 U.S. 155 (1993).

10. *Sale*, 509 U.S. 155 at 156–157.

11. As it concerns the nonrefoulement principle, these foundation documents include the United Nation's 1951 Convention and the 1967 Protocol Relating to the Status of Refugees which were both ratified by the US government. See António Guterres, *The 1951 Convention Relating to the Status of Refugees and its 1967 Protocol* (Geneva: United Nations High Commission on Refugees, 2011).

12. Thomas Gammeltoft-Hansen and Nikolas Tan, "The End of the Deterrence Paradigm - Future Directions for Global Refugee Policy," *Journal on Migration and Human Security* 5, no. 1 (2017): 28–56. Although Gammeltoft-Hansen and Tan speculate on the impending demise of the deterrence paradigm, my analysis pays attention to its continuing significance and shows that it is very much alive and well, as a feature of US immigration and refugee policy.

13. Gammeltoft-Hansen and Tan, "The End of the Deterrence Paradigm," 38–40. The shift toward the use of Temporary Protected Status over asylum is discussed in more detail in chapter 6.

14. Gammeltoft-Hansen and Tan, "The End of the Deterrence Paradigm," 37–38.

15. Patrisia Macías-Rojas, "Immigration and the War on Crime: Law and Order Politics and the *Illegal Immigration Reform and Immigrant Responsibility Act of 1996*," *Journal on Migration and Human Security* 6, no. 1 (2018): 1–25 at 5.

16. Ibid., 5–6.

17. Ibid; Anita Sinha, "Slavery By Another Name: 'Voluntary' Immigrant Detainee Labor and the Thirteenth Amendment," *Stanford Journal of Civil Rights & Civil Liberties* 11, no. 1 (2015): 1–44 at 5–6.

18. Macías-Rojas, "Immigration and the War on Crime," 12–14.

19. Juliet Stumpf, "The Crimmigration Crisis: Immigrants, Crime and Sovereign Power," *American University Law Review* 56, no. 2 (2006): 367–419 at 383–384; Sarah Tosh, "Defending the 'Bad Immigrant:' Aggravated Felonies, Deportation, and

Legal Resistance at the Crimmigration Nexus" (PhD Diss., CUNY, John Jay College of Criminal Justice, 2019), 41–70.

20. Macías-Rojas, "Immigration and the War on Crime," 6–13.

21. Subhash Kateel and Aarti Shahani, "Families for Freedom: Against Deportation and Delegalization," in *Keeping Out the Other: A Critical Introduction to Immigration Enforcement Today*, eds. David Brotherton and Philip Kretsedemas (New York: Columbia University Press, 2008), 204–240; Tosh, "Defending the 'Bad Immigrant,'" 2–9.

22. John Higham, *Strangers in the Land; Patterns of American Nativism, 1860–1925* (New York: Atheneum, 1963).

23. Macías-Rojas, "Immigration and the War on Crime," 9–16; Sinha, "Slavery by Another Name," 6–7.

24. *Immigration Reform and Control Act*, Pub.L 99–603, 100 Stat. 3359 (1986). Kristina Shull, "Nobody Wants These People: Reagan's Immigration Crisis and America's First Private Prisons" (PhD diss,University of California-Irvine, 2014), 49–58.

25. 1990 *Immigration Act* (Pub.L. 101–649, 104 Stat. 4978) and the 1996 *Illegal Immigration and Immigrant Responsibility Act* (Pub.L. 104–208, 110 Stat. 3009 aka 110 Stat. 3009–546). Carl Lindskoog, *Detain and Punish: Haitian Refugees and the Rise of the World's Largest Immigration Detention System* (Gainesville, FL: University Press of Florida, 2018), 82 and 133–136.

26. Kelly Oliver, *Carceral Humanitarianism: Logics of Refugee Detention* (Minneapolis, MN: University of Minnesota Press, 2017).

27. Gary Palmer, "Guarding the Coast: Alien Migrant Interdiction Operations at Sea," *International Law Studies* 72, no. 1 (1998): 157–179 T 164–165.

28. *Haitian Centers Council v. Sale*, 823 F. Supp. 1028 (E.D.N.Y. 1993) at 1036 and 1038–1039.

29. Luca Mavelli, "Governing Populations Through the Humanitarian Government of Refugees: Biopolitical Care and Racism in the European Refugee Crisis," *Review of International Studies* 43, no. 5 (2017): 809–832 at 810.

30. Hannah Arendt, *The Origins of Totalitarianism* (New York: Harcourt, 1966), 286–288.

31. Ibid., 286.

32. Stumpf, "The Crimmigration Crisis," 396–400.

33. Ibid., 379–395.

34. Malcolm Feeley and Jonathan Simon, "The New Penology: Notes on the Emerging Strategy of Corrections and Its Implications," *Criminology* 30, no. 4 (1992): 449–474 at 467.

35. Ibid.

36. Michelle Alexander, *The New Jim Crow: Mass Incarceration in the Age of Colorblindness* (New York: The New Press, 2010); Bruce Western, *Punishment and Inequality in America* (New York: Russell Sage Foundation, 2006).

37. Dorothy Roberts, "Crime, Race, and Reproduction," *Tulsa Law Review* 67 (1992): 1945–1977.

38. Lisa Marie Cacho, *Social Death: Racialized Rightlessness and the Criminalization of the Unprotected* (New York University Press, 2012), 6.

39. Feeley and Simon, "The New Penology," 454–455.

40. *Haitian Refugee Center. v. Civiletti*, 503 F. Supp. 442 (S.D. Fla. 1980) at 517–518.

41. *Johnson v. Eisentrager*, 339 U.S. 763 (1950) at 770–771. See chapter 3 for a more detailed discussion of this case.

42. Jared Sexton, "The Social Life of Social Death: On Afro-Pessimism and Black Optimism," *In/Tensions Journal* 5 (2011): 1–47 at n1 at 37.

43. Alexander, *The New Jim Crow*, 97–177.

44. Frank Wilderson, "The Prison Slave as Hegemony's (Silent) Scandal," *Social Justice* 30, no. 2 (2003): 18–27 at 19–20.

45. Mary Waters, *Black Identities: West Indian Immigrant Dreams and American Realities* (Cambridge, MA: 1999); Tekle Woldemikael, "A Case Study of Race Consciousness Among Haitian Immigrants," *Journal of Black Studies* 20 (1989): 224–239.

46. Alejandro Portes and Alex Stepick, *City on the Edge: The Transformation of Miami* (Berkeley: University of California Press, 1993) 38–60.

47. Michel Foucault, *Society Must Be Defended: Lectures at the Collège de France, 1975–1976* (New York: Macmillan, 2003), 43–64.

48. Ladelle McWhorter, for example, has produced a Foucauldian theory of racism and the control of sexuality, which she distinguishes from an intersectional approach to this subject matter. For McWhorter, race and sexuality are mutually constitutive features of the same system of control, rather than relatively autonomous histories of oppression that "intersect." One implication of this analysis is that there can never be a heteronormative, sexist, or classist iteration of the binary that is *not* also racist. Ladelle McWhorter, *Racism and Sexual Oppression in Anglo-America* (Bloomington, IN: University of Indiana Press, 2009), 1–15.

49. This observation is derived from reading across several sources including: Foucault, *Society Must Be Defended*, 239–264; Bruno Latour, *We Have Never Been Modern* (Cambridge, MA: Harvard University Press, 1993), 1–46; John Jackson and Nadine Weidman, *Race, Racism, and Science: Social Impact and Interaction* (Camden, NJ: Rutgers University Press, 2005), 61–96.

50. See Robert Hodge and Gunther Kress, *Social Semiotics* (Ithaca, NY: Cornell University Press, 1988), 13–18.

51. See Saidiya Hartman, *Scenes of Subjection: Terror, Slavery, and Self-Making in Nineteenth-Century America* (New York: Oxford University Press, 2007); McWhorter, *Racism and Sexual Oppression in Anglo-America*; Walter Rodney, *How Europe Underdeveloped Africa* (Washington, DC: Howard UP, 1981).

52. Jared Sexton, "People of Color Blindness: Notes on the Afterlife of Slavery," *Social Text* 103, no. 28:2 (2010): 31–53 at 45–49.

53. Mavelli, "Governing Populations Through the Humanitarian Government of Refugees," 811–812.

54. Jackson and Weidman, *Race, Racism, and Science*, 112–118, 122–126.

55. Mavelli, "Governing Populations Through the Humanitarian Government of Refugees," 815.

56. Cacho, *Social Death*; Khalil Saucier and Tryon Woods, "Ex Aqua The Mediterranean Basin, Africans on the Move and the Politics of Policing," *Theoria* 141, no. 61 (2014): 55–75; Jared Sexton, "Unbearable Blackness," *Cultural Critique* 90, no. 90 (2015): 159–178.

57. Jackson and Weidman, *Race, Racism, and Science*, 16–24.

58. *Cuban American Bar Association (CABA)* 43 F.3d 1412, 1419.

59. Christina Frohock, "'Brisas del Mar': Judicial and Political Outcomes of the Cuban Rafter Crisis in Guantánamo," *Harvard Latino Law Review* 15, no.39 (2012), 39–83 at 42–43.

60. In August 1994, approximately 8,000 Cuban refugees appeared on the shores of South Florida in a matter of a week—a number that was more than double the amount of Cuban refugees who had been intercepted by the Coast Guard in the first half of the year. The interdiction operations that responded to refugee crisis ended up compounding approximately 33,000 Cuban refugees in camps at Guantanamo Bay Cuba and Panama. The 1980 Mariel Boatlift, by comparison, rescued approximately 125,000 Cuban and 25,000 Haitian refugees. Frohock, "'Brisas del Mar,'" 43 and 45.

61. Frohock, "'Brisas del Mar,'" 42.

62. Ibid., 43–44 and 47.

63. Ibid., 42 and 53. *Cuban Adjustment Act*, Pub. L. 89–732, 80 Stat. 1161 (1966).

64. Frohock, "'Brisas del Mar,'" 43–44.

65. Haitian interdictions massively outnumbered Cuban interdictions throughout 1982–1993, ranging anywhere from a ratio of 2:1, to over 100:1. Year 1994 was the first year in which Cuban interdictions outpaced Haitian interdictions—with over 37,000 Cubans being interdicted compared to approximately 25,000 Haitians. US Department of Homeland Security, USCG Migrant Interdiction Statistics "Table 534. Coast Guard Migrant Interdictions by Nationality of Alien," Originally accessed May 2011: http://www.uscg.mil/hq/cg5/cg531/AMIO/FlowStats /currentstats.asp/. Reposted at this link and accessed November 21, 2020: https:// view.officeapps.live.com/op/view.aspx?src=http%3A%2F%2Fwww2.census .gov%2Flibrary%2Fpublications%2F2011%2Fcompendia%2Fstatab%2F131ed %2Ftables%2F12s0534.xls.

66. *Jean*, 472 U.S. 846; *Sale*, 509 U.S. 155. See chapters 2–4 for a discussion of the INS parole policies for Haitian refugees that were upheld by both of these decisions.

67. Frohock, "'Brisas del Mar,'" 47–48.

68. *CABA*, 43 F.3d 1412, 1419 at 1420–1421.

69. Frohock, "'Brisas del Mar,'" 51.

70. Ibid.

71. Fred Kaplan, *Lincoln and the Abolitionists* (New York: HarperCollins, 2017), 138–140.

72. Frohock, "'Brisas del Mar,'" 49–50.

73. The 500 Cuban refugees who were paroled by Reno's policy amount to a small fraction of 1 percent of the total Cuban-Mariel detainee population at Guantanamo (approximately .015 or 15 percent of 1 percent of the total population).

74. Frohock, "'Brisas del Mar,'" 59 and 62. A District Court ruling required Attorney General Reno to extend the parole policy devised for Cuban refugees to Haitian unaccompanied minors, in an attempt to counter the AG's initial refusal to extend the policy to Haitians. This District Court ruling was eventually overturned by the Eleventh Circuit Court which made the final decision on the case.

75. *CABA*, 43 F.3d 1412, 1419 at 1418–1419.

76. *CABA*, 43 F.3d 1412, 1419 at 1424–1426 and 1427–1428.

77. Katherine Strandburg, "Official Notice of Changed Country Conditions in Asylum Adjudication: Lessons from International Refugee Law," *Georgetown Immigration Law Journal* 11, no. 1 (1996): 45–82.

78. Frohock, "'Brisas del Mar,'" 40. The government described the detainees as "migrants" that it had "temporarily granted safe haven."

79. Frohock, "'Brisas del Mar,'" 54.

80. Calvin Warren, *Ontological Terror: Blackness, Nihilism and Emancipation* (Durham, NC: Duke University Press, 2018), 64–66.

81. Frohock, "'Brisas del Mar,'" 51.

82. *CABA*, 43 F.3d 1412, 1419 at 1419. There were approximately 12,000 Haitian detainees being held at Guantanamo by the time of the District Court decision and that number had dwindled further, to approximately 8,000 by the time of the Eleventh Circuit Court decision. Frohock, "'Brisas del Mar,'" 45, 51 and 58–59.

83. Frohock, "'Brisas del Mar,'" 45.

84. *CABA*, 43 F.3d 1412, 1419 at 1419.

85. *CABA v. Christopher*, No. 94-2183 (S.D. Fla. Oct. 24, 1994).

86. *CABA*, 43 F.3d 1412, 1419 at 1419–1420.

87. *CABA*, 43 F.3d 1412, 1419 at 1420.

88. Ibid.

89. Ibid.

90. *CABA*, 43 F.3d 1412, 1419 at 1424–1430.

91. *CABA*, 43 F.3d 1412, 1419 at 1424n9, citing *HRC v. Baker*, 953 F.2d 1498 (11th Cir., 1992); *Jean v. Nelson*, 727 F.2d 957 (11th Cir. 1984); *Sale v. HCC*, U.S. ___, 113 S.Ct. 2549, 125 L.Ed.2d 128 (1993).

92. *CABA*, 43 F.3d 1412, 1419 at 1424–1426.

93. *Haitian Refugee Center, Inc. v. Gracey*, 600 F. Supp. 1396 (D.D.C. 1985) at 1404; *Haitian Refugee Center v. Baker*, 953 F.2d 1498 (11th Cir. 1992) at 1555–1557; *Sale v. HCC*, 509 U.S. 155 (193) at 156 and 179–182.

94. *CABA*, 43 F.3d 1412, 1419 at 1418–1419 and 1430–1431.

95. Frohock, "'Brisas del Mar,'" 45.

96. In its decision the Eleventh Circuit confirmed that the Guantanamo detainees were being denied asylum screenings and had no legal right to demand them. CABA, 43 F.3d 1412, 1419 at 1426.

97. Frohock, "'Brisas del Mar,'" 48.

98. Ibid., 47.

99. Ibid., 48–49.

100. Ibid., 50.

101. Ibid., 45–56n, 44–51.

102. Ibid., 49.

103. *CABA*, 43 F.3d 1412, 1419 at 1426–1427.

104. Ibid.

105. *CABA*, 43 F.3d 1412, 1419 at 1427.

106. Giorgio Agamben, *Homo Sacer: Sovereign Power and Bare Life* (Stanford, CA: Stanford University Press, 1998), 119–125.

107. *CABA*, 43 F.3d 1412, 1419 at 1427.

108. Hartman, *Scenes of Subjection*, 86–90.

109. *CABA*, 43 F.3d 1412, 1419 at 1418.

110. These implications are communicated by the court's repeated references to the government's humanitarian motivations (anchored by its description of the interdiction and detention program as a "gratuitous humanitarian act" as well as being an "American tradition of humanitarian concern and conduct") that were undertaken out of concern for saving the lives of fleeing Haitians and Cubans, but not out of any enforceable obligation to US or international law. *CABA*, 43 F.3d 1412, 1419 at 1418, 1426–1428 and 1430.

111. *Baker*, 953 F.2d 1498.

112. *CABA*, 43 F.3d 1412, 1419 at 1424–1425.

113. *CABA*, 43 F.3d 1412, 1419 at 1425 citing *Baker*, 953 F.2d at 1514; id. at 1510 and 1516–1517.

114. Koh and Wishnie, "The Story of *Sale v. Haitian Centers Council*," 386; Frohock, "'Brisas del Mar,'" 42.

115. Frohock, "'Brisas del Mar,'" 49.

116. *CABA*, 43 F.3d 1412, 1419 at 1427–1429.

117. Ibid, citing *Jean*, 727 F.2d 957.

118. *Jean v. Nelson*, 472 U.S. 846 (1985) at 848.

119. *Jean*, 472 U.S. 846 at 855–857.

120. *CABA*, 43 F.3d 1412, 1419 at 1427, citing *Jean*, 727 F.2d at 972.

121. *CABA*, 43 F.3d 1412, 1419 at 1427, citing *Jean*, 727 F.2d at 978n30.

122. *Chinese Exclusion Case*, 130 U.S. 581 (1889). See discussion in chapter 4.

123. *Jean*, 727 F.2d 957 at 964, 965 and 977. For citations of Jean in CABA, see n156–157.

124. *CABA*, 43 F.3d 1412, 1419 at 1428.

125. Frohock, "'Brisas del Mar,'" 80–81.

126. Ibid., 81.

127. Ibid., 80–82. Also see Alberto Perez, "Note and Comment: Wet Foot, Dry Foot: The Recurring Controversy," *Nova Law Review* 28 (2004) 437–460.

128. Ibid.

129. Perez, "Note and Comment: Wet Foot, Dry Foot," 15–17.

130. Gammeltoft-Hansen and Tan, "The End of the Deterrence Paradigm."

131. Mark Duffield, "Racism, Migration and Development: the Foundations of Planetary Order," *Progress in Development Studies* 6, no. 1 (2006): 68–79. See discussion in chapter 1.

132. Feeley and Jonathan Simon, "The New Penology."

133. Ibid.

134. Hartman, *Scenes of Subjection*, 189–206; Roberts, "Crime, Race, and Reproduction," Warren, *Ontological Terror*.

135. Foucault, *Society Must Be Defended*, 43–64.

136. Fred Moten, "Blackness and Nothingness," *The South Atlantic Quarterly* 112, no. 4 (2013): 737–780; Khalil Saucier and Tryon Woods eds., *Conceptual Aphasia in Black* (Lanham, MD: Lexington Press, 2016); Sexton, "The Social Life of Social Death"; Sebastian Weier, "Consider Afro-Pessimism," *Amerikastudien/ American Studies* 59, no. 3 (2014): 419–433.

137. Yanira Madrigal-Garcia and Nancy Acevedo-Gil, "The New Juan Crow in Education," *Journal of Hispanic Higher Education* 15, no. 2 (2016): 154–181; Irene Browne and Mary Odem, "'Juan Crow' in the Nuevo South?" *Du Bois Review* 9, no. 2 (2012): 321–337.

138. Kateel and Shahani, "Families for Freedom," 258–290.

139. Kevin Bales, *Disposable People: New Slavery in the Global Economy* (Berkeley, CA: University of California Press, 2012); Ramona Vijeyarasa, and Jose Miguel Bello, "Modern-day Slavery? A Judicial Catchall for Trafficking, Slavery and Labour Exploitation: A Critique of Tang and Rantsev," *Journal of International Law & International Relations* 9, no. 1 (2013): 38–76.

140. Shull, "Nobody Wants These People," 13–40.

141. *CABA*, 43 F.3d 1412, 1419 at 1424n9.

142. Frohock, "'Brisas del Mar,'" 80–82.

143. Kevin Johnson, "Doubling Down on Racial Discrimination: The Racially Disparate Impacts of Crime-Based Removals," *Case Western Reserve Law Review* 66, no. 4 (2016): 993–1038.

144. Ibid., 1028–1029.

145. Arendt, *Origins of Totalitarianism*, 286–288.

146. Tamara Nopper, "Why Black Immigrants Matter: Refocusing the Discussion on Racism and Immigration Enforcement," in *Keeping Out the Other: A Critical Introduction to Immigration Enforcement Today*, eds. David Brotherton and Philip Kretsedemas (New York: Columbia University Press, 2008), 204–240.

Chapter 6

The Radical Exclusion of Haitian, African, and Central American Refugees in the Trump Era

The entry of large numbers of aliens into the United States unlawfully between ports of entry on the southern border is contrary to the national interest. . . . Other presidents have taken strong action to prevent mass migration. In Proclamation 4865 of September 29, 1981 (*High Seas Interdiction of Illegal Aliens*), in response to an influx of Haitian nationals traveling to the United States by sea, President Reagan suspended the entry of undocumented aliens from the high seas and ordered the Coast Guard to intercept such aliens before they reached United States shores and to return them to their point of origin. In Executive Order 12807 of May 24, 1992 (*Interdiction of Illegal Aliens*), in response to a dramatic increase in the unlawful mass migration of Haitian nationals to the United States, President Bush ordered additional measures to interdict such Haitian nationals and return them to their home country. The Supreme Court upheld the legality of those measures in *Sale v. Haitian Centers Council, Inc.*, 509 U.S. 155 (1993). I am similarly acting to suspend, for a limited period, the entry of certain aliens in order to address the problem of large numbers of aliens traveling through Mexico to enter our country unlawfully or without proper documentation.—*Donald Trump*[1]

Just a few days into our 14-day quarantine and without receiving our COVID-19 test results, my family and I were removed from quarantine without explanation and sent off to be deported. . . . The officers locked us in an unfamiliar cell with about three other Haitian families and told us not to go anywhere. . . . When we saw the airplane landing in the complex, everyone started crying. Because the officers had told us we were going to another immigration prison, seeing the airplane at the complex seemed like confirmation that we were not actually being transferred. None of the officers ever confirmed that we were being deported. No one would even say the word deportation. None of them, through this whole process. All the families were crying on the bus, for over an hour. My husband and others kept asking what was going on, if they were deporting us. They would not tell us anything despite our desperation. It was all extremely emotional.—*Abigale's story*[2]

REMAIN-IN-MEXICO AND TITLE 42

On November 9, 2018, President Trump announced that the US-Mexico border was going to be closed to most migrants and asylum seekers for a period of ninety days. Trump's proclamation overlooked statistics which show that the size of the unauthorized migrant population has been trending downward since the peak it reached in 2008, and that it had dipped to its lowest total in over a decade, in the very same year that Trump took office.[3] There is evidence, however, that the unauthorized migrant population experienced a modest increase in 2018, amounting to a growth rate of approximately 2 percent.[4] Much of this increase was driven by Central American migrants and asylum seekers who were fleeing violence and instability in their home nations.[5] Not surprisingly, this population became a focal point of the Trump administration's border enforcement practices.

Trump's November proclamation amplified the signals that had been sent by the zero tolerance border policy, that had been announced by Attorney General Jeff Sessions in June 2018, and also by the practice of holding migrant parents and children in separate detention facilities (aka "family separations") which had begun in early 2017.[6] President Trump also made a point of citing the Haitian interdiction operations of the Reagan-Bush era to establish legal precedents for this new direction in US-Mexico border policy.[7] In fact, the *only* legal and policy precedents that Trump cited as a justification for the new border policy were Presidential orders and court decisions concerning the Haitian interdictions.[8]

Two and half months later, on January 25, 2019, the Trump administration introduced the Migrant Protection Protocols (MPP), which became more popularly known as the remain-in-Mexico policy.[9] The remain-in-Mexico policy has all the hallmark features of an interdiction operation, with the exception that it is being implemented within the territorial borders of another nation rather than on the high seas. Under the new policy, most migrants and asylum seekers who are apprehended at the US-Mexico border are sent back to Mexico as they wait for their case to be heard and are only allowed to enter the United States to attend their immigration court hearings.[10] The government of Mexico has consented to this arrangement by way of a diplomatic agreement which is similar to the one that the Haitian government entered into with the US government in the early 1980s. One distinguishing feature of this enforcement operation, however, is that it does not apply to Mexican nationals.[11] The remain-in-Mexico policy requires the Mexican government to assist with the deterrence and detention of migrants—primarily from Central America—who pass through Mexico on the way to the US border.[12]

There are also many Haitians, including parents with children, trying to enter the United States through the US-Mexico border. Many of these families were displaced by the 2010 earthquake in Haiti, granted shelter by Latin American nations, and decided to make the trek to the US border when life became too difficult for them in these nations.[13] Abigale, whose story I used to open this chapter, belongs to one of these families.

Abigale's family, like most Haitians at the US-Mexico border, was not processed through the remain-in-Mexico policy. Her family was repatriated to Haiti under a policy that was initiated by the US Center for Disease Control in March 2020, titled "Order Suspending Introduction of Certain Persons from Countries Where a Communicable Disease Exists."[14] This policy is often referred to as the "Title 42 policy" because Trump administration officials justified it through reference to Title 42 of the US Code (42 U.S.C. § 265) which authorizes the government to implement emergency mitigation strategies and other special measures during a public health crisis.[15]

The Title 42 policy is similar to the travel ban on HIV-positive migrants that the US government introduced in the 1980s.[16] Both of these policies were broadly framed as efforts to safeguard public health, but their implementation was narrowly focused on a particular and timely health crisis—the HIV/AIDS epidemic in the case of the travel ban and the COVID-19 pandemic in the case of the Title 42 policy. Most significantly, both policies targeted Haitian migrants and asylum seekers. The HIV travel ban was exclusively used to block the entry of Haitian noncitizens. The Title 42 policy has not been used in such a blatantly discriminatory way. Even so, advocacy groups have observed that Haitian asylum seekers compose the overwhelming majority of people who are being removed from the United States under the auspices of Title 42.[17] And as Abigale explains, some of these Haitian families have been removed before they receive the results of their COVID-19 tests.

The relationship between the remain-in-Mexico and the Title 42 policy recalls the treatment of Cuban and Haitian Guantanamo detainees that I examined in the last chapter. Central American asylum seekers have to contend with a border enforcement operation of unprecedented severity which has been directly influenced by policies and legal precedents that were used to roll out the Haitian interdictions. But the government has devised another border security policy, of even greater severity, which targets Haitians. The unequal treatment of these asylum seeker populations has become more obvious in the early months of the Biden administration.

Within two months of taking office, the Biden administration began to reopen the US-Mexico border for the Central American migrants that had been targeted by the remain-in-Mexico policy. Although the Biden administration attempted to terminate the policy, it has been kept alive by court challenges issued by state governmemts.[18] In contrast, no effort has been made to end the Title 42 policy.[19] Since the Biden administration took office, repatriations of Haitian noncitizens (including but not limited to Title 42) have increased significantly. Within the first few months of taking office, the Biden administration removed more Haitians than did the Trump administration during its last year in office.[20]

This is yet another example of how draconian policies that were first applied to black populations have been extended to a larger, nonblack population, but without altering the black/nonblack binary. Conditions get worse for nonblack people, but blacks are still singled out for an exclusionary treatment that is even more severe than what is normally meted out to nonblacks. Asylum granting rates under the remain-in-Mexico program, for example, were abysmally low in the Trump era—at less than one half of 1 percent of the entire caseload.[21] The Title 42 policy, on the other hand, has imposed a near-absolute ban on access to asylum. A policy report titled, *The Invisible Wall*, sums up the situation this way:

> The Title 42 policy categorically denies entry to all migrants trying to cross the border without travel documents, whether by [port of entry] or apprehended after entering without authorization, and authorizes their immediate expulsion (to Mexico or their home country) without ever screening them for asylum or other humanitarian protection under the law.[22]

The only exception to this ban on asylum rights are screenings authorized by the Convention Against Torture (CAT), which have to be requested by the asylum seekers and only if they can contact an attorney who is able to request the screening on their behalf. The attorney, however, is not allowed to be present at the screening, the asylum seeker is not provided with a written record of their interview, and they are also unable to appeal the asylum officer's decision.[23]

The government has not released data on the number of asylum seekers who have asked for CAT screenings, and there is no record of any of them receiving asylum on the basis of these screenings.[24] It is also significant that the Title 42 policy recognizes two categories of asylum seekers, those who can be immediately repatriated or returned to another location in Mexico, and those who have to be detained for a period of time before they are repatriated or returned.[25] There is no category for people who might qualify for asylum, similar to the way that the Haitian program contained no category, on its ledger sheets, for Haitians granted asylum.[26] The Title 42 policy is also like the Haitian program in another way.

The policy has created a hierarchy of rightlessness within the excludable alien category, with Haitian asylum seekers occupying the bottom rung. Asylum seekers apprehended under the remain-in-Mexico policy are also "excludables" but they can claim more rights under statutory law than the people who have been apprehended under Title 42. It is not even necessary for the government to show that an asylum seeker has COVID-19 or any other communicable disease to justify their repatriation. The Title 42 policy allows the government to refuse asylum to anyone it chooses on the grounds that the COVID-19 pandemic has impaired the ability of the immigration system to screen them.[27]

For asylum seekers like Abigale, it is a gross injustice to be put through a fourteen-day quarantine, to have yourself and your family take a COVID-19 test, and then be repatriated to Haiti anyway, before the government determines whether or not you actually pose a health risk. But the policy is written in such a way that it allows for this kind of treatment. In a similar vein, the policy does not name Haitians as a target group, but it gives the government broad discretion to invoke Title 42 as a reason for refusing entry to any noncitizen that it believes falls under its public health mandate—and there is nothing in the language of the policy that expressly forbids the government from using this discretion to target particular national origin groups.

Two years before the CDC announced its Title 42 policy, Trump White House officials were making plans to terminate Temporary Protected Status (TPS) for Haitians and also for some African and Central American nationals.[28] Most of the Haitians who were at risk of losing TPS and who were being repatriated under the Title 42 policy came from the same group of refugees who had been displaced by the 2010 earthquake. Haitians also figured prominently in a series of public, racist statements, made by President Trump, that were connected to the deliberations over the TPS cancellations.[29]

In the rest of the chapter, I take a closer look at all of these policies, with an eye for the black/nonblack distinctions that they deployed and reinforced. I am going to use the Title 42 policy as a window into a history of antiblack sentiment that is most directly related to the US government's Haitian refugee policies. Even so, the bulk of my discussion focuses on the legal dispute over the remain-in-Mexico policy and the TPS cancellations, because my main goal is to build on the analysis I introduced in the last chapter. I want to show how policies that were first applied to blacks can be extended to nonblacks, but without changing the fundamentals of the black/nonblack binary. In the next several sections of the chapter, I provide a more detailed treatment of the antiblack subtext for the TPS cancellations and the remain-in-Mexico policy, using the Title 42 policy as a guiding thread. These sections are followed by a comparative analysis of the legal challenges to both policies.

A BRIEF HISTORY OF TPS AND DETERRENCE
STRATEGIES TARGETING HAITIANS
IN THE NEW MILLENNIUM

One of the more obvious differences between TPS and the remain-in-Mexico policy is that TPS holders are officially recognized as "being here," whereas the subjects of the remain-in-Mexico have not been granted the right of entry. TPS is also much closer to a conventional refugee relief policy, in that it is intended to give shelter to displaced people. Remain-in-Mexico, on the other hand, is closer to a deterrence strategy. When US immigration officials boast about the success of the remain-in-Mexico policy, they focus on its effectiveness in decreasing and diverting unwanted migration.

The Department of Homeland Security credited the remain-in-Mexico policy for returning over 55,000 migrants and asylum seekers to Mexico within the first nine months of its operation and also for reducing unauthorized migration by as much as 64 percent during this same period of time. The MPP has also been credited for curbing the controversial practice of family separations. Under the remain-in-Mexico policy, families with children are returned to Mexico to await their court dates rather than being separated and held in detention facilities at the US border. After implementing this policy, the DHS reported an 80 percent reduction in the number of migrant families attempting to cross the border without authorization.[30]

On the other hand, one of the connecting threads between these policies is their appeal to humanitarian values. To underscore this humanitarian mandate, the US government has pledged to involve international relief organizations in the MPP to ensure that all of the asylum seekers "are provided access to humanitarian care and assistance, food and housing, work permits, and education."[31] But there are other aspects of this humanitarian mandate that recall the paradigm of carceral humanitarianism that I discussed in the last chapter.

Under the MPP, appeals to humanitarianism are mobilized in tandem with enforcement and population management strategies that limit the noncitizen's access to the law and to encourage their repatriation. Similar to the Title 42 policy, the MPP does not require border patrol officers to question all migrants to see if they have a plausible case for asylum. The officer is granted the discretionary authority to determine whether a particular individual is "more likely than not" to face persecution, based on their interactions with them. If a migrant fears being persecuted, they are expected to raise these concerns of their own accord in their initial interview with border patrol.[32] US Citizenship and Information Services has advised the DHS to use this policy as a way of keeping asylum claims to a minimum.[33]

TPS can also be understood as a program, guided by a humanitarian mandate, which has scaled back the asylum rights of displaced people and diverts them from seeking asylum. TPS provides relief to people who are fleeing disparate situations, but it does not give them a pathway to permanent legal status or access to the same kinds of support services that are granted to officially designated refugee populations.[34] One important privilege granted to TPS recipients is the right to live and work in the United States for a duration of six to eighteen months. This temporary status is often renewed for a period of years due to worsening conditions in the home nations of TPS holders. As a result, many TPS holders become de facto residents who put down roots in local communities and adjust to living life in the United States under an indefinitely renewable temporary status. This experience of legal precarity has become an increasingly common feature of the US migrant experience from the 1980s onward, which is shared by international students, work visa holders, and more recently, by unauthorized migrant youth who became beneficiaries of the Deferred Action for Childhood Arrivals (DACA) program that was created by the Obama administration.[35]

TPS was introduced to US law by the 1990 Immigration Act.[36] However, the beginnings of TPS as a policy mechanism can be traced a few years earlier to an out-of-court settlement between the US government and refugee rights advocates who were contesting the treatment of Nicaraguan and Salvadoran asylum seekers.[37] Throughout the 1980s the US government was very resistant to granting asylum to these people, mainly because of the political context for US involvement in Central America.[38] Most of these refugees were fleeing violent conditions that the US government had helped to create, with its funding of contra forces that were trying to destabilize Nicaragua's socialist government, as well as combating the influence of left-leaning movements in other parts of Central America.[39]

The 1997 *Nicaraguan Adjustment and Central American Relief Act* (NACARA), which was made possible by the activism of refugee rights constituencies, played an important role in changing the US government's treatment of Central American asylum seekers.[40] But as I have just noted, the US government began issuing TPS to Central American refugees for almost a full decade prior to NACARA. The issuance of TPS to Central Americans, and for refugees of many other nationalities, also began to outpace asylum grants from the 1990s onward.

By 2017, the US government had ceased issuing asylum grants under NACARA.[41] In that same year a little over 53,000 refugee arrivals were documented by Department of Homeland Security and approximately 26,500 people were granted asylum by the US immigration courts.[42] By comparison, the US population of TPS holders in 2017 numbered approximately 325,000 people, and approximately 250,000 of these people were

Honduran or Salvadoran.[43] So by the time that the Trump administration began its practice of family separations at the US-Mexican border, TPS had become the primary form of relief that the US government was granting to displaced people—especially to people from Central American nations. TPS was not supplementing the asylum grants of the immigration courts and the state department, instead, TPS had become the new normal for refugee relief.

Haitians were excluded from TPS throughout the 1990s and the early 2000s.[44] Things might have continued this way indefinitely were it not for the devastating Haitian earthquake of January 2010.[45] As Naomi Paik has explained, the earthquake was not just a natural disaster.[46] The quake tremors aggravated a bundle of preexisting, interconnected structural inequities produced by over two centuries of economic exploitation, political alienation, and neo-imperialist interventions, which resulted in over half of the Haitian population losing their homes, over a quarter million people were killed outright, and over five million were displaced.[47] The damage wrought by the earthquake was so severe that it was diplomatically impossible for the international community to stand by and do nothing. The United States, Canada, and Mexico, along with many South American nations, opened their borders to Haitians who were displaced by the earthquake.[48]

In response to the crisis, the Obama administration pledged $100 million in funding for relief efforts in Haiti and granted TPS to tens of thousands of Haitians.[49] But this relief was issued in tandem with yet another maritime interdiction operation that was designed to suppress a mass exodus of Haitian refugees. The Coast Guard was enlisted to interdict Haitians on the high seas, space was cleared at Guantanamo and holding facilities in Miami to prepare for a new wave of detainees, and radio messages were broadcast to Haiti, warning earthquake victims that they would be intercepted and returned to Haiti if they attempted to flee to the United States without authorization.[50]

This post-earthquake interdiction strategy was in keeping with the Haitian-specific enforcement practices that the US government continued into the new millennium. For example, the George W. Bush administration implemented a secret Haitian policy in 2001, after the terrorist attacks on the Pentagon and the World Trade Center, which directed all immigration enforcement officers to detain Haitians who arrived in the United States, regardless of their asylum eligibility.[51] As a consequence of this program, the Haitian detainee population exploded and asylum grants for Haitians dropped by almost 90 percent.[52] The George W. Bush administration implemented another Haitian-specific interdiction operation to manage a mass exodus that was expected to occur in the wake of the second coup against the Aristide administration, on February 29, 2004.[53]

Throughout the 2000s and 2010s, US policy continued to be more exclusionary for Haitians than other interdicted refugees. For example, interdicted

Haitians are not asked whether they have any fears of being persecuted if they are repatriated to Haiti. Similar to the Title 42 policy, Haitian fears of persecution are only documented if refugees go out of their way to raise them with US officers and in order to do so, they usually have to shout these concerns from one vessel to the other (a process that has come to be known as the "shout test").[54] Cuban and Chinese interdictees, on the other hand, are granted asylum interviews and are told they can raise their fears of persecution with the Coast Guard or DHS officers.[55]

The damage caused by Hurricane Matthew contributed to a new surge in Haitian interdictions between 2016 and 2017.[56] Although this increase occurred in the early years of the Trump administration, its causes can be traced to the Obama era. The Obama administration held to the same Haitian refugee policies as the George W. Bush administration, which included a continuation of the "no screen" policy for interdicted Haitians that began with the 1991 Kennebunkport Order, mandatory detention of Haitian refugees, and mass deportation.[57]

Around this same period of time, the fall out of the Haitian earthquake began to converge with issues that were setting the stage for a more draconian policy at the US-Mexico border. Haitians that had been welcomed by Brazil, after the 2010 earthquake, were alienated by the aftershocks of a national recession which lead many of them to migrate northward to the United States.[58] By 2015, US officials were aware of a significant increase in Haitians attempting to enter the United States along the US-Mexico border.[59] The Obama-era DHS responded with a deterrence strategy that clamped down on the migratory routes that Haitians were using to travel across Latin America to the US-Mexico border. As a result, more Haitian migrants were forced to take the more dangerous route, across the Caribbean Sea, as a means of entry to the United States.[60]

These desperate conditions are an important part of the backdrop for the Trump administration's TPS cancellations.[61] The DHS terminated TPS for Haitian, Sudanese, Nicaraguan, and Salvadoran populations in a series of decisions spanning November 2017 through January 2018.[62] During this same period of time, the DHS extended TPS for four other nationalities.[63] But statements issued by DHS officials also indicated that the TPS cancellations were a precursor for a broader agenda to phase out TPS for all displaced people.[64]

A few days after the DHS announced its plans to revoke TPS, President Trump made some public, racist, remarks about these very same groups. The most infamous of these statements was his rhetorical speculation—issued in January 2018—about why the United States was admitting so many people from "shithole countries," making specific reference to Haiti and African nations.[65] At this same meeting, he told lawmakers that migrants from Haiti must be "left out of any deal"[66] concerning immigration or refugee policy and about six months prior, he asserted that recent immigrants from Haiti "all have AIDS"[67] and also that once Nigerians had a taste of life in the United States they would "never go back to their huts in Africa."[68] Trump also made racist remarks about Mexican immigrants and Arab-Muslim refugees, as well as making statements that cast aspersions on all migrants and refugees.[69] But black migrants and refugees, and Haitians in particular, cropped up repeatedly, as targets of his racist animus.

As I explained in chapter 2, black people are one of the smallest segments of the US migrant and refugee population. Although the black migrant and refugee population has grown by leaps and bounds from the late 1980s onward, it still composes little more than 9 percent of the US foreign-born population.[70] In contrast, black populations compose half of the national origin groups that were targeted by the Trump administration's TPS cancellations. Trump's racist statements about migrants and refugees were also inordinately focused on black populations. Forty percent of the examples used by the District Court of Northern California, to establish Trump's racist animus toward TPS holders, focused on black migrants and refugees.[71] This pattern of antiblack racism begs the question—why all the concern about such a tiny fragment of the US foreign-born population?

Trump's statements about the unsuitability of black people for admission to the United States cannot be explained by restrictionist anxieties about teeming "numbers" of racialized migrants that are threatening to steal jobs and overwhelm public services that are funded by taxpayer dollars.[72] As I have explained in prior chapters, (anti)blackness is more central to issues of ontological security than other kinds of racial otherness, due to the role it has played in constituting the modern idea (through its absence and violent expulsion).

Antiblack sentiments do not have to be justified through reference to objectively existing social problems that are associated with black populations, although there are coded discourses on racism that operate in this manner.[73] These discursive tactics are sufficient but not necessary for the expression of antiblack sentiments. Antiblack sentiments can also be expressed without any coherent justification, because blackness poses a problem that, in the racist imagination, is innate to itself and which dramatizes the distinction between the human and subhuman like no other kind of racial otherness.

Trump, for example, stigmatized Mexican and Central American migrants by associating them with criminality and Arab-Muslims with terrorism. But to establish black otherness he only had to reference the civilizational inferiority of the "hut-dweller," who could very well be a "law-abiding person" and a "hard-worker" but is undesirable nonetheless. In a similar vein, the threat that the black body poses to society is innate to the body itself ("they all have AIDS"), which operates outside of any concept of political/ideological difference (associated with terrorism and other forms of extremist violence) and which does not even require evidence of a malicious intent to do harm (like the threat of violent property crimes). Once AIDS is associated with "all Haitians," it no longer functions as a description of a potential public health crisis, but as a metaphor about the pollution that blackness introduces to a white or nonblack social body. Even though the Title 42 policy had nothing to do with HIV/AIDS, it is not difficult to see how the association that Trump made between Haitian bodies and communicable disease is reflected in the inexplicable targeting of Haitians (above all other national origin groups) as possible carriers of the COVID-19 virus—or as a national origin group (above all other groups) that strained the government's ability to process asylum claims in the context of the pandemic.

UNDERSTANDING REMAIN-IN-MEXICO AND THE REVOCATION OF TPS AS EXAMPLES OF RADICAL EXCLUSION

The racist subtext for the TPS cancellations connects to the argument that I introduced in chapter 3 about the difference between radical exclusion and deportability. To briefly recap, deportability is a disciplinary regime that uses the threat of removal to exploit migrants with a precarious legal status.[74] Deportable migrants live in constant fear, but this fear conditions their behavior while they are still living and working "here" in the United States. Radical exclusion, on the other hand, targets a racial other who is not allowed to be "here" and is not even desired as an exploitable worker. The aim of radical exclusion is not to create exploitable and disposable subjects but to deny entry to social types that are absolutely intolerable.

Radical exclusion became a more transparent feature of just about every aspect of US immigration policy in the Trump era, whether it concerns the Arab-Muslim travel ban, efforts to cancel the DACA program, moratoriums on green cards (that were justified by the COVID-19 pandemic), efforts to clamp down on the growth of the refugee population, and efforts to restrict the size of the work visa population.[75] The overarching goal of all of these policy maneuvers has been to exclude for the sake of excluding, rather than to cultivate flows of exploitable migrant labor.

Leo Chavez's analysis of the Latino threat provides a better starting point for understanding this predicament than De Genova's thesis on illegality and deportability.[76] De Genova produces a theory that could be applied to any migrant—regardless of their race, nationality, or gender—with a precarious legal status. Chavez, on the other hand, describes a discourse that targets a specific racialized population and which has been used to construct this population as a problem, irrespective of whether the people in question are undocumented, admitted with temporary visas, are permanent residents, or native-born citizens.

I am, admittedly, accentuating the differences between Chavez and De Genova's scholarship for the sake of my argument. I could just as easily trace points of agreement and continuity between their theories.[77] The differences, however, still matter—especially when it comes to advancing a critical race analysis. Simply put, Chavez's meditations on the Latino threat discourse require a race analysis, whereas De Genova's deportability theory does not. Chavez also engages the problem of racism in a way that is more consistent with the analysis of radical exclusion than that of migrant exploitation. The specter of racial otherness that is conjured by the Latino threat discourse is similar to the predicament of blackness that I have described in the prior chapters. Under the grips of this racist animus, Latinx populations are no longer viewed as exploitable but tolerable candidates for social membership; they are viewed as absolutely intolerable others who pose a threat to the ontological security of the United States.

Trump's derogatory remarks about TPS holders are a good example of the racist commonsense that informs acts of radical exclusion—and also of how this racist subtext is anchored by antiblack sentiments. There is a similar, but less explicit, chain of associations, between anti-immigrant sentiment, antiblackness, and radical exclusion, at work in the remain-in-Mexico policy.

Muzaffar Chishti and Jessica Bolter were among the first migration policy analysts to notice the connections between the MPP and the US government's Haitian interdiction operations.[78] Whereas the Haitian interdictions attracted a great deal of public attention, Chishti and Bolter observe that the remain-in-Mexico policy "has been implemented gradually, with less visibility, and still allows some access to asylum procedures."[79] On this last point, it also bears noting that the MPP is governed by US statutory law.

One of the legal foundations for the MPP is a section of the Immigration and Nationality Act that was added in 1996, as part of the reforms implemented under the IIRIRA.[80] This section of the INA

> provides that aliens arriving by land from a foreign contiguous territory (i.e., Mexico or Canada)—whether or not at a designated port of entry—generally may be returned, as a matter of enforcement discretion, to the territory from which they are arriving.[81]

People who are subject to these returns can still apply for asylum, but their access to asylum rights is very limited and, according to recent data, the overwhelming majority of them are not granted asylum.

Expedited removals were introduced to US immigration law by IIRIRA.[82] As the name implies, expedited removals make it possible for the immigration courts and enforcement agents to process removal cases more quickly, with this speed-up being made possible by curtailments on due process rights and access to asylum law. In January 2017, President Trump expanded on the scope of these removals by introducing a policy that allowed US border patrol to apply expedited removal procedures to all unauthorized migrants.[83] But the remain-in-Mexico policy went a step further.

One of the reasons why the MPP has been challenged by immigrant rights advocates is because it has maneuvered Central American asylum seekers into a situation in which they have even less rights than people who are subjected to expedited removal.[84] The end result is a hierarchy of rightlessness, with people subject to full removal proceedings sitting at the top of the hierarchy (regular deportables), people subjected to expedited removals sitting below (second class deportables), and people targeted for contiguous removal under the remain-in-Mexico policy near the bottom (excludables). There is also the disproportionately Haitian population of asylum seekers who are targeted by the Title 42 policy that are sitting below the people on the lowest rung of the remain-in-Mexico policy (second class excludables).

Around the same time that the Trump administration implemented the MPP, it was also working to expand its Safe Third Country policy, which requires refugees to seek asylum in any eligible nation that they have to pass through before entering the United States.[85] Canada has signed an agreement with the US government to be a Safe Third Country as has Mexico (though the Mexican government has insisted its hand was forced by threats of trade tariffs). At the time of this writing, the Trump administration was looking to enlist several other Central American and Caribbean nations in this policy.[86]

Another precedent for the MPP is Operation Gatekeeper which was initiated in 1994—the same year as Operation Sea Signal, which I discussed in the last chapter.[87] Operation Gatekeeper could be described as a land-border counterpart to the maritime interdictions that were being carried out under Sea Signal. As Joseph Nevins has explained, Operation Gatekeeper was used to advance a national-scale border control strategy that was unprecedented in its scope and rigor.[88] Typical of US border enforcement strategies, Operation Gatekeeper was focused only on the United States' southern border and it contributed to a racialized commonsense that equated "illegality" with brown and black migrant bodies.

Nevins explains that the enforcement practices that were being used under Operation Gatekeeper "helped to create the illegal through the construction of the boundary and the expansion of the federal government's enforcement capacity."[89] Viewed in this light, illegality is not an objectively existing problem, it is a policy and enforcement discourse that rationalizes the marginality and exploitation of a vulnerable migrant population.[90] This discourse on illegality can be combined with tactics of selective enforcement that varies according to labor market demand for unauthorized migrants. But according to Nevins, the overarching goal of Operation Gatekeeper was to "rid US territory of those without state sanction to be within its boundaries," out of respect for "the almost sacred nature" of the national border.[91] Once again, these goals are a better fit for the imperatives of radical exclusion than migrant exploitation. They are about affirming a concept of absolute difference—the profanity of illegality on one hand and the sacredness of the national territory on the other.

This kind of border control is invested in a symbolic politics that stretches far beyond practical concerns about public safety. It is one of the many ways that US law and policy has been used to answer Samuel Huntington's question: "Who are we?"[92] This question invites the same kinds of ontological distinctions that are evoked by antiblack sentiments. Although Operation Gatekeeper was not set up to target black populations, it relied on absolute distinctions between "us" and "them" that have a special historical relationship to the history and ontological moorings of antiblackness. Put another way, Gatekeeper is an important tipping point in a larger process whereby the policing of the US southern border becomes increasingly informed by a problem of racial otherness that can trace its beginnings to antiblack animus. Nevins makes a comparable point in his analysis. He observes that many researchers have used the concept of global apartheid to describe these kinds of border enforcement practices, but they do not connect the dots between "global apartheid" and the South African apartheid system.[93]

Nevins's argument resonates with ones that have been made by Afropessimist scholars. The concept of "global apartheid" establishes an abstract equivalence between (anti)black segregation and the border controls of the present day, but without tracing the historical relationship between these two kinds of apartheid. Nevins points out that black apartheid has to be factored into the explanation of "global apartheid," which means acknowledging how antiblack animus precedes and shapes racist animus against immigrants. Nevins goes on to provide an explanation of the racist binary that is consistent with the Foucauldian analysis that I discussed in chapter 5. Here is a sample.

> "Black" and "white"—and other racial categories—are not first and foremost about distinctions of skin color or pigmentation or phenotype . . . what are effectively racial distinctions often exist between groups with no discernable physical

differences. In this sense "race" is first and foremost based on power imbued differences related to notions of ancestry and geographic origins. Racism—what Stuart Hall . . . and Ruth Wilson Gilmore . . . have both characterized as a fatal coupling of power and difference—reflects and shapes who gets what, who call the shots, and how one lives and dies.[94]

Nevins's explanation of race-as-power is consistent with my argument about the black/nonblack binary as a circuitry of institutional power. He explains mobility in a similar way, as a "product and producer . . . of power" that constitutes group boundaries and identities.[95] But like many migration scholars, Nevins's analysis of mobility is anchored in a contrast between a restricted and a more expansive kind of mobility. As a result, his agenda for change is focused on reforms that will change the way borders are defined and regulated, with the aim of making them more open to migrants.[96]

The problem with this analysis is that it overlooks the distinction between restricted and controlled mobility. Restricted mobility can be conceptualized, quantitatively, in terms of the scope and distance that a person is able to travel. Controlled mobility, on the other hand, has less to do with the scope of a person's mobility, and more to do with their capacity for autonomous movement. As I explained in chapter 1, there is an intimate relationship between controlled mobility and antiblackness. The targets of controlled mobility are constituted as objects that are incapable of free movement. These people can move far and wide so long as their movement is not self-directed. This predicament is epitomized by the case of Dred Scott, who could be compelled to travel through both free and slave states, but remained a slave no matter where he happened to reside.[97]

In order to challenge this kind of mobility it is not enough to call for open borders, it is also necessary to interrogate the ontological distinction between the human and subhuman that informs border policy and enforcement practices. It is not just a geopolitical border that is being policed, or even for that matter, a legal status, but a racialized concept of social membership. This aspect of border control is about policing the movement of categorically different kinds of bodies. It should be viewed through the lens of radical exclusion, which is animated by a desire to deter the entry of people who are deemed innately unfit for membership.

OPERATION STREAMLINE AND THE OBAMA-ERA TICKET SYSTEM

Radical exclusion became a more prominent feature of US border patrol activities throughout the first decades of the new millennium. A good case in point is Operation Streamline, which was initiated in 2005 by the George W. Bush administration.[98]

The regulation of unauthorized migration by the Bush administration prior to Operation Streamline was derivative of the instrumentalist explanation of migrant exploitation that has been advanced by many scholars.[99] Although the Bush administration presided over a massive expansion of hiring and funding for immigration enforcement and border control especially, the unauthorized migrant population grew faster in this era than during any other period of US history.[100] It is also important to note that the historic peak for border enforcement actions occurred in the final year of the Clinton administration, and this peak was never exceeded by the Trump administration.[101]

Border enforcement actions dropped dramatically after George W. Bush took office in 2000—during the same time that unauthorized migration was undergoing a massive expansion.[102] The fact that Bush had been governor of Texas just prior to be taking the president's office is also of some significance. For many decades, the regulation of unauthorized migration was governed by an informal policy dubbed the "Texas proviso" that effectively legalized the employment of unauthorized migration, while still holding that unauthorized presence, itself, was a legal violation—the upshot being that the migrant was legally culpable for their unauthorized status but not their employer.[103] George W. Bush also played a leading role in the last attempt to enact a comprehensive immigration reform law. He endorsed a bill, along with Senators John McCain and Ted Kennedy, that would have, among other things, regularized a large cross section of the unauthorized population (granting a renewable temporary status, but which offered no guaranteed pathway to permanent residence) and instituted a new process whereby unauthorized migrants can apply for a permanent legal status.[104] The Bush administration's support for these kinds of immigration reforms aggravated tensions with the right-wing nationalists and immigration control hawks in the Republican base who, at the time, were concentrated in the House of Congress.[105] These immigration control hardliners may have been fringe elements of the Republican Party during the George W. Bush years, but their agenda was mainstreamed by the Trump administration.[106]

This context underscores why Operation Streamline is so significant. Although it was inaugurated by the George W. Bush administration, it was a dramatic departure from the pragmatic, enforcement-heavy approach to immigration that defined most of its immigration policy positions. Under Operation Streamline, the Bush administration relied on a section in the Immigration and Nationality Act that authorized the federal government to criminally prosecute migrants for unauthorized entry.[107] Prior to this time, unauthorized entry had been treated, mainly, as a civil offense and the debate over the intersections of criminal and immigration enforcement was focused on the role of local police.[108] The dominant opinion that emerged from this debate was that local police were only authorized to conduct activities pertaining to immigration enforcement if it was in the context of an ongoing criminal investigation or if they were partnering with federal enforcement.

Operation Streamline departed from this entire field of debate because it was a federal enforcement operation. Under Streamline, unauthorized migrants were apprehended almost immediately after crossing the border, were criminally prosecuted for their immigration violations, served time in federal prison, and were removed from the United States as soon as they finished their sentences.[109] Within a few years of the beginning of this program, federal prosecutions for "immigration crimes" began to equal and exceed the annual number of prosecutions for drug-related crimes.[110] During this same period of time, Latinx people became the largest racial-ethnic segment of the US federal prison population, establishing a trend that continues to this day.[111]

The mainstream pro-immigration discourse of the early 2000s (which was endorsed by the Bush and Obama administrations) justified these kinds of enforcement practices by insisting they were targeting criminals and not law-abiding, hardworking people.[112] But the migrants who were apprehended and removed under Operation Streamline were given no opportunity to become "hardworking" immigrants. They were apprehended and criminalized before they had a chance to get a job (or commit a crime, other than unauthorized entry) and were tracked into a pipeline of detention and incarceration that would result in their removal.

Operation Streamline established the policy and legal foundations for the practice of family separations and the zero tolerance border policy that the Trump administration rolled out between 2017 and 2018. As some policy analysts have explained, these Trump-era policies were not simply influenced by Operation Streamline, they were a direct continuation of the border enforcement practices that had been initiated by Streamline.[113] So although the Trump administration's remain-in-Mexico policy was unprecedented in some ways, it also amplified an enforcement agenda that dates to the early years of the new millennium. Obama-era policies on Haitian refugees are another important precursor for the remain-in-Mexico policy.

As I noted previously, after the 2010 earthquake, many Haitians who had been admitted to South America migrated northward to the US-Mexico border. In 2016, US Customs and Border Patrol initiated a new policy that was tailored for these Haitian asylum seekers. Like the remain-in-Mexico policy, this arrangement granted Haitians a "ticket" for an appointment with Customs and Border Patrol (to determine their eligibility for entry) and gave them permission to be paroled in Mexico as they waited for this appointment.[114]

Naomi Paik has explained that this system of "humanitarian parole," which was used to facilitate the petitions for Haitian asylum seekers, was extended to Central American and Mexican migrants.[115] One conclusion that Paik draws from this comparison is that a policy that was, on the whole, beneficial for Haitians was used to undermine the asylum rights of Central American and Mexican nationals.[116] But there is another report, generated by a coalition of Haitian-run, black activist and migrant rights nonprofits, that I cited earlier in this chapter, which tells a different story.[117] According to this report, the policy that the Obama administration devised for Haitian and African asylum seekers at the US-Mexico border was deeply problematic. Instead of being beneficial for Haitian asylum seekers, it is described as a discriminatory precursor to the Title 42 policy.[118] This report also points out that the "ticket" or "metering" system that was devised for Haitian asylum seekers became the subject of an antidiscrimination lawsuit.[119]

The insights from Paik's analysis and the report that I have just summarized point toward a set of propositions that I introduced earlier in this chapter. Policies for black populations often become precursors for policies that are rolled out for nonblack, populations (with the Haitian ticket system preceding the remain-in-Mexico policy). And policies for black populations tend to be more exclusionary than policies applied to nonblack populations (as demonstrated by the Title 42 policy).

But as I noted at the beginning of this chapter it is very difficult to make room for this kind of analysis in a court of law. It poses a problem for the legal arguments that are used both by the defenders and critics of government policy. I am going to provide a more detailed account of this problem in the next section, which focuses on the legal challenge to the MPP.

CHALLENGING THE REMAIN-IN-MEXICO POLICY

The Trump-era legal challenge to the remain-in-Mexico policy revolved around four federal court decisions which include an initial decision by a Northern California District Court, two decisions issued by the Ninth Circuit Court of Appeals, and an order issued by the Supreme Court.[120]

The first federal court to rule on the legality of the MPP was the District Court of Northern California—in *Innovation Law Lab v. Nielsen* (2019), decided by Judge Immergut. Immergut's decision, like that of many of the District Courts judges who ruled on the government's Haitian refugee polices, was sympathetic to the plaintiffs. Immergut's argument was also very similar to the one used by Judge Spellman in *Louis v. Nelson* (1982), which I discussed in chapters 2 and 3.[121]

Spellman acknowledged that the government's treatment of Haitian refugees raised some important questions about due process and equal protection—but he concluded that Haitian refugees were unable to appeal to constitutional law because they were excludable aliens.[122] So instead of making an argument that hinged on the legal rights of the Haitian plaintiffs, he charged INS officials for violating the APA.

In *Innovation Law Lab v. Nielsen*, Judge Immergut observed that the two key issues at the stake in the legal challenge concerned whether the practice of contiguous return was authorized by the Immigration and Nationality Act (in the way it was being implemented under the MPP) and whether the government was violating the nonrefoulement principle.[123] The former argument had to do with whether the remain-in-Mexico policy had been reconciled to existing law (as required by the APA). The latter argument had to do with whether the government was violating the rights of the migrants it was processing under the MPP, as defined by international law—and also by the 1980 Refugee Act, which contained language on nonrefoulement that was patterned after the 1951 Refugee Convention.

Immergut ruled that, in both instances, the government was in violation of the law, but he also insisted that the APA argument was sufficient, on its own, to justify an injunction against the MPP.[124] This argument was different than Spellman's, because it acknowledged that migrants targeted by the MPP actually did have rights under US statutory law and international refugee law. But Immergut's decision was similar to Spellman's in that it did not rely on a strong rights-based argument. As a result, Immergut's decision contributed to a history of argumentation that runs through many of the sympathetic court decisions that I reviewed in the prior chapters.

Practical steps are taken to block government policies that are injurious to migrants and refugees, but using arguments that tacitly cede ground to their rightlessness. The argument that was most central to Immergut's decision had to do with the way that the targets of the MPP were classified by the government under statutory law.

The practice of contiguous return is authorized by section 1225 of the Immigration and Nationality Act.[125] This section gives the US government the authority to require that migrants and refugees reside in a territory adjacent to the United States while they wait to be summoned to the United States to have their case heard by the immigration courts. The MPP stipulates that several categories of noncitizens are excluded from this contiguous return policy, including unaccompanied minors, migrants with known physical or mental health issues, and returning legal permanent residents.[126] The legal category that was most relevant to the legal dispute over the MPP, however, were noncitizens who are being processed for expedited removal.

People who are subject to expedited removal can be exempted from the practice of contiguous return. They have the right to express concern about being returned to their home nation, or to contiguous territory, at which point asylum officers are obligated to grant them an interview to determine if they have a credible fear of persecution.[127] Once this process begins, these people are tracked directly into the immigration court system, rather than being required to wait for months in Mexico for their case to be heard by the immigration courts. As subjects of these proceedings, these petitioners have "substantial procedural safeguards against being removed to a place where he or she may face persecution."[128] Effectively, these people are applying defensively for asylum and are only removed from the United States if their asylum petition is not granted.

The petitioners that I have just described fall under a class of noncitizens that are described in section 1225 b(1) of the INA.[129] But there is another class of noncitizens, described by the next section, 1225 b(2) who *can* be subjected to the practice of contiguous return.[130] Border patrol and asylum officers are not required to ask these people if they fear persecution on return to their home nation or to Mexico.[131] Even if these people raise concerns about persecution, they are evaluated using a stricter standard than credible fear (which is the criterion that they will "more likely than not" face persecution on return).[132] If the asylum petitions of these people are denied, they are not "deported" or "removed" from the United States. Instead, they are simply not granted the right to enter. Meanwhile, as they wait for lengthy periods of time for their case to be heard, they can be exposed to hazards that are even worse than what migrants experience in US detention centers, as well as being given incentives to drop their petition and return home.[133] So overall, the asylum rights of a 1225 b(2) class person are much weaker than the rights of people who are grouped into the 1225 b(1) class.

The migrants and migrant service organizations that raised the legal challenge in *Innovation Law Lab v. Nielsen* argued that the remain-in-Mexico policy was assigning people to these legal classes in distorted ways, which grossly increased the number of people who were subject to contiguous return.[134] Migrants who had credible asylum claims and qualified for expedited removal were tracked into the 1225 b(2) class—for contiguous removal. The government also argued that the discretionary authority it enjoyed to prosecute people under full or expedited removal proceedings under the 1225 b(1) class also granted it discretionary authority to switch people from the 122b b(1) to the b(2) class.[135]

These were all very complicated arguments, but they all revolved around a basic point of dispute, over whether the government had the authority to push large numbers of Central American migrants further down the hierarchy of rightlessness. The government's legal machinations can be explained in light of the deterrence paradigm. The law was being manipulated for the purpose of restricting the entry of as many Central American migrants and refugees into the United States as possible. Going a step further, this stratagem can be viewed through the lens of radical exclusion, which relies on an extra-legal authority that is fueled by a racist animus, to constantly push the law beyond its established limits. The arguments used by Judge Immergut in *Innovation Law Labs v. Wolf* did not cut to the heart of this problem. The same is true for the Ninth Circuit, which heard the government's appeal of the District Court's decision.

Like Judge Immergut, the Ninth Circuit produced a decision that was sympathetic to the plaintiffs. The Ninth Circuit also made a stronger rights-based argument that placed more weight on the government's violation of the nonrefoulement principle.[136] It also agreed with Judge Immergut that the government's interpretation of contiguous return under the Immigration and Nationality Act was incorrect and was a violation of the APA, though it declined to rule on whether this APA argument extended to other aspects of the government's policy.[137] The Ninth Circuits concluded by affirming Immergut's decision to levy an injunction against the MPP that would take effect across the entirety of the US-Mexico border.[138]

A few days later, however, the Ninth Circuit issued another decision which limited the geographic scope of this injunction to border sectors that fell under its territorial jurisdiction.[139] Consequently, the government was prohibited from carrying out the remain-in-Mexico policy across sections of the US border that ran through the states of Arizona and California but not through Texas and New Mexico. This qualified support for the District Court's injunction was completely eliminated a week later when the Supreme Court weighed in on the case. The court issued a brief, one paragraph, order—with no legal argument—that overrode the Ninth Circuit's opinion and allowed the government to continue the remain-in-Mexico along the entirety of the US-Mexico border until the case was heard on appeal.[140]

Eight months after the Supreme Court issued this order, the political landscape for the remain-in-Mexico policy changed significantly, due to the results of the US Presidential election. Shortly after the election, President Biden indicated that his administration was considering dismantling the remain-in-Mexico policy.[141,142] Days before issuing this decision, the Department of Homeland Security also announced that it was ending the practice of family separations and the zero tolerance border policy, which had been introduced by the Trump administration.[143] These decisions aimed to restore the asylum rights of Central American refugees. But as I noted at the beginning of this chapter, there has been no change to the Title 42 policy, which has been quietly used to bar the entry of Haitian asylum seekers.

This treatment of Haitian refugees is distinguished, not just by its severity, but by the silence that surrounds it. There is no mention of Title 42 in the legal dispute over the MPP or the TPS cancellations, even though these policies are being applied to similar populations and with a similar aim of restricting asylum rights and repatriating "unwanted people." The Obama-era "ticket" or "metering" system that was designed for Haitian asylum seekers has been subjected to a similar silence. To illustrate further, I will return to Judge Immergut's decision for *Innovation Law Labs v. Wolf.*

One of the most important issues that Immergut had to resolve was whether there was a viable legal precedent for the practice of contiguous return, as it was being interpreted by the Trump administration. The government argued that there was a BIA decision—*Matter of Sanchez-Avila*—that provided the precedent it needed to justify practice.[144] Immergut was not persuaded. She observed that the plaintiff in Sanchez-Avila was very different than the asylum seekers who were challenging the remain-in-Mexico policy.[145] Sanchez-Avila was not an unauthorized migrant who had a plausible case for asylum. He was a resident alien commuter who was denied (re)entry to the United States, due to his "involvement with controlled substances."[146] On these grounds, Immergut went on to argue that *Matter of Sanchez-Avila* did not provide a clear precedent for why the plaintiffs in *Innovation Law Lab v. Wolf* should be subjected to contiguous return.

Immergut made a good point, but neither she nor the government's attorneys made any mention of the Obama-era "ticket" system. As Paik has explained, this policy used a technique of managing Haitian asylum seekers that was very similar to contiguous return which was developed several years before the Trump administration created the MPP.[147] It bears noting, however, that the ticket system only supplies a policy precedent, created by the discretionary authority of the executive office, and not a legal precedent that was established by the courts or the legislature. This is, very likely, the main reason why the ticket system does not show in the government's argument, and why Immergut did not bother to address it. But the "irrelevance" of the ticket system also speaks to a history of controls on black mobility that have been enabled by policies, practices, and sentiments that operate on the margins of the law. The silence surrounding these practices makes it possible for them to proliferate without leaving a trace on the public record, which is yet another example of the aphasiac cloud that surrounds the problem of black rightlessness. In the next section, I explain how similar silences played out in the legal dispute over the Trump administration's efforts to cancel TPS.

CHALLENGING THE CANCELLATION OF TPS

The legal challenge to the Trump administration's efforts to cancel TPS met the same fate as the challenge to the remain-in-Mexico policy. The challenge began with District Court decisions that affirmed the rights of the plaintiffs, and these sympathetic decisions were overturned by the higher courts.[148] There is, however, a subtle but important difference in both of these case histories.

The legal challenge to remain-in-Mexico met with more support from the appellate courts than the legal challenge to the cancellation of TPS. Whereas the challenge to the MPP received sympathetic decisions from both district and circuit courts, the challenge to the TPS cancellations was shut down at the circuit court level. It is also important to note that both challenges were heard by the Ninth Circuit Court of Appeals. So the same circuit court that pushed back against the Trump administration in the challenge to the MPP ended up defending the Trump administration when it came to the TPS cancellations.

But the Ninth Circuit's argument ended up being of no practical consequence of the policy it was defending. After taking office, President Biden reversed the Trump administration's plans to cancel TPS and extended TPS protections to more displaced populations.[149] The debate over TPS has shifted, from whether it will be canceled, to whether TPS holders should be granted the right to apply for green cards.[150] At the time of this writing, the government is waiting for the Supreme Court to set a date to decide this issue.

This turn of affairs lends more credence to Harold Koh's strategy for using legal challenges to angle for a political solution rather than waiting on a sympathetic decision from the higher courts.[151] Koh has shown how policy battles that seemed "unwinnable" in the courts could be pursued by building networks that pressure the executive office to use its discretionary powers. The decision of the Clinton administration to parole HIV-positive Haitian detainees from Guantanamo to the US mainland is one of the most impressive outcomes that Koh achieved with this strategy.[152] The decision of the Biden administration to end the remain-in-Mexico policy, revoke the TPS cancellations, and many other aspects of Trump-era immigration and refugee policy further underscore the power and political clout of the executive office. But these developments also beg the question: why do the courts matter?

My answer to this question is that the courts matter because their decisions illustrate how the law is reconciled to a sovereign decision that is vested with the power to commit acts of radical exclusion. The federal courts—and the appellate courts especially—tend to serve a conservative function when it comes to the relationship between these forces. In other words, the courts generally respect the sovereign power that the executive office wields over immigration and refugee law—producing a jurisprudence that tends to preserve rather than disturb the exercise of this supra-legal authority. Since radical exclusion is enabled by the sovereign authority that the law is obliged to protect, it festers in the aphasiac silences of the law. Radical exclusion could be described as a hollow space in the law—a condition of extreme rightlessness—that, if viewed in a certain light, would seem to be antithetical to the rule of law, but has also been systemically replicated and enabled by the bodies of legal opinion that guide the evolution of the law.

The analysis of the law matters because it calls attention to this problem. Even after reversing the Trump-era TPS cancellations, the relationship between the law, the sovereign power, and radical exclusion will not have changed. This relationship has to be surfaced in order to problematize the racist undercurrents of the law and call attention to the singularly important role that antiblack animus plays in anchoring these racist undercurrents. In the remainder of this section I am going to examine the federal court decisions about the TPS cancellations, with an eye for this problem.

The first two federal court decisions that evaluated the TPS legal challenge were heard by Judge Edward Chen of the District Court of Northern California. Judge Chen's first decision, for this case, in *Ramos v. Nielsen* (issued August 2018) blocked the government's attempt to dismiss the legal challenge.[153] In his second decision for this case (issued October 2018), Judge Chen issued an injunction against the cancellation of TPS, which was intended to remain in effect while the case was being adjudicated.[154] My discussion is going to focus on Judge Chen's first decision, because it raises issues that make for an interesting comparison with the litigation over the US government's Haitian refugee policies, going back to the era of the Haitian program.

In his opening statement of his first decision, Judge Chen summarized the grievances of the plaintiffs into four points.[155] First, the US citizen children of TPS holders were having their due process rights violated, because they were being forced to leave the United States with their parents despite having a legal right to remain. Second,[156] the due process rights of TPS holders were also being violated by the government's assumption that they had no legal grounds to contest their removal. This argument recalls the distinction between deportable subjects and excludable aliens that was officially eliminated by IIRIRA in 1996, but which continues to haunt litigations over migrant and refugee rights.

With this second point, Chen was insisting that TPS holders had due process and procedural rights that the government was bound to respect, due to their history of residence in the United States. These are the same rights that would accrue to a deportable unauthorized migrant. TPS holders would, arguably, have an even more compelling claim on these rights since they have a legal status, even if it is temporary. In contrast, the Trump administration insisted on treating TPS holders like excludable aliens who had never been granted entry to the United States. According to this line of argument, TPS holders were in the same rightless predicament as the Haitian refugees from the litigation of the Haitian program in the early 1980s.[157]

The third point of contention raised by Judge Chen further underscored his argument that TPS holders were US residents and rights-bearing subjects. In this third point, Chen directly addressed President Trump's racist statements about TPS holders and immigrants in general, and observed that these statements were pertinent to the plaintiffs argument that the cancellation of TPS had been informed by discriminatory sentiments that violated the equal protection clause of the Fourteenth Amendment.[158] Fourth, and finally, Chen observed that Trump administration officials had dramatically altered the criteria that prior administrations had used to make decisions about continuing or cancelling TPS, and that these changes could be violations of the APA.[159]

All of these complaints should be familiar to the reader by now. Arguments about APA violations, violations of (Fifth Amendment) due process rights, and the (Fourteenth Amendment) equal protection clause are recurring themes of challenges to the US government's Haitian refugee policies. But the case from this history that is most relevant to Judge Chen's decision is the first one I discussed in chapter 2: the *Haitian Refugee Center v. Civiletti* decision that was decided by Judge King in 1980.[160]

Chen's decision combines an APA argument with a strongly worded constitutional rights argument that was reminiscent of the decision Judge King delivered n the Civiletti case. In some ways, Chen's analysis of racism is more uncompromising than King's as well as that of Judge Carter who used the construct of invidious discrimination to criticize the parole decisions of INS officials (see the discussion of *Vigile v. Sava*[161] in chapter 3). Although Chen does not reference the concepts of institutional or structural racism, he describes a "cat's paw" dynamic whereby the opinions of President Trump established a context and set of imperatives that influenced the decisions of the DHS and White House officials who issued the cancellation of TPS.[162] This argument differs from Judge King's critique of racism as a kind of individual-psychological deviance that is typical of liberal bias theory. It also differs from Judge Carter's application of the jurisprudence on "invidious discrimination" which revolved around an illegitimate bias that lower-level officials introduce into presumably race-neutral policies and practices that have been devised by their superiors.[163] In different ways, King and Carter advanced a bottom-up analysis of racism (or a "bad apple" theory) in which causal primacy is ceded to the beliefs and actions of deviant individuals. Chen, on the other hand, produced a top-down analysis of racism. Chen's analysis can still account for the possibility that President Trump's racist statements are a reflection of his personality traits and life history, but it also accounts for how Trump's attitudes shaped federal policy due to the position he occupied in a chain of authority.

Chen grounded this argument in a jurisprudence established by the 1977 Supreme Court decision for *Arlington Heights v. Metropolitan Housing*

Corps.[164] According to Arlington Heights, violations of the equal protection clause that effect a particular group do not require evidence of how another comparable group has been treated. In order to show proof that a violation has occurred, it is sufficient for the plaintiff to provide evidence of discriminatory intent, which is what Judge Chen did with his "cat's paw" theory.

Arlington Heights focused on complaints of housing discrimination by US-born black populations, but it is comparable to the standard of "strict scrutiny" that the 1972 *Graham v. Richardson* decision introduced for cases involving discrimination on the basis of noncitizen status.[165] As I explained in chapter 2, the Graham standard was premised on the idea that noncitizens are a "discrete and insular minority"—a construct that is derived from post-civil rights-era jurisprudence that has been used to protect racial minorities. Chen's use of the Arlington Heights decision invited comparisons between these two kinds of minority statuses, since the plaintiff group for *Ramos v. Nielsen* were composed of people who were TPS holders and also members of black/African and Latinx populations.

But it could also be argued that Chen's decision did not hinge on the protections offered by Graham, since he was not really arguing that Haitian, Sudanese, Nicaraguan, and Salvadoran TPS holders were discriminated against *as* TPS holders. Chen emphasized that these people were discriminated against because they were viewed as a particularly undesirable kind of TPS holder (i.e., people from "shithole countries"). Put another way, they were being discriminated against because they were racial-ethnic minorities. This is why his argument was framed by the Arlington Heights decision, which dealt with the complaints of African Americans. By referencing Arlington Heights, Chen was saying that the injustice suffered by the TPS holders was no different than the kind of discrimination suffered by US-born racial minorities.

Having acknowledged all of this, it is still possible to see how the Graham decision connects to the argument advanced by Chen. To trace these connections, it is important to consider the genealogy of Supreme Court decisions in which Graham is located—which can be traced to the 1886 Supreme Court decision for *Yick Wo v. Hopkins.*[166] I discussed this decision in more depth in chapter 2. The important point, for the purpose of this discussion, is the insistence of the Yick Wo court that all people residing on US soil are protected by the Constitution regardless of their legal status. It is also important to note that Judge Chen cited Yick Wo in his decision.[167] With this citation Chen underscored the point that TPS holders have the right to complain about racial discrimination because they are US residents—because this is the same argument that was advanced in Yick Wo. This is also why Chen's use of the Arlington Heights precedent is a little deceiving.

Although there is compelling evidence that the TPS holders in *Ramos v. Nielsen* were targets for racist discrimination, their right to complain about this treatment hinged on their status as US residents, and not simply on their status as racial minorities. Radical exclusion operates along this distinction, between the noncitizen who is viewed as having a legitimate right to "be here" and racialized noncitizens who are denied entry and treated as if they "never entered" even if they are physically present on US soil. This is why the racial otherness that was salient for the Arlington Heights decision does not adequately describe the kind of racialized rightlessness that has been perpetuated by the US government's immigration and refugee policies—and especially, by its Haitian refugee policies.

The distinction between racial minorities and majority groups members, as conventionally defined under law, presumes that all of these people are rights-bearing subjects, by virtue of their status as US citizens or long-term residents. But when radical exclusion gets a grip on immigration policy, it uses the distinction between the (deportable) resident and the excludable as a way of targeting "undesirables" who do not even have the right to raise complaints about racial discrimination. This is the predicament of the Haitian refugee which I recounted in all of the prior chapters (and especially in chapters 2–4). This is also why it is very significant that Trump administration officials rebutted the complaints of the plaintiffs by insisting that TPS holders had never been granted entry to the United States.[168] According to this line of argument, the plaintiff group for *Ramos v. Nielsen* was composed of people who, legally speaking, were not "really here" in the United States. Consequently, they were put in a similar predicament as the CABA detainees and the refugees targeted by the Haitian program.

The government drew on the legal precedent established by the *Trump v. Hawaii* decision to support its argument for why it could terminate TPS without regard for the constitutional rights of TPS holders.[169] In *Trump v. Hawaii*, the Supreme Court defended the legality of the third, revised version of President Trump's travel ban on nationals from Arab-Muslim nations. The arguments of the plaintiffs in this case paralleled the challenge to the TPS cancellations, because they drew on many of Trump's derogatory public statements about Islam and Arab-Muslim people to substantiate their argument about the biased and unlawful nature of the travel ban.[170] It also bears noting that several of the nations that had been included in the travel ban, at one point or another, were predominantly Arab-Muslim and black/African (including Chad, the Sudan, and Somalia).[171] The plaintiffs in this case, however, relied on the Establishment Clause of the First Amendment to press their claims and not the equal protection clause of the Fourteenth Amendment—to underscore their argument about being targeted on the basis of their religion and not race.[172] For the purpose of this discussion, what is most significant about *Trump v. Hawaii* is the way it deployed arguments about rightlessness and excludability that were tacitly affirmed by Judge Chen in his attempt to push back against the TPS cancellations.

Chen offered a number of reasons for why *Trump v. Hawaii* had no bearing on the case he was deciding. He observed that the upholding of the travel ban, in *Trump v. Hawaii*, was justified by national security and foreign policy considerations that did not apply to the plaintiffs in *Ramos v. Nielsen*.[173] He also pointed out that the Supreme Court's decision was justified as an interpretation of statutory law that granted the government much broader discretionary authority than it has under the legislation that created TPS. But most importantly, Chen insisted that the plaintiff group for *Trump v. Hawaii* was composed of noncitizens who were not physically present in the United States.[174] In making this point, Chen insisted that TPS holders "are not aliens abroad seeking entry or admission who—have no constitutional right of entry," and as "aliens within the United States [they] have greater constitutional protections than those outside who are seeking admission for the first time."[175]

With this statement, Chen was appealing to a kind of naïve realism which presumes that there is a strict correspondence between physical presence and the fact of entry. Even if he personally disagreed with the Trump administration's travel ban, he was willing to concede that the noncitizens effected by this ban had no rights (or at least had less rights than the TPS plaintiffs) because they had not yet entered the United States. TPS holders, on the other hand, actually were present in the United States and many of them had been living "here" for a great many years, raising families, working jobs, and becoming responsible members of their local communities.

The legal commonsense underlying Chen's appeal is rooted in the argument established by *Yick Wo v. Hopkins*, which is that anyone residing in the United States, regardless of their legal status, had a right to claim the protections of the law. The problem with this is argument is that it turns a blind eye to the way radical exclusion works. As I explained in chapter 3, the question of entry is better understood as a sociopolitical construction which is informed by ideas about the desirability of the noncitizen who is attempting to enter—rather than a straightforward assessment of whether they are "actually here." This is another reason why the case of *Louis v. Nelson*, decided by Judge Spellman in 1982, is so significant.[176]

All of the Haitian plaintiffs in *Louis v. Nelson* were being held in detention centers on US soil, but were still classified as excludables who had not been granted the right of entry to the United States. This is why Spellman declined to use a constitutional rights argument in defense of these Haitian refugees, even though he sympathized with their plight. It is also important to recall that *Yick Wo v. Hopkins* has been enlisted by the government in its efforts to defend its interdiction operations—using Yick Wo to make the point that constitutional law only applies to noncitizens who are present on US soil rather than on the high seas.[177] In *CABA v. Christopher* the Eleventh Circuit Court of Appeals used a similar argument to deny the protections of constitutional, statutory, and international law to Haitian and Cuban detainees at Guantanamo Bay.[178] But about a decade later, the Supreme Court issued a series of decisions concerning the treatment of Arab-Muslim "enemy combatants" which reached the opposite conclusion—that the US base at Guantanamo Bay actually did fall under the legal jurisdiction of the US government and that Guantanamo detainees were entitled to due process and procedural rights.[179] These wildly divergent decisions show how the federal courts can differ over how the legal and territorial jurisdiction of the United States is defined, which carries implications for the question of entry—and how some noncitizens can be granted access to the law even if they have not been granted the right of entry.

The Supreme Court's 1893 decision for *Fong Yue Ting v. US* provides an even more compelling example of how laws that are used to police "resident alien" populations can blur the lines between the expulsion of people who are "already here" and the exclusion of people who are being denied entry (see chapter 3).[180] Although Fong Yue Ting was decided over 120 years ago, the decision has never been overturned, and it can be regarded as an early precursor for the deterrence paradigm that began to take shape in the mid-1990s.[181] The way that Fong Yue Ting blurred the lines between expulsion and exclusion anticipates the elimination of the legal distinction between excludables and deportables that was introduced by IIRIRA in 1996.[182] The practical outcome of this erasure is that migrants who are "actually here" in the United States can be plunged into a rightless predicament that is barely distinguishable from that of the excludable alien of years past. IIRIRA was an apex point in a series of reforms traceable to the anti-drug abuse laws of the 1980s, which created this new kind of migrant rightlessness.[183]

Judge Chen discussed *Fong Yue Ting v. US* in his second decision for *Ramos v. Nielsen*, but he used this discussion to make a point that was similar to his reading of *Yick Wo v. Hopkins*. He took issue with the way that the Trump administration had interpreted a legal precedent that relied on Fong Yue Ting to support its argument about the excludability of TPS holders.[184]

Chen dismissed this argument because, in his opinion, it relied on outdated ideas about the government's sovereign right to expel or exclude aliens. He went on to explain that this sovereign authority to expel and exclude "does not detract from evolved and well-established authority that aliens lawfully within the United States have rights from those seeking admission in the first instance into the United States."[185] Chen also cited the Supreme Court's 2001 decision for *Zadvydas v. Davis*[186] to support his argument, but he used this decision to make a point that is traceable to Yick Wo precedent, which is that any alien who is present in the United States, regardless of legal status, should enjoy the protections of the law.

This argument presumes that *Yick Wo v. Hopkins* is a more accurate reflection of contemporary jurisprudence than *Fong Yue Ting v. US*, despite the fact that neither of these two decisions has been overturned. But unfortunately, Fong Yue Ting is a "living" feature of the law just as much as Yick Wo, and as I have argued throughout this book, the radical exclusion that was pioneered by Fong Yue Ting lived on through the arguments that were used to defend the Haitian interdictions.

Chen's reading of Yick Wo is also limited by a premise—which pervades legal scholarship on racism and immigration law[187]—that sovereign authority is always, necessarily, used to exclude migrants and restrict immigrant rights. But in chapter 2, I showed that the constitutional rights argument advanced in Yick Wo was accompanied by a federal supremacy argument that affirmed the sovereign authority of the government over immigration law.[188] Viewed in this light, the sovereign authority argument is not as outdated as Chen suggests and is also not really antithetical to the legal principles that Chen was using to anchor his argument. In the end, Chen produces an argument that contains the same flaw as Judge King's impassioned critique of the racist treatment of Haitian refugees, in his Civiletti decision.

In both cases, racist and exclusionary practices are criticized on the presumption that they deviate from well-established norms that are more inclusive and egalitarian. Both judges failed to produce an argument which can account for radical exclusion as an active feature of immigration law and policy that has been enabled by the actions of the government and the courts. This problem recalls the treatment of racism in the Supreme Court's decision for *Jean v. Nelson*, which had the final word on the cases that had been first decided by Judge Spellman.[189] The reader may recall that when *Jean v. Nelson* was heard by the Supreme Court, it responded to the charge of racism by insisting that INS policy on denying parole to Haitian refugees was being carried out in a race-neutral manner.[190] The Supreme Court appeared to agree that US law should abide by the same egalitarian norms that were affirmed by Judges King and Chen. But the court affirmed these norms for the sake of dismissing their significance for the case at hand.

According to the Supreme Court's argument for *Jean v. Nelson*, the government was not obligated to respect the rights of Haitian refugees, but its treatment of these rightless people still conformed to established legal norms on the subject of racial discrimination. In this context, the commitment to antidiscrimination is something akin to the "gratuitous humanitarian act" described by the Eleventh Circuit in *CABA v. Christopher*, which affirms an ethics that does not come with any legal obligations.[191] This reasoning was used to make a very different legal argument than that of Judge Chen, but it appeals to a similar idea, about the egalitarian norms that inform the interpretation and implementation of law and policy.

When the Ninth Circuit Court of Appeals heard the government's appeal of Judge Chen's decisions, it made an argument which echoed that of the Supreme Court in *Jean v. Nelson*. The appellate court rejected Chen's decision and focused its argument on two features of the plaintiff's claims: violations of administrative procedure and violations of the equal protection clause, having to do with racial discrimination.[192]

On the first matter, the court found that the decision of DHS secretary Nielsen to terminate TPS for the designated national origin groups fell within the scope of her discretionary authority.[193] In effect, the court insisted that she was not obligated to follow the criteria that prior administrations had used to determine whether TPS should be extended, which accounted for new and ongoing conditions of instability in the home nations of TPS holders. The court also agreed with the Trump administration that TPS holders are people who have not been granted entry to the United States, which also means they are not entitled to due process or to equal protection.[194]

The Ninth Circuit's decision in this case relied on an understanding of the US government's authority over immigration law, which is consistent with the Plenary Power doctrine. But the structure of the argument followed a pattern that was similar to the Eleventh Circuit's decision for *CABA v. Christopher*—in which the Plenary Power doctrine is never directly referenced, though it appears in the genealogy of precedential decisions that was cited by the majority opinion.[195]

So, the Plenary Power doctrine lingered in the backdrop of the Ninth Circuit's decision for *Ramos v. Wolf*: the same ghostly presence that haunted the CABA decision. Within the space of this ghostly presence, the Ninth Circuit paid deference to the norms of antidiscrimination and race-neutrality. It acknowledged that President Trump had made racially charged statements, around the same time that the TPS cancellations were issued, but it did not attempt to defend these statements. Instead, the court insisted that there was no evidence that Trump's statements had influenced Nielsen's policy decisions or that if any other White House or DHS official who was involved in the TPS decision.[196] According to this line of argument, Trump's statements were unacceptable, but they were limited to a few isolated incidents and there was no "cat's paw" connecting these racist statements to the government's policy decisions.[197]

Once again, we are faced with an argument that affirms the government's discretionary authority over immigration law, but which also insists that racial discrimination had nothing to do with the government's exercise of this discretionary authority—even though the legal precedents the court cited in support of its argument authorize the government to exclude noncitizens for any reason it chose. I have already explained why the Supreme Court's decision for *Jean v. Nelson* is an important template for this evasive line of argument. It also bears noting that the Jean decision is cited by the Ninth Circuit in *Ramos v. Wolf*, but curiously enough, it was cited by the dissenting judge and not by the majority opinion.

The Ninth Circuit's decision in this case was decided by a panel of three judges, two of whom were Republican appointees.[198] The dissent was issued by the lone Democratic appointee on the panel, Judge Christen. Her dissent echoed many of the themes of Chen's earlier decisions and reached a similar conclusion.[199] But Christen's argument also appealed to a legal pragmatism that undermined the salience of race and racism.

Judge Chen produced a robust analysis of the problem of institutional racism that fell short when it came to acknowledging the continuing salience of racist exclusions and sovereign powers that he had resigned to the dustbin of history. Judge Christen, on the other hand, avoided the matter entirely. She acknowledged that Trump had made concerning statements that raised important questions about equal protection, but that this argument was ultimately unnecessary for the legal challenge.[200]

Christen quoted excerpts from internal emails and memos (that Chen had also featured in his earlier decisions) which showed that government officials had rewritten and radically altered recommendations for the renewal of TPS made by prior DHS workers.[201] Christen argued that this turnabout in official opinion about the TPS renewals had not been justified by criteria that were plausibly related to the legislation governing TPS or by established policy guidelines. Instead, it appeared that the only reason for the sudden change in opinion was due to political pressure that DHS officials were receiving from their administrative superiors.[202]

Judge Christen found that all of this evidence made for a clear-cut case that the Trump administration's new policy on TPS was in violation of the APA.[203] She also argued that it would be unwise for the plaintiffs to pursue their complaints about racial discrimination, and she cited *Jean v. Nelson* to support this position.[204] Christen agreed with the Jean court that there was no need to reach questions of constitutional law if there were other equally plausible (non-constitutional) arguments available to press an argument.

In the Supreme Court's decision for Jean, this argument was used to counter the Eleventh Circuit's insistence that the government had a constitutionally protected right-to-be-racist when it came to immigration law. When Christen cited Jean, she was deflecting Chen's argument that the government had interjected racist animus into its policy decisions in a way that clearly violated constitutional law. But the end result in both cases was the same; the analysis of racism was kept at a distance from the evaluation of immigration policy decisions. The end result is a strange consensus in which defenders and detractors of the government's immigration policies agree that it is unwise to make racism an issue of contention, even if they happen to personally disagree about the salience of racism for the case in question. As this case demonstrates, and as I have noted throughout the book, these race-averse tendencies get more pronounced as legal challenges move from the arena of the district courts, and upward through the appellate court system.

HIERARCHIES OF OTHERNESS

There is a racist subtext for the remain-in-Mexico policy that helps to explain why it was introduced and how it was implemented. Even so, the migrants and refugees who challenged the MPP did not make racism a central feature of their legal arguments. By comparison, the charge of racism was more central to the complaints that were raised against the Trump administration's TPS cancellations.[205] Both of these legal challenges were unsuccessful, but the TPS challenge failed harder. It ran up against a body of legal opinion that halted the case at the circuit court level. In contrast, the challenge to the MPP received a sympathetic hearing from the same circuit court that quashed the contentions over TPS. Meanwhile, the discriminatory outcomes of the Title 42 policy have still not been subjected to legal scrutiny. The federal courts have called the policy to task for its treatment of unaccompanied minors, but the courts have yet to hear a case that raises questions about the policy's inordinate focus on Haitian refugees.[206]

One lesson to draw from all of these legal deliberations is that complaints about racial discrimination—especially complaints that touch on the anti-black racism underlying government policy—face a hard time in the federal court system. This is a problem that can be traced to the earliest challenges to the government's Haitian refugee policies. There was also a pronounced tendency, even among judges who were critical of the government's policies, to evade the problem of racism or to deal with it in a truncated way. So on one hand, there are legal arguments, both for and against these policies, that are unable to grapple with the problem of antiblack racism, and on the other, there is a macro-institutional process unfolding in which controls that had once been imposed, exclusively, on black mobility have been streamlined to a larger nonblack population.

In this chapter I have tried to show how a theory of the black/nonblack binary can be used to bring this process, more clearly into view, and to problematize it. I have shown how the nether-zones of black rightlessness can become an incubator for exclusionary policies and practices that are extended to nonblack populations. This is why the legal precedents used to justify the government's Haitian interdiction operations and other policy precedents (like the Obama-era "ticket system") have to be factored into the prehistory of the remain-in-Mexico policy. Building on insights from chapter 5, I have also emphasized that the black/nonblack binary is not erased just because black rightlessness is mainstreamed to nonblack populations. Bodies and populations that are coded as "black" can still suffer from a kind of rightlessness that sets them apart from "nonblacks," even as the distance between these racial categories is narrowed by draconian policies.

For example, although the remain-in-Mexico policy was influenced, in part, by the legacy of the Haitian interdictions, Haitian refugees are largely absent from the refugee caseload that is being processed under this policy. Instead, they are overconcentrated in the refugee population that has been denied entry by the more draconian Title 42 policy. It also took well over two decades before Haitians were included in the TPS program, in significant numbers, and they were top of the list of groups to cut out of TPS when the Trump administration attempted to end the program. Antiblackness also figured into the policy history of the remain-in-Mexico policy in a different way than the attempted TPS cancellations.

The Central American refugees targeted by the remain-in-Mexico policy could be described as a "population problem" that had a family resemblance to the problem posed by the mass exodus of Haitian refugees and triggered a similar policy response. Even so, the remain-in-Mexico policy did not produce a condition of rightlessness that was as severe as the government's Haitian interdiction operations. Antiblackness was a feature of the policy history that abstractly defined the problem that the MPP was designed to control, but antiblack animus did not factor into this legal dispute in a palpable way, as it did in the challenge to the government's TPS policy—with Presidential remarks that expressed a clear distaste for black migrants and refugees simply because they were black.[207]

For a point of contrast, it is worth considering the legal dispute over the future of DACA which was occurring around the same time—in 2019 and 2020.[208] This program was similar to TPS in that it provided a temporary renewable status—to migrants who would otherwise be deportable—which did not provide a guaranteed pathway to permanent residence. Unlike TPS, however, the beneficiaries of this program were not people displaced by wars and natural disasters but unauthorized migrant youth who were deemed to be good candidates for integration. To qualify for DACA, migrant youth cannot have a criminal record and should have skill sets and history of achievements that would make them good candidates as military recruits or college students.[209]

One of the most significant things about the struggle over the future of DACA is that it ended with a Supreme Court decision in June 2020 (*Wolf v. Vidal*) that prevented the Trump administration from moving forward with its cancellation of the program.[210] In this case, the Supreme Court argued that the government's motives for cancellation were arbitrary and capricious, and in violation of the APA.[211] I am not going to enter into a detailed analysis of this decision. For the purpose of this discussion it is important, mainly, as a point of contrast for the remain-in-Mexico policy and the TPS cancellations.

DACA recipients fit the description of the "good" immigrant, which has been criticized by immigrant rights activists as an oppressive construct that justifies the mass removal of "bad" immigrants.[212] But it would probably be more accurate to say that DACA recipients are being treated as eligible candidates for the "good" immigrant category. They are beneficiaries of a precarious inclusion that is conditioned by the threat of deportation, but which also holds out the promise of receiving a permanent status and becoming an American success story. This situation is well described by the predicament of deportability. The remain-in-Mexico program and the cancellation of TPS, on the other hand, are better examples of radical exclusion—which is focused on deterring or removing migrants and refugees who are not viewed as suitable candidates for social membership, even under the most precarious conditions.

The unequal valuation of these migrants is reflected in the way the federal courts have ruled on all three programs—with DACA being protected by a bipartisan majority of the Supreme Court (which includes Clarence Thomas who usually opposes litigation that favors migrant rights[213]), the challenge to remain-in-Mexico being nullified by a bipartisan majority of Supreme Court justices (with Justice Sotomayor being the lone objector[214]), and the challenge to the TPS cancellations not even making it to the Supreme Court due to the opposition it faced at circuit court level.

Central American nationals are distributed across all three of these migrant groups, but this distribution is by no means even. The migrants targeted by the remain-in-Mexico policy are overwhelmingly Central American. The struggle over TPS policy, in contrast, involved a cluster of national origin groups that were evenly divided between Central American and black/African populations (though it bears noting that almost 80 percent of TPS holders are Central American[215]). The DACA population, on the other hand, is predominantly composed of Mexican nationals (approximately 80 percent), barely 10 percent of Central American nationals, barely 1 percent of black African or Caribbean nationals, and there is no Haitian presence in this population of any statistical merit.[216]

The treatment of these migrant groups by the government cannot be strictly explained at the level of the racial-ethnic population—with "brown"[217] people receiving an entirely different kind of treatment than black people. Instead there are inequalities that loosely correlate with population demographics but which are also guided by racialized constructs that are specific to each policy.

DACA recipients evoke the romance of the hardworking immigrant that has been historically defined by the European migrant experience and more recently, by other nonblack categories of upwardly mobile newcomers. The migrants targeted by the remain-in-Mexico program fit, more easily, into the "bad" immigrant/refugee category that is associated with criminality, sloth, and wasteful fiscal expenditures. The "bad" immigrant category also helps to explain why Haitian, Sudanese, Nicaraguan, and Salvadoran TPS holders were singled out for cancellation—or as forerunners for a wave of cancellations that would have been extended to other groups. But as I explained earlier in this chapter, there was an element to Trump's invectives against these TPS holders, and migrants in general, that required no pragmatic rationalization.

TPS holders did not have to be criminals or a burden to the economy (and on this latter point Judge Chen pointed out that the opposite is true[218]). They were undesirable simply because of what they were, not because of what they could or could not do, and the racist denigration of the very being of these people was most pronounced in Trump's statements about black migrants.

These differences cannot be explained by the workings of a single, uniform, black/nonblack binary. Instead, as I noted in the last chapter, these differences are products of differentialist and dichotomizing schemas that rely on superior/inferior (or good/bad) distinctions which can take on different configurations within different iterations of state policy. This is another way of saying that (anti)blackness is not the property of a body or a population, but of institutional circuitries of power that are used to code and control bodies and populations. As I have argued throughout the book, these circuitries of power flow through the law—as well as state policy—but they are not creatures of the law. There is also a social ontology that acts as the backdrop for the law, which determines which kinds of populations are more deserving of its protections than others. Although black populations compose a tiny minority of the migrants and refugees attempting to enter the United States on an annual basis, it is still important to consider how antiblack animus continues to anchor the ideas about deservingness of these populations and the potential threat that they pose to the wider/whiter society. If you take these issues seriously, it should be more apparent that questions of immigration reform and border control are intimately bound up with questions of social membership, political community, and the way power is put in the service of these ideas. In the next and final chapter, I am going to provide an exploratory discussion of these issues I have just raised, along with some concluding remarks, which are informed by the legal and policy history that I have examined throughout the book.

NOTES

1. Presidential Proclamation No. 9822, 83 Fed. Reg. 221 (November 9, 2018).

2. Nicole Phillips and Tom Ricker, *The Invisible Wall: Title 42 and its Impact on Haitian Migrants*, Haitian Bridge Alliance, Quixote Center and UndocuBlack Network, March 25, 2021, accessed September 19, 2021, file:///C:/Users/pkret/On eDrive/Documents/Writing%20&%20Research/Black%20Interdictions/Chapter%20Drafts/Completed%20Drafts/The-Invisible-Wall.pdf,164.

3. Jeffrey Passel and D'Vera Cohn, "U.S. Unauthorized Immigrant Total Dips to Lowest Level in a Decade," *Pew Research Center*, November 15, 2018, accessed January 8, 2021, https://www.pewresearch.org/hispanic/2018/11/27/u-s-unauthorized -immigrant-total-dips-to-lowest-level-in-a-decade/.

4. At the time of this writing there are no estimates available for the national size of the unauthorized migrant population past 2018. The Migration Policy Institute has estimated a population total of approximately 11 million for 2018, which amounts to an increase of approximately 300,000 over 2017 estimates of 10.7 million (which is equivalent to a 2 percent increase in size). Since these estimates are derived from different sources (MPI versus the Pew Research Center) it is also possible that the margin of difference between these years is indicative of how the population was measured and not due to a real increase in the size of the population (or that there was a marginally larger increase in its size). Migration Policy Institute, "Unauthorized Immigrant Population Profiles," accessed, January 8, 2021, https://www.migrationpolicy.org/ programs/us-immigration-policy-program-data-hub/unauthorized-immigrant-popula- tion-profiles?gclid=EAIaIQobChMI-_PowsiM7gIVYsyzCh1VdQvIEAAYASAAE gInLPD_BwE; Passel and Cohn, "U.S. Unauthorized Immigrant Total Dips to Lowest Level in a Decade."

5. John Agnew, "The Asymmetric Border: The United States' Place in the World and the Refugee Panic of 2018," *Geographical Review* 109, no. 4 (2019): 507–526.

6. Department of Justice (DoJ), "Attorney General Announces Zero-Tolerance Policy for Criminal Illegal Entry," *Office of Public Affairs*, April 6, 2018, accessed December 31, 2020, https://www.justice.gov/opa/pr/attorney-general-announces-zero -tolerance-policy-criminal-illegal-entry; Committee on the Judiciary U.S. House of Representatives, *The Trump Administration's Family Separations Policy: Trauma, Destruction and Chaos* (Washington, DC: Committee of the Judiciary U.S. House of Representatives, 2020), accessed December 31, 2020, https://judiciary.house.gov/ uploadedfiles/the_trump_administration_family_separation_policy_trauma_destruc- tion_and_chaos.pdf?utm_campaign=4526-519, 6.

7. Ibid. All of the legal precedents relevant to the Haitian interdictions are listed in the excerpt from the proclamation that was used to introduce this chapter.

8. In the latter part of the proclamation, President Trump cited several sections from the Immigration and Nationality Act that authorized the enforcement actions that he was calling for in the proclamation. For the purpose of this discussion, I distinguish the authorizing function of these sections of the INA (which are discussed

in more detail later in this chapter) from the government's Haitian refugee policies which were cited as precedents for the policies that the Trump White House was planning to create (which has to do with how the law is translated into strategies for deterring migrant flows). Ibid.

9. Department of Homeland Security, "Guidance for Implementing Section 235(b) (2)(C) of the Immigration and Nationality Act and the Migrant Protection Protocols," *Policy Memorandum, U.S. Citizenship and Immigration Services*, January 28, 2018, accessed January 1, 2020, https://www.uscis.gov/sites/default/files/document/memos /2019-01-28-Guidance-for-Implementing-Section-35-b-2-C-INA.pdf; "Policy Guidance for Implementation of the Migrant Protection Protocols," *Memorandum from Kristjen M. Nielsen*, January 25, 2019, accessed December 31, 2020, https://www.dhs.gov/sites/default /files/publications/19_0129_OPA_migrant-protection-protocols-policy-guidance.pdf.

10. Department of Homeland Security, "Policy Guidance for Implementation of the Migrant Protection Protocols," 3–4.

11. Ibid., 2; *Haitian Centers Council, Inc. v. Sale*, 823 F. Supp. 1028 (E.D.N.Y. 1993) at 1042, citing *Haitian Centers Council, Inc. v. McNary*, 969 F.2d 1350 (2d Cir. 1992) at 1343.

12. Department of Homeland Security, "Assessment of the Migrant Protection Protocols (MPP)," *Publications Library*, October 28, 2019, accessed January 1, 2021, https://www.dhs.gov/publication/assessment-migrant-protection-protocols-mpp, 4–6.

13. Naomi Paik, "Between Rights and Rightlessness: Haitian Migrants and the Elusive Promises of Humanitarianism," *E-misferica* 14, no. 1 (2019), accessed January 1, 2021, https://hemisphericinstitute.org/en/emisferica-14-1-expulsion/14-1 -essays/between-rights-and-rightlessness-haitian-migrants-and-the-elusive-promises -of-humanitarianism.html; Phillips and Ricker, *The Invisible Wall*, 18–20.

14. Phillips and Ricker, *The Invisible Wall*, 11. This order was devised by Trump administration officials and has been continued by the Biden administration. The order was originally issued for thirty days and then extended indefinitely on April 20, 2020. It was replaced by the Order Suspending the Right to Introduce Certain Persons from Countries where a Quarantinable Communicable Disease Exists that was issued on October 13, 2020.

15. Ibid.

16. See chapter 4 for a discussion of the HIV travel ban.

17. Phillips and Ricker, *The Invisible Wall*, 25.

18. Ibid., 21; Priscilla Alvarez, "Biden Administration Formally Ends 'Remain in Mexico' Policy after Suspending It Earlier This Year," *CNN.com*, June 1, 2021, accessed September 22, 2021. https://www.cnn.com/2021/06/01/politics/immigration -remain-in-mexico/index.html; Muzzafar Chishti and Jessica Bolter, "Court-Ordered Re-Launch of Remain-in-Mexico Policy Tweaks Predecessor Program, but Faces Similar Challenges," Migration Policy Institute, December 2, 2021, accessed January 2, 2022, www.migrationpolicy.org/article/court-order-relaunch-remain-in-mexico,

19. Phillips and Ricker, *The Invisible Wall*, 21.

20. Julian Borger, "Haiti Deportations Soar as Biden Administration Deploys Trump-Era Health Order," *The Guardian*, March 25, 2021, accessed September 22, 2021, https://www.theguardian.com/us-news/2021/mar/25/haiti-deportations-soar-as -biden-administration-deploys-trump-era-health-order.

21. Gustavo Solis, "Asylum Grant Rates under Remain in Mexico are Far Below Historic Average," *San Diego Union Tribune*, December 26, 2019, accessed September 22, 2021, https://www.sandiegouniontribune.com/news/immigration/story/2019-12-26/asylum-grant-rates-under-remain-in-mexico-are-far-below-historic-average.

22. Phillips and Ricker, *The Invisible Wall*, 12.

23. Ibid.

24. Ibid.

25. Ibid.

26. Discussed in more detail in chapter 2. See also *HRC v. Civiletti*, 503 F. Supp. 442 (S.D. Fla. 1980), 516.

27. Phillips and Ricker, *The Invisible Wall*, 12–13.

28. Suzanne Gamboa and Reuters, "Court Rules Trump can End Temporary Protected Status for Immigrant Families," *NBC News*, September 14, 2020, accessed September 22, 2021, https://www.nbcnews.com/news/latino/court-rules-trump-can-end-temporary-protected-status-immigrant-families-n1240072.

29. Ali Vitali, Kasie Hunt and Frank Thorp, "Trump Referred to Haiti and African Nations as 'Shithole' Countries," *NBC News*, January 11, 2018, accessed September 22, 2021, https://www.nbcnews.com/politics/white-house/trump-referred-haiti-african-countries-shithole-nations-n836946; Leighton Akio Woodhouse, "Trump's Shithole Countries Remark is at the Center of a Lawsuit to Reinstate Protections for Immigrants," *The Intercept*, June 28, 2018, accessed September 22, 2021, https://theintercept.com/2018/06/28/trump-tps-shithole-countries-lawsuit/.

30. Department of Homeland Security, "Assessment of the Migrant Protection Protocols (MPP)," *Publications Library*, October 28, 2019, accessed January 1, 2021, https://www.dhs.gov/publication/assessment-migrant-protection-protocols-mpp.

31. Department of Homeland Security, "Assessment of the Migrant Protection Protocols (MPP)," 4.

32. Department of Homeland Security, "Guidance for Implementing Section 235(b)(2)(C) of the Immigration and Nationality Act and the Migrant Protection Protocols," *Policy Memorandum, U.S. Citizenship and Immigration Services*, January 28, 2018, accessed January 1, 2020, https://www.uscis.gov/sites/default/files/document/memos/2019-01-28-Guidance-for-Implementing-Section-35-b-2-C-INA.pdf.

33. Department of Homeland Security, "Assessment of the Migrant Protection Protocols (MPP)," 6.

34. Department of Homeland Security, "Temporary Protected Status," *U.S. Citizenship and Immigration Services: Humanitarian Policies*, accessed January 1, 2021, https://www.uscis.gov/humanitarian/temporary-protected-status.

35. Philip Kretsedemas, *The Immigration Crucible: Transforming Race, Nation and the Limits of the Law* (New York: Columbia University Press, 2012), 13–46; Roberto Gonzales, Veronica Terriquez and Stephen Ruszczyk, "Becoming DACAmented," *The American Behavioral Scientist* 58, no. 14 (2014): 1852–1872 at 1852–1857.

36. *The Immigration Act of 1990*, Pub.L. 101–649, 104 Stat. 4978 (1990).

37. *American Baptist Churches (ABC) v. Thornburgh*, 760 F. Supp. 796 (N.D. Cal. 1991). For an account of the role that *ABC v. Thornburgh* played in the evolution of TPS, see Susan Bibler Coutin, "Falling Outside: Excavating the History of Central American Asylum Seekers," *Law & Social Inquiry* 36, no. 3 (2018): 569–596 at 578–579. Also see Paik, "Between Rights and Rightlessness."

38. Coutin, "Falling Outside," 574–576.

39. Jennifer Lundquist and Douglas Massey, "Politics or Economics? International Migration during the Nicaraguan Contra War," *Journal of Latin American Studies* 37, no. 1 (2005): 29–53 at 30–31.

40. *Nicaraguan Adjustment and Central American Relief Act*, Pub.L. 105–100, 111 Stat. 2160 (1997).

41. 2016 is the last year in which NACARA adjustments are recorded by DHS statistics. See Department of Homeland Security, "Table 6. Persons Obtaining Lawful Permanent Resident Status by Type and Major Class of Admission: Fiscal Years 2015 to 2017," *2017 Immigration Yearbook* (Washington, DC: DHS, 2018).

42. "Table 13: Refugee Arrivals: Fiscal Years 1980 to 2017" and "Table 16. Individuals Granted Asylum Affirmatively or Defensively: Fiscal Years 1990 to 2017," *2017 Immigration Yearbook* (Washington, DC: DHS, 2018).

43. Robert Warren and Darren Kerwin, "A Statistical and Demographic Profile of the US Temporary Protected Status Populations from El Salvador, Honduras, and Haiti," *Journal on Migration and Human Security* 3, no. 3 (2017): 577–592 at 577–578 and 582.

44. In 1997, the Clinton administration created a special program designed for Haitians which granted relief comparable to TPS but weaker, via the Haitians Deferred Enforced Departure policy, which offered relief for one year only. Barring this exception, Haitians were excluded from TPS until the time of the 2010 earthquake. Stephen Lendman, "US Discriminatory Immigration Policies Toward Haitians," *StephenLendman.org*, February 27, 2009, accessed January 1, 2021, https://stephenlendman.org/2009/02/us-discriminatory-immigration-policy/.

45. Muzaffar Chishti and Claire Bergeron, "Haiti Tragedy Raises Important Immigration Issues for the United States," *Migration Policy Institute: Policy Beat*, February 16, 2010, accessed January 1, 2021, https://www.migrationpolicy.org/article/haiti-tragedy-raises-important-immigration-issues-united-states; Lendman, "US Discriminatory Immigration Policies Toward Haitians."

46. Paik, "Between Rights and Rightlessness."

47. Disasters Emergency Committee, "Haiti Earthquake: Facts and Figures," June 2, 2015, accessed January 1, 2021, https://www.dec.org.uk/articles/haiti-earthquake-facts-and-figures.

48. Patricia Weiss Fagen, *Receiving Haitians in the Context of the 2010 Earthquake* (Geneva: The Nansen Initiative, 2013) accessed, January 8, 2021, http://www.nanseninitiative.org/wp-content/uploads/2015/03/DP_Receiving_Haitian_Migrants_in_the_Context_of_the_2010_earthquake.pdf, 6–9 and 14–21.

49. The US Haitian population increased by approximately100,000 people between 2010 and 2018, with much of this increase being attributed to displacement due to the 2010 earthquake. The current population of Haitian TPS holders—most

of whom are earthquake victims—has been estimated at approximately 55,000. Kira Olsen-Medina and Jeanne Batalova, "Haitian Immigrants in the United States," *Migration Policy Institute: Spotlight,* August 12, 2020, accessed January 1, 2021, https://www.migrationpolicy.org/article/haitian-immigrants-united-states-2018?gclid =CjwKCAiArbv_BRA8EiwAYGs23L9yM0xKj3EIxOvGTDjgFdVYb0qsdJ7hjFI k80LKJLsHmgxnqNNaOBoCLB4QAvD_BwE.

50. Paik, "Between Rights and Rightlessness."

51. Lendman, "US Discriminatory Immigration Policies Toward Haitians."

52. Ibid.

53. Ibid; Joann van Selm and Betsy Cooper, *The New "Boatpeople": Ensuring Safety and Determining Status* (Washington, DC: Migration Policy Institute, 2005), 76.

54. van Selm and Cooper, *The New "Boatpeople,"* 77.

55. Ibid.

56. Paik, "Between Rights and Rightlessness."

57. Lendman, "US Discriminatory Immigration Policies Toward Haitians."

58. Paik, "Between Rights and Rightlessness."

59. Ibid.

60. Paik, "Between Rights and Rightlessness."

61. Jonathan Blitzer, "The Battle Inside the Trump Administration Over TPS," *The New Yorker,* May 12, 2018, https://www.newyorker.com/news/daily-comment/ the-battle-inside-the-trump-administration-over-tps.

62. *Ramos,* No. 18-16981 (9th Cir. 2020) at 3.

63. *Ramos,* No. 18-16981 at 15.

64. *Ramos,* No. 18-16981 at 25–27.

65. *Ramos v. Nielsen,* 18-cv-01554-EMC (N.D. Cal, October 2018) at 30–31.

66. Ibid.

67. Ibid.

68. Ibid.

69. Ibid.

70. Monica Anderson and Gustavo Lopez, "Key Facts About Black Immigrants in the U.S." *Pew Research Center,* last modified, January 24, 2018, https://www .pewresearch.org/fact-tank/2018/01/24/key-facts-about-black-immigrants-in-the-u-s/.

71. Two of the five incidents of racist statements by President Trump about migrants and refugees included references to black populations, with Haitians and Africans being specifically referenced in each of these examples. *Ramos,* 18-cv-01554-EMC (Oct 18) at 30–31.

72. Kitty Calavita, "The New Politics of Immigration: 'Balanced-Budget Conservatism' and the Symbolism of Proposition 187," *Social Problems* 43, no. 3 (1996): 284–305.

73. As evidenced by racialized discourses on crime, welfare dependency, urban culture, and so on. For a concise review of this history of (barely) coded anti-black discourse in the late twentieth century, see Robin D. G. Kelley, *Yo' Mama's Disfunktional!: Fighting the Culture Wars in Urban America* (Boston: Beacon Press, 1998).

74. In chapter 3, I used De Genova's scholarship as the focal point for my critique of deportability theory, building an argument first developed by Saucier and Woods. Nicholas De Genova, "Migrant 'Illegality' and Deportability in Everyday Life," *Annual Review of Anthropology* 31, no. 1 (2002): 419–447; Khalil Saucier and Tryon Woods, "Ex Aqua The Mediterranean Basin, Africans on the Move and the Politics of Policing," *Theoria* 141, no. 61 (2014): 55–75.

75. ACLU Washington, "Timeline of the Muslim Ban," accessed January 4, 2021, https://www.aclu-wa.org/pages/timeline-muslim-ban; BBC News, "Coronavirus: Trump Signs Order on Immigration Green Card Suspension," April 23, 2020, accessed January 4, 2021, https://www.bbc.com/news/world-us-canada-52391678; Adam Liptak and Michael Shear, "Trump Can't Immediately End DACA, Supreme Court Rules," *New York Times*, June 18, 2020, accessed January 4, 2021, https://www.nytimes.com/2020/06/18/us/trump-daca-supreme-court.html; Michael Shear and Miriam Jordan, "Trump Suspends Visas Allowing Hundreds of Thousands of Foreigners to Work in the US," *New York Times*, June 22, 2020, accessed January 4, 2021, https://www.nytimes.com/2020/06/22/us/politics/trump-h1b-work-visas.html ?auth=login-google.

76. Leo Chavez, *The Latino Threat: Constructing Immigrants, Citizens, and the Nation* (Stanford, CA: Stanford University Press, 2013); De Genova, "Migrant 'Illegality' and Deportability in Everyday Life."

77. Both theories, for example, can be used to explain enforcement actions that are consistent with Gammeltoft-Hansen and Tan's theory of the deterrence paradigm (Gammeltoft-Hansen and Tan, "The End of the Deterrence Paradigm"). In this case, the threat of deportation does not only facilitate the exploitation of migrants who are "already here." It also sends signals that encourage these migrants to "self-deport" and deter Latin American emigration—consistent with the "attrition enforcement" strategies advanced by immigration control advocates. See Luis Plascencia, "Attrition Through Enforcement and the Elimination of a 'Dangerous Class,'" in *Latino Politics and Arizona's Immigration Law SB 1070*, eds. Lisa Magaña and Erik Lee (New York: Springer, 2013), 93–127. But once the threat of deportation is viewed in this light, it is no longer a theory of deportability as explained by De Genova. Instead it ends up becoming a theory of deportation as viewed through the lens of radical exclusion.

78. Muzaffar Chishti and Jessica Bolter, "Remain in Mexico Plan Echoes Earlier U.S. Policy to Deter Haitian Migration," *Migration Policy Institute: Policy Beat*, March 28, 2019, accessed January 1, 2020, https://www.migrationpolicy.org/article/ remain-mexico-plan-echoes-earlier-us-policy-deter-haitian-migration.

79. Chishti and Bolter, "Remain in Mexico Plan Echoes Earlier U.S. Policy."

80. This being Section 235(b)(2)(C). Department of Homeland Security, "Guidance for Implementing Section 235(b)(2)(C) of the Immigration and Nationality Act and the Migrant Protection Protocols."

81. Ibid.

82. American Immigration Council, "A Primer on Expedited Removal," July 22, 2019, accessed January 1, 2021, https://www.americanimmigrationcouncil.org/ research/primer-expedited-removal.

83. Ibid.

84. *Innovation Law Lab v. Nielsen*, 366 F.Supp.3d 1110 (2019) at 1115–1117.

85. Claire Felter and Amelia Cheatham, "Can 'Safe Third Country' Agreements Resolve the Asylum Crisis?" *Council on Foreign Relations*, August 29, 2019, accessed January 4, 2021, https://www.cfr.org/in-brief/can-safe-third-country-agreements-resolve-asylum-crisis#:~:text=Asylum%20seekers%20are%20required%20to,them%20back%20to%20that%20country.

86. Ibid.

87. Joseph Nevins, *Operation Gatekeeper and Beyond: The War on Illegals and the Remaking of the US - Mexico Boundary* (New York: Taylor & Francis Group, 2010), 3.

88. Nevins, *Operation Gatekeeper and Beyond*, 17–46.

89. Nevins, *Operation Gatekeeper and Beyond*, 12.

90. Calavita, *Inside the State*; De Genova, "Migrant 'Illegality' and Deportability in Everyday Life," 160–160; Mae Ngai, "The Strange Career of the Illegal Alien: Immigration Restriction and Deportation Policy in the United States, 1921–1965," *Law and History Review* 21, no. 1 (2003): 69–108. I have made a comparable argument in Philip Kretsedemas, "Immigration Enforcement and the Complication of National Sovereignty: Understanding Local Enforcement as an Exercise in Neoliberal Governance," *American Quarterly* 60, no. 3 (2008): 553–573.

91. Nevins, *Operation Gatekeeper and Beyond*, 153.

92. Samuel Huntington, *Who Are We?: The Challenges to America's National Identity* (New York: Simon & Schuster, 2004). For a critical introduction to the concept of ontological security, see Catarina Kinnvall, Ian Manners and Jennifer Mitzen, "Introduction to 2018 Special Issue of European Security: 'Ontological (In)Security in the European Union,'" *European Security* 27, no. 3 (2018): 249–265.

93. Nevins, *Operation Gatekeeper and Beyond*, 205.

94. Nevins, *Operation Gatekeeper and Beyond*, 207.

95. Nevins, *Operation Gatekeeper and Beyond*, 207–208, citing the work of Tim Creswell, *On the Move: Mobility in the Modern Western World* (New York: Routledge, 2006), 1, 2, and 6.

96. Nevins, *Operation Gatekeeper and Beyond*, 208–210.

97. Calvin Warren, *Ontological Terror: Blackness, Nihilism and Emancipation* (Durham, NC: Duke University Press, 2018), 76–87.

98. Michael Corradini et al., "Operation Streamline: No Evidence that Criminal Prosecution Deters Migration," *Vera Institute of Justice*, June 2018, accessed January 4, 2021, https://www.immigrationresearch.org/report/other/operation-streamline-no-evidence-criminal-prosecution-deters-migration.

99. Durand and Massey, "Evolution of the Mexico-US Migration System"; Julie Phillips and Douglas Massey, "The New Labor Market: Immigrants and Wages after IRCA," *Demography* 36, no. 2 (1999): 233–46. Also see n80.

100. Durand and Massey, "Evolution of the Mexico-US Migration System," 38.

101. Philip Kretsedemas, "The Limits of Control: Neo-Liberal Policy Priorities and The US Non-Immigrant Flow," *International Migration* 50, no. s1 (2011): e1–18 at e10. The high point of approximately 1.6 million border enforcement actions

documented by the chart in this article for 2000 has not been exceeded to this day (as of year-end of 2020), although the chart only presents data up to 2009.

102. Ibid.

103. Manuel Garcia y Griego, "The Bracero Program," *Rural Migration News* 9, no. 2 (2003), accessed January 4, 2021, https://migration.ucdavis.edu/rmn/more.php?id=10. The economic pragmatism of the Texas Proviso is also summed up by Senator McCarran's approving comments about "illegal" Mexican migrant labor in the Senate hearings over the framing of what would become the 1952 Immigration and Nationality Act. Mae Ngai, *Impossible Subjects: Illegal Aliens and the Making of Modern America* (Princeton: Princeton University Press, 2014), 273–274.

104. David Leal, "Stalemate: United States Immigration Reform Efforts 2005 to 2007," *People and Place* 17, no. 3 (2009): 1–17.

105. Kretsedemas, *Immigration Crucible*, 137–143.

106. Philip Kretsedemas and David Brotherton, "Introduction: Immigration Policy in an Age of Punishment," in *Immigration Policy in the Age of Punishment*, eds. David Brotherton and Philip Kretsedemas (New York: Columbia University Press, 2018), 1–34.

107. Corradini et al., "Operation Streamline: No Evidence that Criminal Prosecution Deters Migration."

108. Kretsedemas, *Immigration Crucible*, 79–83.

109. Corradini et al., "Operation Streamline: No Evidence that Criminal Prosecution Deters Migration."

110. Mark Motivans, "Federal Justice Statistics 2009," *Bureau of Justice Statistics*, December 2011, accessed January 4, 2021, https://www.bjs.gov/content/pub/pdf/fjs09.pdf/.

111. Philip Kretsedemas, *Migrants and Race in the US* (New York: Routledge, 2013), 17.

112. Tanya Golash-Boza, "President Obama's Legacy as 'Deporter in Chief,'" in *Immigration Policy in the Age of Punishment*, eds. David Brotherton and Philip Kretsedemas (New York: Columbia University Press, 2018), 37–56 at 41–45.

113. Corradini et al., "Operation Streamline: No Evidence that Criminal Prosecution Deters Migration."

114. Paik, "Between Rights and Rightlessness"; Philips and Ricker, *The Invisible Wall*, 21.

115. Paik, "Between Rights and Rightlessness."

116. Ibid.

117. Philips and Ricker, *The Invisible Wall*.

118. Ibid., 20–22.

119. Ibid., 21. *Al Otro Lado v. Wolf*, No. 3:17-cv-02366-BAS-KSC (S.D. Cal. February 18, 2021).

120. *Innovation Law Lab*, 366 F.Supp.3d 1110, 1114; *Innovation Law Lab v. Wolf*, 951 F.3d 1073 (9th Cir., 2020); *Innovation Law Lab v. Wolf*, 951 F.3d 986 (9th Cir., 2020); *Wolf v. Innovation Law Lab*, 589 U.S. (2020).

121. *Louis v. Nelson*, 544 F. Supp. 973 (S.D. Fla., 1982).

122. *Louis*, 544 F. Supp. 1004 at 998–999 and 1003–1004.

123. *Innovation Law Lab*, 366 F. Supp. 3d 1110, 1114 at 1115–1117 and 1126–1128.

124. *Innovation Law Lab*, 366 F. Supp. 3d 1110, 1114 at 1128.

125. Department of Homeland Security, "Guidance for Implementing Section 235(b)(2)(C) of the Immigration and Nationality Act and the Migrant Protection Protocols."

126. Customs and Border Protection, "MPP Guiding Principles," January 28, 2019, accessed January 5, 2021, https://www.cbp.gov/sites/default/files/assets/documents/2019-Jan/MPP%20Guiding%20Principles%201-28-19.pdf.

127. *Innovation Law Lab*, 366 F. Supp. 3d 1110, 1114 at 1115–1116.

128. *Innovation Law Lab*, 366 F. Supp. 3d 1110, 1114 at 1122.

129. *Innovation Law Lab*, 366 F. Supp. 3d 1110, 1114 at 1122–1123.

130. *Innovation Law Lab*, 366 F. Supp. 3d 1110, 1114 at 1123–1124.

131. *Innovation Law Lab*, 366 F. Supp. 3d 1110, 1114 at 1115–1116.

132. Department of Homeland Security, "Guidance for Implementing Section 235(b)(2)(C) of the Immigration and Nationality Act and the Migrant Protection Protocols."

133. Department of Homeland Security, "Assessment of the Migrant Protection Protocols," 3; Human Rights Watch, "US: Investigate 'Remain in Mexico' Program."

134. *Innovation Law Lab*, 366 F. Supp. 3d 1110, 1114 at 1122–1124.

135. *Innovation Law Lab*, 366 F. Supp. 3d 1110, 1114 at 1124–1125.

136. *Innovation Law Lab*, 951 F.3d 1073 at 1088–1089.

137. *Innovation Law Lab*, 951 F.3d 1073 at 1094.

138. *Innovation Law Lab*, 951 F.3d 1073 at 1095.

139. *Innovation Law Lab*, 951 F.3d 986 at 989.

140. *Wolf*, 589 U.S.

141. Nick Miroff and Maria Sacchetti, "Biden Says He'll Reverse Trump Immigration Policies But Wants 'Guardrails' First," *Washington Post*, December 22, 2020, accessed January 5, 2021, https://www.washingtonpost.com/national/biden-immigration-policy-changes/2020/12/22/2eb9ef92-4400-11eb-8deb-b948d0931c16_story.html.

142. Olafimihan Oshin and Rafael Bernal, "Biden Formally Ends Trump-era 'Remain in Mexico' Immigration Program," *The Hill*, June 1, 2021, accessed September 22, 2021, https://thehill.com/latino/556371-biden-formally-ends-trump-era-remain-in-mexico-immigration-program.

143. Ibid.

144. *Innovation Law Lab*, 951 F.3d 1073 at 1125–1126.

145. Ibid.

146. *Innovation Law Lab*, 951 F.3d 1073 at 1125.

147. Paik, "Between Rights and Rightlessness."

148. *Ramos*, 18-cv-01554-EMC (Aug. 2018); *Ramos*, 18-cv-01554-EMC (October 2018); *Ramos*, No. 18-16981.

149. Nicole Narea, "A Federal Court Ruling Could Allow Trump to Deport 400,000 Immigrants Next Year," *Vox*, September 14, 2020, accessed January 5, 2021, https://www.vox.com/policy-and-politics/2020/9/14/21436633/ninth-circuit

-tps-trump-temporary-protected-status; Marcia Brown, "TPS For All," *American Prospect*, December 9, 2020, accessed January 5, 2021, https://prospect.org/day-one -agenda/temporary-protected-status-for-all-immigration/; Ted Hesson and Laura Gottesdiener, "Exclusive: Biden Team Weighs Deportation Relief For More Than 1 Million Hondurans, Guatemalans," *Reuters*, December 21, 2020, accessed January 5, 2021, https://www.reuters.com/article/us-usa-immigration-biden/exclusive-biden -team-weighs-deportation-relief-for-more-than-1-million-hondurans-guatemalans -idUSKBN28V2IN.

150. John Fritze, "Supreme Court to Debate Immigration Case as Biden Wrestles with Crisis at Southern Border," *USA Today*, April 16, 2021, accessed September 22, 2021, https://www.usatoday.com/story/news/politics/2021/04/16/supreme-court -debate-tps-immigration-case-biden-confronts-border/7110295002/.

151. Harold Koh, "The 'Haiti Paradigm' in United States," *Yale Law Review* 103 (1993): 2391–2455 at 2400–2401.

152. Koh, "The Haiti Paradigm," 2397.

153. *Ramos*, 18-cv-01554-EMC (August 2018).

154. *Ramos*, 18-cv-01554-EMC (October 2018).

155. *Ramos*, 18-cv-01554-EMC (August 2018) at 2.

156. I am placing this claim second because it follows, logically, after the first claim though it actually appears fourth in Chen's summary. Ibid.

157. *Ramos*, 18-cv-01554-EMC (August 2018) at 49–53.

158. *Ramos*, 18-cv-01554-EMC (August 2018) at 42–43.

159. *Ramos*, 18-cv-01554-EMC (August 2018) at 24–32.

160. *Haitian Refugee Center v. Civiletti*, 503 F. Supp. 442 (S.D. Fla. 1980).

161. *Vigile*, 535 F. Supp. 1020.

162. *Ramos*, 18-cv-01554-EMC (August 2018) at 43–45.

163. *Vigile*, 535 F. Supp. 1020 at 1007.

164. *Ramos*, 18-cv-01554-EMC (August 2018) at 44-47; *Arlington Heights v. Metropolitan Housing Corps* 429 U.S. 252 (1977).

165. *Graham v. Richardson*, 403 U.S. 365 (1971).

166. *Yick Wo v. Hopkins*, 118 U.S. 356 (1886).

167. *Ramos*, 18-cv-01554-EMC (October 2018) at 53.

168. *Ramos*, 18-cv-01554-EMC (August 2018) at 49–53.

169. Ibid; *Trump v. Hawaii*, 585 U.S. ___, 138 S.Ct. 2392 (2018);

170. *Trump*, 585 U.S. ___ at 27–29.

171. *Trump*, 585 U.S. ___ at 1 and 5.

172. *Trump*, 585 U.S. ___ at 26–28.

173. *Ramos*, 18-cv-01554-EMC (August 2018) at 51.

174. *Ramos*, 18-cv-01554-EMC (August 2018) at 51–52.

175. *Ramos*, 18-cv-01554-EMC (August 2018) at 51.

176. *Louis*, 544 F. Supp. 973.

177. *Yick Wo v. Hopkins*, 118 U.S. 356 (1886), cited by *Johnson v. Eisentrager*, 339 U.S. 763 (1950) at 771; *United States v. Verdugo-Urquidez*, 494 U.S. 259 (1990) at 271.

178. *CABA v. Christopher*, 43 F.3d 1412, 1419.

179. *Boumediene v. Bush*, 553 U.S. 723 (2008); *Hamdan v. Rumsfeld*, 548 U.S. 557, 576–577 (2006); *Rasul v. Bush*, 542 U.S. 466 (2004).

180. *Fong Yue Ting v. US*, 149 U.S. 698 (1893).

181. As discussed by Gammeltoft-Hansen and Tan, "The End of the Deterrence Paradigm."

182. Gary Palmer, "Guarding the Coast: Alien Migrant Interdiction Operations at Sea," *International Law Studies* 72, no. 1 (1998):157–179 at 173.

183. Epitomized by the use of the "aggravated felony" as a trigger for deportation proceedings, within immigration law. See Sarah Tosh, "Defending the 'Bad Immigrant:' Aggravated Felonies, Deportation, and Legal Resistance at the Crimmigration Nexus" (PhD Diss., CUNY, John Jay College of Criminal Justice, 2019), 62–70.

184. *Ramos*, 18-cv-01554-EMC (October 2018) at 39–41, citing *Trump*, 585 U.S. ___ at 30–31, citing *Fiallo v. Bell*, 430 U.S. 787 (1977).

185. *Ramos*, 18-cv-01554-EMC (October 2018) at 40.

186. Ibid, citing *Zadvydas v. Davis*, 533 U.S. 678 (2001) at 693.

187. The general tendency is to equate sovereign authority with the Plenary Power doctrine, without acknowledging that Plenary Power is just one iteration of the sovereign authority that the US government has exerted over immigration law. This tendency is not specific to the scholarship on racism and the law, but it is very concentrated in this aspect of legal studies, and especially in critical research on the law, racism, and Asian American populations. Robert Chang, *Disoriented: Asian Americans, Law and the Nation-State* (New York: NYU Press, 1999), 37–38; Jamel Thamkul, "The Plenary Power-Shaped Hole in the Core Constitutional Law Curriculum: Exclusion, Unequal Protection, and American National Identity," *California Law Review* 96, no. 2 (2008): 553–593. Motomura's analysis of the Plenary Power doctrine and the US government's Haitian refugee policies which I discussed in chapter 2 is another good example, though it does not fit squarely in the subfield of racism and legal studies. I also want to emphasize that this feature of Motomura's analysis does not take away from its strengths. Motomura's theory of phantom norms provides an important scaffolding of my argument about the antiblack undercurrents of the law, though my reading of this argument takes it in a different direction than the one intended by Motomura. Hiroshi Motomura, "Immigration Law after a Century of Plenary Power: Phantom Constitutional Norms and Statutory Interpretation," *Yale Law Journal* 100, no. 3 (1990): 546–613.

188. See chapter 2 for a recounting of this argument and also Philip Kretsedemas, "The Controlled Expansion of Local Immigration Laws," in *Immigration Policy in the Age of Punishment*, eds. David Brotherton and Philip Kretsedemas (New York: Columbia University Press, 2018), 140–164.

189. *Jean*, 472 U.S. 846 at 855–857.

190. *Jean*, 472 U.S. 846 at 855–857.

191. *CABA*, 43 F.3d 1412, 1419 at 1427. Also see Oliver, *Carceral Humanitarianism*; Paik, "Between Rights and Rightlessness."

192. *Ramos*, No. 18-16981.

193. *Ramos*, No. 18-16981 at 35–39.

194. *Ramos*, No. 18-16981 at 45–47. But the court also went to onto argue that even using the Arlington Heights standard, deployed by Judge Chen, the plaintiffs had not been victims of racial discrimination. *Ramos*, No. 18-16981 at 47–53.

195. In CABA, the Eleventh Circuit, citing from *Jean v. Nelson*, observed that, "there is little question that the Executive has the power to draw distinctions among aliens based on nationality." *CABA*, 43 F.3d 1412, 1419 at 1427. This excerpt is taken from a portion of the Jean decision in which the court cites the overtly racist rationale from the *Chinese Exclusion Case* to support its argument, though this case is not cited in the CABA decision itself. *Jean*, 727 F.2d 957 at 960–965. The connecting threads between the Plenary Power doctrine and the Ninth Circuit's decision for *Ramos v. Wolf* are more abstruse. The Ninth Circuit cited *Trump v. Hawaii* to support its argument about the sovereign right to exclude, which cited *Knauff v. Shaughnessy*, which cites *Fong Yue Ting v. US*, which cited the *Chinese Exclusion Case*. *Ramos*, No. 18-16981 at 45–47, citing *Trump v. Hawaii*, 585 U.S. ___ (2018) at 8, citing *Knauff v. Shaughnessy*, 338 U.S. 537, 542–543 (1950) at 542–543, citing *Fong Yue Ting*, 149 U.S. 698 at , citing *Chinese Exclusion Case*, 130 U.S. 581 (1889) at 734, 738, 745 and 756.

196. *Ramos*, No. 18-16981 at 50–51.

197. *Ramos*, No. 18-16981 at 49.

198. The three judges on the panel included Consuelo M. Callahan (who issued the decision, and was appointed by George W. Bush), Ryan D. Nelson (who issued a concurring opinion, and was appointed by Donald Trump), and Morgan Christen (who issued the dissent, and was appointed by Barack Obama). *Ramos*, No. 18-16981 at 2. The composition of the panel may explain the different positions that the Ninth Circuit took on the remain-in-Mexico policy versus the TPS cancellations. The panel for *Innovation Law Lab v. Wolf* was "stacked" in the opposite way, with two Democrat appointees (Judge's Fletcher and Paez, appointed by Bill Clinton) and one Republican appointee (Judge Fernandez, appointed by George W. Bush, who issued the dissent in that case). *Innovation Law Lab*, 951 F.3d 1073 at 1077. This correlation between partisan affiliation and case outcomes has been observed by research on asylum grants in the immigration courts and at the appellate level. See Jaya Ramji-Nogales, Andrew Schoenholtz, and Philip Schrag, "Refugee Roulette: Disparities in Asylum Adjudication," *Stanford Law Review* 60 (2007): 295. These disparate outcomes also suggest that there is a political process that determines how judicial panels are assembled and which cases appellate courts are willing to hear. There may be greater pressure to ensure that some cases, like the TPS cancellations, are heard by a panel of judges that are friendly to the position of the Executive Office—consistent with Mark Dow's observations about the informal pressures that the Executive Office has exerted on immigration judges. See Mark Dow, "Unchecked Power Against Undesirables," in *Keeping Out the Other*, eds. David Brotherton and Philip Kretsedemas (Columbia University Press: NY, 2008), 29–43. These pressures may also explain why the Eleventh Circuit was allowed to have the final word on *CABA v. Christopher*, despite its history of disagreement with the Supreme Court over the interpretation of the Plenary Power doctrine, the result being that Cuban and Haitian Guantanamo detainees were alienated from the rule

of law. But several years later, the Supreme Court decided several cases—lead by a liberal-leaning majority—which insisted that Guantanamo detainees, held as "enemy combatants" under the post 9/11 "War on Terror," were protected by constitutional law (see discussion in chapter 5 and also, Frohock, "'Brisas del Mar,'" 63–72). The reason why Supreme Court opinion had the final say on these cases, but not on *CABA v. Christopher*, may have been influenced by signals from the Executive Office, that the CABA case was a pressing matter of national security that should not be disturbed by Supreme Court opinion. This is, admittedly, speculation, but it is consistent with Harold Koh's observations about the deferential posture that the federal courts, and especially the Supreme Court, have taken toward the Executive Office on cases that touch on issues of national security and the government's authority over immigration law, which is exemplified by the litigation of the Haitian interdictions. Koh, "The Haiti Paradigm," 2413–2415.

199. *Ramos*, No. 18-16981 at 67–107.

200. *Ramos*, No. 18-16981 at 104–107.

201. *Ramos*, No. 18-16981 at 97–100; *Ramos*, 18-cv-01554-EMC (October 2018) at 30–37.

202. *Ramos*, No. 18-16981 at 100–101.

203. *Ramos*, No. 18-16981 at 91–95 and 103–104.

204. *Ramos*, No. 18-16981 at 106–107.

205. *Ramos*, 18-cv-01554-EMC (August 2018) at 12–13; *Ramos*, 18-cv-01554-EMC (October 2018) at 30–31.

206. American Immigration Council, "A Guide to Title 42 Expulsions at the Border," March 29, 2021, accessed September 22, 2021, https://www.americanimmigrationcouncil.org/research/guide-title-42-expulsions-border.

207. *Ramos*, 18-cv-01554-EMC (August 2018) at 12–13; *Ramos*, 18-cv-01554-EMC (October 2018) at 30–31.

208. Adam Liptak and Michael Shear, "Trump Can't Immediately End DACA, Supreme Court Rules," *New York Times*, June 18, 2020, accessed January 4, 2021. https://www.nytimes.com/2020/06/18/us/trump-daca-supreme-court.html.

209. US Citizenship and Immigration Services, "Consideration of Deferred Action for Childhood Arrivals (DACA)," accessed January 5, 2021, https://www.uscis.gov/humanitarian/humanitarian-parole/consideration-of-deferred-action-for-childhood-arrivals-daca.

210. *Wolf v. Vidal*, 591 U.S. ___ (2020).

211. Ibid.

212. For an introduction to the immigrant rights critique of the good/bad immigrant dichotomy, see Subhash Kateel and Aarti Shahani, "Families for Freedom: Against Deportation and Delegalization," in *Keeping Out the Other: A Critical Introduction to Immigration Enforcement Today*, eds., David Brotherton and Philip Kretsedemas (New York: Columbia University Press, 2008), 258–290.

213. Thomas was among the group of dissenters who opposed the Supreme Court majority opinions in *Zadvydas*, 533 U.S. 678 that limited the detention powers of the US government. Thomas was also among the dissenters for decisions that affirmed due process rights for Guantanamo detainees in *Boumediene*, 553 U.S. 723 and *Rasul*,

542 U.S. 466 (also see Frohock, "Brisas del Mar," 61n201) and he also sided with the majority opinions that upheld the government's Haitian interdiction operations. See Harold Koh and Michael Wishnie, "The Story of *Sale v. Haitian Centers Council*: Guantanamo and Refoulement," in *Human Rights Advocacy Stories*, eds. Margaret Satterthwaite and Deena Hurwitz (Eagan, MN: Westlaw and Foundations Press, 2008), 385–432 at 395–396.

214. *Wolf*, 589 U.S.

215. Hondurans and Salvadorans compose over 326,000 of the approximately 411,000 TPS holders that compose the TPS population according to 2020 statistics. Jill Wilson, "Temporary Protected Status: Overview and Current Issues," *Congressional Research Service*, Updated October 6, 2020, accessed January 10, 2021, https://fas.org/sgp/crs/homesec/RS20844.pdf, 6.

216. Gustavo Lopez and Jens Manuel Krogstad, "Key Facts About Unauthorized Immigrants Enrolled in DACA," *Pew Research Center*, September 25, 2017, accessed January 6, 2021, https://www.pewresearch.org/fact-tank/2017/09/25/key-facts-about-unauthorized-immigrants-enrolled-in-daca/.

217. I have put "brown" in scare quotes because the academic scholarship on brownness has been used to advance a different explanation of race than that of the black/nonblack binary. In news journalism, the "brown" category is used as a matter-of-fact description of Latinx (and sometimes South Asian) populations. For Latinx populations in particular, it is used to describe a history of inequality of racialization that is different than but also analogous to the black population (in which brown-ness and blackness are treated as different instances of the same basic kind of racial marginality). This is also the approach taken by many of the studies that I critically discussed at the beginning of this book (see the introduction and chapters 1 and 2), which posit an equivalence between the alienation of the racialized migrant and the native black person, which is never explicitly theorized. There are also South Asian discourses on brownness that are used to affirm racist hierarchies (in which brownness is tacitly positioned "above" black). See Vijay Prashad, *The Karma of Brown Folk* (Minneapolis, MN: University of Minnesota Press, 2000). There are other discourses on brownness as a kind of hybridity that complicates and undermines the kinds of hierarchical distinctions that are described by the black/nonblack binary. In the context of these discourses, brownness is on the side of a cultural agency which inveighs "against race," rather than being in the service of an analysis that is being used to explain racism and racial inequality. It also bears noting that some of these discourses on brown hybridity tend in a neoconservative direction. See Michael Garcia, "The Inauthentic Ethnic: Richard Rodriguez's Brown and Resisting Essentialist Narratives of Ethnic Identity," *Prose Studies* 34, no. 2 (2012): 129–150.

218. Chen observed, drawing for support from several amicus briefs, that mass deportations resulting from the cancellation of TPS would create economic hardship for many US communities. *Ramos*, 18-cv-01554-EMC (October 2018) at 10.

Chapter 7

A Legal Strategy for the End
of the World and Beyond

The picture is that in Haiti the same people who organized the invasion in 2004 . . . they are still there. Eighty nine hundred soldiers or so plus forty four hundred police officers more or less, spending fifty one million US dollars a month in a country where seventy percent of the population have less than a dollar a day to live. It's a paradise for them. Once we had the colonization of Haiti and now we have a neocolonial occupation. They don't want me back in Haiti in my point of view because they still want to occupy Haiti Before the coup I was calling for dialogue so we could have inclusion not exclusion, so we could have cohesion not explosion of the social structures. They decided to go for a coup and the result is for bad to worse. [My] return is part of the solution not part of the problem.—Jean-Bertrand Aristide, Interview: November 2010[1]

ARISTIDE'S ANALYSIS, MOISE'S ASSASSINATION AND THE JANUARY INSURRECTION

Throughout this book I have directed the readers' attention to durable inequalities and exclusionary policies that have been suffered by Haitian refugees. The interview excerpt cited above provides another perspective on these problems. Former president Aristide describes a neocolonial structure of economic power that survived the Duvalier regime and which, in his view, had something to do with both of the coups that ousted him from office in 1991 and 2004. Recent events in Haiti suggest that little has changed since the time of this interview.

On July 7, 2021, Haitian president Jovenel Moise was assassinated by a group of armed men who may have been hired by some of Moise's political rivals.[2] Moise did not enjoy the same broad support from the Haitian

population as did Aristide, and his Presidency became controversial when he
decided to forestall the holding of new elections for a period of months and
rule by executive decree in the interim.³ All of these questions about Moise's
leadership style were eclipsed by the controversy that was stirred up by his
assassination.

Shortly after the assassination, a Haitian gang leader took to the streets
to protest, claiming that the assassination was carried by the "stinking bour-
geoise" of Haiti who had decided to sacrifice Moise to serve their own inter-
ests.⁴ One of the men accused of masterminding the coup d'etat claimed that
the mission "was supposed . . . to save Haiti from hell, with the support of the
U.S. government."⁵ Although this man—who is a South Florida-based pastor
and doctor—was featured prominently in world news reports as one of the
main conspirators, subsequent reports have suggested that he probably would
not have approved of murdering the president.⁶ Meanwhile, the investigation
into the assassination identified several prominent Haitian government officials, including a Supreme Court justice, the head of the president's security
service, and even the current prime minister, who had been appointed by
Moise, as other possible conspirators.⁷

Although Moise's Presidency had been criticized in the months prior to his
assassination, it is not clear what the political motives of the assassins were
or why Moise was viewed as a liability by some Haitian elites. One thing that
is clear, however, is that the assassination intensified the anxieties that many
Haitians already had about their personal safety and the political stability of
Haiti—and that this all contributed to the new flows of Haitian refugees that
were being interdicted by the Biden administration.

Shortly after these events unfolded, the Biden administrative resumed the
US government's longstanding policy of interdicting Haitian refugees at sea.
The rationale given by DHS secretary Alejandro Mayorkas was very similar
to the one used by Clinton-era immigration officials.⁸ The interdictions were
justified as a humanitarian effort that was in the best interest of the refugees
themselves. But as I have explained in the prior chapters, these humanitarian
overtures also underscore the rightlessness of the refugees and they can be
situated within a history of controlled mobility that targets black populations.
Throughout the book, I have connected the dots between these present-day
policies and antiblack sentiments, enabled by the workings of sovereign
power, that can be traced to the inception of the US republic. I have also
emphasized that antiblack desire is not just another kind of interest-seeking
behavior.

As I explained in the introduction and in chapter 1, antiblackness describes
the constitutive exterior of the modern: the demi-human substrata that have
to be controlled as a precondition for order, reason, and the pursuit of private
happiness. This way of understanding blackness—not just as the attribute of

a population or a morphological attribute of the body, but as an imaginary through which the ontological foundations of the modern order are rendered immanent and mapped on to populations, places, and bodies—helps to explain the excessive and seemingly irrational tendencies of antiblackness.

In this closing chapter, I am going to sum up the composite features of the analysis that I used to advance this argument, paying special attention to what this all means for a theory of the law and for antiracist legal strategy. This discussion also confronts a number of questions that I have raised throughout the book: Who is the law intended for? How does one extend the rule of law to people for whom it was not intended? And how does one surface this problem in a public sphere that lapses into awkward silences and evasive rationalizations whenever it is forced to confront it?

The insurrection at the US White House that occurred on January 6, 2021, provides another perspective on these questions. It could be described as the distorted mirror image of the situation in Haiti. The Moise assassination shines a light on a necropolitics that has been fostered by centuries of colonization. The January insurrection, on the other hand, shines a light on the sovereign desires that animated this history of colonization.

President Trump's electoral defeat triggered a legitimacy crisis for the US government. In the eyes of the insurrectionists, the government had fallen into the hands of people who would extend the protections of the law to people for whom it was never intended—the illegalized, the criminalized, and other "problem populations." So you end up with rioters brandishing Blue Lives Matters placards storming the Capitol and vacillating between harassing the police who are trying to protect the building, fraternizing with many of these same police officers, complaining bitterly when they are arrested by the police for breaking the law, and insisting all the while that they are on the side of the police.[9]

This bizarre scenario can be explained by Calvin Warren's distinction between the Law of Being and the being of the law that I have referenced throughout this book.[10] The storming of the Capitol may have violated the being of the law, but it also was also carried out in fealty to the Law of Being—the sovereign accord—that authorizes the law. This is also why the January insurrection can be regarded as Justice Taney's revenge on a political system that had betrayed the racist commonsense he articulated in *Dred Scott v. Sandford* over 150 years ago.[11]

According to Justice Taney, black people were innately unfit for citizenship and this understanding was so deeply entrenched in the opinions of the white citizenry that it did not have to be written into law. Throughout his Presidency, Trump appealed to similar sentiments, with Tweets and other public statements that depicted a traditional American social order that was under a state of siege by a host of racialized folk devils.[12] As I explained in chapter 6, the specter of the black immigrant figured prominently in this racist rhetoric, in gross disproportion to the presence of blacks in the US immigrant and refugee population. As many pundits and journalists have observed, this racist imaginary helped to set the stage for the panicked arguments about electoral fraud that set the stage for the insurrection.[13]

Although the public condemnation of the insurrection could be a sign that this vision of American society is in crisis, the fact that the insurrection occurred at all is a testament to the continuing salience of Justice Taney's views on race, nation, and citizenship. Meanwhile, we still have to contend with a public culture that lapses into silences and confused evasions when it is forced to confront its racist history and, especially, its emotional investments in antiblack sentiment. So how do you convert (anti)blackness from a repressed subtext into a means of explaining the fields of law, politics, and policy from which it is routinely excluded? I have been answering this question throughout the book, in the way I have gone about my analysis. In the next section I discuss its defining features in a little more detail.

THE EXPLANATORY VALUE OF BLACKNESS: EPISTEMOLOGICAL MEDITATIONS ON ANTIBLACK ANIMUS AND CONTROLLED MOBILITY

If the goals of my analysis could be fit into a single sentence it would be that (anti)blackness has much greater explanatory value than it is usually given credit for by the scholarly community. Legal storytelling is the epistemological perspective that I have used to advance this argument. I have aimed to provide an intensive explanation of the relationship between several different histories of law and policy—by tracing patterns of argumentation across federal court decisions on Haitian refugee policy, situating them in light of other decisions pertaining to race and sovereign power that predate these policies, and also in light of other policies, practices, and bodies of opinion that have not been subjected to the law. I have also tried to show that the connecting threads between these layers of legal opinion and extra-level discretionary authority are easier to see when antiblackness is brought into view.

Intensity and Chronology

My explanation of the relationship between blackness and the law can be boiled down to four components. The first component has to do with the intensity of oppression. Deprivations that are associated with blackness are more extreme and absolute than those experienced by racial categories that are constructed at a distance from blackness. So the excessive nature of antiblack sentiment and black oppression helps to explain the relative privilege of nonblackness. Throughout the book, I have called attention to this relationship, by showing how policies applied to Haitian refugees have been more punitive and "unprecedented" than policies applied to nonblack refugee populations.

For example, INS director Charles Sava used his discretionary authority to keep the vast majority of Haitian asylum seekers under his charge locked up in detention centers, but allowed nonblack asylum seekers, who fit the same profile as many of the Haitians he had locked up, to be paroled into the United States as their cases went through the immigration courts.[14] The detention policy that Sava devised for the New York District INS mirrored the policies used by Florida INS officials that were challenged by the *Louis v. Nelson* cases that were heard by Judge Spellman.[15] These policies were unprecedented, not only because they singled out Haitians, but because they mark the first time in the history of US refugee law in which the US government began a practice of systematically denying parole to asylum seekers.

The second component of my analytic approach has to do with the chronological sequencing of black and nonblack exclusions. Although I am not advancing a positivist argument, this chronological feature maps, easily enough, onto a conventional understanding of causality, in which a change in factor Y is preceded, and explained by, a change in factor X.[16] I have provided many examples of how the draconian policies that were first imposed on Haitians were gradually expanded to a larger, mostly nonblack, population of migrants and refugees. The US government's maritime interdiction operations, which began in 1981 with an exclusive focus on Haitians, were expanded to over twenty national origin groups, and eventually became standard practice for how the US government dealt with all refugees trying to access the United States by sea.[17] The mandatory detention policies that were exclusively imposed on Haitian refugees—under the auspices of the Haitian program—also, eventually, became standard practice for the entire immigration system.[18]

The open arms policy that the US government had originally devised to welcome and resettle Cuban refugees was eventually dismantled and replaced by an interdiction and detention policy that was directly informed by the US government's Haitian refugee policy.[19] The Executive Orders and Supreme Court decisions that inaugurated and defended the Haitian interdictions also set legal precedents that were used by the Trump administration to justify the remain-in-Mexico policy, which became a centerpiece of its strategy for deterring Central American migrant and refugee flows.[20]

In all of these instances, policies first used to control the mobility of Haitians were precursors for policies that were applied to a larger group of mostly nonblack migrants and refugees. These policies can also be situated within a chronology of controls on black mobility that is traceable to the early postbellum and antebellum era. I drew attention to these connections in chapters 2–4, by explaining how the arguments that were used to justify black immobility in *Dred Scott v. Sandford* and *Plessy v. Ferguson* echo through the Circuit and Supreme Court decisions that were used to defend the government's Haitian refugee policies.[21]

I have also shown that even when oppressive practices migrate from black to nonblack populations, black bodies and populations are still treated more harshly than nonblacks. The Trump administration's remain-in-Mexico policy, for example, was patterned after the Haitian interdictions, but the Central American migrants who were detained under the remain-in-Mexico policy still had a greater claim on the law than Haitian interdictees.[22] This unequal treatment of Haitian refugees is underscored by the Title 42 policy that was created under the Trump administration and continued by the Biden administration.[23] Like the HIV travel ban of the 1980s, Title 42 uses COVID-19-related public health concerns to grant the government broad discretionary authority to any migrant or refugee of its choosing—and Haitians were the main population targeted by both policies.[24]

In a similar vein, the interdiction and detention of Cuban and Haitian refugees in the mid-1990s (under Operation Sea Signal) was a turning point moment, in which the US government's policy for Cuban refugees began to look more like its policy for Haitians.[25] But the legal challenge to Operation Sea Signal also ended with the US government's roll out of its "wet foot dry foot" policy, which perpetuated the unequal treatment of Cuban and Haitian asylum seekers.[26]

The examples I have just described help to clarify the difference between the two explanatory features I have just discussed: the intensity of antiblack oppression, on one hand, and chronological sequencing on the other. Oppressive practices can proliferate, chronologically, from black to nonblack populations, but black populations still suffer from these practices in a more intense way than nonblack populations. The relationally defined nature of nonblack privilege persists through all of these transformations. Even though things may be getting worse for most migrants and refugees, these worsening conditions can still be organized in a way that preserves nonblackness as a category that is defined by its distance, no matter how precarious, from the misery of black populations.

Circuitries of Power

A third component of my analysis has to do with the locus of antiblack sentiment. I have argued that blackness is not really a property of bodies and populations; it is a stigma produced by antiblack sentiments that emanates from institutional circuitries of power. For the purposes of this book, these circuitries of power are tied up with the policies and enforcement practices of the executive office, federal jurisprudence and, to a lesser extent, laws enacted by the Congress. I must qualify this statement by emphasizing a point made by many Afropessimist scholars that antiblackness emanates from the organization of the social rather than being a unique product of the state.[27] So, it is important to be mindful of the mutually constituting nature of state and society when it comes to antiblack sentiment.

My empirical focus has been on the legal and policy discourse of the state, but I want to emphasize that I am not making a theoretical argument about the primacy of this official discourse for my explanation of antiblack sentiment. For my purposes, this official discourse just served as a convenient way of illustrating the strange, disjunctive relationship between antiblackness and the law—keeping in mind all the while that antiblackness is not a sui generis creation of the law.

It is also important to note that, while government policies can be held accountable to the law, they are not, strictly speaking, products of the law. This observation is especially pertinent for the refugee policy-making powers of the Executive branch which are protected by a well-established body of legal opinion about the government's sovereign powers over immigrant admissions. As I have shown throughout this book, the Supreme Court and many Circuit Courts have been very consistent about defending the government's discretionary authority to craft and implement its Haitian refugee policies.

Hence, government policy can be understood as a medium that grants immigration officials the ability to craft new regulatory strategies with a degree of freedom from the strictures of the law. This is one reason why the study of policy is important for research on antiblackness and other exclusionary sentiments that are normally excised from public speech. Furthermore, if we understand antiblackness as a prism of intelligibility for conceptualizing and ordering the social world, it becomes possible to see how antiblack sentiment can take on different meanings and be put to different ends from one policy to the next. This is why I have repeatedly insisted that blackness is a field of visibility, generated by the workings of institutions, that informs policy and practice.

There is a history of antiblack sentiment, for example, that is specific to the US government's Haitian refugee policies. The INS did not deny parole to all black asylum seekers during the era of the Haitian program,[28] and this is because antiblack sentiment is not a legal edict that is transparently applied to all black bodies because they are black. Antiblackness is not the law itself, but a subtext and sentiment that ripples through the law, which is another reason why it has to be decoded in light of a history and a context that is specific to a given policy, law, or court decision.

Silences and Radical Exclusion

A fourth component of my explanation is the work of silences. The intensity, chronology, and locus of antiblack sentiment mainly has to do with powers, concentrated in the executive branch of government, that create policy. Silences, on the other hand, have more to do with the distortions that are produced by the law when it has to confront the sovereign authority of the state and the stubborn reality of antiblack racism. Unlike the government's Haitian refugee policies, these silences do not always work to exclude black people; they also crop up in legal arguments that are used to strengthen their rights. But an important caveat is in order. These rights arguments abstract black refugees from the fact of the blackness—converting the Haitian into a refugee or displaced person who happens to be black rather than the reverse. Judge Christen's dissent in the Ninth Circuit decision for *Ramos v. Wolf*, which I discussed in chapter 6, is a good example.

In her dissent, Christen argued that there was no merit to the Trump administration's effort to cancel TPS for Haitian, African, and Central Americans. But she also insisted that the charge of racism added nothing of consequence to the legal arguments of the plaintiffs.[29] Christen's dissent was in agreement with the District Court decisions issued by Judge Chen—with the notable exception of Chen's position on race and racism which reached the same constitutional question on the matter of unlawful discrimination and the equal protection clause that Christen wanted to avoid.[30] Her argument begs some important questions about the core issue at stake in the case.

Judge Christen did not share the majority opinion's position that Judge Chen's argument about institutional racism—his "cat's paw" theory[31]—was baseless. Her argument against the cat's paw theory was balanced on a finer point: that it may be valid but that it was unnecessary and, perhaps, a liability. According to Christen, the TPS cancellations could be refuted, more efficiently and with fewer consequences for established precedent, by limiting the complaint to the APA: mirroring an argument used by Judge Spellman several decades earlier in *Louis v. Nelson*.[32] As a result, arguments about racism had to be excised from the complaints of the plaintiffs as a precondition for taking their legal challenge seriously.

Others judges, like Judge Chen and Carter, brought the problem of racism before the law, but without specifically naming antiblack sentiment or confronting the problem of black rightlessness. I have tried to show that these aphasiac moments end up being complicit in enabling the exclusionary forces they refuse to acknowledge. It is these progressive arguments more so than the overtly exclusionary policies of the state which underscore how thoroughly alienated blackness is from the law. They mark the difference between the legible and the illegible, by refusing to acknowledge, or by only half acknowledging, exclusions and exclusionary sentiments that have been relegated to the nether regions of the law.

There is a relationship between these silences and the workings of radical exclusion, which I introduced in chapter 3. The silences of the law foster a misdiagnosis of this problem. The effects that radical exclusion produces within the law are treated as if they are wholly internal to the law. They are challenged and corrected with arguments that rely on established legal precedent and federal jurisprudence. But radical exclusion operates in excess of established precedent. One example is the residency-check requirements for Chinese immigrants that were defended by the Supreme Court decision in *Fong Yue Ting v. US*, which made it possible for deportable migrants to be treated no differently than "excludables" who had never been granted entry to the United States.[33] Another example is the Haitian program of the late 1970s, which introduced a practice of mandatory detention which was unprecedented for its time and created a new kind of extreme rightlessness within the "excludable alien" population.[34] The Haitian interdiction operations of the 1980s and 1990s took the guiding imperatives of the Haitian program one step further—creating enforcement operations that relied on the existence of a new kind of exterritorial space that lay outside of the protections of US and international law.[35]

All of these policies and practices were defended by arguments that appealed to established legal precedent. But they were also used to maneuver racialized migrants and refugees into a space of abject rightlessness, and they relied on legal precedents that deferred to a sovereign authority that was not subject to the law. These latter arguments provide an insight into the motivating impulse of radical exclusion, which acts on a desire to exclude that hales from outside the law. This is also why radical exclusion and controlled mobility can be regarded as different iterations of the same phenomenon.

Radical Exclusion and Controlled Mobility

Radical exclusion hollows out the law. It is the eruption of a supra-legal paradigm of power within the law. Controlled mobility, on the other hand, can operate perfectly well outside of the law. Laws like the *Fugitive Slave Acts*[36] may reinforce and legitimize the paradigm of power on which controlled mobility relies. Even so, controlled mobility does not originate within the law; it emanates from a private sphere of power that is usually left unregulated by the law.[37] This private sphere of power is also the space in which commodified black bodies have been subjected to the discretionary authority of white, male property holders.

I have spent most of the book discussing radical exclusion, because it is more relevant to the way that the sovereign desire to exclude manifests within the law. Controlled mobility is still important, however, because it highlights the genealogy of power that makes it possible to trace connections between the rightlessness of racialized migrants in the present day and the techniques of control that constituted the black slave as an object of power.

Even the most progressive of legal arguments have had a hard time grappling with these genealogies of power. As I have emphasized this throughout the book, this shortcoming cannot be blamed on a failure of nerve among the judges and attorneys who challenged the government's Haitian refugee policies. This pattern of silences—the stuttering of the law in the face of the sovereign decision—is symptomatic of a problem that is coextensive with the law itself. To challenge antiblack desire is to call into question the social order over which the law presides—or at least this is how it appears when antiblack desire is allowed to persist as an unquestioned commonsense.

What antiblackness signals, better than any other kind of racial otherness, is the distinction between the rights-bearing subject and the radically depersonalized ground on which this subject stands.[38] The analysis of antiblackness is useless if it cannot lift back the curtain on these relations of domination and critique them. Ultimately, this is a distinction between people who have been turned into commodities, or even worse, into a detritus that is not even useful as a commodity—and a discourse on rights and freedoms that addresses itself to a universal subject, but which turns its head away from its reliance on these commodified, depersonalized others whose lives have been excluded from the official transcript. This problem may not be unique to (anti)blackness, but blackness is one of the most salient points of entry into it.

In the end, blackness explains everything and nothing. Because of its deontological status, blackness is denied the capacity to make any meaning of its own. But for this same reason, it becomes the site of invention, a fungible instrument that prepares the way for new techniques of control and orderings of social space. So, to insist on the explanatory value of blackness, as I have done throughout this book, is to insist on a paradox. It means that the very stuff that has been denied the capacity for self-definition can explain the identity and evolution of all the things from which it has been excluded. If you take this message to heart, you also have to understand that I am not just using the explanatory value of blackness to advance a conventional social science methodology, though I am not opposed to such a project. I am using the explanatory value of blackness to inveigh against a social ontology which points to a future that is necessarily white, and which associates death and nonbeing with blackness. In order to counter this social ontology, it will be necessary to craft meta-narratives that exceed even the ambitions of legal storytelling. There is a need for new stories that can reach beyond the confines of the law and rethink the "master" narratives about progress, democratic governance, and republican society that have served as the conscience of the law for the past several centuries.

A LEGAL STRATEGY FOR THE END
OF THE WORLD AND BEYOND

The task of creating a new meta-narrative about blackness, modernity, and the law lies beyond the ambitions of this book. What I will try to do, instead, is offer some insights into a legal strategy that could prepare the way for these kinds of narratives. My starting point is Derrick Bell's critical race theory and, especially, his paradoxical pessimism, which I introduced in the introduction. As I explained in that discussion, Bell's writing and his politics provides a great illustration of how a pessimistic race analysis can avoid the dead ends of fatalism. Bell uses the premise that "racism is permanent" as the foundation for a legal strategy and a radical democratic politics.[39]

These features of Bell's race analysis can be clarified further through a comparison with the legal strategy proposed by Harold Koh. As I explained in chapter 4, Koh argued several of the landmark cases that challenged the US government's Haitian interdiction policies. At the end of that chapter I critiqued the limitations of Koh's race analysis, but there are also some noteworthy continuities between Koh's and Bell's approach to the law.

The reader may recall that Koh did not expect that the federal courts would be sympathetic to the legal challenges he was leading. In other words, Koh was pessimistic about his chances of getting a "winning decision" from the higher courts. According to Koh, the goal of the legal challenge was to set the stage for a political victory that could be implemented by the executive office rather than the courts. He used the legal challenge for *Sale v. HCC* to keep the cause of the Haitian refugees alive in the public sphere, in the hopes that Bill Clinton would terminate the Bush-era Kennebunkport interdiction policy if he was elected president.[40] Although President Clinton did not change course on interdiction policy, Koh claimed Clinton's decision to allow the parole over 300 HIV-positive Haitian Guantanamo detainees into the United States as a political win.[41] Clinton's decision to return Aristide to power in 1993 with the backing of US troops could be counted as another political win that had been influenced, in part, by the attention that had been drawn to the plight of Haitian refugees by high profile legal challenges.[42] Koh, along with attorneys for the Cuban American Bar Association, adopted a similar strategy when they argued *CABA v. Christopher*. They did not expect that the appeals process would result in a favorable decision. Instead, they planned to use the sympathetic arguments of lower courts as framing strategies for a campaign that would be waged in the media and meetings with elected officials that were intended to get President Clinton to use his executive authority on behalf of the Guantanamo detainees.[43] At least as it concerns the Cuban Guantanamo detainees, this strategy seemed to have worked.

As I have already noted, this legal strategy was pragmatically pessimistic about the federal court system. Derrick Bell shares Koh's pessimism about the US legal system. But whereas Koh's pessimism was counter-balanced by his reliance on political pressure and moral suasion, Bell did not think the US political system would be any more receptive to a counter-racist legal strategy than the legal system. You could say that Bell's pessimism was more pervasive than Koh's. Bell also produced a legal analysis that, at times, seemed to operate in the opposite direction of Koh.

According to Bell's interest convergence theory, it is possible for the law to produce beneficial outcomes for blacks and other racialized populations, but the political motives for these beneficent laws are not what they seem.[44] Whereas Koh counted on the political process to achieve goals that would never pass muster with the courts, Bell argued that the courts could be counted on to make brave decisions, but that the progressive impact of these decisions is usually curtailed by a self-interested politics. The dismantling of Jim Crow segregation, for example, could be explained in light of an interest that US elites had in countering anti-US Soviet propaganda on the global stage, and also pacifying a large population of white, middle class, liberal-minded American citizens who had been disillusioned by the public spectacle of racist violence against black civil rights protestors.[45] In these moments, blacks end up being the third party beneficiaries of negotiations overpower that are being driven by contending factions of whites. This argument helps to explain why de facto patterns of racial segregation in many parts of the United States were just as severe after the dismantling of Jim Crow than before, and why black unemployment and mass incarceration escalated.[46]

According to Bell, the optics of desegregation were intended, mainly, for a nonblack audience. Because black interests were not factored into these desegregation practices in any meaningful way, it is not surprising that they were unable to counter the social forces that ended up undermining them and introducing new forms of de facto segregation. According to Bell, we seem to be faced with a politics that is hopelessly racist. But this does not mean that change is impossible. It underscores the need for a more thorough analysis.

Afropessimist scholarship explains state racism as an outgrowth of the organization of the social sphere.[47] There are precursors for this analysis in the work of Hannah Arendt, whose writing on republican democracy revolves around the antagonistic relationship between the despotic necessities of social organization (and societal reproduction) and the relatively "freer" relations of the political sphere.[48] Although Arendt is much more optimistic, than Afropessimist scholars, about the egalitarian possibilities of political life, they share a basic agreement on the existence of an oppressive sphere of social relations that tends to stifle and overdetermine the political sphere. Both analyses point in the same direction.

If there is any hope for a better politics, the social foundations of the political order have to be problematized and reconfigured. No counter-racist politics worth its salt can hope to make a lasting impact if it does not have a sober analysis of these social foundations. Koh's optimistic attitude toward the political sphere is hampered by this problem. Because Koh does not interrogate the racist organization of the social sphere (at least not in the same thoroughgoing way as Bell), he ends up with a politics that is capable of delivering narrowly circumscribed wins, but is unable to challenge the racist commonsense that gives rise to the Haitian interdictions.

Bell approaches this problem in the opposite way, by producing a legal strategy that is directed at the racist, social foundations of the political sphere. It is also important to note that Bell's analysis of these social foundations is informed by an analysis of economic relations. But the "economic," as Bell understands it, is not just a quantifiable material resource that can be abstracted from social relations. Economic justice is not just a matter of resource redistribution. It is about black communities[49] recovering the collective capacity to generate value and meet their material needs, which is a process that requires a transformation of social relations within these communities and the relationship between these communities and the wider society.

Bell's socioeconomic analysis is well illustrated by his proposal for a hypothetical piece of legislation that he calls the Racial Preferences Licensing Act (RPLA).[50] The goal of the RPLA is to generate public funds from the acts of racial discrimination that Bell thought were an inevitable feature of US society. Under the RPLA, employers and other private citizens could obtain a license that allows them to legally discriminate against blacks and other racialized populations for any reason they chose, so long as they paid their licensing fees.[51] The aim of this legislation is obviously not to win the hearts and minds of the white racist or of a larger, politically ambiguous nonblack population. It also does not rely on the idea that the law can be counted on to advance an egalitarian, antiracist set of principles. Instead, the RPLA advances a legal strategy which accounts for the durability of the racist interests that, according to Bell, are enabled by the law even when it appears to championing racial justice.

Bell's discussion of the RPLA can be read as a work of social satire more so than a serious legislative agenda. It also bears noting that Bell uses the

RPLA to enter into a devil's advocate discussion with one of his favorite alter egos, Geneva Crenshaw, about the goals of legal activism in the post-civil rights era.[52] All of this goes to underscore that the RPLA is useful, primarily as an exercise in legal storytelling that Bell is using to offer a new paradigm of legal strategy.

By channeling RPLA funds into black communities, Bell signals his concern for changing the unequal socioeconomic relations that the racist politics of the public sphere is committed to perpetuating. Although it may appear otherwise, Bell's strategy does not hinge on a politics of redistribution. It is always possible for resources to be redistributed in a way that does nothing to change the political marginality of black populations. Being mindful of this possibility, Bell advances a tactics of redistribution that is geared toward enhancing black, collective agency.

If you read the RPLA proposal in light of Bell's other writings it will be readily apparent that his interest in improving the socioeconomic standing of black communities is not informed by an integrationist ideology.[53] He is more concerned with creating opportunities for black communities to collaborate and share resources that is not overdetermined by the existing organization of power. In other words, Bell advances a redistributive agenda with an eye for its political implications.

The legal strategy I am going to propose is not as focused on resource redistribution as Bell's, and this is mainly because challenges to US refugee policy usually turn on questions of rights and access to the law. By keeping the focus on these questions of rights and access to law, it is also possible to show how Bell's critical sensibility can be used to expand on Koh's legal strategy. Koh has explained how his team expected to get sympathetic decisions from the lower courts, even if they were not expecting a win at the level of the Circuit or Supreme Courts. Koh and his allies used the language from these sympathetic decisions to establish a normative framework for the issues at stake in these legal challenges and mobilize support in the public sphere and in the political establishment.[54] Bell's analysis of racism and the law points to the need for a more far-reaching strategy, but which can proceed in a similar way.

The first and most important condition is that litigators have to be prepared to make arguments that focus on the problem of antiblack racism. It is quite likely that these arguments will receive no sympathetic decisions even at the District Court level. Similar to Koh's strategy, however, the aim would not be to secure a win but to use these court battles to generate a language that can be taken outside of the theater of the law, to raise awareness about a problem. In this case, it is likely that the language of most use to legal and social activists will not be the decision of the court itself, but the arguments raised by plaintiffs, accompanied by a critical analysis of the court's rejections of these arguments. And whereas Koh used this legal language to mobilize political support for his cause, the interventions that I am describing would have to raise questions about the social foundations of the contemporary political sphere. This language would be intended for networks and constituencies that are searching for a new paradigm of the political.

The quest for a new and better politics has always been a pressing concern for black intellectuals and movements in the United States, which have not simply advanced a politics, but raised questions about the limits of the political and about whether something like a black politics is even viable. The competing visions of Marcus Garvey, W. E. B. Dubois, and Booker T. Washington in the early twentieth century; the black power critique of the mainstream civil rights movement in the 1960s; the black feminist critique of white feminist politics (which has been extended by black queer and postcolonial feminist scholars); and the more recent debates over political strategy between the black civil rights establishment and the activism of the post-Ferguson era are just a few examples.[55] This is the point at which Julius Scott's *Common Wind* and Paul Gilroy's *Black Atlantic* become relevant, as a counter-history of black agencies that are constantly resisting the dictates of antiblack racism.[56] Within the networks of refugee, migrant, and human rights activists, similar kinds of transgressive discussions are occurring.[57]

These discussion spaces, fragile as they may be, are framing the problems of the day in new ways. There are advocacy agendas, for example, that are organized around a very understandable question: Why isn't the US government helping more displaced people? As well-intended as it may be, this question takes the fact of displacement for granted and fails to probe another equally important question: Why is there so much displacement to begin with? David Bacon has reframed this dilemma with his restatement of an injustice frame that has welled up from the political consciousness of Latin American labor rights activists: All people may have a right to migrate, but what about the right to stay home?[58] Wouldn't these two rights have to be coequally protected in order for them to have any meaning at all? The right *not* to migrate is really about the right to be protected from displacement. It is the right to earn a fair wage where you are living right now, in a way that is safe and healthy for yourself, and the right to participate in the social and political life of your local community without fear of persecution. It is only when this right is respected, to be able to make a life for yourself where you were born or raised, in a safe and sustainable, that migration can be genuinely framed as a choice. If these conditions are absent, then much of what is described as migration can be recategorized as a variety of displacement: population movements that are forced more than free and conditioned by the panic of necessity rather than reasoned choice.

There is a relationship between the pessimistic scenario I have just described and histories of controlled mobility. The fundamental problem of the enslaved African is not that their right to migrate had been violated, but that they were subjected to an extremely cruel system of forced migration. Even though migrants should not be analogized to enslaved Africans, it is important to be mindful of the coercions that are masked by volitional discourses on migration. The connection between the dehumanizing treatment of the contemporary migrant and the excessive violence that produces the black slave is genealogical not analogical. These two predicaments are not equivalent; the latter precedes, and helps to explain, the former. This is just another way of saying that the cruelties of antiblack racism are always spilling over the threshold of the black/nonblack binary.

The worsening climate of policy and public opinion that has gathered around the figure of the contemporary migrant offers a tragically apt example of this expanding circle of cruelties. One way of describing this climate— as translated through an analysis of antiblack racism—is that the distance between blackness and nonblackness, that used to work to the benefit of the migrant and the refugee, has narrowed. One consequence of this narrowing is an increasingly coercive experience of mobility.

It has become more difficult to tell migrants from refugees. Government policy makers often prefer to describe asylum seekers as "unauthorized migrants" or even as "illegal aliens," because the problem of displacement has become a more pervasive feature of the migrant experience, and on a scale that overflows the remedies and resources that had been established to help the refugee, as this subject has been defined by international law. So the pincers of coercion operate on mobility from all angles: through the forces that lead people to flee to the United States, in the arsenal of deterrence strategies that are used to deny them entry, in the interior enforcement practices that track their movements once they are "inside" the nation, and in the way they are removed.

There are no easy solutions to these problems that can be worked out in advance of the conversations and mobilizations that will be needed to bring about change. This same understanding is reflected in my proposed legal strategy, which is more concerned with generating arguments that push at the boundaries of the possible, rather than seeking wins that operate within the confines of established possibilities. I have interrogated the silences, evasions, and contorted rationalizations of the law in order to raise questions about the racist commonsense and techniques of control that it refuses to acknowledge even as they are being enabled and replicated by its pronouncements. I have tried to interrupt this flow of meaning with an analysis that questions the inevitability and necessity of it all. But I want to emphasize that the goal of my analysis is just to create the critical distance that is needed to engage these issues and conditions in a new way. The question of how to act and what kinds of narratives are needed to guide these actions is another matter which exceeds the goals of this book and, in some ways, exceeds the possibilities of the written text. These are matters that, for the time being, I leave the reader to decide.

NOTES

1. Nicolas Rossier, "Conversation Part 2: Jean-Bertrand Aristide on Haiti in the Earthquake's Aftermath," *The Nation/Grit TV*, November 22, 2010, accessed September 19, 2021, https://www.youtube.com/watch?v=1EP_hrhRgg0.

2. At the time of this writing, the men directly involved in the assassination have been identified but the people who hired them and planned the assassination have yet to be formally charged. *BBC News*, "Haiti President's Assassination: What We Know So Far," September 15, 2021, accessed September 19, 2021, https://www.bbc.com/news/world-latin-america-57762246.

3. Peter Beaumont and Julian Borger, "Haiti in Fresh Crisis Amid Coup Claims and Dispute Over President's Term," *The Guardian*, February 10, 2021, accessed March 11, 2021, https://www.theguardian.com/world/2021/feb/10/haiti-coup-attempt -allegations-jovenel-moise-president-term.

4. Andre Paultre and Sarah Marsh, "Americas Gang Boss Wades into Haiti tur-moil, Sees Conspiracy behind President's Killing," *Reuters*, July 11, 2021, accessed September 19, 2021, https://www.reuters.com/world/americas/rival-haitian-leaders -battle-power-after-presidents-assassination-2021-07-10/.

5. Juliana Bedoya, "Emmanuel Sanon, the Pastor Doctor Accused of Masterminding Jovenel Moïse's Assassination in Haiti," *Al Dia*, July 14, 2021, accessed September 19, 2021, https://aldianews.com/articles/politics/emmanuel -sanon-pastor-doctor-accused-masterminding-jovenel-moises-assassination.

6. Ibid.

7. Reuters, "Haiti Police Say Former Supreme Court Judge Suspect in President's Killing," July 31, 2021, accessed September 19, 2021, https://www.reuters.com/world/americas/haiti-police-say-former-supreme-court-judge-suspect-presidents-kill-ing-2021-07-31/. Sarah Marsh, "Haiti PM, a Suspect in Murder of President Moise, Replaces Justice Minister," *Reuters*, September 15, 2021, accessed September 19, 2021, https://www.reuters.com/world/americas/haiti-official-resigns-over-pms-links -suspect-presidents-slaying-2021-09-15/.

8. Department of Homeland Security, "Secretary Mayorkas Overviews U.S. Maritime Migrant Interdiction Operations," July 13, 2021, accessed September 19, 2021, https://www.dhs.gov/news/2021/07/13/secretary-mayorkas-overviews-us -maritime-migrant-interdiction-operations.

9. Justin Boggs, "Capitol Officer: They Beat Law Enforcement with 'Blue Lives Matter' Flags," *E.W. Scripps National Desk*, February 22, 2021, accessed March 2, 2021, https://www.thedenverchannel.com/news/national/capitol-officer-they-beat -law-enforcement-with-blue-lives-matter-flags; Nathalie Baptiste, "The Mob at the

Capitol Proves That Blue Lives Have Never Mattered to Trump Supporters," *Mother Jones*, January 8, 2021, accessed March 2, 2021, https://www.motherjones.com/politics/2021/01/the-mob-at-the-capitol-proves-that-blue-lives-have-never-mattered-to-trump-supporters/.

10. Calvin Warren, *Ontological Terror: Blackness, Nihilism and Emancipation* (Durham: Duke University Press, 2018), 62–109.

11. *Dred Scott v. Sandford*, 60 U.S. 393 (1856). See also the discussion of this case in chapter 1.

12. Hatem Bazian, "Islamophobia, Trump's Racism and 2020 Elections," *Islamophobia Studies Journal* 5, no. 1 (2019): 8–10; Lawrence Bobo, "Racism in Trump's America: Reflections on Culture, Sociology, and the 2016 US Presidential Election," *The British Journal of Sociology* 68 (2017): S85–S104; Paula Ioanide, *The Emotional Politics of Racism: How Feelings Trump Facts in an Era of Colorblindness* (Stanford, CA: Stanford University Press, 2015).

13. Marcus Nevius, "The Legacy of Racial Hatred in the January 6 Insurrection," *JSTOR Daily*, February 24, 2021, accessed March 2, 2021, https://daily.jstor.org/the-legacy-of-racial-hatred-in-the-january-6-insurrection/; Grace Tatter and Meghna Chakrabarti, "The Racist Roots of the Capitol Insurrection," *WBUR*, January 14, 2021, accessed March 2, 2021, https://www.wbur.org/onpoint/2021/01/14/the-racist-roots-of-the-capitol-insurrection.

14. As documented in *Vigile v. Sava* 535 F. Supp. 1020 (S.D.N.Y. March 5, 1982) and *Bertrand v. Sava*, Nos. 81 Civ. 7371, 81 Civ. 7372 (S.D.N.Y. April 5, 1982). Discussed in chapter 3.

15. As documented in *Louis v. Nelson*, 544 F. Supp. 973 (S.D. Fla. 1982) and *Louis v. Nelson*, 544 F. Supp. 1004 (S.D. Fla. 1982). Discussed in chapter 2.

16. But it also bears noting that there are approaches to social science methodology that have questioned the positivist concept of causality as being descriptive more so than explanatory. According to these methodological perspectives, a rigorous explanation (whether or not it deploys the language of "causality") requires a theoretically informed treatment that accounts for the singularity—rather than the generality—of the contexts and history in which ones "factors" are interacting. Although it is possible to convert this analysis into numerical data that can be used to describe patterns across many cases, it relies on acts of judicious interpretation, on the part of the researcher, that are more conducive to a qualitative than quantitative methodology. See Charles Ragin, *Fuzzy Set Social Science* (Chicago, IL: University of Chicago Press, 2000); Andrew Sayer, *Method in Social Science* (New York: Routledge, 1992), 85–117.

17. See the introduction and chapter 4 for a more involved discussion. It also bears noting that the interdiction operations that were inaugurated in 1981 were originally titled the HMIO and were later changed to the Alien Migrant Interdiction Operation (AMIO). In the first year of the program, all of the interdictees (171 in all) were Haitian. In the second year (1982), over 500 Haitians were interdicted, along with six Dominicans and forty four Cubans, and over the next ten years, the roster of "alien" interdictees expanded to include Chinese, Mexican, and Ecuadoran nationals as well as several other Asian and Latin American nationalities were grouped in the "other"

category. Throughout this time, however, Haitians remained the predominant focus of the interdiction operations, being outpaced, occasionally by interdictions of Cuban and Dominican nationals. See US Department of Homeland Security, USCG Migrant Interdiction Statistics, "Table 534. Coast Guard Migrant Interdictions by Nationality of Alien." Originally accessed May 2011: http://www.uscg.mil/hq/cg5/cg531/AMIO /FlowStats/currentstats.asp/ Reposted at this link and accessed November 21, 2020. https://view.officeapps.live.com/op/view.aspx?src=http%3A%2F%2Fwww2.census.gov%2Flibrary%2Fpublications%2F2011%2Fcompendia%2Fstatab%2F131ed %2Ftables%2F12s0534.xls.

18. Referring once more to the policies that were discussed in chapters 2 and 3 and were contested in the following cases—*Vigile* 535 F. Supp. 1020; *Bertrand*, 684 F.2d 204; *Louis*, 544 F. Supp. 973; *Louis*, 544 F. Supp. 1004—and which resurfaced in the deliberations that culminated in *Haitians Center Council v. McNary*, 807 F. Supp. 928 (E.D.N.Y. 1992) that were discussed in chapter 4; and *CABA*, 43 F.3d 1412, 1419 that was discussed in chapter 5.

19. As discussed in chapter 5. See also Christina Frohock, "'Brisas del Mar': Judicial and Political Outcomes of the Cuban Rafter Crisis in Guantánamo," *Harvard Latino Law Review* 15, no. 39 (2012), 39–83.

20. As discussed in chapter 6, the key precedents being Executive Order No. 12324 (*Interdiction of Illegal Aliens*) 3 C.F.R. 46 FR 48109 (1981), Comp., p. 180, and *Sale v. Haitian Centers Council, Inc.*, 509 U.S. 155 (1993).

21. *Dred Scott* 60 U.S. 393; *Plessy v. Ferguson* 163 U.S. 537 (1896) with two critical points of comparison being *Jean v. Nelson* 727 F.2d 957 (11th Cir. 1984) and *Haitian Refugee Center v. Baker*, 112 S. Ct. 1245 (1992). Also see Thomas Jones, "Haitian Refugee Center, Inc. v. James Baker, III: The Dred Scott Case of Immigration Law," *Penn State International Law Review* 11, no. 1 (1992).

22. Whereas the government argued that Haitian interdictees had no claim on US constitutional or international law (see chapter 4), the issues at stake in the debate over the remain-in-Mexico policy revolved around contrasting interpretations of the Immigration and Nationality Act—with this debate tacitly affirming that the migrants in question had some access to the law. See chapter 6 for a more involved discussion. For brief overview, see Muzaffar Chishti and Jessica Bolter, "Remain in Mexico Plan Echoes Earlier U.S. Policy to Deter Haitian Migration," *Migration Policy Institute: Policy Beat*, March 28, 2019, accessed January 1, 2020, https://www.migrationpolicy .org/article/remain-mexico-plan-echoes-earlier-us-policy-deter-haitian-migration.

23. Nicole Phillips and Tom Ricker, *The Invisible Wall: Title 42 and its Impact on Haitian Migrants*, Haitian Bridge Alliance, Quixote Center and UndocuBlack Network, March 25, 2021, accessed September 19, 2021, file:///C:/Users/pkret/On eDrive/Documents/Writing%20&%20Research/Black%20Interdictions/Chapter% 20Drafts/Completed%20Drafts/The-Invisible-Wall.pdf, 6–9.

24. Ibid. Also see the discussion of the HIV travel ban and treatment of HIV-positive Haitian refugees in chapter 4.

25. As discussed in chapter 5 and recounted in the deliberations over *CABA*, 43 F.3d 1412, 1419. See also Frohock, "'Brisas del Mar.'"

26. Frohock, "'Brisas del Mar.'" See chapter 5 for a more involved discussion.

27. Saidiya Hartman, *Scenes of Subjection: Terror, Slavery, and Self-Making in Nineteenth Century America* (Oxford: Oxford University Press, 1997), 168–171; Frank Wilderson, "The Prison Slave as Hegemony's (Silent) Scandal," *Social Justice* 30, no. 2 (2003): 18–27.

28. In the case of female genital cutting (FGC) the US courts have actually seemed willing to make special exceptions for African migrants and has made legal precedents established by these cases central to its jurisprudence on asylum law. *Matter of Kasinga*, 21 I&N Dec. 357 (BIA 1996); *Matter of C-A*, 23 I&N Dec. 951 (BIA 2006) at 955; *Matter of M-E-V-G*, 26 I&N Dec. 227 (BIA 2014) at 247; *Matter of W-G-R*, 26 I&N Dec. 208 (BIA 2014) at 219. But as Connie Oxford has explained, the concern for FGC victims can also be explained by a discourse on "exotified harm" that relies on racialized and ethnocentric ideas about the otherness of the cultures from which these migrant women are being "rescued." This tendency, in which blackness and non-Western otherness can factor into decisions that are beneficial for refugees, underscores my overarching point about the need to situate (anti)blackness within the specific histories of policy and lawmaking. Connie Oxford, "Protectors and Victims in the Gender Regime of Asylum," *NWSA Journal* 17 (2005): 18–38.

29. *Ramos v. Wolf*, No. 18-16981 at 106–107.

30. *Ramos v. Nielsen*, 18-cv-01554-EMC (August 2018). See chapter 6 for a more involved discussion.

31. *Ramos*, No. 18-16981 at 97–100; *Ramos*, 18-cv-01554-EMC (August 2018) at 43–45.

32. *Ramos*, No. 18-16981 at 106–107.

33. *Fong Yue Ting v. US*, 149 U.S. 698 (1893) at 699–705. See chapter 3 for a more involved discussion.

34. For a more involved discussion, see chapters 2 and 3. See also n14 and 15.

35. See chapter 4.

36. *Fugitive Slave Act*, Pub.L. 31–60, 9 Stat. 462 (1850).

37. See the discussion of the privately organized deportation strategies of the ACS in chapter 2, as well as my discussion of (anti)blackness and the law (informed by the work of Hartman, Tuitt, and Warren) from chapter 1.

38. It also bears emphasizing how this line of argument, in Afropessimist theory, connects to the Foucauldian and poststructuralist critique of personhood. McWhorter, "Persons and Sovereigns in Ethical Thought"; Warren, *Ontological Terror*; Wilderson, *Afropessimism*; "The Prison Slave as Hegemony's (Silent) Scandal."

39. Derrick Bell, *Faces at the Bottom of the Well: The Permanence of Racism* (New York: Basic Books, 1992).

40. Harold Koh, "The 'Haiti Paradigm' in United States," *Yale Law Review* 103 (1993): 2391–2455 at 2400–2401.

41. Ibid., 2412–2413.

42. Ibid., 2397–2398.

43. Frohock, "'Brisas del Mar'"; Harold Koh and Michael Wishnie, "The Story of Sale v. Haitian Centers Council: Guantanamo and Refoulement," in *Human Rights Advocacy Stories*, eds. Margaret Satterthwaite and Deena Hurwitz (Eagan, MN: Westlaw and Foundations Press, 2008), 385–432 at 416–419.

44. Derrick Bell, *"Brown v. Board of Education* and the Interest Convergence Dilemma," in *The Derrick Bell Reader*, eds. Richard Delgado and Jean Stefancic (New York: NYU Press, 2005), 33–39.

45. Ibid.

46. Michelle Alexander, *The New Jim Crow: Mass Incarceration in the Age of Colorblindness* (New York: The New Press, 2012), 35–58.

47. Hartman, *Scenes of Subjection*; Wilderson, "The Prison Slave as Hegemony's (Silent) Scandal."

48. Hannah Arendt, *The Human Condition* (Chicago: University of Chicago Press, 1958). See also Rebecca Adami, "Human Rights For More Than One Voice: Rethinking Political Space Beyond the Global/Local Divid," *Ethics & Global Politics* 7, no. 4 (2014): 163–180; Mira Siegelberg, "Things Fall Apart: J.G.A. Pocock, Hannah Arendt, and the Politics of Time," *Modern Intellectual History* 10, no. 1 (2013): 109.

49. I am using the term "communities" and not "population" to respect the emphasis that Bell places on black agency and collective self-sufficiency in his work. This can also be understood as a distinction between a self-defined and externally imposed category (similar to the Hegelian an sich/fur sich distinction that Karl Marx famously appropriated in his discussion of class consciousness). See Bertell Ollman, "Toward Class Consciousness Next Time: Marx and the Working Class," *Politics & Society* 3, no. 1 (1972): 1–24.

50. Derrick Bell, "The Racial Preference Licensing Act," in *The Derrick Bell Reader*, eds. Delgado and Stefancic, 46–54.

51. Ibid.

52. Ibid.

53. For two examples, see Derrick Bell, "The Real Cost of Racial Equality," in *The Derrick Bell Reader,* eds. Richard and Stefancic, 223–225; "Time for Teachers: Putting Educators Back to Work in the *Brown* Remedy," in *The Derrick Bell Reader*, eds. Delgado and Stefancic, 226–231.

54. Koh, "The 'Haiti Paradigm' in United States," 2398–2409.

55. Carmichael/Toure and Hamilton, *Black Power: The Politics of Liberation in America*; Dewey Clayton, "Black Lives Matter and the Civil Rights Movement: A Comparative Analysis of Two Social Movements in the United States," *Journal of Black Studies* 49, no. 5 (2018): 448–480; Bell hooks, "Sisterhood: Political Solidarity Between Women," *Feminist Review* 23, no. 1 (1986): 125–138; Keith Johnston and Elwood Watson, "The W. E. B. DuBois and Booker T. Washington Debate: Effects Upon African American Roles in Engineering and Engineering Technology," *The Journal of Technology Studies* 30, no. 4 (2004): 65–70.

56. Both of these books were briefly referenced at the beginning of chapter 1, as a counterpoint for my theory of controlled mobility. Paul Gilroy, *The Black Atlantic: Modernity and Double Consciousness* (Cambridge, MA: Harvard University Press, 1993); Julius Scott, *The Common Wind: Afro-American Currents in the Age of the Haitian Revolution* (New York: Verso, 2018).

57. Ida Danewid, "White Innocence in the Black Mediterranean: Hospitality and the Erasure of History," *Third World Quarterly* 38, no. 7 (2017): 1674–1689;

Monisha Gupta, "'Don't Deport Our Daddies!': Gendering State Deportation Practices and Immigrant Organizing," *Gender and Society* 28, no. 1 (2014): 83–109; Martin Manalansan, "Queer Intersections: Sexuality and Gender in Migration Studies," *The International Migration Review* 40, no. 1 (2006): 224–49; Rachel Silvey, "Transnational Rights and Wrongs: Moral Geographies of Gender and Migration," *Philosophical Topics* 37, no. 2 (2009): 75–91.

58. David Bacon, *The Right to Stay Home: How US Policy Drives Mexican Migration* (New York: Penguin/Random House, 2014).

Bibliography

Aberra, Nesima. "The Supreme Court's Travel Ban Decision Explained." *The Center for Public Integrity*. Last updated June 29, 2018. Accessed September 19, 2021, https://publicintegrity.org/inequality-poverty-opportunity/immigration/the -supreme-courts-travel-ban-decision-explained/?gclid=Cj0KCQiA_qD_BRDiARI sANjZ2LDCHde0hFedfMEfTmOvk5T4ULzeiinnrcNDgj_5GBLWPSNx_zv7YK-gaAqFcEALw_wcB.

ACLU Washington. "Timeline of the Muslim Ban." Accessed January 4, 2021, https://www.aclu-wa.org/pages/timeline-muslim-ban.

Adami, Rebecca. "Human Rights For More Than One Voice: Rethinking Political Space Beyond the Global/Local Divide." *Ethics & Global Politics* 7, no. 4 (2014): 163–180.

Agamben, Giorgio. *State of Exception*. Chicago: University of Chicago Press, 2004.

———. *Homo Sacer: Sovereign Power and Bare Life*. Stanford, CA: Stanford University Press, 1998.

Agnew, John. "The Asymmetric Border: The United States' Place in the World and the Refugee Panic of 2018." *Geographical Review* 109, no. 4 (2019): 507–526.

Aje, Lawrence. "Fugitive Slave Narratives and the (Re) presentation of the Self? The Cases of Frederick Douglass and William Brown." *L'Ordinaire Des Amériques* 215 (2013): 1–45.

Alexander, Michelle. *The New Jim Crow: Mass Incarceration in the Age of Colorblindness*. New York: The New Press, 2012.

Alvarez, Priscilla. "Biden Administration Formally Ends 'Remain in Mexico' Policy after Suspending It Earlier This Year." *CNN.com*. June 1, 2021. Accessed September 22, 2021. https://www.cnn.com/2021/06/01/politics/immigration -remain-in-mexico/index.html.

Amar, Akhil. "Plessy v. Ferguson and the Anti-canon (Supreme Mistakes)." *Pepperdine Law Review* 39, no. 1 (2011): 75–89.

American Immigration Council. "A Guide to Title 42 Expulsions at the Border." March 29, 2021. Accessed September 22, 2021, https://www.americanimmigration council.org/research/guide-title-42-expulsions-border.

Anderson, Monica and Gustavo Lopez. "Key Facts About Black Immigrants in the U.S." *Pew Research Center.* Last modified January 24, 2018. Accessed September 19, 2021, https://www.pewresearch.org/fact-tank/2018/01/24/key-facts-about-black-immigrants-in-the-u-s/.

Arendt, Hannah. *Crises of the Republic.* New York: Harcourt & Brace, 1969.

———. *The Origins of Totalitarianism.* New York: Harcourt, 1966.

———. *The Human Condition.* Chicago: University of Chicago Press, 1958.

Audige, Jerome. "Prepared Statement of Jerome Audige, Executive Director, New Jersey Haitian/American Cultural Foundation." Hearing Before the Subcommittee on Immigration Refugees, and International Law of Committee of the Judiciary. House of Representatives, Ninety-Eighth Congress. Second Session on H.R. 4853 Cuban/Haitian Adjustment. Serial No, 64. May 9, 1984.

Bacon, David. *The Right to Stay Home: How US Policy Drives Mexican Migration.* New York: Penguin/Random House, 2014.

Bales, Kevin. *Disposable People: New Slavery in the Global Economy.* Berkeley, CA: University of California Press, 2012.

Balibar, Etienne. *Violence and Civility: On the Limits of Political Philosophy.* New York: Columbia University Press, 2015.

Balot Ryan and Larissa Atkison. "Women and Slaves in Greek Democracy." In *A Companion to Greek Democracy and the Roman Republic,* edited by Dean Hammer, 387–404. New York: Wiley, 2015.

Baptist, Edward. *The Half Has Never Been Told: Slavery and the Making of American Capitalism.* New York: Basic Books, 2016.

Baptiste, Nathalie. "The Mob at the Capitol Proves That Blue Lives Have Never Mattered to Trump Supporters." *Mother Jones.* January 8, 2021. Accessed March 2, 2021, https://www.motherjones.com/politics/2021/01/the-mob-at-the-capitol-proves-that-blue-lives-have-never-mattered-to-trump-supporters/.

Barlow, Michael. "Addressing Shortcomings in Afro-Pessimism." *Inquiries* 8, no. 9 (2016): 2/2. Accessed March 3, 2021, http://www.inquiriesjournal.com/articles/1435/2/addressing-shortcomings-in-afro-pessimism.

Barmaki, Reza. "Criminals/Refugees in the Age of Welfareless States: Zygmunt Bauman on Ethnicity, Asylum and the New 'Criminal.'" *International Journal of Criminology and Sociological Theory* 2, no. 1 (2009): 251–226.

Bashi, Vilna. "Globalized Anti-Blackness: Transnationalizing Western Immigration Law, Policy, and Practice." *Ethnic and Racial Studies* 27, no. 4 (2004): 584–606.

Bauman, Zygmunt. *Liquid Modernity.* New York: Polity, 2000.

Bazian, Hatem. "Islamophobia, Trump's Racism and 2020 Elections." *Islamophobia Studies Journal* 5, no. 1 (2019): 8–10.

BBC News. "Haiti President's Assassination: What We Know So Far." September 15, 2021. Accessed September 19, 2021, https://www.bbc.com/news/world-latin-america-57762246.

———. "Coronavirus: Trump Signs Order on Immigration Green Card Suspension." April 23, 2020. Accessed January 4, 2021, https://www.bbc.com/news/world-us-canada-52391678.

Beaumont, Peter and Julian Borger. "Haiti in Fresh Crisis Amid Coup Claims and Dispute Over President's Term." *The Guardian.* February 10, 2021. Accessed March 11, 2021, https://www.theguardian.com/world/2021/feb/10/haiti-coup-attempt-allegations-jovenel-moise-president-term.

Bedoya, Juliana. "Emmanuel Sanon, the Pastor Doctor Accused of Masterminding Jovenel Moïse's Assassination in Haiti." *Al Dia.* July 14, 2021. Accessed September 19, 2021, https://aldianews.com/articles/politics/emmanuel-sanon-pastor-doctor-accused-masterminding-jovenel-moises-assassination.

Bell, Derrick. "*Brown v. Board of Education* and the Interest Convergence Dilemma." In *The Derrick Bell Reader*, edited by Richard Delagdo and Jean Stefancic, 30–39. New York: NYU Press, 2005.

———. "The Racial Preference Licensing Act." In *The Derrick Bell Reader*, edited by Delgado and Stefancic, 46–54. New York: NYU Press, 2005.

———. "Chronicle of the Space Traders." In *The Derrick Bell Reader*, edited by Richard Delagdo and Jean Stefancic, 57–72. New York: NYU Press, 2005.

———. "The Real Cost of Racial Equality." In *The Derrick Bell Reader*, edited by Richard and Stefancic, 223–225. New York: NYU Press, 2005.

———. "Time for Teachers: Putting Educators Back to Work in the Brown Remedy." In *The Derrick Bell Reader*, edited by Delgado and Stefancic, 226–231. New York: NYU Press, 2005.

———. "Trying to Teach the White Folks." In *The Derrick Bell Reader*, edited by Richard and Stefancic, 385–396. New York: NYU Press, 2005.

———. "Beyond Despair." In *The Derrick Bell Reader*, edited by Richard and Stefancic, 417–420. New York: NYU Press, 2005.

———. *Faces at the Bottom of the Well: The Permanence of Racism.* New York: Basic Books, 1992.

Benhabib, Seyla. "Identity, Perspective and Narrative in Hannah Arendt's 'Eichmann in Jerusalem.'" *History and Memory* 8, no. 2 (1996): 35–59.

Berlin, Isaiah. *Philosophy in an Age of Pluralism: The Philosophy of Charles Taylor in Question.* Cambridge: Cambridge University Press, 1994.

Bernstein, Richard, Alessandro Ferrara, Volker Kaul, and David Rasmussen. "Cultural Pluralism." *Philosophy & Social Criticism* 41, no. 4–5 (2015): 347–356.

Blackmon, Douglas. *Slavery by Another Name: The Reenslavement of Black Americans from the Civil War to WWII.* New York: Anchor Books, 2008.

Blitzer, Jonathan. "The Battle Inside the Trump Administration Over TPS." *The New Yorker.* May 12, 2018. Accessed September 19, 2021, https://www.newyorker.com/news/daily-comment/the-battle-inside-the-trump-administration-over-tps.

Bobo, Lawrence. "Racism in Trump's America: Reflections on Culture, Sociology, and the 2016 US Presidential Election." *The British Journal of Sociology* 68 (2017): S85–S104.

Bobo, Lawrence and Camille Zubrinsky. "Race in the American Mind: From the Moynihan Report to the Obama Candidacy." *The Annals of the American Academy of Political and Social Science* 621, no. 1 (2009): 243–259.

Boggs, Justin. "Capitol Officer: They Beat Law Enforcement with 'Blue Lives Matter' Flags." *E.W. Scripps National Desk.* February 22, 2021. Accessed March 2, 2021, https://www.thedenverchannel.com/news/national/capitol-officer-they -beat-law-enforcement-with-blue-lives-matter-flags.

Bonilla-Silva, Eduardo. *Racism Without Racists: Color-blind Racism and the Persistence of Racial Inequality in the United States.* Lanham, MD: Rowman & Littlefield, 2003.

———. "We are all Americans!: The Latin Americanization of racial Stratification in the USA." *Race and Society* 5, no. 1 (2002): 3–16.

———. "Rethinking Racism: Toward a Structural Interpretation." *American Sociological Review* 62, no. 3 (1997): 465–480.

Bonilla-Silva, Eduardo and David Dietrich. "The Sweet Enchantment of Color-Blind Racism in Obamerica." *The Annals of the American Academy of Political and Social Science* 634, no. 1 (2011): 190–206.

Borger, Julian. "Haiti Deportations soar as Biden Administration Deploys Trump-Era Health Order." *The Guardian.* March 25, 2021. Accessed September 22, 2021, https://www.theguardian.com/us-news/2021/mar/25/haiti-deportations-soar -as-biden-administration-deploys-trump-era-health-order.

Borjas, George. *Friends or Strangers: the Impact of Immigrants on the US Economy.* New York: Basic Books, 1990.

Brodkin, Karen. *How Jews Became White Folks and What That Says about Race in America.* Brunswick, NJ: Rutgers UP, 1998.

Brotherton, David and Philip Kretsedemas, eds., *Keeping Out the Other: A Critical Introduction to Immigration Enforcement Today.* New York: Columbia University Press, 2008.

Brown, Marcia. "TPS For All." *American Prospect.* December 9, 2020. Accessed January 5, 2021, https://prospect.org/day-one-agenda/temporary-protected-status -for-all-immigration/.

Brown, William Wells. *Narrative of William W. Brown, a Fugitive Slave. Written by Himself.* Boston: The Anti-slavery office, 1847.

Browne, Irene, and Odem, Mary. "'Juan Crow' in the Nuevo South?" *Du Bois Review* 9, no. 2 (2012): 321–337.

Brutus, Wilkine. *A Boat Voyage: A Haitian Refugee Story.* "Episode 1 - Child of the Sea: Haiti to Cuba." May 3, 2018. Accessed September 26, 2021, https://www .himalaya.com/album/a-boat-a-voyage-a-haitian-refugee-story-1760211.

Bureau of Transportation Statistics. "Table 5.1 US Coast Guard Migrant Interdictions at Sea, Calendar Years 1991–2001." Accessed November 21, 2020, https://www.bts.gov/archive/publications/maritime_trade_and_transpor-tation/2002/table_05_01.

Burin, Eric. *Slavery and the Peculiar Solution: A History of the American Colonization Society.* Gainesville, FL: University Press of Florida, 2003.

Bryce-Laporte, Roy. "Black Immigrants: The Experience of Invisibility and Inequality." *Journal of Black Studies* 3, no. 1 (1972): 29–56.

Cacho, Lisa Marie. *Social Death: Racialized Rightlessness and the Criminalization of the Unprotected.* New York: NYU Press, 2012.

Calavita, Kitty. "The New Politics of Immigration: 'Balanced-Budget Conservatism' and the Symbolism of Proposition 187." *Social Problems* 43, no. 3 (1996): 284–305.

———. *Inside the State: The Bracero Program, Immigration, and the INS.* New York: Routledge, 1992.

Carens, Joseph. "Realistic and Idealistic Approaches to the Ethics of Migration." *The International Migration Review* 30, no. 1 (1996): 156–170.

———. "Aliens and Citizens: The Case for Open Borders." *The Review of Politics* 49, no. 2 (1987): 251–273.

Carmichael, Stokely (Kwame Toure) and Charles Hamilton. *Black Power: The Politics of Liberation in America.* New York: Vintage, 1967.

Caygle, Heather, Sarah Ferris and Laura Barron-Lopez. "'It Would be Very Difficult': Dems Prepare for Heartburn Over Biden Immigration Plan." *Politico.* February 11, 2021. Accessed March 11, 2021, https://www.politico.com/news/2021/02/11/house-democrats-biden-immigration-plan-468720.

Cell, John. *The Highest Stage of White Supremacy: The Origins of Segregation in South Africa and the American South.* Cambridge, UK: Cambridge University Press, 1982.

Central Intelligence Agency. "Central America: Cuba." *World Factbook.* December 28, 2020, https://www.cia.gov/library/publications/the-world-factbook/geos/cu.html.

Cervenak, Sarah Jane, and J. Kameron Carter. "Untitled and Outdoors: Thinking with Saidiya Hartman." *Women & Performance: A Journal of Feminist Theory* 27, no. 1 (2017): 45–55.

Chang, Robert. *Disoriented: Asian Americans, Law and the Nation-State.* New York: NYU Press, 1999.

Charles, Jacqueline. "Biden Accused Trump of Ignoring Haiti. As Turmoil Deepens, Will He Change U.S. Policy?" *Miami Herald.* February 14, 2021. Accessed March 11, 2021, https://www.miamiherald.com/news/nation-world/world/americas/haiti/article249213495.html.

Charles, Jacqueline, Michael Wilner and Monique Madan. "Biden Team Under Fire for Deportation Uptick, Backing Moise as Haiti Tensions Multiply." *Miami Herald.* February 5, 2021. Accessed March 11, 2021, https://www.miamiherald.com/article249046215.html.

Chauvin, Sébastien and Blanca Garcés-Mascareñas. "Beyond Informal Citizenship: The New Moral Economy of Migrant Illegality." *International Political Sociology* 6, no. 3 (2012): 241–259.

Chavez, Leo. *The Latino Threat: Constructing Immigrants, Citizens, and the Nation.* Stanford, CA: Stanford University Press, 2013.

Chishti, Muzaffar and Claire Bergeron. "Haiti Tragedy Raises Important Immigration Issues for the United States." *Migration Policy Institute: Policy Beat.* February 16, 2010. Accessed January 1, 2021, https://www.migrationpolicy.org/article/haiti-tragedy-raises-important-immigration-issues-united-states.

Chishti, Muzaffar and Jessica Bolter. "Court Ordered Relaunch of Remain-in-Mexico Tweaks Predecessor Program, but Faces Similar Challenges." Migration Policy

Institute. December 2, 2021. Accessed Jamuary 2, 2022, https: www.migra-tionpolicy.org/article/court-order-relaunch-remain-in-mexico. "Remain in Mexico Plan Echoes Earlier U.S. Policy to Deter Haitian Migration." *Migration Policy Institute: Policy Beat.* March 28, 2019. Accessed January 1, 2020, https://www.migrationpolicy.org/article/remain-mexico-plan-echoes-earlier-us-policy-deter-haitian-migration.

Chomsky, Aviva. *"They Take Our Jobs!" and 20 Other Myths About Immigration.* Boston, MA: Beacon Press, 2007.

Clayton, Dewey. "Black Lives Matter and the Civil Rights Movement: A Comparative Analysis of Two Social Movements in the United States." *Journal of Black Studies* 49, no. 5 (2018): 448–480.

CNN. "Aristide Says US deposed Him in 'Coup D'etat.'" *CNN.com.* March 1, 2004. Accessed September 19, 2021, https://www.cnn.com/2004/WORLD/americas/03/01/aristide.claim/.

Cohen, Howard. "Coast Guard Repatriates 110 Haitians Aboard an Overloaded Boat on the Caribbean Coast." *Miami Herald.* December 23, 2020. Accessed March 11, 2021, https://www.miamiherald.com/news/nation-world/world/americas/haiti/article248050925.html.

Cole, David. "Enemy Aliens." *Stanford Law Review* 54, no. 5 (2002): 953–1004.

———. *No Equal Justice.* New York: New Press, 1999.

Committee on the Judiciary U.S. House of Representatives. *The Trump Administration's Family Separations Policy: Trauma, Destruction and Chaos.* Washington, DC: Committee of the Judiciary U.S. House of Representatives, 2020. Accessed December 31, 2020, https://judiciary.house.gov/uploadedfiles/the_trump_administration_family_separation_policy_trauma_destruction_and_chaos.pdf?utm_campaign=4526-519.

CONCORD Europe. *European Union Emergency Trust Fund for Africa: Partnership or Conditionality?* Brussels, Belgium: CONCORD Europe, 2017. Accessed December 26, 2020, https://migracnikonsorcium.cz/wp-content/uploads/2018/01/CONCORD_EUTF_Monitoring_short.pdf.

Conlon, Deirdre. "Becoming Legible and 'Legitimized': Subjectivity and Governmentality Among Asylum Seekers in Ireland." In *Migrant Marginality: a Transnational Perspective*, edited by P. Kretsedemas, J. Capetillo and G. Jacobs, 186–204. New York: Routledge, 2013.

Cooper, Erica. "One 'Speck' of Imperfection—Invisible Blackness and the One-Drop Rule: An Interdisciplinary Approach to Examining *Plessy v. Ferguson* and *Jane Doe v. State of Louisiana.*" PhD diss., Indiana University, 2008.

Corradetti, Claudio. "Constructivism in Cosmopolitan Law: Kant's Right to Visit." *Global Constitutionalism* 6, no. 3 (2017): 412–441.

Corradini, Michael, Jonathan Allen Kringen, Laura Simich, Karen Berberich, and Meredith Emigh. "Operation Streamline: No Evidence that Criminal Prosecution Deters Migration." *Vera Institute of Justice.* June 2018. Accessed January 4, 2021, https://www.immigrationresearch.org/report/other/operation-streamline-no-evidence-criminal-prosecution-deters-migration.

Coutin, Susan Bibler. "Falling Outside: Excavating the History of Central American Asylum Seekers." *Law & Social Inquiry* 36, no. 3 (2018): 569–596.

Cullors, Patrisse. "Abolition and Reparations: Histories of Resistance, Transformative Justice, and Accountability." *Harvard Law Review* 132 (2018): 1684.

Cunningham, Vinson. "The Argument of 'Afropessimism.'" *The New Yorker.* July 13, 2020. Accessed September 19, 2021, https://www.newyorker.com/magazine /2020/07/20/the-argument-of-afropessimism.

Customs and Border Protection. "MPP Guiding Principles." January 28, 2019. Accessed January 5, 2021, https://www.cbp.gov/sites/default/files/assets/docu-ments/2019-Jan/MPP%20Guiding%20Principles%201-28-19.pdf.

Dainotto, Roberto. *The Mafia: A Cultural History.* London: Reaktion Books, Ltd, 2011.

Dandy, Justine and Rogelia Pe-Pua. "The Refugee Experience of Social Cohesion in Australia." *Journal of Immigrant & Refugee Studies* 13, no. 4 (2015): 339–357.

Danewid, Ida. "White Innocence in the Black Mediterranean: Hospitality and the Erasure of History." *Third World Quarterly* 38, no. 7 (2017): 1674–1689.

Danso, Ransford. "From 'There' to 'Here': An Investigation of the Initial Settlement Experiences of Ethiopian and Somali Refugees in Toronto." *GeoJournal* 56, no. 1 (2002): 3–14.

Danticat, Edwidge. "Children of the Sea." In *Krik? Krak!,* edited by Edwidge Danticat, 1–29. New York: Soho Press, 1995.

Dávila, Arlene. *Latino Spin: Public Image and the Whitewashing of Race.* New York: NYU Press, 2008.

Davis, Jim. "Leathernecks Provide Security For Operation Sea Signal." *Quantico* 77, no. 9 (1994): 32.

de Boer, Tom. "Closing Legal Black Holes: The Role of Extraterritorial Jurisdiction in Refugee Rights Protection." *Journal of Refugee Studies* 28, no. 1 (2014): 118–134.

De Genova, Nicholas. "Migrant 'Illegality' and Deportability in Everyday Life." *Annual Review of Anthropology* 31, no. 1 (2002): 419–447.

De Genova, Nicholas and Nathalie Peutz, eds., *The Deportation Regime.* Durham, NC: Duke University Press, 2010.

Deleuze, Gilles. *Pure Immanence: Essays on a Life.* New York: Zone Books, 2005.

Deleuze, Gilles and Feliz Guattari. *A Thousand Plateaus: Schizophrenia and Capitalism.* Minneapolis, MN: University of Minnesota Press 1996 [1987].

Delgado, Richard, and Jean Stefancic. *Critical Race Theory: An Introduction,* 3rd ed. New York: NYU Press, 2017.

———, eds. *The Derrick Bell Reader.* New York: NYU Press, 2005.

———. "Derrick Bell's Chronicle of the Space Traders." *Univ of Colorado Law Review* 62 (1991) 321.

Department of Homeland Security. "Secretary Mayorkas Overviews U.S. Maritime Migrant Interdiction Operations." July 13, 2021. Accessed September 19, 2021, https://www.dhs.gov/news/2021/07/13/secretary-mayorkas-overviews-us-mari-time-migrant-interdiction-operations.

———. "Temporary Protected Status." *U.S. Citizenship and Immigration Services: Humanitarian Policies.* Accessed January 1, 2021, https://www.uscis.gov/humani-tarian/temporary-protected-status.

———. "Assessment of the Migrant Protection Protocols (MPP)." *Publications Library.* October 28, 2019. Accessed January 1, 2021, https://www.dhs.gov/publi-cation/assessment-migrant-protection-protocols-mpp.

———. "Guidance for Implementing Section 235(b)(2)(C) of the Immigration and Nationality Act and the Migrant Protection Protocols." *Policy Memorandum, U.S. Citizenship and Immigration Services.* January 28, 2018. Accessed January 1, 2021, https://www.uscis.gov/sites/default/files/document/memos/2019-01-28-Guidance-for-Implementing-Section-35-b-2-C-INA.pdf.

———. "Policy Guidance for Implementation of the Migrant Protection Protocols." *Memorandum from Kristjen M. Nielsen.* January 25, 2019. Accessed December 31, 2020, https://www.dhs.gov/sites/default/files/publications/19_0129_OPA_migrant-protection-protocols-policy-guidance.pdf.

———. USCG Migrant Interdiction Statistics. "Table 534. Coast Guard Migrant Interdictions by Nationality of Alien." Originally accessed May 2011: http://www.uscg.mil/hq/cg5/cg531/AMIO/FlowStats/currentstats.asp/. Reposted and accessed November 21, 2020: https://view.officeapps.live.com/op/view.aspx?src=http%3A%2F%2Fwww2.census.gov%2Flibrary%2Fpublications%2F2011%2Fcompendia%2Fstatab%2F131ed%2Ftables%2F12s0534.xls.

———. *2017 Immigration Yearbook.* Washington, DC: DHS, 2018.

———. *2015 Immigration Yearbook.* Washington, DC: DHS, 2016.

———. *2014 Immigration Yearbook.* Washington, DC: DHS, 2015.

———. *2011 Immigration Yearbook.* Washington, DC: DHS, 2012.

———. *2006 Immigration Yearbook.* Washington, DC: DHS, 2007.

———. *2004 Immigration Yearbook.* Washington, DC: DHS, 2005.

———. *2000 Immigration Yearbook.* Washington, DC: DHS, 2001.

Department of Justice (DoJ). "Attorney General Announces Zero-Tolerance Policy for Criminal Illegal Entry." *Office of Public Affairs.* April 6, 2018. Accessed December 31, 2020, https://www.justice.gov/opa/pr/attorney-general-announces-zero-tolerance-policy-criminal-illegal-entry.

Dienstag, Joshua. "Nietzsche's Dionysian Pessimism." *American Political Science Review* 95, no. 4 (2001): 923–937.

Disasters Emergency Committee. "Haiti Earthquake: Facts and Figures." June 2, 2015. Accessed January 1, 2021, https://www.dec.org.uk/articles/haiti-earthquake-facts-and-figures.

Dow, Mark. "Unchecked Power Against Undesirables." In *Keeping Out the Other*, edited by David Brotherton and Philip Kretsedemas, 29–43. Columbia University Press: NY, 2008.

———. *American Gulag: Inside US Immigration Prisons.* Berkeley, CA: University of California Press, 2005.

Dowling, Julie and Jonathan Xavier Inda, eds., *Governing Immigration Through Crime: A Reader.* Stanford, CA: Stanford University Press, 2013.

Dubey, Madhu. "The 'True Lie' of the Nation: Fanon and Feminism." *Differences* 10, no. 2 (1998): 1–12.

Duffield, Mark. "Racism, Migration and Development: the Foundations of Planetary Order." *Progress in Development Studies* 6, no. 1 (2006): 68–79.

Dupuy, Alex. "Commentary Beyond the Earthquake: A Wake-Up Call for Haiti." *Latin American Perspectives* 37, no. 3 (2010): 195–204.

Durand, Jorge and Douglas Massey. "Evolution of the Mexico-US Migration System: Insights from the Mexican Migration Project." *The Annals of the American Academy of Political and Social Science* 684, no. 1 (2019): 21–42.

Duval, Jerome. "Haiti: From Slavery to Debt." *Counterpunch.* November 10, 2017. Accessed September 19, 2021, https://www.counterpunch.org/2017/11/10/haiti -from-slavery-to-debt.

Eliassi, Barzoo, "Statelessness in a World of Nation-States: the Cases of Kurdish Diasporas in Sweden and the UK." *Journal of Ethnic and Migration Studies* 42, no. 9 (2016): 1403–1419.

EUNAVFOR MED. "Operation SOPHIA Six Monthly Report: June, 22nd to December, 31st 2015." Accessed December 26, 2020, https://migrantsatsea.org/ tag/maritime-interdiction/.

Ewing, Philip and Brian Naylor. "Biden Says Capitol Attack Was 'Culmination' Of Trump's Assaults On Democracy." *NPR.* January 7, 2021. Accessed March 2, 2021, https://www.npr.org/sections/biden-transition-updates/2021/01/07/954404473/ biden-is-set-to-introduce-merrick-garland-as-his-attorney-general-pick.

Fagen, Patricia Weiss. *Receiving Haitians in the Context of the 2010 Earthquake.* Geneva: The Nansen Initiative, 2013. Accessed January 8, 2021, http://www.nans- eninitiative.org/wp-content/uploads/2015/03/DP_Receiving_Haitian_Migrants_in _the_Context_of_the_2010_earthquake.pdf.

Fanon, Frantz. *Black Skin, White Masks.* New York: Grove Press, 1967.

———. *Wretched of the Earth.* New York: Grove Press, 1961.

Farah, Douglas, "Aristide Returns to Acclaim in Haiti." *The Washington Post.* October 16, 1994. Accessed September 19, 2021, https://www.washingtonpost .com/archive/politics/1994/10/16/aristide-returns-to-acclaim-in-haiti/685e4e3e -918d-4bfb-9d65-6be3db9ead7f/.

Feagin, Joe and Sean Elias. "Rethinking Racial Formation Theory: A Systemic Racism Critique." *Ethnic and Racial Studies* 36, no. 6 (2013): 931–960.

Feeley, Malcolm and Jonathan Simon. "The New Penology: Notes on the Emerging Strategy of Corrections and Its Implications." *Criminology* 30, no. 4 (1992): 449–474.

Fekete, Liz. "The Emergence of Xeno-Racism." *Race & Class* 43, no. 2 (2001): 23–40.

Fernandez, Ronald. *America Beyond Black and White: How Immigrants and Fusions Are Helping Us Overcome the Racial Divide.* Ann Arbor, MI: University of Michigan Press, 2007.

Fitzgerald, Jennifer, David Leblang, and Jessica Teets. "Defying the Law of Gravity: The Political Economy of International Migration." *World Politics* 66, no. 3 (2014): 406–445.

Foner, Eric. "End of Slave Trade Meant New Normal for America." Interview by Michel Martin, *Tell Me More, NPR.* January 10, 2008. Audio, 11:18. Accessed September 19, 2021, https://www.npr.org/templates/story/story.php?storyId=17988106.

Fritze, John. "Supreme Court to Debate Immigration Case as Biden Wrestles with Crisis at Southern Border." *USA Today.* April 16, 2021. Accessed September 22,

2021, https://www.usatoday.com/story/news/politics/2021/04/16/supreme-court -debate-tps-immigration-case-biden-confronts-border/7110295002/.

Frohock, Christina. "CABA v. Christopher: Twentieth Anniversary of the Guantánamo Refugees Litigation." *Cuban American Bar Association Blog*, Miami, FL. Last Modified, October 23, 2015. Accessed September 19, 2021, https://cabaonline .com/2015/10/23/caba-v-christopher-twentieth-anniversary-of-the-guantanamo -refugees-litigation/.

———. "'Brisas del Mar': Judicial and Political Outcomes of the Cuban Rafter Crisis in Guantánamo." *Harvard Latino Law Review* 15, no. 39 (2012): 39–83.

Foucault, Michel. *Security, Territory, Population: Lectures at the College de France, 1977–1978.* New York: Palgrave-Macmillan, 2007.

———. *Society Must be Defended: Lectures and the College de France, 1975–1976.* New York: Picador, 2003.

Gamboa, Suzanne and Reuters. "Court rules Trump Can End Temporary Protected Status for Immigrant Families." *NBC News.* September 14, 2020. Accessed September 22, 2021, https://www.nbcnews.com/news/latino/court-rules-trump-can -end-temporary-protected-status-immigrant-families-n1240072.

Gammeltoft-Hansen, Thomas and Nikolas Tan. "The End of the Deterrence Paradigm -Future Directions for Global Refugee Policy." *Journal on Migration and Human Security* 5, no. 1 (2017): 28–56.

Gans, Herbert. "The Moynihan Report and its Aftermaths: A Critical Analysis." *Du Bois Review* 8, no. 2 (2011): 315–327.

———. "Second-Generation Decline: Scenarios for the Economic and Ethnic futures of the Post-1965 American Immigrants." *Ethnic and Racial Studies* 15, no. 2 (1992): 173–192.

Garcia, Michael. "The Inauthentic Ethnic: Richard Rodriguez's Brown and Resisting Essentialist Narratives of Ethnic Identity." *Prose Studies* 34, no. 2 (2012): 129–150.

Garcia y Griego, Manuel. "The Bracero Program." *Rural Migration News* 9, no. 2 (2003). Accessed January 4, 2021, https://migration.ucdavis.edu/rmn/more.php?id =10.

Gavigan, Patrick. "Migration Emergencies and Human Rights in Haiti." Paper prepared for the Conference on Regional Responses to Forced Migration in Central America and the Caribbean, September 30–October 1, 1997. Accessed September 24, 2021, https://www.oas.org/juridico/english/gavigane.html.

Gilroy, Paul. *There Ain't No Black in the Union Jack: The Cultural Politics of Race and Nation.* New York: Routledge Classics, 2002.

———. *The Black Atlantic: Modernity and Double Consciousness.* Cambridge, MA: Harvard University Press, 1993.

Giuffré, Mariagiulia. "State Responsibility Beyond Borders: What Legal Basis for Italy's Push-Backs to Libya?" *International Journal of Refugee Law* 24, no. 4 (2012): 692–734.

Glazer, Nathan and Daniel Moynihan. *Beyond the Melting Pot the Negroes, Puerto Ricans, Jews, Italians, and Irish of New York City*, 2nd ed. Cambridge, MA: MIT, 1970.

Go, Julian, ed. *Rethinking Obama.* Bingley, UK: Emerald Group Publishing, 2011.

Golash-Boza, Tanya. "President Obama's Legacy as 'Deporter in Chief.'" In *Immigration Policy in the Age of Punishment*, edited by David Brotherton and Philip Kretsedemas, 37–56. New York: Columbia University Press, 2018.

———. *Deported: Immigrant policing, Disposable Labor and Global Capitalism.* New York: NYU Press, 2015.

Golash-Boza, Tanya and Eduardo Bonilla-Silva. "Rethinking Race, Racism, Identity and Ideology in Latin America." *Ethnic and Racial Studies* 36, no. 10 (2013): 1485–1489.

Gonzales, Roberto, Veronica Terriquez and Stephen Ruszczyk. "Becoming DACAmented." *The American Behavioral Scientist* 58, no. 14 (2014): 1852–1872.

Grisales, Claudia. "How Pro-Trump Insurrection At The U.S. Capitol Affected Electoral Vote Certification." *NPR.* January 6, 2021. Accessed March 2, 2021, https://www.npr.org/2021/01/06/954216224/how-pro-trump-insurrection-at-the-u -s-capitol-affected-electoral-vote-certificat.

Guantanamo Public Memory Project. "Ronald Auborg: At Guantanamo, 1991." New York: Columbia University's Institute for the Study of Human Rights. Accessed September 24, 2021, https://gitmomemory.org/stories/ronald-aubourg/.

———. "Natalie and Gregory Beau Brun: At Guantanamo, 1992." New York: Columbia University's Institute for the Study of Human Rights. Accessed September 24, 2021, https://gitmomemory.org/stories/natalie-and-gregory-beaubrun/.

Gupta, Monisha. "'Don't Deport Our Daddies!': Gendering State Deportation Practices and Immigrant Organizing." *Gender and Society* 28, no. 1 (2014): 83–109.

Guterres, António. *The 1951 Convention Relating to the Status of Refugees and its 1967 Protocol.* Geneva: United Nations High Commission on Refugees, 2011.

Hahamovitch, Cindy. *No Man's Land: Jamaican Guestworkers in America and the Global History of Deportable Labor.* Princeton: Princeton University Press, 2011.

Hart, David. "Constellations: Capitalism, Antiblackness, Afro-Pessimism, and Black Optimism." *American Journal of Theology & Philosophy* 39, no. 1 (2018): 5–33.

Hartman, Saidiya. *Scenes of Subjection: Terror, Slavery, and Self-Making in Nineteenth-Century America.* New York: Oxford University Press, 2007.

Harvey, David. *A Brief History of Neoliberalism.* London: Oxford University Press, 2007.

Hatton, Timothy and Jeffrey Williamson. *Global Migration and the World Economy: Two Centuries of Policy and Performance.* Cambridge, MA: MIT Press, 2005.

Hearing Before the Subcommittee on Immigration Refugees, and International Law of Committee of the Judiciary. House of Representatives, Ninety-Eighth Congress. Second Session on H.R. 4853 Cuban/Haitian Adjustment. Serial No, 64. May 9, 1984.

Hein, Jeremy. "Refugees, Immigrants, and the State." *Annual Review of Sociology* 19 (1993): 43–59.

Herder, Johann. *JG Herder on Social and Political Culture.* Cambridge: Cambridge University Press, 1969.

Hersch, Joni. "Profiling the New Immigrant Worker: The Effects of Skin Color and Height." *Journal of Labor Economics* 26, no. 2 (2008): 345–386.

Hesse, Barnor. "Preface: Counter Racial Formation Theory." In *Conceptual Aphasia in Black: Displacing Racial Formation*, edited by P. Khalil Saucier and Tryon Woods, vii–xi. Lanham, MD: Lexington Press, 2016.

Hesson, Ted and Laura Gottesdiener. "Exclusive: Biden Team Weighs Deportation Relief For More Than 1 Million Hondurans, Guatemalans." *Reuters.* December 21, 2020. Accessed January 5, 2021, https://www.reuters.com/article/us-usa-immigration-biden/exclusive-biden-team-weighs-deportation-relief-for-more-than-1-million-hondurans-guatemalans-idUSKBN28V2IN.

Higham, John. *Strangers in the Land; Patterns of American Nativism, 1860–1925.* New York: Atheneum, 1963.

Hill, Linda Kelly. "The Gangs of Asylum." *Georgia Law Review* 46 (2012): 639–655.

Hodge, Robert and Gunther Kress. *Social Semiotics.* Ithaca, NY: Cornell University Press, 1988.

Hofstadter, Richard. *Social Darwinism in American Thought.* Boston: Beacon Press, [1944] 1992.

Holland, Kenneth. "A History of Chinese Immigration in the United States and Canada." *American Review of Canadian Studies* 37, no. 2 (2007): 150–160.

Hollifield, James, Philip Martin, and Pia Orrenius, eds., *Controlling Immigration: A Global Perspective.* Stanford, CA: Stanford University Press, 2014.

hooks, bell. "Sisterhood: Political Solidarity Between Women." *Feminist Review* 23, no. 1 (1986): 125–138.

Hope, Megan. "The Rise and Fall of Comprehensive Immigration Reform." *Annunciation House.* December 1, 2007. Accessed March 11, 2021, https://annunciationhouse.org/2007/12/01/immigration-reform/.

Horne, Gerald. *Confronting Black Jacobins: The United States, The Haitian Revolution and the Origins of the Dominican Republic.* New York: Monthly Review Press, 2015.

Hovil, Lucy and Lutz Oette. "Tackling the Root Causes of Trafficking and Human Smuggling From Eritrea." International Refugee Rights Initiative: SIHA Network and SOAS University of London, November 2017. Accessed November 29, 2020, http://refugee-rights.org/wp-content/uploads/2017/11/IRRI-KP-final.pdf.

Ignatief, Noel. *How the Irish Became White.* New York: Routledge, 1995.

Ioanide, Paula. *The Emotional Politics of Racism: How Feelings Trump Facts in an Era of Colorblindness.* Stanford, CA: Stanford University Press, 2015.

Jackson, John and Nadine Weidman, *Race, Racism and Science: Social Impact and Interaction.* Camden, NJ: Rutgers University Press, 2005.

Jamaica: Travel and Culture.com. "Lover's Leap." Accessed November 29, 2020: http://www.jamaicatravelandculture.com/destinations/st_elizabeth/lovers-leap.htm.

James, CLR. *Mariners, Renegades, and Castaways: The Story of Herman Melville and the World We Live In.* Lebanon, NH: UPNE/Dartmouth College Press, [1953] 2001.

———. *The Black Jacobins: Toussaint L'Ouverture and the San Domingo Revolution.* New York: Vintage, 1989.

James, CLR, Grace Lee Boggs and Raya Dunayevskaya. *State Capitalism and World Revolution.* New York: Charles H. Kerr, 1986.

James, Joy, ed., *States of Confinement : Policing, Detention and Prisons.* New York: St. Martin's Press, 2000.

Jaymes, Gregory. "Thirty-Three Haitians Drown as Boat Capsizes Off Florida." *New York Times.* October 7, 1981. Accessed September 26, 2021, https://www.nytimes.com/1981/10/27/us/33-haitians-drown-as-boat-capsizes-off-florida.html.

Jenkins, Craig and Susanne Schmeidl. "Flight from Violence: The Origins and Implications of the World Refugee Crisis." *Sociological Focus* 28, no. 1 (1995): 63–82.

Johnson, Kevin. "Doubling Down on Racial Discrimination: The Racially Disparate Impacts of Crime-Based Removals." *Case Western Reserve Law Review* 66, no. 4 (2016): 993–1038.

———. "Immigration in the Supreme Court 2009–2013." *Oklahoma Law Review* 68, no. 57 (2015): 87–91.

Johnston, Keith and Elwood Watson. "The W. E. B. DuBois and Booker T. Washington Debate: Effects Upon African American Roles in Engineering and Engineering Technology." *The Journal of Technology Studies* 30, no. 4 (2004): 65–70.

Jones, Thomas. "*Haitian Refugee Center, Inc. v. James Baker, III*: The Dred Scott Case of Immigration Law." *Penn State International Law Review* 1, no. 1 (1992): 1–48.

Joseph, Tiffany. *Race on the Move: Brazilian Migrants and the Global Reconstruction of Race.* Stanford, CA: Stanford University Press, 2015.

Judy, Ronald. *(Dis)Forming the American Canon: African-Arabic Slave Narratives and the Vernacular.* Minneapolis: University of Minnesota Press, 1993.

Jung, Moon-Kie. "The Enslaved, the Worker and Du Bois's Black Reconstruction: Toward an Underdiscipline of Antisociology." *Sociology of Race and Ethnicity* 5, no. 2 (2019): 157–168.

Kahn, Jeffrey. "The Caribbean Roots of European Maritime Interdiction." *Society for Cultural Anthropology: Refugees and the Crisis of Europe.* Last modified June 28, 2016. Accessed September 19, 2021, https://culanth.org/fieldsights/the-caribbean-roots-of-european-maritime-interdiction.

———. *Islands of Sovereignty: Haitian Migration and the Borders of Empire.* University of Chicago Press, 2019.

Kanstroom, Daniel. *Deportation Nation.* Cambridge, MA: Harvard University Press, 2009.

Kant, Immanuel. "This Fellow was Quite Black . . . a Clear Proof that What He Said Was Stupid." In *Race and the Enlightenment: A Reader*, edited by Emmanuel Eze, 38–64. New York: Wiley-Blackwell, 1997.

Kaplan, Fred. *Lincoln and the Abolitionists.* New York: HarperCollins, 2017.

Kateel, Subhash and Aarti Shahani. "Families for Freedom: Against Deportation and Delegalization." In *Keeping Out the Other: A Critical Introduction to Immigration Enforcement Today*, edited by David Brotherton and Philip Kretsedemas, 258–290. New York: Columbia University Press, 2008.

Kelley, Alexandra. "0.1 Percent of Immigrants Receive Asylum at the Border." *The Hill.* December 17, 2019. Accessed January 5, 2021, https://thehill.com/changing -america/resilience/refugees/474857-01-percent-of-immigrants-receive-asylum-at -the-border.

Kelley, Robin D.G. *Yo' Mama's Disfunktional!: Fighting the Culture Wars in Urban America.* Boston: Beacon Press, 1998.

Kelsie, Amber. "Blackened Debate at the End of the World." *Philosophy & Rhetoric* 52, no. 1 (2019): 63–70.

Kent, Mary. "Immigration and America's Black Population." *Population Reference Bureau.* Last modified, December 10, 2007. Accessed September 19, 2021, https:// www.prb.org/blackimmigration/.

Kim, Claire Jean, "The Racial Triangulation of Asian Americans." *Politics & Society* 27, no. 1 (1999): 105–138.

King, Katrina Quisumbing. "Recentering U.S. Empire: A Structural Perspective on the Color Line." *Sociology of Race and Ethnicity* 5, no. 1 (2019): 11–25.

King, Richard and Dan Stone, eds., *Hannah Arendt and the Uses of History: Imperialism, Nation, Race, and Genocide.* New York: Berghahn Books, 2007.

Klarreich, Kathy. "New Haitian Exodus? Same Old US Treatment of Refugees." *Christian Science Monitor.* February 3, 2004. Accessed March 11, 2021, https:// www.csmonitor.com/2004/0203/p09s02-cogn.html.

Kleingeld, Pauline. "Kant's Second Thoughts on Race." *The Philosophical Quarterly* 57, no. 229 (2007): 573–592.

Kline, David. "The Pragmatics of Resistance: Framing Anti-Blackness and the Limits of Political Ontology." *Critical Philosophy of Race* 5, no. 1 (2017): 51–69.

Koh, Harold. "The Human Face of the Haitian Interdiction Program." *Virginia Journal of International Law* 33 (1993): 483–490.

———. "The 'Haiti Paradigm' in United States." *Yale Law Review* 103 (1993): 2391–2455.

Koh, Harold and Michael Wishnie. "The Story of Sale v. Haitian Centers Council: Guantanamo and Refoulement." In *Human Rights Advocacy Stories*, edited by Margaret Satterthwaite and Deena Hurwitz, 385–432. Eagan, MN: Westlaw and Foundations Press, 2008.

Koopman, Colin. *Genealogy as Critique: Foucault and the Problems of Modernity.* Indianapolis, IN: Indiana University Press, 2013.

Kretsedemas, Philip. "The Controlled Expansion of Local Immigration Laws." In *Immigration Policy in the Age of Punishment*, edited by David Brotherton and Philip Kretsedemas, 140–164. New York: Columbia University Press, 2018.

———. *Migrants and Race in the US.* New York: Routledge, 2013.

———. *The Immigration Crucible: Transforming Race, Nation and the Limits of the Law.* New York: Columbia University Press, 2012.

———. "The Limits of Control: Neo-Liberal Policy Priorities and The US Non-Immigrant Flow." International Migration 50, s1 (2011): e1–18.

———. "Immigration Enforcement and the Complication of National Sovereignty: Understanding Local Enforcement as an Exercise in Neoliberal Governance." *American Quarterly* 60, no. 3 (2008): 553–573.

———. "Language Barriers and Perceptions of Bias: Ethnic Differences in Immigrant Encounters with Welfare System." *Journal of Sociology & Social Welfare* 32 (2005): 109–123.

———. "Avoiding the State: Haitian Immigrants and Welfare Services in Miami-Dade County." In *Immigrants, Welfare Reform, and the Poverty of Policy*, edited by Philip Kretsedemas and Ana Aparicio, 107–136. Westport, CY/London: Greenwood-Praeger, 2004.

———. "Haitian Immigrants and Welfare Services in Miami-Dade County." W.K. Kellogg Foundation website, July 2001, accessed September 29, 2021, file:///C:/Users/pkret/Downloads/1623706%20(3).PDF.

———. "Discussing Development in Jamaica: Talk Radio, Public Discourse, and the Politics of the Poor." PhD diss, University of Minnesota, 1997.

Kretsedemas, Philip and David Brotherton. "Introduction: Immigration Policy in an Age of Punishment." In *Immigration Policy in the Age of Punishment*, edited by David Brotherton and Philip Kretsedemas, 1–34. New York: Columbia University Press, 2018.

Ladner, Joyce, ed. *The Death of White Sociology*. New York: Random House, 1973.

Laguerre, Michel. *Diasporic Citizenship: Haitian Americans in Transnational America*. New York: Springer, 2016.

Lamphere, Louise, Alex Stepick and Guillermo Grenier. *Newcomers In Workplace: Immigrants and the Restructuring of the US Economy*. Philadelphia, PA: Temple University Press, 2011.

Latour, Bruno. *We Have Never Been Modern*. Cambridge, MA: Harvard University Press, 1993.

Leal, David. "Stalemate: United States Immigration Reform Efforts 2005 to 2007." *People and Place* 17, no. 3 (2009): 1–17.

Lee, Stacey. *Unraveling the "Model Minority" Stereotype: Listening to Asian American Youth*. New York: Teachers College Press, 2015.

Lendman, Stephen. "US Discriminatory Immigration Policies Toward Haitians." *StephenLendman.org*. February 27, 2009. Accessed September 19, 2021, https://stephenlendman.org/2009/02/us-discriminatory-immigration-policy/.

Lewicki, Aleksandra and Shooman, Yasemin. "Building a New Nation: Anti-Muslim Racism in Post-unification Germany." *Journal of Contemporary European Studies* 28, no. 1 (2020): 30–43.

Lindskoog, Carl. *Detain and Punish: Haitian Refugees and the Rise of the World's Largest Immigration Detention System*. Gainesville, FL: University Press of Florida, 2018.

Liptak, Adam and Michael Shear. "Trump Can't Immediately End DACA, Supreme Court Rules." *New York Times*. June 18, 2020. Accessed January 4, 2021. https://www.nytimes.com/2020/06/18/us/trump-daca-supreme-court.html.

Lloyd, Jenna and Alison Mount. "The Caribbean Roots of U.S. Migration Policy." *NACLA Report on the Americas* 51, no. 1 (2019) 78–84. Accessed September 19, 2021, https://www.tandfonline.com/doi/abs/10.1080/10714839.2019.1593695?journalCode=rnac20.

Lobo, Bethany. "Women as a Particular Social Group: A Comparative Assessment of Gender Asylum Claims in the United States and United Kingdom." *Georgetown Immigration Law Journal* 26 (2012): 361–405.

Lopez, Gustavo and Jens Manuel Krogstad. "Key Facts About Unauthorized Immigrants Enrolled in DACA." *Pew Research Center.* September 25, 2017. Accessed January 6, 2021, https://www.pewresearch.org/fact-tank/2017/09/25/key -facts-about-unauthorized-immigrants-enrolled-in-daca/.

Lowe, Lisa. *Immigrant Acts: On Asian American Cultural Politics.* Durham, NC: Duke University Press, 1996.

Loescher, Gilburt and John Scanlan. "Human Rights, U.S. Foreign Policy, and Haitian Refugees." *Journal of Interamerican Studies and World Affairs* 26, no. 3 (1984): 313–356.

Luhmann, Niklas. *Law As a Social System.* Oxford: Oxford University Press, 2004.

Lundquist, Jennifer and Douglas Massey. "Politics or Economics? International Migration during the Nicaraguan Contra War." *Journal of Latin American Studies* 37, no. 1 (2005): 29–53.

Macías-Rojas, Patrisia. "Immigration and the War on Crime: Law and Order Politics and the Illegal Immigration Reform and Immigrant Responsibility Act of 1996." *Journal on Migration and Human Security* 6, no. 1 (2018): 1–25.

Mackinnon, Amy and Robbie Gramer. "Political Crisis in Haiti Poses Challenge for Biden's Democracy Push." *Foreign Policy.* February 10, 2021. Accessed March 11, 2021, https://foreignpolicy.com/2021/02/10/haiti-political-crisis-biden-state -department-challenge/.

Madrigal-Garcia, Yanira and Acevedo-Gil, Nancy. "The New Juan Crow in Education." *Journal of Hispanic Higher Education* 15, no. 2 (2016): 154–181.

Maidment, Richard. "Plessy v. Ferguson Re-Examined." *Journal of American Studies* 7, no. 2 (1973): 125–132.

Malešević, Siniša. *The Sociology of War and Violence.* London: Cambridge University Press, 2010.

Mamdani, Mahmood. *When Victims Become Killers: Colonialism, Nativism, and the Genocide in Rwanda.* Princeton: Princeton University Press, 2001.

Manalansan, Martin. "Queer Intersections: Sexuality and Gender in Migration Studies." *The International Migration Review* 40, no. 1 (2006): 224–249.

Mann-Hamilton, Ryan. "What Rise from the Ashes: Nation and Race in the African American Enclave of Samana." In *Migrant Marginality: A Transnational Perspective*, edited by Philip Kretsedemas, Jorge Capetillo and Glenn Jacobs, 222–238. New York: Routledge, 2013.

Mars, Perry. "Ethnic Conflict and Political Control: The Guyana Case." *Social and Economic Studies* 39, no. 3 (1990): 65–94.

Marsh, Sarah. "Haiti PM, a suspect in murder of President Moise, replaces justice minister." *Reuters.* September 15, 2021. Accessed September 19, 2021, https:// www.reuters.com/world/americas/haiti-official-resigns-over-pms-links-suspect -presidents-slaying-2021-09-15/.

Massey, Douglas and Karen Pren. "Unintended Consequences of US Immigration Policy: Explaining the Post-1965 Surge from Latin America." *Population and Development Review* 38, no. 1 (2012): 1–29.

Massey, Douglas, Jorge Durand and Karen Pren. "Explaining Undocumented Migration to the US." *International Migration Review* 48, no. 4 (2014): 1028–1061.

Mavelli, Luca. "Governing Populations Through the Humanitarian Government of Refugees: Biopolitical Care and Racism in the European Refugee Crisis." *Review of International Studies* 43, no. 5 (2017): 809–832.

Maxwell, Andrew. "The Underclass, 'Social Isolation' and 'Concentration Effects' 'The Culture of Poverty' Revisited." *Critique of Anthropology* 13, no. 3 (1993): 231–245.

Mazrui, Ali. "The African State as a Political Refugee: Institutional Collapse and Human Displacement." *International Journal of Refugee Law* 7 (1995): 21–36.

McWhorter, Ladelle. "Persons and Sovereigns in Ethical Thought." *Genealogy* 1, no. 4 (2017): 21; Accessed September 19, 2021, https://doi.org/10.3390/genealogy1040021.

———. *Racism and Sexual Oppression in Anglo-America: A Genealogy.* Bloomington, IN: University of Indiana Press, 2009.

Merriam-Webster Online. "Strand." Accessed November 29, 2020, https://www.merriam-webster.com/dictionary/strand#h3.

Migration Policy Institute. "Once Again: Prospects for a U.S. Legalization Program and the Unauthorized Immigrant Groups that Could Factor in the Debate." *MPI Webinar.* February 4, 2021. Accessed March 11, 2021, https://www.migrationpolicy.org/multimedia/prospects-us-legalization-program-and-unauthorized-immigrant-groups-could-factor-debate.

———. "Data Hub: Number and Share of Total U.S. Population, 1850–2017." Accessed December 3, 2020. https://www.migrationpolicy.org/programs/data-hub/us-immigration-trends.

———. "Unauthorized Immigrant Population Profiles." Accessed January 8, 2021, https://www.migrationpolicy.org/programs/us-immigration-policy-program-data-hub/unauthorized-immigrant-population-profiles?gclid=EAIaIQobChMI-_PowsiM7gIVYsyzCh1VdQvIEAAYASAAEgInLPD_BwE/.

Milton, Abul Hasnat, Mijanur Rahman, Sumaira Hussain, Charulata Jindal, Sushmita Choudhury, Shahnaz Akter, Shahana Ferdousi, Tafzila Akter Mouly, John Hall and Jimmy Efird. "Trapped in Statelessness: Rohingya Refugees in Bangladesh." *International Journal of Environmental Research and Public Health* 14, no. 8 (2017): 942.

Miroff, Nick and Maria Sacchetti. "Biden Says He'll Reverse Trump Immigration Policies But Wants 'Guardrails' First." *Washington Post.* December 22, 2020. Accessed January 5, 2021, https://www.washingtonpost.com/national/biden-immigration-policy-changes/2020/12/22/2eb9ef92-4400-11eb-8deb-b948d0931c16_story.html.

Moten, Fred. "Blackness and Nothingness." *The South Atlantic Quarterly* 112, no. 4 (2013): 737–780.

Motivans, Mark. "Federal Justice Statistics 2009." *Bureau of Justice Statistics.* December 2011. Accessed January 4, 2021, https://www.bjs.gov/content/pub/pdf/fjs09.pdf/.

Motomura, Hiroshi. "Haitian Asylum Seekers: Interdiction and Immigrant Rights." *Cornell International Law Journal* 26 (1993): 695.

————. "Immigration Law After a Century of Plenary Power: Phantom Constitutional Norms and Statutory Interpretation." *Yale Law Journal* 100, no. 3 (1990): 546–613.

Narea, Nicole. "A Federal Court Ruling Could Allow Trump to Deport 400,000 Immigrants Next Year." *Vox.* September 14, 2020. Accessed January 5, 2021, https://www.vox.com/policy-and-politics/2020/9/14/21436633/ninth-circuit-tps -trump-temporary-protected-status.

National Archives Foundation. "Refugee Act of 1980." Accessed September 24, 2021, https://www.archivesfoundation.org/documents/refugee-act-1980/.

National Immigration Law Center (NILC). "What the Federal Courts Said About President Trump's Refugee and Muslim Ban 2.0." Last updated April 11, 2017. Accessed September 19, 2021, https://www.nilc.org/issues/immigration-enforce-ment/federal-court-rulings-on-refugee-muslim-ban2/.

Ndaula, Malik with Debbie Satyal. "Rafiu's Story: An American Immigrant Nightmare." In *Keeping Out the Other: a Critical Introduction to Immigration Enforcement Today*, edited by David Brotherton and Philip Kretsedemas, 241–257. New York: Columbia University Press, 2008.

Nevins, Joseph. *Operation Gatekeeper and Beyond: The War On "Illegals" and the Remaking of the US-Mexico Boundary.* New York: Routledge, 2001.

Nevius, Marcus. "The Legacy of Racial Hatred in the January 6 Insurrection." *JSTOR Daily.* February 24, 2021. Accessed March 2, 2021, https://daily.jstor.org/the -legacy-of-racial-hatred-in-the-january-6-insurrection/.

Newby, C. Alison and Julie Dowling. "Black and Hispanic: The Racial Identification of Afro-Cuban Immigrants in the Southwest." *Sociological Perspectives* 50, no. 3 (2007): 343–366.

Ngai, Mae. *Impossible Subjects: Illegal Aliens and the Making of Modern America.* Princeton: Princeton University Press, 2014.

————. Mae Ngai. "The Strange Career of the Illegal Alien: Immigration Restriction and Deportation Policy in the United States, 1921–1965." *Law and History Review* 21, no. 1 (2003): 69–108.

Nghe, Linh, James Mahalik, and Susana Lowe. "Influences on Vietnamese Men: Examining Traditional Gender Roles, the Refugee Experience, Acculturation, and Racism in the United States." *Journal of Multicultural Counseling and Development* 31, no. 4 (2003): 245–261.

Nopper, Tamara. "Why Black Immigrants Matter: Refocusing the Discussion on Racism and Immigration Enforcement." In *Keeping Out the Other: A Critical Introduction to Immigration Enforcement Today*, edited by David Brotherton and Philip Kretsedemas, 204–240. New York: Columbia University Press, 2008.

Ocaña, Damarys "An Unfortunate Icon." *The Guardian.* December 10, 2008. Accessed September 19, 2021, https://www.theguardian.com/commentisfree/cifamerica/2008/dec/10/scarface-al-pacino-anniversary-latinos.

Ogbu, John. *Black American Students in an Affluent Suburb a Study of Academic Disengagement.* Mahwah, NJ: L. Erlbaum Associates, 2003.

Olaloku -Teriba, Annie. "Afro-Pessimism and the (Un)Logic of Anti-Blackness." *Historical Materialism* 26, no. 2 (2018). Accessed December 7, 2020, https://www .historicalmaterialism.org/articles/afro-pessimism-and-unlogic-anti-blackness.

Oliver, Kelly. *Carceral Humanitarianism: Logics of Refugee Detention*. Minneapolis, MN: University of Minnesota Press, 2017.

Ollman, Bertell. "Toward Class Consciousness Next Time: Marx and the Working Class." *Politics & Society* 3, no. 1 (1972): 1–24.

Olsen-Medina, Kira and Jeanne Batalova. "Haitian Immigrants in the United States." *Migration Policy Institute: Spotlight*. August 12, 2020. Accessed January 1, 2021, https://www.migrationpolicy.org/article/haitian-immigrants-united-states-2018?gclid=CjwKCAiArbv_BRA8EiwAYGs23L9yM0xKj3EIxOvGTDjgFdVYb0qsdJ7hjFIk80LKJLsHmgxnqNNaOBoCLB4QAvD_BwE.

Omi, Michael, and Howard Winant. *Racial Formation in the United States*, 3rd ed. New York: Routledge, 2014.

Ong, Aiwha. *Buddha is Hiding: Refugees, Citizenship, the New America*. Berkeley, CA: University of California Press, 2003.

Ong Hing, Bill. *Defining America Through Immigration Policy*. Philadelphia: Temple University Press, 2003.

Online Etymology Dictionary. "Strand." Accessed November 29, 2020, https://www.etymonline.com/word/strand.

Orrenius, Pia and Madeline Zavodny. "Do Amnesty Programs Reduce Undocumented Immigration? Evidence from IRCA." *Demography* 40, no. 3 (2003): 437–450.

Oshin, Olafimihan and Rafael Bernal. "Biden Formally Ends Trump-Era 'Remain in Mexico' Immigration Program." *The Hill*. June 1, 2021. Accessed September 22, 2021, https://thehill.com/latino/556371-biden-formally-ends-trump-era-remain-in-mexico-immigration-program.

Oxfam. *An Emergency for Whom? The EU Emergency Trust Fund for Africa – Migratory Routes and Development Aid in Africa*. Cowley, Oxford: Oxfam Great Britain, 2017. Accessed December 26, 2020, https://www.oxfam.org/en/research/emergency-whom-eu-emergency-trust-fund-africa-migratory-routes-and-development-aid-africa.

Oxford, Connie. "Protectors and Victims in the Gender Regime of Asylum." *NWSA Journal* 17 (2005): 18–38.

PBS News Hour. "Handling Haitian Refugees." October 30, 2002. Accessed September 29, 2021, https://www.pbs.org/newshour/show/handling-haitian-refugees.

Paik, Naomi. "Between Rights and Rightlessness: Haitian Migrants and the Elusive Promises of Humanitarianism." *E-misferica* 14, no. 1 (2019). Accessed January 1, 2021, https://hemisphericinstitute.org/en/emisferica-14-1-expulsion/14-1-essays/between-rights-and-rightlessness-haitian-migrants-and-the-elusive-promises-of-humanitarianism.html.

———. "Carceral Quarantine at Guantanamo Legacies of US Imprisonment of Haitian Refugees, 1991–1994." *Radical History Review* 115 (2013): 142–168.

Painter, Matthew, Malcolm Holmes, and Jenna Bateman. "Skin Tone, Race/Ethnicity, and Wealth Inequality Among New Immigrants." *Social Forces* 94, no. 3 (2016): 1153–1185.

Palmer, Gary. "Guarding the Coast: Alien Migrant Interdiction Operations at Sea." *International Law Studies* 72, no. 1 (1998): 157–179.

Pamphile, Leon. "The Haitian Response to the John Brown Tragedy." *Journal of Haitian Studies* 12, no. 2 (2006): 135–142.

Pan, Ying. "The Impact of Legal Status on Immigrants' Earnings and Human Capital: Evidence from the IRCA 1986." *Journal of Labor Research* 33, no. 2 (2012): 119–142.

Papastergiadis, Nikos. "The Invasion Complex: The Abject Other and Spaces of Violence." *Geografiska Annaler. Series B, Human Geography* 88, no. 4 (2006): 429–442.

Park, Robert. "Racial Assimilation in Secondary Groups With Particular Reference to the Negro." *American Journal of Sociology* 19, no. 5 (1914): 606–623.

Passel, Jeffrey and D'Vera Cohn. "U.S. Unauthorized Immigrant Total Dips to Lowest Level in a Decade." *Pew Research Center.* November 15, 2018. Accessed January 8, 2021, https://www.pewresearch.org/hispanic/2018/11/27/u-s-unauthorized-immigrant-total-dips-to-lowest-level-in-a-decade/.

Patterson, Cynthia. "Citizenship and Gender in the Ancient World." In *Migrations and Mobilities*, edited by Judith Resnick and Seyla Benhabib, 47–75. New York: NYU Press, 2009.

Patterson, Orlando. *Slavery and Social Death: A Comparative Study.* Cambridge: Harvard University Press, 1982.

Paultre, Andre and Sarah Marsh. "Americas Gang boss wades into Haiti turmoil, sees conspiracy behind president's killing." *Reuters.* July 11, 2021. Accessed September 19, 2021, https://www.reuters.com/world/americas/rival-haitian-leaders-battle-power-after-presidents-assassination-2021-07-10/.

Perea, Juan. "A Brief History of Race and the US-Mexico Border." *UCLA Law Review* 51 (2003) 283.

Perez, Alberto. "Note and Comment: Wet Foot, Dry Foot: The Recurring Controversy." *Nova Law Review* 28 (2004) 437–460.

Perrow, Charles. "Disaster after 9/11 The Department of Homeland Security and the Intelligence Reorganization." *Homeland Security Affairs* 2, no. 1 (2006): 1–29.

Phillips, Julie and Douglas Massey. "The New Labor Market: Immigrants and Wages after IRCA." *Demography* 36, no. 2 (1999): 233–246.

Phillips, Nicole and Tom Ricker. *The Invisible Wall: Title 42 and its Impact on Haitian Migrants.* San Diego, CA: Haitian Bridge Alliance, Quixote Center and UndocuBlack Network, 2021. Accessed September 19, 2021, file:///C:/Users/pkr et/OneDrive/Documents/Writing%20&%20Research/Black%20Interdictions/Cha pter%20Drafts/Completed%20Drafts/The-Invisible-Wall.pdf.

Pilkington, Ed. "Outcry as More Than 20 Babies and Children Deported by US to Haiti." *The Guardian.* February 8, 2021. Accessed March 11, 2021, https://www .theguardian.com/us-news/2021/feb/08/us-ice-immigration-customs-enforcement -haiti-deportations?CMP=Share_iOSApp_Other.

Pitts, Darren. *A Guantanamo Diary – Operation Sea Signal.* Washington, DC: Institute for National Strategic Studies, 1995.

Plascencia, Luis. "Attrition Through Enforcement and the Elimination of a 'Dangerous Class.'" In *Latino Politics and Arizona's Immigration Law SB 1070*, edited by Lisa Magaña and Erik Lee, 93–127. New York: Springer, 2013.

Plummer, Brenda Gayle. *Haiti and the Great Powers, 1902–1915.* Baton Rouge: Louisiana State University Press, 1988.

Polgreen, Lydia and Tim Weiner. "Haiti's President Forced Out; Marines Sent to Keep Order." *The New York Times.* February 29, 2004. Accessed September 19, 2021, https://www.nytimes.com/2004/02/29/international/americas/haitis-president-forced-out-marines-sent-to-keep.html.

Portes, Alejandro, and Alex Stepick. *City on the Edge: The Transformation of Miami.* Berkeley: University of California Press, 1993.

Portes, Alejandros and Min Zhou. "The New Second Generation: Segmented Assimilation and Its Variants." *The Annals of the American Academy of Political and Social Science* 530, no. 1 (1993): 74–96.

Posner, Michael. *Violations of Human Rights in Haiti.* A Report of the Lawyers Committee for International Human Rights to the Organization of American States. November 1980. Accessed September 25, 2021, https://ufdc.ufl.edu/AA00001006/00001/2j.

Prashad, Vijay. *The Karma of Brown Folk.* Minneapolis, MN: University of Minnesota Press, 2000.

Prestianni, Sara. "Steps In the Process of Externalisation of Border Controls to Africa, From the Valletta Summit to Today." *ARCI/Open Society Foundations.* 2016. Accessed November 29, 2020, http://www.integrationarci.it/wp-content/uploads/2016/06/analysisdoc_externalisation_ARCI_ENG.pdf.

Ragin, Charles. *Fuzzy Set Social Science.* Chicago, IL: University of Chicago Press, 2000.

Ralph, David. "Haitian Interdiction on the High Seas: The Continuing Saga of the Rights of Aliens Outside United States Territory." *Maryland. J. Int'l L. & Trade* 17 (1993) 227.

Ramji-Nogales, Jaya, Andrew Schoenholtz and Philip Schrag. "Refugee Roulette: Disparities in Asylum Adjudication." *Stanford Law Review* 60 (2007): 295–411.

Reid, Ira. *The Negro Immigrant.* New York: Columbia University Press, 1939.

Relief Web. "Refugee Voices: Haiti Asylum Seekers – Haiti." *OCHA Services.* July28, 2004. Accessed September 24, 2021, https://reliefweb.int/report/haiti/refugee-voices-haiti-asylum-seekers.

Renwick, Lucille. "Haiti Memories: Searching for a New Life, Hundreds of Refugees Have Arrived in L.A. With Their Stories of Despair and Brutal Treatment Back Home." *LA Times.* August 21, 1994. Accessed September 24, 2021, https://www.latimes.com/archives/la-xpm-1994-08-21-ci-29766-story.html.

Reuters. "Haiti Police Say Former Supreme Court Judge Suspect in President's Killing." July 31, 2021. Accessed September 19, 2021, https://www.reuters.com/world/americas/haiti-police-say-former-supreme-court-judge- suspect-presidents-killing-2021-07-31/.

Roberts, Dorothy. *Killing the Black Body: Race, Reproduction, and the Meaning of Liberty.* New York: Vintage, 1998.

———. "Crime, Race, and Reproduction." *Tulsa Law Review* 67 (1992): 1945–1977.

Rodman, Hyman. *Lower-Class Families; the Culture of Poverty in Negro Trinidad.* New York: Oxford University Press, 1971.

Rodney, Walter. *How Europe Underdeveloped Africa.* Washington, DC: Howard UP, 1981.

Roediger, David. *The Wages of Whiteness: Race and the Making of the American Working Class.* London/New York: Verso, 1999.

Roldan, Concha. "Perpetual Peace, Federalism and the Republic of the Spirits: Leibniz Between Saint-Pierre and Kant." *Studia Leibnitiana* 43, no. 1 (2011): 87–102.

Rosenblum, Marc and Idean Salehyan. "Norms and Interests in US Asylum Enforcement." *Journal of Peace Research* 41, no. 6 (2004): 677–697.

Rossier, Nicolas. "Conversation Part 2: Jean-Bertrand Aristide on Haiti in the Earthquake's Aftermath." *The Nation/Grit TV.* November 22, 2010. Accessed September 19, 2021, https://www.youtube.com/watch?v=1EP_hrhRgg0.

Rustin, Bayard. "Prepared Statement of Bayard Rustin, Chairman, A. Philip Randolph Institute." Hearing Before the Subcommittee on Immigration Refugees, and International Law of Committee of the Judiciary. House of Representatives, Ninety-Eighth Congress. Second Session on H.R. 4853 Cuban/Haitian Adjustment. Serial No, 64. May 9, 1984.

Sachs, Jeffrey. "From His First Day in Office, Bush Was Ousting Aristide." *Los Angeles Times.* March 4, 2004. Accessed September 19, 2021, https://www.latimes.com/archives/la-xpm-2004-mar-04-oe-sachs4-story.html.

Sahoo, Ajaya, Dave Sangha, and Melissa Kelly. "From 'Temporary Migrants' to 'Permanent Residents': Indian H-1B Visa Holders in the United States." *Asian Ethnicity* 11, no. 3 (2010): 293–309.

Sakuma, Amanda. "Obama Leaves Behind a Mixed Legacy on Immigration." *NBC News.* January 18, 2007. Accessed March 11, 2021, https://www.nbcnews.com/storyline/president-obama-the-legacy/obama-leaves-behind-mixed-legacy-immigration-n703656.

Sassen, Saskia. *Territory, Authority, Rights: From Medieval to Global Assemblages.* Princeton, NJ: Princeton University Press, 2008.

———. *Guests and Aliens.* New York: New Press, 1999.

———. *Globalization and Its Discontents.* New York: New Press, 1999.

Saucier, P. Khalil and Tryon Woods, eds. *Conceptual Aphasia in Black.* Lanham, MD: Lexington, 2016.

———. "Introduction: Racial Optimism and the Drag of Thymotics." In *Conceptual Aphasia in Black*, edited by P. Khalil Saucier and Tryon Woods, 1–34. Lanham, MD: Lexington Press, 2016.

———. "Ex Aqua The Mediterranean Basin, Africans on the Move and the Politics of Policing." *Theoria* 141, no. 61 (2014): 55–75.

Sayer, Andrew. *Method in Social Science.* New York: Routledge, 1992.

Schiller, Nina Glick, Linda Basch, and Cristina Szanton Blanc. "From Immigrant to Transmigrant: Theorizing Transnational Migration." *Anthropological Quarterly* 68, no. 1 (1995): 48–63.

Scott, Julius. *The Common Wind: Afro-American Currents in the Age of the Haitian Revolution.* New York: Verso, 2018.

Sepulveda, Maria. "Barring Extraterritorial Protection for Haitian Refugees Interdicted on the High Seas." *Catholic University Law Review* 44, no. 1 (1994) 321–362.

Sexton, Jared. "The Vel of Slavery: Tracking the Figure of the Unsovereign." *Critical Sociology* 42, no. 4–5 (2016): 583–597.

———. "Unbearable Blackness." *Cultural Critique* 90, no. 90 (2015): 159–178.

———. "The Social Life of Social Death: On Afro-Pessimism and Black Optimism." *In/Tensions Journal* 5 (2011): 1–47.

———. "People of Color Blindness: Notes on the Afterlife of Slavery." *Social Text* 103, no. 28:2 (2010): 31–53.

———. "Proprieties of coalition: Blacks, Asians, and the politics of policing." *Critical Sociology* 36, no. 1 (2010): 87–108.

Shamir, Ronen. "Without Borders? Notes on Globalization as a Mobility Regime." *Sociological Theory* 23, no. 2 (2005): 197–217.

Shear, Michael and Miriam Jordan. "Trump Suspends Visas Allowing Hundreds of Thousands of Foreigners to Work in the US." *New York Times.* June 22, 2020. Accessed January 4, 2021, https://www.nytimes.com/2020/06/22/us/politics/trump-h1b-work-visas.html?auth=login-google.

Shelby, Tommie. *We Who are Dark: the Philosophical Foundations of Black Solidarity.* Cambridge: Harvard University Press, 2005.

Sherry, Frank. *Raiders and Rebels: The Golden Age of Piracy.* New York: HarperCollins, 2008.

Shull, Kristina. "Nobody Wants These People: Reagan's Immigration Crisis and America's First Private Prisons." PhD diss, University of California-Irvine, 2014.

Siegelberg, Mira. "Things Fall Apart: J.G.A. Pocock, Hannah Arendt, and the Politics of Time." *Modern Intellectual History* 10, no. 1 (2013): 109.

Silvey, Rachel. "Transnational Rights and Wrongs: Moral Geographies of Gender and Migration." *Philosophical Topics* 37, no. 2 (2009): 75–91.

Simon, Jonathan. "Refugees in a Carceral Age: The Rebirth of Immigration Prisons in the United States." *Public Culture* 10, no. 3 (1998): 577–607.

Sinha, Anita. "Slavery By Another Name: 'Voluntary' Immigrant Detainee Labor and the Thirteenth Amendment." *Stanford Journal of Civil Rights & Civil Liberties* 11, no. 1 (2015): 1–44.

Smith, Dorothy. *Writing the Social: Critique, Theory, and Investigations.* Toronto: University of Toronto Press, 2000.

Smith, Robert. *Mexican New York.* Berkeley: University of California Press, 2006.

So, Linda, Andrea Januta and Mike Berens. "Off-Duty Cops, Other Officials Face Reckoning After Rallying For Trump in D.C." *Reuters.* January 13, 2021. Accessed March 2, 2021, https://www.reuters.com/article/us-usa-trump-protest-officials-insight/off-duty-cops-other-officials-face-reckoning-after-rallying-for-trump-in-d-c-idUSKBN29I315.

Solis, Gustavo. "Asylum grant rates under Remain in Mexico are far below historic average." *San Diego Union Tribune.* December 26, 2019. Accessed September 22,

2021, https://www.sandiegouniontribune.com/news/immigration/story/2019-12-26
/asylum-grant-rates-under-remain-in-mexico-are-far-below-historic-average.

Spivak, Gayatri Chakravorty. "Can the subaltern speak?." *Die Philosophin* 14, no.
27 (2003): 42–58.

Srikanth, Anagha. "Babies and Children Deported to Haiti in Apparent Defiance of
Biden Order: Report." *Changing America.* February 9, 2021. Accessed March 11,
2021, https://thehill.com/changing-america/resilience/refugees/537987-babies-and
-children-deported-to-haiti-in-apparent.

Standing, Guy. "The Precariat: From Denizens to Citizens?" *Polity* 44, no. 4 (2012):
588–608.

Statista. "Number of Asylum Applicants in Germany in 2020, by Country of Origin."
December 8, 2020. Accessed September 19, 2021, https://www.statista.com/statis-
tics/911586/country-origin-asylum-applicants-germany/.

Strandburg, Katherine. "Official Notice of Changed Country Conditions in Asylum
Adjudication: Lessons from International Refugee Law." *Georgetown Immigration
Law Journal* 11, no. 1 (1996): 45–82.

Stumpf, Juliet. "The Crimmigration Crisis: immigrants, crime and sovereign power."
American University Law Review 56, no. 2 (2006): 367–419.

Sweet, Frank. *The Legal History of the Colorline.* Palm Coast, FL: Backintyme, 2005.

Tampio, Nicholas. "Rawls and the Kantian Ethos." *Polity* 39, no. 1 (2007): 79–102.

Tassinari, Virginia, Francesca Piredda, and Elisa Bertolotti. "Storytelling in Design
for Social Innovation and Politics: a Reading Through the Lenses of Hannah
Arendt." *The Design Journal* 20, no. sup1 (2017): S3486–S3495.

Tatter, Grace and Meghna Chakrabarti. "The Racist Roots Of The Capitol Insurrection."
WBUR. January 14, 2021. Accessed March 2, 2021, https://www.wbur.org/onpoint
/2021/01/14/the-racist-roots-of-the-capitol-insurrection.

Taylor, Dan. "The Reasonable Republic? Statecraft, Affects, and the Highest Good
in Spinoza's Late Tractatus Politicus." *History of European Ideas* 45, no. 5 (2019):
645–660.

Temple University Directory. "Jan Ting: Professor Emeritus." Accessed September
29, 2021, https://law.temple.edu/contact/jan-ting/.

Thamkul, Jamel. "The Plenary Power-Shaped Hole in the Core Constitutional Law
Curriculum: Exclusion, Unequal Protection, and American National Identity."
California Law Review 96, no. 2 (2008): 553–593.

The Dialogue: Leadership for the Americas. "Congressional Testimo New York: Haiti
on the Brink – Assessing US Policy Toward a Country in Crisis." December 11,
2019. Accessed March 11, 2021, https://www.thedialogue.org/analysis/congres-
sional-testimony-haiti-on-the-brink-assessing-us-policy-toward-a-country-in-crisis/.

Tompkin, Cheryl. "Criminal at the Gate: A Case for the Haitian Refugee." *Black Law
Journal* 7 (1981): 387–410.

Torres-Saillant, Silvio. "The Tribulations of Blackness: Stages in Dominican Racial
Identity." *Latin American Perspectives* 25, no. 3 (1998): 126–146.

Tosh, Sarah. "Defending the 'Bad Immigrant:' Aggravated Felonies, Deportation,
and Legal Resistance at the Crimmigration Nexus." PhD Diss., CUNY, John Jay
College of Criminal Justice, 2019.

Tuitt, Patricia. *Race, Law, Resistance.* New York: Taylor & Francis Group, 2004.

Tushnet, Mark. "Critical Legal Studies: A Political History." *Yale Law Journal* 100 (1990): 1515.

United Nations High Commission on Refugees (UNHCR). "Global Trends in Forced Displacement, 2019." Accessed November 29, 2020. https://www.unhcr.org/globaltrends2019/.

———. "Global Trends: Forced Displacement in 2010." Accessed December 26, 2020. https://www.unhcr.org/statistics/country/4dfa11499/unhcr-global-trends-2010.html.

United Network. "The Fatal Policies of Fortress Europe." Accessed December 26, 2020, http://unitedagainstrefugeedeaths.eu/about-the-campaign/about-the-united-list-of-deaths/.

U.S. Citizenship and Immigration Services. "Consideration of Deferred Action for Childhood Arrivals (DACA)." Accessed January 5, 2021, https://www.uscis.gov/humanitarian/humanitarian-parole/consideration-of-deferred-action-for-childhood-arrivals-daca.

Valles, Dario. "'Cuando llegaron los Haitianos': Black and Central American Migration, Respectability, and the Asylum Crisis in Tijuana, México." *Journal of Latin American Geography* 19, no. 2 (2020): 288–298.

van Selm, Joanne, Betsy Cooper and Kathleen Newman. *The New 'Boat People': Ensuring Safety and Determining Status.* Washington, DC: Migration Policy Institute, 2005.

Varsanyi, Monica. *Taking Local Control: Immigration Policy Activism in US Cities and States.* Stanford, CA: Stanford University Press, 2010.

Vijeyarasa, Ramona and Jose Miguel Bello. "Modern-day Slavery? A Judicial Catchall for Trafficking, Slavery and Labour Exploitation: A Critique of Tang and Rantsev." *Journal of International Law & International Relations* 9, no. 1 (2013): 38–76.

Vitali, Ali, Kasie Hunt and Frank Thorp. "Trump referred to Haiti and African nations as 'shithole' countries." *NBC News.* January 11, 2018. Accessed September 22, 2021, https://www.nbcnews.com/politics/white-house/trump-referred-haiti-african-countries-shithole-nations-n836946.

Vosko, Leah, Valerie Preston, and Robert Latham, eds. *Liberating Temporariness? Migration, Work, and Citizenship in an Age of Insecurity.* Montreal: McGill-Queen's Press, 2014.

Wacquant, Loic. "Crafting the Neoliberal State: Workfare, Prisonfare, and Social Insecurity." *Sociological Forum* 25, no. 2 (2010): 197–220.

Wang, Peter. *Legislating Normalcy: The Immigration Act of 1924.* San Francisco: R & E Research Associates, 1975.

Waring, Marilyn. *If Women Counted: A New Feminist Economics.* San Francisco: Harper & Row, 1988.

Warren, Calvin. *Ontological Terror: Blackness, Nihilism and Emancipation.* Durham, NC: Duke University Press, 2018.

Warren, Robert and Darren Kerwin. "A Statistical and Demographic Profile of the US Temporary Protected Status Populations from El Salvador, Honduras, and Haiti." *Journal on Migration and Human Security* 3, no. 3 (2017): 577–592.

Wasem, Ruth. *US Immigration Policy on Haitian Migrants.* Darby, PA: Diane Publishing, 2011.

———. *US Immigration Policy on Haitian Migrants.* Washington, DC: Congressional Research Service, 2011.

Waters, Mary. *Black Identities: West Indian Immigrant Dreams and American Realities.* Cambridge, MA: 1999.

Weier, Sebastian. "Consider Afro-Pessimism." *Amerikastudien/American Studies* 59, no. 3 (2014): 419–433.

Western, Bruce. *Punishment and Inequality in America.* New York: Russell Sage Foundation, 2006.

White House. "FACT SHEET: President Biden Outlines Steps to Reform Our Immigration System by Keeping Families Together, Addressing the Root Causes of Irregular Migration, and Streamlining the Legal Immigration System." *White House Statements and Releases.* February 2, 2021. Accessed March 11, 2021, https://www.whitehouse.gov/briefing-room/statements-releases/2021/02/02/fact-sheet-president-biden-outlines-steps-to-reform-our-immigration-system-by-keeping-families-together-addressing-the-root-causes-of-irregular-migration-and-streamlining-the-legal-immigration-syst/.

———. "Press Briefing by CBP Acting Commissioner Mark Morgan." *Press Briefings: Immigration.* September 9, 2019. Accessed January 1, 2021, https://www.whitehouse.gov/briefings-statements/press-briefing-cbp-acting-commissioner-mark-morgan/.

Whitfield, Harvey. "The Development of Black Refugee Identity in Nova Scotia, 1813–1850." *Left History* 10, no. 2 (2005): 9–31.

Wilderson, Frank. *Afropessimism.* New York: Liveright Publishing/W.W. Norton, 2020.

———. *Red, White and Black: Cinema and the Structure of US Antagonisms.* Durham, NC: Duke University Press, 2010.

———. "The Prison Slave as Hegemony's (Silent) Scandal." *Social Justice* 30, no. 2 (2003): 18–27.

Wilson, Jill. "Temporary Protected Status: Overview and Current Issues." *Congressional Research Service.* Updated October 6, 2020. Accessed January 10, 2021, https://fas.org/sgp/crs/homesec/RS20844.pdf.

Wimmer, Andreas and Nina Glick Schiller. "Methodological Nationalism and Beyond: Nation–State Building, Migration and the Social Sciences." *Global Networks* 2, no. 4 (2002): 301–334.

Winston, Susanna and Curt Beckwith. "The Impact of Removing the Immigration Ban on HIV-Infected Persons." *AIDS Patient Care and STDs* 25, no. 12 (2011): 709–711. doi: 10.1089/apc.2011.0121. Epub 2011 Jun 28.

Woldemikael, Tekle. "A Case Study of Race Consciousness Among Haitian Immigrants." *Journal of Black Studies* 20 (1989): 224–239.

Woodhouse, Akio Leighton. "Trump's shithole countries remark is at the center of a lawsuit to reinstate protections for immigrants." *The Intercept.* June 28, 2018 Accessed September 22, 2021, https://theintercept.com/2018/06/28/trump-tps-shit-hole-countries-lawsuit/.

Wu, Ellen. *The Color of Success: Asian Americans and the Origins of the Model Minority*. Princeton: Princeton University Press, 2013.

Wu, Frank. *Yellow: Race in America Beyond Black and White*. New York: Basic Books, 2002.

Young, Robert. *Darwin's Metaphor: Nature's Place in Victorian Culture*. Cambridge: Cambridge University Press, 1985.

Yousef, Nancy. "Wollstonecraft, Rousseau and the Revision of Romantic Subjectivity." *Studies in Romanticism* 38, no. 4 (1999): 537–557.

Yuval-Davis, Nira. "Dialogical Epistemology—An Intersectional Resistance to the 'Oppression Olympics.'" *Gender & Society* 26, no. 1 (2012): 46–54.

Zelizer, Viviana. "How I Became a Relational Economic Sociologist and What Does That Mean?" *Politics & Society* 40, no. 2 (2012): 145–174.

Zolberg, Aristide. *A Nation by Design*. Cambridge, MA: Harvard University Press, 2009.

Index

About the Author

Philip Kretsedemas is professor of Sociology at UMass-Boston. His research and theory has examined migrant racialization and the politics of immigration and social policy. His current work is focused on reorienting migration and refugee studies around the problem of antiblack racism. He is also interested in foregrounding the significance of temporary migration for the neoliberal migration regime and using migration politics as a starting point for examining extreme violence. Some of his books include *Immigration Policy in the Age of Punishment* (coedited with David Brotherton, Columbia University Press), *Migrants and Race in the US* (Routledge), and *The Immigration Crucible* (Columbia). He has published in *American Quarterly, International Migration, Journal of African American Studies*, and *Stanford Law and Policy Review* and has also published book chapters in projects published by New York University Press, Canadian Scholars Press, and Greenwood-Praeger. His forthcoming work includes the edited project (with Jamella Gow) *Modern Migrations, Black Interrogations: Revisioning Migrants and Mobilities Through the Critique of Antiblackness* (Temple University Press) and (with Payal Banerjee) a special issue of the journal *International Migration* on the subject "Visa Holders, Legal Precarity, Labor and the Immigration Enforcement After the Penal Turn."

www.ingramcontent.com/pod-product-compliance
Lightning Source LLC
Chambersburg PA
CBHW022300280326
41932CB00010B/927